Alaska

a travel survival kit

D0974475

Alaska – a travel survival kit

Published by
Lonely Planet Publications
PO Box 88, South Yarra, Victoria 3141, Australia
PO Box 2001A, Berkeley, CA 94702, USA

Cover photograph
Alaskan Eskimo (Alaska Division of Tourism)

Other photographs
Jim DuFresne, Ellen Du Fresne, Peggy Zwers, Doug Richmond, Alaska Division of Tourism

Illustrations
John Svenson

Logos
Alaska Division of Tourism

First published
June 1983

This edition
October 1986

National Library of Australia
Cataloguing-in-Publication Data

DuFresne, Jim
    Alaska – a travel survival kit.

    2nd edition
    Previous edition : South Yarra, Vic.:
    Lonely Planet, 1983.
    Includes index.
    ISBN 0 908086 77 6

    1. Alaska – Description and Travel – 1981
    – Guidebooks. I. Title.

917.98'045

Jim DuFresne

Jim Dufresne is a former sports and outdoors editor of the *Juneau Empire* and the first Alaskan sportswriter to win a national award from Associated Press. He is presently a freelance writer, specialising in outdoor and travel writing. His previous books include *Tramping In New Zealand* (Lonely Planet) and wilderness guides to Isle Royale, Voyageurs and Glacier Bay National Parks.

John Svenson

Artist mountaineer John Svenson has lived in Alaska for the past 18 years but his woodcuts, water colours and illustrations of the mountain image have appeared in national outdoor magazines as well as art galleries throughout the Northwest. During the summer he works as a climbing guide, and though his trade has taken him to the summits of four continents, Alaska has always remained his inspirational mecca.

Acknowledgements In Alaska, a friend is more than somebody you have a beer with once a week. He or she becomes a lifelong acquaintance; warm relief during the long, dark winters; a brother you are roped to on a glacier and your saviour if you slip. I have been blessed with many friends from the 49th State and they have made this poor writer a rich man. They also aided me considerably in the second edition of *Alaska – A Travel Survival Kit*.

My deepest appreciation goes to my old Juneau housemates Jeff and Sue Sloss, whose spare room was my home base during the summer of '85. Likewise Jim Moore, a former writer for the *Anchorage Daily News* who assisted me greatly while I was shuffling through Seattle, putting together a summer in Alaska. Others from Juneau who gave me their time and insight on this special state were Ken Leghorn, Ed Fogel, Pete Hettinger, Frank and Janie Homan, Fred Hiltner, Patty Cooper, Heidi Snow and Kara in Gustavus.

My travelling partners included Tot and Joanne Heffelfinger, Chip Bishop, Bob Zupancis and Anne Fredricks, whose backpack could never be too heavy for her. I am indebted to Bill Marchese and David Stewart of the Alaska Division of Tourism, Jim Johnson of Alaska Airlines and Carl Sampson of the *Juneau Empire* for supplying photos, information and encouragement.

At the other end of the world in Australia, Tony Wheeler and Jim Hart of Lonely Planet gave me the encouragement to enlarge this travel guide while Elizabeth Kim cleaned it up from their California office.

But in the end this book is written for three women who have always inspired me to travel and experience Alaska: to my wife, Peggy; to Bonnie of Alaska Discovery; and most of all to my sister, Ellen (1949-1978), who lost her life in the land she loved. May Alaska always cherish her soul.

This Edition

As with all LP books, many hands contributed to the production of *Alaska – a travel survival kit*. Elizabeth Kim did the editing in the LP California office. On the other side of the Pacific in Melbourne, Ann Logan did the typesetting, Graham Imeson took care of the maps and paste-up while Hugh Finlay did the final proofreading and indexing.

A Warning & a Request

All travel guides rely on new information to stay up-to-date. Things change – prices go up, good places go bad, new places open up – nothing stays the same. If you find things better, worse, cheaper, more expensive, recently opened or closed, or simply different, please write and tell us about them and help make the next edition even better. We love getting letters from travellers out 'on the road' and, as usual, the most useful letters will be rewarded with a free copy of the next edition, or another LP guide if you prefer.

Although the author and publisher have tried to make the information as accurate as possible we accept no responsibility for any loss, injury or inconvenience sustained by any traveller using this book.

Lonely Planet Newsletter

To make the most of all the letters and information that come into Lonely Planet we publish a quarterly newsletter with extracts from many of the letters we get, plus other facts on air fares, visas, etc. It's packed with down-to-earth information from writers with the best possible qualifications – they've been there. Whether you want the latest facts, travel stories, or simply to reminisce, the LP Newsletter will keep you in touch with what is going on. It comes out in February, May, August and November (approximately).

To subscribe, write to Lonely Planet in either Australia or the USA; a year's subscription costs A$10 in Australia, US$10 in the USA (1986 prices, subject to change):

Lonely Planet Publications,
PO Box 88,
South Yarra,
Victoria 3141,
Australia
   or
Lonely Planet Publications,
PO Box 2001A,
Berkeley,
CA 94702,
USA

Contents

Introduction

It's not the mountains, the sparkling lakes or the frozen face of a glacier that draws travellers to Alaska every year; it's the magic in the land, an irresistible force that tugs on those who dream about the North Country.

No area in the United States possesses the mystical pull this land does. It ignites the imagination of people who live in the city but long to wander in the woods. Its mythical title of 'the final frontier' is as true today as it was yesterday when Alaska's promise of adventure and the lure of quick wealth brought the first invasion of visitors to the state in 1898 – the miners of the Klondike gold rush. Today they have been replaced by travellers and backpackers, but the spirit is the same.

They are drawn to Alaska by its colourful reputation, stunned by the grandeur of what they see, and often return home penniless. There are mountains, glaciers and rivers in other places in North America, but few are on the same scale or as overpowering as those in Alaska. To look at two mountain ranges slashed by a sloping valley and see a brown bear rambling up one side; to sit in a kayak and watch a five-mile-wide glacier continually calve ice off its face – these are experiences of nature's beauty that permanently change your way of thinking.

If nature's handiwork doesn't affect you, the state's overwhelming size and numbers will. Everything in Alaska is big; everything except its population, that is. Of the total population of 460,000 almost half live in one city, Anchorage,

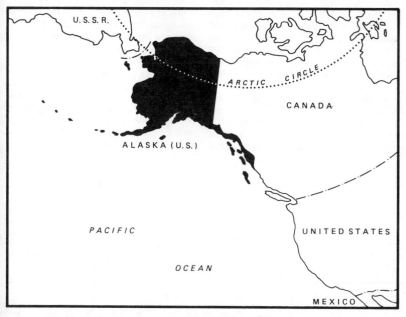

yet the state covers an area of 591,004 square miles (1,536,610 square km) which makes it one-fifth the size of the remainder of the United States; as big as England, France, Italy and Spain together; or 120 times larger than Rhode Island.

Alaska has the third-longest river in North America, 17 of the 20 highest peaks in the US and 5000 glaciers – one larger than Switzerland. It also has arctic winters that are one long night and arctic summers that are one long day. You can find king crabs that measure three feet (one metre) from claw to claw, brown bears that stand over 12 feet (four metres) tall and farmers who grow 70-lb (31 kg) cabbages and 30-lb (13 kg) turnips after a summer of 20-hour days.

Two things that have reached legendary proportions in Alaska are the state's mosquitoes and its prices. There are always tales among travellers about a plate of eggs, toast and potatoes costing $20 or insects so large that campers beat them back with sticks, but myths are spread by those who went home bug-bitten and broke. For most people, a good bottle of bug dope will keep the mosquitoes away, while the aim of this book is to show you how to avoid many of the high prices and still see the wonders of the North Country.

Despite Alaska's reputation for high prices, it's still possible for backpackers and overseas travellers to experience the land on a so-called 'budget trip' because the greatest things the state has to offer –

prime wilderness, abundant wildlife, clear water, miles of hiking trails, in general the great outdoors – are either free or cost little to do or see. If you are low on funds but are willing to camp, hike or sit on a mountain peak to soak up the sunshine and scenery, then you can afford a trip to Alaska. If, on the other hand, you insist on staying in hotels, eating in restaurants and dancing in nightclubs, then legendary Alaskan prices will quickly become reality.

Within the state – ranging 1400 miles (2240 km) from north to south and 2400 miles (3840 km) from east to west – are several regions which make up Alaska's character, each as distinctive as the countries in Europe. You can begin your travels in the rainy, lush south-east and end at the Arctic tundra – a vast, treeless plain where the sun never sets during the summer. In between, the weather and scenery change dramatically. In the summer, the temperatures can range from a cool 50°F (10°C) in Glacier Bay to a sizzling 95°F (35°C) on a hot August afternoon in Fairbanks. Rainfall can measure less than two inches (51 mm) some years above the Arctic Circle, or more than 300 inches (7600 mm) at the little town of Port Walter in the Southeast.

For the purpose of budget travel, the state has been divided into six regions in this book, with the main focus on five which can be easily reached either by road or by the State Marine Ferry system.

Facts about Alaska

HISTORY

Alaska's history is a strange series of spurts and stutters. Today it is viewed as a wilderness paradise, but often in the past it was regarded as a frozen wasteland, suitable only for Eskimos and polar bears. When some resource was uncovered, however, there followed a short period of prosperity and exploitation; first of sea otter skins, then of gold, salmon, oil and most recently, untouched wilderness. After each was exhausted the land slipped back into oblivion.

The first Alaskans migrated from Asia to North America 30,000 to 40,000 years ago during an ice-age that lowered the sea level and gave rise to a 900-mile (1450 km) land-bridge spanning Siberia and Alaska. The nomadic groups were not bent on exploring the new world but on following the animal herds that provided them with food and clothing. Although many tribes continued deep into North and South America, four ethnic groups – the Athabascans, Aleuts, Eskimos and the coastal tribes of Tlingits and Haidas – remained in Alaska and made the harsh wilderness their homeland.

The first written record of the state was made by Virtus Bering, a Dutch navigator sailing for the Czar of Russia. Bering's trip in 1728 proved that America and Asia were two separate continents, and 13 years later, on a second voyage, he went ashore near Cordova to become the first European to set foot in Alaska. The explorer and many of his crew were killed in a shipwreck during that journey, but the survivors brought back fur pelts and tales of fabulous seal and otter colonies – Alaska's first boom was underway. The Russians wasted little time in over-running the Aleutian Islands and quickly established a settlement on Kodiak Island. Chaos followed as bands of Russian hunters robbed and murdered each other for furs while the peaceful Aleutian Indians, living near the hunting grounds, were almost annihilated.

By the 1790s, Russia had organised the Russian American Company to regulate the fur trade and ease the violent competition. However, tales of the enormous wealth of Alaskan wildlife brought several other countries to the frigid waters. Spain claimed the entire North American west coast, including Alaska, and sent several explorers to the Southeast region. These early visitors took boat loads of furs but left neither settlers nor forts, only a few Spanish names.

The British arrived when Captain James Cook began searching the area for the mythical north-west passage between the Pacific and Atlantic oceans. The French sent Jean de La Perouse, who in 1786 made it as far as Lituya Bay along the outside coast. By the 1790s Cook's shipmate, George Vancouver, had returned on his own and charted the complicated waters of Southeast's Inside Passage.

After depleting the fur colonies in the Aleutians, the Russians moved their territorial capital from Kodiak to Sitka in the Southeast and built a second fort near the mouth of the Stikine River in 1834 to prevent the British from moving into the area. That fort, which was named St Dionysius at the time, would eventually evolve into the small lumbering/fishing town of Wrangell. When a small trickle of American adventurers began to arrive, four nations had a foot in the Panhandle of Alaska. Spain and France were squeezed out of the area by the early 1800s while the British were reduced to leasing selected areas from the Russians.

By the 1860s, the Russians found themselves badly over-extended. Their involvement in Napoleon's European

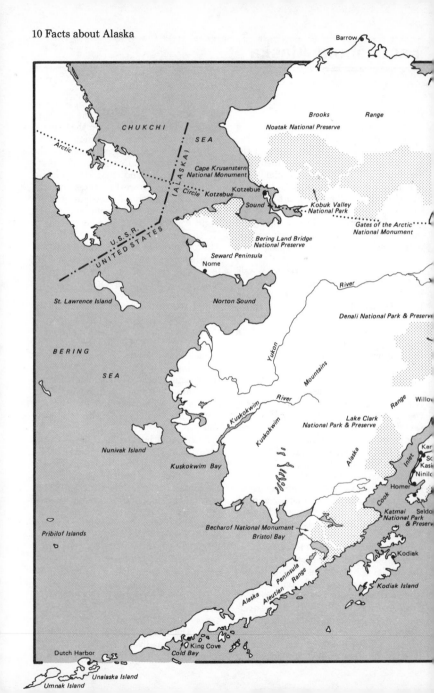

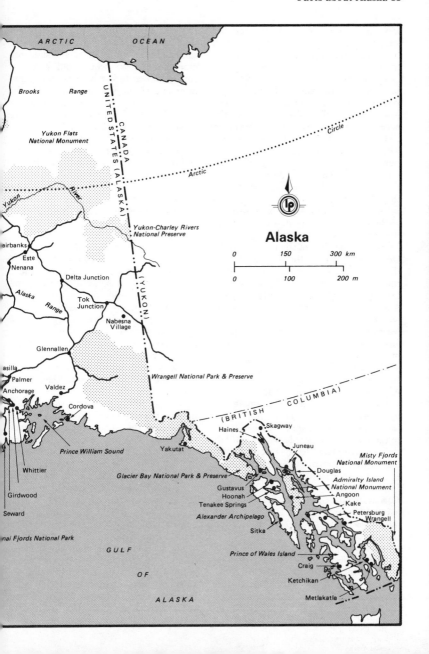

wars, a declining fur industry and the long lines of shipping between Sitka and the heartland of Russia were draining their national treasury. The country made several overtures to the US for the sale of Alaska and fishermen from Washington State pushed for it. The American Civil War delayed the negotiations and it wasn't until 1867 that Secretary of State William H Seward, with extremely keen foresight, signed a treaty to purchase the state for $7.2 million, or less than two cents an acre. By then the US public was in an uproar over the 'Frozen Wasteland'. Newspapers called it 'Seward's Ice Box' or 'Walrussia' while one senator heatedly compared Alaska to a 'sucked orange' now that there was little left of the rich fur trade. On the Senate floor the debate to ratify the treaty was a six-month battle before the sale was approved. On 18 October 1867 the formal transfer of Alaska to the Americans took place in Sitka, while nearby Wrangell, a town both the Russians and the British controlled at one time, changed flags for the third time in its short existence.

Alaska remained a lawless, unorganised territory for the next 20 years, with the US Army in charge at one point and the Navy at another. This great land, remote and inaccessible to all but a few hardy settlers, remained a dark, frozen mystery to the majority of people. Eventually its riches were uncovered one by one. First it was whales, taken mostly in the Southeast and later in the Bering Sea and the Arctic Ocean. Next the phenomenal salmon-runs were tapped, with the first canneries being built in 1878 in Klawock. Both industries brought a trickle of people and prosperity to Alaska.

What brought the land into the world limelight, however, was gold. The promise of quick riches and the adventure of the frontier became the most effective lure Alaska ever had. Gold was discovered in the Gastineau Channel in the 1880s and overnight the towns of Juneau and

Douglas sprang up, living off the very productive Treadwell and Alaska-Juneau mines. Circle City in the Interior suddenly emerged in 1892 when gold was discovered in nearby Birch Creek. Four years later one of the world's most colourful gold rushes took place when the metal was unearthed in the Klondike of the Yukon Territory in Canada.

Often called 'the last grand adventure', the Klondike gold rush took place when the country and much of the world was suffering through a severe recession. Thousands quit their jobs and sold their homes to finance a trip through Southeast Alaska to the newly created boom town of Skagway. From the tent city almost 30,000 stampeders tackled the steep Chilkoot Trail to Lake Bennett, where they built crude rafts to float the rest of the way to the gold-fields. An equal number returned home along the same route, broke and disillusioned. The number of miners who made a fortune was small, but the tales and legends that emerged were endless. The Klondike stampede, though it lasted only from 1896 to the early years of the 1900s, was Alaska's most colourful era and thrust the state permanently into the role of America's last frontier.

By the 1900s, the attention of the miners shifted from the Klondike to Nome and then to Fairbanks, a boom town that was born when Felix Pedro discovered gold 12 miles north of the area in 1902. The gold mines and the large Kennecott copper mines north of Cordova stimulated the state's growth, and the 1900 census estimated the state's population to be 60,000, including 30,000 non-natives. Alaskans, who moved their capital from Sitka to Juneau that year, began to clamour for more say in their future. The US Congress first gave them a non-voting delegate to Washington in 1906 and then set up a territorial legislature that met in Juneau in 1913. Three years later the territory submitted its first statehood bill to Congress.

Statehood was set aside when many of Alaska's residents departed south for high-paying jobs created by WW I. Ironically, it took another war (WW II) to push the land firmly into the 20th century.

The US experienced its only foreign invasion on home soil during WW II, when the Japanese attacked the Attu Islands and bombed Dutch Harbor in the Aleutian Islands. Congress and military leaders panicked and rushed to develop and protect the rest of Alaska. Large army and airforce bases were built and thousands of military personnel were sent to man them.

The famous Alcan – the Alaska Highway – was the single most important project of the military build-up. The 1520-mile (2450 km) road was a major engineering feat and became the only overland link between Alaska and the rest of the country. It was built by the military but the residents were the ones who benefited from it, as the road stimulated the development of Alaska's natural resources. The growth led to a new drive for statehood to cure what many felt was Alaska's status of 'second-class citizenship' in Washington DC. Early in 1958, Congress approved a statehood act which Alaskans quickly accepted, and on 3 January 1959 President Dwight Eisenhower proclaimed the land the USA's 49th state.

Alaska entered the 1960s full of promise, when disaster struck; one of the most powerful earthquakes ever recorded in the US hit Southcentral Alaska on Good Friday morning in 1964. Over 100 lives were lost and the damage was estimated at $500 million. In Anchorage, office buildings sank below ground while a tidal wave wiped out the entire community of Valdez. In Kodiak and Seward, 32 feet (10 metres) of coastline slipped into the Gulf of Alaska while Cordova lost its entire harbour to a 16-foot (five metre) rise.

If the natural catastrophe left the new state in a shambles, then it was a gift from nature that rushed it to recovery and beyond. Alaska's next boom took place in 1968 when massive oil deposits were discovered underneath Prudhoe Bay in the Arctic Ocean. The value of the oil doubled after the world-wide Arab oil embargo of 1973, but it couldn't be touched until there was a pipeline to transport it to the warm-water port of Valdez. The pipeline, in turn, couldn't be built until the US Congress, which still administered most of the land, settled an intense controversy between industry, environmentalists and native Indians with historical claims.

The Native Claims Settlement Act of 1971 was an unprecedented piece of legislation that opened the way for a group of oil companies to undertake the construction of the 789-mile (1270 km) pipeline. The oil began to flow in 1977, but during the brief years of pipeline construction Anchorage bloomed into a fully-fledged modern city and Fairbanks burst at the seams as it was the transportation hub for much of the project. Along with four-digit weekly salaries, there was an astronomical rise in prices for basic items in Fairbanks, like housing and food, that some residents feel never came down with the wages.

In the end, however, oil gave Alaska an economic base that is the envy of many other states, as its residents enjoy the highest per-capita income in the country. The state's budget is in the billions and legislators in Juneau have transformed Anchorage into a stunning city with sports arenas, libraries and performing-arts centres while awarding virtually every Bush town with a million-dollar school. Like the fur trade and the whale hunts, all this will end someday, but for now it is difficult for Alaska residents to see beyond the gleam of the oil dollar.

Alaska is experiencing in the 1980s what might be its last boom – exploitation of the wilderness. Industry, conservationists and government came head to head over an issue known simply as d-2. The name refers to a single paragraph in the Native Claims Settlement that called for the preservation of 80 million acres (32 million hectares) of Alaska wilderness. Most residents used it to cover the entire issue of federal interference with the state's resources and future. The resulting battle was a tug-of-war session on how much land the US Congress would preserve, to what extent industries such as mining and logging would be allowed to develop, and what the permanent resident would be allowed to purchase. The fury over wilderness reached a climax when on the eve of his departure from office, lame-duck president Jimmy Carter signed the Alaska Lands Bill into law in 1980, setting aside over 100 million acres (40 million hectares) for national parks and preserves with a single stroke of the pen.

At the core of the issue was both 'locking up the land' and federal interference in the lives of Alaskans. Largely as the result of their remoteness, Alaskans have always been extremely independent, and they resented anyone who travelled north with a book of rules and regulations. This was especially true at the turn of the century, and that touch of frontier can still be found today. To most Alaskans, Washington DC is a foreign capital.

Today's Alaskans tend to be young and spirited in work and play. They are individualistic in their lifestyles, following few outside trends and adhering only to what their environment dictates. They are lovers of the outdoors, though they don't always seem to take care of it, and generally extend a warm welcome to travellers. Occasionally you might run into one who is boastfully loud as he spins and weaves tales of unbelievable feats while slapping you on the back. In this land of frontier fable, that's not being obnoxious – that's being colourful.

THE NATIVE HERITAGE

Long before Bering's journeys to Alaska, other groups of people had made their

way there and established a culture and life-style in some of the harshest environments in the world. The first major invasion across the land bridge was by the Tlingits and Haidas (who settled throughout the Southeast and British Columbia) and the Athabascans (a nomadic tribe that lived in the Interior). The other two major groups were the Aleuts of the Aleutian Islands and the Eskimos who settled on the coast of the Bering Sea and the Arctic Ocean. Both groups were believed to have migrated only 3000 years ago but were well established by the time the Europeans arrived.

The Tlingit and Haida cultures were advanced ones, as the tribes had permanent settlements including large clan-houses. They were noted for their excellent woodcarving, most notably poles – called *totems* – that can still be seen today in most Southeast communities. The Tlingits were spread throughout the Southeast in strong numbers and occasionally went as far south as Seattle in their large dugout canoes. Both groups had few problems gathering food as fish and game were plentiful in the Southeast.

Not so for the Aleuts and the Eskimos. With much colder winters and cooler summers, both groups had to develop a highly effective sea-hunting culture to sustain life in the harsh regions of Alaska. This was especially true for the Eskimos who could not have survived the winters without their amazing ice-hunting abilities. In the spring, these people, armed with only jade-tipped harpoons in skin-covered boats called *kayaks* and *umiaks*, stalked and killed 60-ton bowhead whales. The Aleuts were noted for some of the finest basket weaving in North America, using the highly prized Attu grass of the Aleutian Islands. The Eskimos were unsurpassed carvers of ivory, jade and soapstone and many support themselves today by continuing the art.

The natives, despite their harsh environment, were strong in numbers

before the white people brought guns, alcohol and disease that destroyed the Indians' delicate relationship with nature and wiped out entire villages. At one time there were an estimated 20,000 Aleuts living on almost every island of the Aleutian chain. It took the Russians only 50 years to reduce the population (mainly through forced labour) to less than 2000.

Today there are almost 70,000 natives, of which two-thirds are Eskimos. They are no longer nomadic but live in permanent villages, using modern materials for their houses instead of sod, and in many places using oil and electricity for heating and cooking. The Bush village has replaced the tribe and ranges in size from 30 people to 2900 in Barrow, the largest native centre.

All natives received a boost in 1971 when Congress passed the Native Claims Settlement Act in an effort to allow oil companies to build a pipeline across their traditional lands. The act created the Alaska Native Fund and formed 12 regional corporations, controlled and administered by the local tribes, that invested and developed the $900 million and 44 million acres that the Alaskan natives received for their historical lands. Today all natives hold stock in their village corporation and receive dividends when it turns a profit. Although a few corporations have floundered and lost money, one of them, Sealaska of Juneau, has done so well managing its lands and investing its funds that it is ranked among the 500 largest companies in America.

POPULATION

The largest state in the US has the smallest population. Permanent residents, not including the large influx of seasonal workers in the fishing and tourist industries, number 460,000, with over half of them living in the Anchorage Bowl area. It is estimated that only 20% were born in Alaska while 25% have moved there in the last five years. This means that the average resident is young (median age is 26 to 28), mobile and mostly from the US west coast. Eskimos and other native groups make up only 14% of the total population while ethnic groups of Japanese, Filipinos and blacks represent even less.

The five largest cities are: Anchorage (population 204,216), Fairbanks (59,222), Juneau (27,500), Kodiak (13,080) and Ketchikan (11,373).

GEOGRAPHY

Southeast Also known as the Panhandle, Southeast Alaska is a 500-mile (800 km)

coastal strip from the Dixon Entrance north of Prince Rupert to the Gulf of Alaska. In between are the hundreds of islands of the Alexander Archipelago and a narrow strip of coast separated from Canada's mainland by the glacier-filled Coastal Mountains. Winding through the middle of the region is the Inside Passage waterway, the lifeline for the isolated communities as the rugged terrain prohibits road building. High annual rainfall and mild temperatures have turned the Southeast into a lush rainforest broken up by majestic mountain ranges, glaciers and fjords that surpass Norway's.

The area has many small fishing and lumbering towns as well as the larger communities of Ketchikan, Sitka and Juneau, which is the state capital and considered by many to be the most scenic city in Alaska. Other highlights of the region include the wilderness areas of Glacier Bay, Admiralty Island, Misty Fjord and Tracy Arm. Because the State Marine Ferry connects it to Seattle and Prince Rupert, Southeast is the cheapest and often the first area visited by travellers.

Southcentral This region curves 650 miles (1046 km) from the Gulf of Alaska, past the Prince William Sound to Kodiak Island. Like Southeast, it is a mixture of rugged mountains, glaciers, steep fjords and virgin forests and is centred around the Kenai Peninsula, a superb recreational area for backpacking, fishing and boating. To the south-west is Kodiak Island, home of much of Alaska's crab industry and the Kodiak bear, the largest species of brown bear in the state. To the east of the Kenai Peninsula is the bay known as Prince William Sound, famous for the Columbia Glacier and a mecca for kayakers and adventurers.

The coastline can often be a rainy and stormy region of the state but the summers are usually mild and have their share of sunshine. The peninsula is served by road from Anchorage and by the

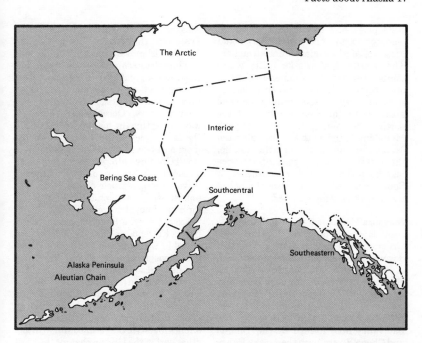

State Marine Ferry across Prince William Sound and to Kodiak.

Highlights of the region are the historical and charming towns of Homer, Seward, Cordova and Hope, while backpackers will find many opportunities for outdoor adventure in the wilderness areas of the Chugach National Forest, Kenai National Wildlife Refuge and the outlying areas around Kodiak, Cordova and Valdez.

Anchorage Because of the city's size and central location, Anchorage has to be viewed as a separate region; one that is passed through whether you want to deal with an urban area or not. At first glance Anchorage appears to be like any other city – billboards, traffic jams, fast-food restaurants and what seems like hordes of people. Among this uncontrolled urban sprawl, however, is a city that in recent years has blossomed on the flow of oil

money. While older cities in the Lower 48 (see 'Alaskan English' section later in this chapter) often worry about a decaying city centre, Anchorage has transformed its downtown area with such capital projects as a sports arena, performing-arts centre and 70 miles (110 km) of bike paths.

Anchorage also has a feature most other cities don't – wilderness at its doorstep. With its nearby Chugach State Park, Turnagain and Knik arms and Matanuska Valley (home of the softball-size radishes), Anchorage is an area worth spending a little time in, if for no other reason than that most travellers have to arrive, depart or pass through it at some stage.

Interior This section includes three major highways – George Parks, Glenn and Richardson – that cut across the centre of the state and touch a variety of forests, state parks and recreational areas, including Denali National Park and Preserve, Alaska's number one attraction. The heartland of Alaska offers warm temperatures in the summer and ample opportunities for outdoor activities in some of the most scenic and accessible areas. With the Alaska Range to the north, the Wrangell and Chugach Mountains to the south and the Talkeetna Mountains cutting through the middle, the Interior has a rugged appearance matching that of either Southeast or Southcentral Alaska but without much of the rain and cloudy weather.

Fairbanks The boom town of both the gold-rush days and later the pipeline construction to Prudhoe Bay has settled down a little but still has retained much of its colourful and hardcore-Alaskan character. A quick trip through Fairbanks is often a disappointment to most travellers, as Alaska's second largest town is a spread-out city. Located in the flat valley floor formed by the Tanana and Chena Rivers, with the Alaska Range and Mt McKinley far off in the distance, Fairbanks lacks the dramatic setting many other areas offer. If sufficient time is spent here, however, the true personality of this free-wheeling frontier town comes out. In the summer, Fairbanks can be an unusually warm place with temperatures often reaching 80-90°F (27-32°C) and a midnight sun that sets for only a few hours.

The surrounding area, especially White Mountains, Circle, Eagle and the North Slope Haul Road to Prudhoe Bay, has some of the most interesting backcountry areas that can still be reached by road. Fairbanks is also the transportation hub for anybody wishing to venture above the Arctic Circle or into the Brooks Range, site of the many new Alaska national parks and wildlife refuges.

The Bush This region covers a vast area that includes the Brooks Range, Arctic Alaska, Western Alaska on the Bering Sea, and the Alaska Peninsula and Aleutian Islands which make up the outreaching western arm of the state. The Bush has a greater area than the other five regions put together and is separated from them by great mountains and mighty rivers. Occasionally there are ways of beating the high cost of getting to the far reaches of the state, but for the most part travelling to the Bush involves small chartered aircraft or 'bush planes'. These airplanes are a common method of travel through much of the state but, unfortunately, are prohibitively expensive for many budget travellers.

Except for the larger communities of Nome, Kotzebue and Barrow, independent travel in Bush villages is difficult unless you have a contact. If you have just stepped off a chartered airplane, the small, isolated villages may appear closed, unfriendly and very limited in their facilities. For those who do make an effort to leave the roads, Bush Alaska offers a life-style that is uncommon in any other part of the US and that for the most part is pure and unaffected by the state's booming summer tourist industry. Climate in the summer can range from chilly temperatures of 40°F (4°C) in the treeless and nightless Arctic tundra to the wet and fog of the Bering Sea coast, where the terrain is a flat land of lakes and slow-moving rivers.

CLIMATE & THE 24-HOUR DAY
It makes sense that a place as large and diverse as Alaska would have a climate to match. The effects of oceans surrounding 75% of the state, the mountainous terrain and the low angle of the sun together give Alaska an extremely variable climate and daily weather that is famous for being unpredictable. Alaskan temperatures can reach both ends of the thermometer, often in the same place. The Interior can top 90°F (32°C) during the summer, yet six months later in the same region, a drop to -60°F (-51°C) is not unusual. Fort

Yukon holds the state record of 100°F (37.7°C) in June 1915 and once recorded -78°F (-60°C).

For the most part Southeast and Southcentral Alaska are high-precipitation areas, with temperatures varying only 40°F (22°C) during the year. Anchorage, shielded by the Kenai Mountains, has an annual rainfall of 15 inches (380 mm) and averages 60° to 70°F (15° to 21°C) from June through to August. Juneau averages 57 inches (1450 mm) of rain or snow, while Ketchikan soars to 154 inches (3900 mm) a year, most of which is rain, as the temperatures are extremely mild even in the winter.

Residents, however, will tell you that averages don't mean a thing. There have been summers when it has rained just about every day, and there have been Aprils when every day has been sunny and dry. A good week in Southcentral and Southeast during the summer will include three sunny days, two overcast ones and two when you will have to pull your rain gear out or duck for cover.

In the Interior and up around Fairbanks, precipitation is light but temperatures can fluctuate by more than 100°F during the year. In the summer, the average daytime temperature can range from 55°F (12°C) to 75°F (23°C) with a brief period in late July to early August where it will top 80° F (27°C) or even 90° F (32°C). At night it can drop sharply to 45°F (7°C) or even lower, and freak snowfalls can occur in the valleys during July or August, with the white stuff lasting a day or two.

The climate in Bush varies. The region north of the Arctic Circle is cool most of the summer with temperatures in the mid-40s F (around 7°C) and less than four inches (100 mm) of precipitation a year. Other areas such as Nome in western Alaska or Dillingham in the south-west aren't much warmer and tend to be foggy and rainy much of the summer.

In most of Alaska, summers are a beautiful mixture of long days and short nights, making the great outdoors even more appealing. At Point Barrow, Alaska's northernmost point, the sun never sets for 2½ months from May through to August. The longest day is 21 June (equinox), when the sun sets for only two hours in Fairbanks, four hours in Anchorage and five to six hours in the Southeast. Even after the sun sets in late June and July, it is replaced, not by night, but by a dusk that still allows good visibility. The midnight sun allows residents and visitors to undertake activities at hours undreamed of in most other places – six-mile hikes after dinner, bike rides at 10 pm or softball games at midnight. It also causes most people, even those with the best window shades, to wake up at 4 or 5 am.

No matter where you intend to travel or what you plan to do, bring protection for Alaska's climate. This should include warm clothing, rain gear and a covering if you are camping out. Alaska's weather is unpredictable, constantly changing and often a shock comes when least expected – don't be left out in the cold.

FESTIVALS & HOLIDAYS

Alaskans do their share of celebrating, much of it during the summer. One of the biggest celebrations in the state is Summer Solstice on 21 June, the longest day of the year. Fairbanks holds the best community festival, with a variety of events including midnight baseball games (played without the use of artificial light) and hikes to local hills to view the midnight sun. Nome stages a week-long Midnight Sun Festival while many towns have unofficial celebrations. Independence Day (4 July) is a popular holiday around the state when the larger communities of Ketchikan, Juneau, Anchorage and Fairbanks sponsor well-planned events. Perhaps even more enjoyable during this time is a visit to a small settlement such as Gustavus, Seldovia or Talkeetna, where you cannot help but be swept along with the local residents in an afternoon of old-fashioned celebrating such as games and square dancing.

Salmon and halibut derbies that end with cash prizes for the heaviest fish caught are regular events around the coastal regions of Alaska, with Juneau and Seward having the largest. State fairs, though small compared to those in the Lower 48, are worth attending if for no other reason than to see what a 70-pound (32 kg) cabbage looks like. They all take place in August and include the Alaska State Fair at Palmer, the Tanana Valley Fair at Fairbanks, the Southeast State Fair at Haines and smaller ones at Kodiak, Delta Junction and Ninilchik.

Regional Festivals & Celebrations
April
International Curling Bonspiel, Fairbanks
Spring Carnival, Mt Alyeska
Alaska Folk Festival, Juneau
Alaska Crab Festival, Whittier
Goldrush Stampede, Skagway

May
Little Norway Festival, Petersburg
Salmon Derby, Ketchikan
Miner's Day Celebration, Talkeetna

Crab Festival, Kodiak
Salmon Derby, Sitka
Polar Bear Swim, Nome
King Salmon Derby, Haines

June
Summer Music Festival, Sitka
Tanana Raft Classic, Nenana
Renaissance Faire, Anchorage
Salmon Derby, Petersburg
Summer Solstice, Fairbanks
Midnight Sun Festival, Nome
All Alaska Logging Championships, Sitka
Whaling Festival, Barrow
Reindeer Round-up, Kotzebue
Halibut Derby, Homer
Nenana River Daze, Nenana

July
Northwest Native Trade Fair, Kotzebue
Moose Dropping Festival, Talkeetna
Renaissance Faire, Fairbanks
Golden Days, Fairbanks
Soapy Smith's Wake, Skagway

August
Summer Arts Festival, Fairbanks
Founder's Day Celebration, Metlakatla
Blueberry Festival, Ketchikan
Tanana Valley Fair, Fairbanks

Southeast Alaska State Fair, Haines
State Fair and Rodeo, Kodiak
Deltana Fair, Delta Junction
Silver Salmon Derby, Valdez
Silver Salmon Derby, Seward
Alaska Seafest, Ketchikan
Golden North Salmon Derby, Juneau
AgriFair, Ninilchik
Blue Grass Festival, Talkeetna
Gold Rush Days, Valdez
Alaska State Fair, Palmer

September
Whittier Days, Whittier
Alaska Festival of Music, Anchorage
Octoberfest, Fairbanks

State Holidays

New Year's Day	1 January
Admission Day	3 January
Lincoln's Day	12 February
President's Day	16 February
Seward's Day	30 March
Easter	April
Memorial Day	25 May
Independence Day	4 July
Labor Day	7 September
Columbus Day	12 October
Alaska Day	18 October
Veteran's Day	11 November
Thanksgiving	26 November
Christmas	25 December

ALASKAN ENGLISH

English is spoken all across this great land but it is tinted with Alaskan phrases and words that make it almost a tongue of its own. Most of these words are of native origin or are a colourful combination coined by some local character. The following list should be of some assistance when you are befuddled but is by no means a complete text of Alaskan English.

Alcan – The Alaska Highway. The only overland link between the state and the rest of the country. Although the highway is almost completely paved now, completing a journey across this legendary road is still a special accomplishment that earns you a slash mark on the side of your pick-up truck.

aurora borealis (or Northern Lights) – A spectacular show on clear nights, possible almost any time of the year. The mystical snakes of light that weave across the sky from the northern horizon are the result of gas particles colliding with solar electrons. Best viewed from the Interior, away from city lights, late summer through winter.

bidarka – A skin-covered sea-kayak used by the Aleuts.

blanket toss – An activity originating with the Eskimos in which a hunter was tossed into the air with a skin so he could search for whales offshore.

blue cloud – What Southeasterners call a break in the clouds.

break-up – A phrase applied to rivers when the ice suddenly begins to disintegrate and flows downstream. Many residents also use it to describe spring in Alaska when the rains come, the snows melt and everything turns to mud and slush.

bunny boots – Large, oversized and usually white plastic boots used extensively in sub-zero weather to prevent feet from freezing.

the Bush – Any area in the state either not connected by road to Anchorage or which does not have a ferry dock in town.

cache – A small hut or storage room built high off the ground to keep supplies and spare food away from roaming bears and wolves. The term, however, has found its way onto the neon signs of everything in the cities from liquor stores to pizza parlours.

cabin fever – A winter condition in which cross-eyed Alaskans go stir-crazy in their one-room cabins because of too little sunlight and too much time spent indoors.

capital move – The political issue that raged in the early 1980s and concerns moving the state capital from Juneau closer to Anchorage. The issue was buried somewhat in a 1982 state election when residents voted down the funding for the move north.

cheechako – Tenderfoot, greenhorn or somebody trying to survive their first year in Alaska.

chum – Not your mate or good buddy but a nickname for the dog salmon.

clearcut – A hated sight for environmentalists, this is an area where loggers have cut every tree, large and small, leaving nothing standing. A traveller's first view of one is often from a state ferry and is a shocking sight.

d-2 – A phrase that covers the lands issue of the late 1970s, pitting environmentalists against developers over the federal government's preservation of 100 million acres of Alaska wilderness as wildlife reserves, forests and national parks.

developers – Those residents of Alaska who favour development of the state natural resources and land through such endeavours as logging and mining, as opposed to preserving it in national parks.

Eskimo ice-cream – A traditional native food made of whipped berries, seal oil and snow.

fish wheel – A wooden trap that scoops salmon or other large fish out of a river into a holding tank by utilising the current as power.

greenies – A nickname for environmentalists and others who celebrated the passage of the Alaska Lands Bill.

humpie – A nickname for the humpback or pink salmon, the mainstay of the fishing industry in the Southeast.

iceworm – A small, thin black worm that thrives in glacial ice. Made famous by a Robert Service poem.

Lower 48 – The way Alaskans describe the continental United States.

mukluks – Lightweight boots of seal skin trimmed with fur, made by the Eskimos.

moose nuggets – Hard, smooth little objects dropped by moose after a good meal. Some enterprising resident in Homer has capitalised on them by baking, varnishing and trimming them with evergreen leaves to sell during Christmas as *Moostletoe*.

muskeg – The bogs in Alaska where layers of matted plantlife float on top of stagnant water. Bad place to hike or pitch a tent.

no-see-um – Nickname for the tiny gnats found throughout much of the Alaska wilderness, especially the Interior and areas in the Brooks Range.

Outside – To residents, any place that isn't Alaska.

permafrost – Permanently frozen subsoil that covers two-thirds of the state.

petroglyphs – Ancient rock carvings.

potlatch – A traditional native gathering held to commemorate any memorable occasion.

qiviut – The wool of the musk ox that is often woven into garments.

scat – Any animal droppings but usually used to describe that of a bear. If it is dark brown or bluish and somewhat square in shape, a bear has passed through. If it is steaming, he's eating blueberries around the next bend.

sourdough – Any old-timer in the state, who some say is 'sour on the country but without enough dough to get out'. More recently arrived residents believe anybody who has survived an Alaskan winter qualifies as a sourdough. The term also applies to a yeasty mixture used to make bread or pancakes rise.

Southeast sneakers – Also known as Ketchikan tennis shoes, Sitka slippers, Petersburg pumps and a variety of other names. These are the tall, reddish-brown rubber boots Southeast residents wear when it rains and often when it doesn't.

taku wind – Juneau's sudden gusts of wind that may exceed 100 miles (160 km) per hour in the spring and fall. Often the winds cause another strange phenomenon – horizontal rain which, as the name indicates, comes straight at you instead falling down on you. In Anchorage and throughout the Interior these sudden rushes of air over or through mountain gaps are called 'williwaws'.

tundra – Often used to refer to the vast, treeless arctic plains.

ulu – A fan-shaped knife that the natives use to chop and scrape meat. Now the gift shops use them to lure tourists.

Facts for the Visitor

VISAS

If you are travelling to Alaska from overseas, one or possibly two things will be needed, depending on your nationality: a passport (except for US and Canadian citizens who only need a driver's licence or voter registration card) and at least one visa, possibly two. Obviously a US visa is needed but if you're taking either the Alaska Highway or the State Marine Ferry from Prince Rupert (British Columbia, Canada) then you will also need a Canadian visa. The Alcan begins in Canada, requiring travellers to pass from the US into Canada and back into the US again.

Travellers from Western Europe and most Commonwealth nations do not need a Canadian visa and can get a six-month travel visa to the US without too much paperwork or waiting. All visitors must have an onward or return ticket to enter the US and sufficient funds to pass into Canada. Those arriving at the Canadian border with less than US$200 will probably be turned back.

No vaccinations are needed for either country and only persons who have been on a farm in the past 30 days will be detained by immigration officials. Travellers are allowed to bring all personal goods (including camping gear or hiking equipment) into either country free of duty along with food for two days personal use and up to 50 cigars, 200 cigarettes (one carton) and 40 ounces (1 litre) of liquor or wine. There are no forms to fill out if you are a foreign visitor bringing in any vehicle, whether it is a bicycle, motorcycle or car; nor are there forms for hunting rifles or fishing gear. The hunting rifle (hand-guns and automatic weapons are prohibited) must be registered in your own country and you should bring proof that it is. There is no limit to the amount of money you can bring, but anything over US$5000 must be registered with customs officials.

A word of warning: overseas travellers should be aware of the procedures to re-enter the US. Occasionally visitors get stuck in Canada without the necessary papers to enter Alaska after passing through the Lower 48. Canadian immigration officers often caution people who they feel might have difficulty returning.

MONEY

Alaskans use the same currency as the rest of the US; they just use a lot more of it. The state is traditionally known for having the highest cost of living in the country, though places like southern California, San Francisco and New York City have caught up and actually exceed it in some areas. There are two reasons for the high prices in Alaska: the long distances needed to transport everything, and the high cost of labour.

To buy a dozen eggs in Fairbanks will cost you more than in other parts of the US – around US$1.30 to $1.60 – but to walk into a café and have two of them cooked and served is where high prices slap you in the face like a July snowfall. In any restaurant, not only are the transportation costs written into the price, but so are the high salaries of the chef, waitress and busboy who put them sunnyside-up on your table.

The trick to budget travel, or to beating the high prices, is to avoid the labour cost – buy your own food in a market and cook it at the Youth Hostel or campsite. Use the mass transit facilities, or better yet, hitch-hike, sleep in the campgrounds and enjoy your favourite brew around a campfire at night. The restaurants, bars, hotels and taxi companies, with their inflated peak-season prices, will quickly drain your money pouch.

A rule of thumb for Alaskan prices is that they are the lowest in Ketchikan and increase gradually as you go north. Overall, the Southeast has the best bargains because of inexpensive barge transportation from Seattle (the supply centre for the area). Barges arrive weekly in the isolated region of Alaska, bringing all the necessities of life. The trip takes several days and fresh foods such as bread and milk are frozen before shipping up. If you walk into a store and find all the milk half frozen, don't be alarmed – the barge just arrived.

Anchorage (and to some extent Fairbanks) are the exceptions to the rule as they have competitive prices due to their large populations and business communities. When travelling in the Bush, on the other hand, be prepared for anything. The cost of fresh food, gasoline or lodging could be two or three times what it is anywhere else in the state. It is here that tales of $15 breakfasts were conjured up, and in some isolated Bush villages those stories might not be too mythical.

On the average a loaf of day-old bread will cost between $1 and $1.20 while locally baked bread will cost from $1.70 to $2.40. Half a gallon (2 litres) of milk costs $1.90 to $2.70, apples cost $0.80-1.20/lb ($1.80-2.60/kg) and hamburger is anywhere from $2/lb ($4.40/kg) in the large cities to over $3.50/lb ($7.70/kg) in a small town. When buying fresh fruit and vegetables, take the time to look over them closely, especially in small town markets. It is not too surprising to buy a stalk of celery and later discover that the middle of it is spoiled.

A US gallon (3.7 litres) of gasoline can cost anywhere from $1.40 in large commercial areas to $2.50 or more at some deserted station off the road. A single room in the cheapest motels or hotels costs $30 to $35 per night while many state and federal campgrounds charge $4 per tent site and privately-owned campgrounds ask anywhere from $7 to $15 a night.

The National Bank of Alaska is the largest bank in the state, with offices in almost every village and town of the heavily-travelled routes. The NBA, open Monday to Friday from 10 am to 3 pm, can meet the needs of most visitors. Many branches of NBA and other banks have night hours on Wednesday and Friday or drive-up windows that stay open late. The popular brands of travellers cheques are widely used around the state and many merchants also accept Canadian money, though they usually burn you on the exchange rate.

Note All prices quoted in this book are in US dollars unless otherwise stated.

INFORMATION
The first place to write to while planning your adventure is the Division of Tourism, where you can request a copy of the annually updated *Alaska Vacation Planner*.

Division of Tourism
    Pouch E
    Juneau, Alaska 99811
    USA
    Tel (907) 465-2010

Travel information is easy to obtain once you are on the road as almost every city, town and village has a tourist contact centre whether it be a visitors bureau, Chamber of Commerce or hut near the ferry dock. They are good sources for free maps, information on local accommodation and directions to the nearest campground or hiking trail.

TIME
In 1983, Alaska reduced its time zones from four to two in an effort to help commerce and communications between its cities. With the exception of four Aleutian Island communities, the entire state shares the same time zone (Yukon Time) which is one hour earlier than the Pacific standard time in which Seattle falls. Telephone area codes are even

simpler in Alaska: the entire state shares 907.

MEDIA

There are 36 daily, weekly and trade newspapers in Alaska, though most are eight pages of local news, softball scores and advertising. The largest daily in the state is the *Anchorage Daily News*, a first-class newspaper that captured the Pulitzer Prize in the 1970s with its stories on the Alaskan pipeline. The next biggest daily is its competitor, the *Anchorage Times*, while the *Fairbanks Daily News Miner* is one of the state's finest papers. The *Seattle Post-Intelligence* is flown into the Southeast daily and the usual news magazines *Time* and *Newsweek* are available, though they are a week old by the time they reach the news stand.

BOOKS

The following publications will aid anybody on a trip to the north. A few of the more popular ones can be found in any good bookstore but most are available only in Alaska or by writing to the publisher. A list of hiking and wilderness guidebooks can be found in the chapter on the Wilderness.

Travel Guides

The Milepost (Alaska Northwest Publishing Company, 130 2nd Avenue South, Edmonds, Washington 98020; 498 pp, $12.95). This travel guide is put out every year and is unquestionably the most popular. While it has good information, history and maps of Alaska and western Canada, its drawbacks are its large size (impossible to slip into the side pocket of a backpack) and the fact that it is written for travellers who are driving. Listings of restaurants, hotels and other businesses are limited to advertisers.

Adventuring In Alaska (Peggy Wayburn, Sierra Club Books, 530 Bush St, San Francisco, California 94108; 314 pp, $10.95). A good general guidebook to the many new national parks and wildlife preserves and other remote regions of Alaska. Also contains excellent 'how-to' information on undertaking wilderness expeditions in the state, whether the mode of travel is canoe, kayak or foot.

Alaska's Southeast: Touring The Inside Passage (Sarah Eppenbach, Pacific Search Press, 222 Dexter Avenue North, Seattle, Washington 98109; 296 pp, $11.95). Although lacking in detailed travel information, the guidebook offers some of the most comprehensive accounts of Southeast's history, culture and colour. It does a superb job of giving you a feeling for each town and area of the Panhandle.

The Inside Passage Traveller (Ellen Searby, Windham Press, Box 1332, Juneau, Alaska 99802; 176 pp, $7.95). Another travel guide devoted to Southeast, written by a former marine ferry crew member. Mediocre overall, but there's good information on the smaller communities that can be reached by the state ferry.

Alaska's Parklands, The Complete Guide (Nancy Simmerman, The Mountaineers, 306 2nd Avenue West, Seattle, Washington 98119; 336 pp, $14.95). The encyclopaedia of Alaska wilderness, covering over 110 state and national parks and wild areas. Lacks detailed travel information and guides to individual canoe and hiking routes but does a thorough job of covering the scenery, location, wildlife and activities available in each preserve.

Alaska Vacation Planner (Alaska State Division of Tourism, Pouch E, Juneau, Alaska 99801; 96 pp, $2 for postage and handling). This guide is updated annually by the state office and is the index of bus companies, air charters, hotels, wilderness lodges and camping facilities as well as a list of state-wide attractions, festivals and guide companies. Prices are included with some business descriptions, but not all. A handy publication to have while planning your trip.

Southeast Alaska Travel Planner (Southeast Alaska Tourism Council, Box 275, Juneau, Alaska 99802; 28 pp, free).

Same as the Alaska Vacation Planner but aimed just at the Southeast.

City Visitor Guides

Various large and small newspapers around the state put out special visitors' guides at the beginning of the summer. All are filled with local history, information, things to do and trails to hike for the area where the newspaper circulates. The guides are free and are usually found at numerous locations (restaurants, bars, hotel lobbies) around town. If you write to them, most newspapers will send you the publication before you depart, though they might charge you a small handling and shipping fee. The various newspaper guides are:

Ketchikan Visitors Guide, Ketchikan Daily News, PO Box 7900, Ketchikan, Alaska 99901.

Juneau Guide, Juneau Empire, 235 Second St, Juneau, Alaska 99801.

Viking Visitor Guide, Petersburg Pilot, PO Box 930, Petersburg, Alaska 99833.

The Wrangell Guide, Wrangell Publishing Inc, PO Box 798, Wrangell, Alaska 99929.

Skagway Alaskan, The Skagway News, PO Box 1898, Skagway, Alaska 99840.

Haines Sentinel, Chilkat Valley News, PO Box 637, Haines, Alaska 99827.

All About Sitka, Daily Sitka Sentinel, 112 Barracks St, Sitka, Alaska 99835.

Valdez/Cordova Visitors Guide, Valdez Vanguard, PO Box 157, Valdez, Alaska 99686.

Interior & Arctic Alaska Visitors Guide, Fairbanks Daily News Miner, Box 710, Fairbanks, Alaska 99707.

Homer Tourist Guide, The Homer News, PO Box 254, Homer, Alaska 99603.

Prince William Sound Pilot, Shoestring Publications, PO Box 601, Whittier, Alaska 99693.

The Anchorage Times Visitors Guide, The Anchorage Times, Box 40, Anchorage, Alaska 99510.

HEALTH

Emergency medical services are available in almost every town of any size at either hospitals or walk-in clinics. If not, the local police will have the means to fly you to the nearest one. The Alaska State Troopers are the state's enforcement agency outside of local police forces and have outposts scattered throughout Alaska that assist in emergencies such as bear maulings, lost hikers or avalanche rescues.

DRUGS

A few words to clear up the myths that surround Alaska's drug laws: technically marijuana is legal when used in the privacy of your home and you are in possession of less than an ounce (about 25 grams). Although it is not a law, the State Supreme Court has ruled that the use of the drug is the right of an individual. Alaska is the only state in the country where marijuana is actually legal, but don't expect a drug paradise when you arrive.

Pot, which comes to Alaska mostly from Hawaii and California, is extremely hard to find and usually quite costly. An ounce of the weed that might sell for $60 in the Lower 48 is pegged as high as $150 to over $200 in Alaska. Many residents who are regular smokers grow their own or purchase it from somebody who does. Home-grown is considerably cheaper but of low quality because of the short growing season in the summer.

It is against the law to smoke marijuana in public places such as parks, bars or the State Marine Ferry, and there are severe penalties for those arrested while doing so. It is also foolhardy to carry the drug when thumbing or driving the Alcan Highway, as you have to pass through the close inspection of immigration officers at two borders.

In recent years state legislators have repeatedly tried to make marijuana illegal but have failed each time. The use of other drugs is against the law and results in severe penalties, especially for cocaine, which is heavily abused in the 49th state.

PLACES TO STAY
Camping

Bring a tent!, then you will never be without inexpensive accommodation in Alaska. There are no cheap bed & breakfasts as found in Europe and the number of Youth Hostels is limited, but there are state, federal and private campgrounds from Ketchikan to Fairbanks. The fee ranges from free to $14 per tent in some of the more deluxe private campgrounds. It is also a widely accepted practice among backpackers to just wander into the woods and find a spot to pitch a tent. With the exception of Anchorage, Fairbanks and one or two other cities, you can walk a mile from most towns and find yourself in an isolated wooded area. It may not be an 'officially designated campsite', but if backpackers are clean and orderly, locals are more than happy to overlook this fact.

The tent should be light (under 5 pounds/2 kg) and complete with a good rainfly. If it has been on more than its share of trips, consider waterproofing it before you leave by recoating the rainfly and tent floor. The new free-standing domes work best, as in many areas of the state the ground is rocky and difficult to sink a peg into. Along with the tent, bring a thin foam sleeping pad (not a bulky air mattress); it will soften the hard ground while helping you keep warm by putting a layer of insulation between your sleeping bag and the moisture that will seep through the tent floor.

Youth Hostels

The once-struggling Alaska Council of American Youth Hostels has grown considerably in the past few years and now has 12 official hostels and one unofficial one scattered throughout the state. Although the number seems to vary from summer to summer, the mainstays of the system are the hostels in Anchorage, Juneau, Ketchikan, Sitka, Haines, Delta Junction, Fairbanks, Soldotna and the unofficial one in Denali National Park. Locations of others in 1985 included Seward, Tok, Alyeska and Talkeetna. The first hostel you check into is the best source of information as to what is open and what has closed down that particular summer. You'll want to check carefully once you arrive, as several chapters are planning to change to a new location within their city, most notably the Anchorage and Fairbanks hostels.

The hostels range from the unheated old freight cars at Denali National Park to the newly refurbished house in Juneau that offers a common room with a fireplace, cooking facilities, showers and a location only four blocks from the capitol building. In between is everything from church basements and metal huts to rustic cabins with wood heat.

ALASKA COUNCIL AMERICAN YOUTH HOSTELS

The fees range from $2 to $8 for a one-night stay, more if you are a non-member. Some hostels accept reservations and others don't; each hostel's particulars will be discussed later in this guide. Be aware that hostelling means separate male and female dormitories, house parents, chores assigned for each day you stay and curfews. Also, the hostels are closed during the day (even when it rains). They are strict about these and other rules such as no smoking, drinking or illegal drugs. Still, Youth Hostels are the best accommodation bargain in Alaska and the best place to meet other budget travellers and backpackers.

For more information on Alaska Youth Hostels before you depart on your trip, write to or call: Alaska Council, PO Box 91226, Anchorage, Alaska 99509; tel (907) 243-3456.

Hotels & Motels
Hotels and motels are the most expensive lodging you can book. Although there are a few bargain bunk-houses, the average single room in an 'inexpensive' hotel is priced from $30 to $35 and a double from $40 to $50. Those are the places down by the waterfront that offer shared bathrooms. Better hotels in each town will be even more costly, with Anchorage's best places charging close to $150 per night.

The other problem with hotel/motels is they tend to be full during much of the summer. Without being part of a tour or having advanced reservations, you may have to search for an available bed in some cities. In small villages, you could be plain out of luck as they are likely to have only one or two places to choose from.

Other Accommodation
Also available are roadhouses located along the highways, wilderness lodges and an expanding network of bed & breakfast places. Authentic roadhouses that combine cabins with a large lodge/dining-room are slowly being replaced by modern motels, but some can still be found and offer rustic cabins which sleep two to four for $40 to $70 per night. A few are charmers, with a roaring blaze in the stone fireplace and an owner who acts as chef, bartender and late-night storyteller.

Wilderness lodges are off the beaten path and usually require a bush plane or boat to reach them. The vast majority need advance booking and offer rustic cabins with saunas and ample opportunities to explore the nearby area by foot, canoe or kayak (they provide the boats). The lodges are designed for people who want to 'escape into the wilderness' without having to endure the 'hardship' of a tent or freeze-dried dinners or a small campstove. The prices range from $100 to $200 per day per person and include all meals.

Visitors can also find accommodation and usually a large breakfast in the private homes of Alaskan residents. In the past few years these bed & breakfast places have popped up throughout the state. Although their rates are below what major hotels will charge, most bed & breakfast places are still above what most budget travellers are willing to pay on a regular basis. Rates vary but are generally between $40 and $50 for a single and $60 and up for a double.

Some bed & breakfast places are in the out-of-the-way communities of Angoon, Pelican, Gustavus or Talkeetna, where staying in a private home in such a small settlement can be a unique and interesting experience. All recommend reservations

AMERICAN YOUTH HOSTELS, INC.

1332 "I" STREET, N.W., SUITE 800
WASHINGTON, D.C. 20005

INDIVIDUAL INTRODUCTORY MEMBERSHIP CARD
Maximum Fee $3.00/Night

VALID FOR UP TO 3 NIGHTS ONLY AT PLACE OF PURCHASE

This Introductory Card is intended to allow an interested individual the opportunity to participate in hosteling before applying for membership in AYH. Valid in U.S. only.

Name _____

Address _____ Zip _____

City/State _____

Date of Birth _____

COUNCIL/AGENCY OR HOSTEL STAMP OF PLACE OF ISSUE

DATE OF ISSUE: JUL 8 1985

X _____
Signature

CARDHOLDER'S COPY

in advance, but it is often possible to obtain a bed the day you arrive. Particular bed & breakfast places will be covered in the regional chapters. For more information before the trip, or to make reservations, contact the following associations:

Southeast
    Southeast Alaska Bed & Breakfast Association, 526 Seward St, Juneau, Alaska 99801, tel (907) 586-2959
Southcentral
    Alaska Private Lodging, PO Box 10135, Anchorage, Alaska 99511, tel (907) 345-2222
Anchorage
    Stay With A Friend, Box 173, Anchorage, Alaska 99503, tel (907) 274-6445
Fairbanks
    Fairbanks Bed & Breakfast, PO Box 74573, Fairbanks, Alaska 99707, tel (907) 452-4967
Ketchikan
    Ketchikan Bed & Breakfast, PO Box 7735, Ketchikan, Alaska 99901, tel (907) 225-3860

FOOD & DRINK

The local supermarket will provide the cheapest food, whether you want to live on a diet of fruit and nuts or cook full meals at the youth hostel. The larger urban centres have markets which offer not only competitive prices but a good selection of fruit and vegetables during the summer. While strolling down the aisles, keep an eye out for fresh Alaskan seafood, especially in Southeast markets. Local seafood is not cheap but it is renowned throughout the country for its superb taste. The most common catches that end up on the fish counter are king salmon steaks at $3-4/lb ($6.60-8.80/kg), whole Dungeness crab at $2-4/lb ($4.40-8.80/kg and prawns at $6-7/lb ($13.20-15.40/kg). The larger markets will have halibut, smoked salmon and cooked king crab.

Alaska is no longer so remote that America's fast-food (and cheapest) restaurants have not reached it. Back in the late 1970s only Anchorage and Fairbanks had a *McDonald's*. Now you can order a Big Mac in Ketchikan, Juneau and Kodiak while other chains such as *Pizza Hut*, *Burger King*, *Wendy's* and *Taco Bell* are just as widespread. There is even a *Dairy Queen* in Kotzebue. Though McDonald's and the other chains are the most inexpensive restaurants you can walk into, the prices still reflect the high cost of living in Alaska, as a Big Mac will cost between $1.80 and $2 and a small order of fries is 75c.

Most of the state, however, is safe from the fast-food invasion and the smaller towns you pass through will offer only a local coffee shop or café. Breakfast, which many places serve all day, is the best bargain, as a plate of eggs, toast and potatoes will cost anywhere from $4 to $6 while a cup of coffee will cost 50 to 75c.

One popular eating event during the summer in most of the state but especially in the Southeast is the salmon bake. A dinner costs from $14 to $18 but it is worth trying at least once if you're up for a full meal. The salmon is caught locally, grilled outside, smothered with somebody's home-made barbecue sauce and served in an all-you-can-eat fashion. One of the best bakes is in Juneau next to the Last Chance Mining Museum, where the meal includes your first beer, live entertainment and beautiful mountain scenery.

The legal drinking age in Alaska is now 21 and only the churches outnumber the bars. Except in a few native towns like Bethel or Angoon where alcohol is prohibited, it is never very difficult to find an open bar or liquor store. That and the long, dark winter explains why Alaska has the highest per capita alcoholism rate in the country, especially among the native people. The hours of bars vary but there are always a few places that open their doors at 9 am and don't close until 5 am.

Bars in the larger cities vary in their decor and many offer live entertainment, music and dancing. Bars in smaller towns are places to have a brew and mingle with fishermen, loggers or other locals. All serve the usual American beer found in the north-west (Miller, Rainier, Olympia) and usually one or two of that fine Canadian brew, charging $1.50 to $2.50 for a 12-oz (360 mm) bottle. During the summer don't be alarmed if you walk into an establishment for a couple of beers while the sun is still up and walk out while it's rising again and you miss the entire night.

WHAT TO WEAR

With nights that freeze and days that fry, layering is the only way to dress for Alaskan summers. It's an accepted fact in the North Country that several light layers of clothing are warmer than a single heavy one. With layers you trap warm air near the body to act as insulation against the cold. Layers are also easy to strip off when the midday sun begins to heat up. Instead of a heavy coat, pack a long-sleeve jersey or woollen sweater and a wind-breaker/parka. It will be easier to pack and more versatile for Alaska's many moods. A woollen hat and mittens are necessary items to fend away the cold night air, freak snowfalls or the chilly rain of the Southeast. Leave the umbrellas at home and instead take a waterproof nylon jacket with a hood for rain protection. Include a pair of rain pants if your plans include day hikes or wilderness expeditions.

The number of luxury restaurants, hotels and entertainment spots is growing in large Alaskan cities. Even in Juneau there is now a bar with a dress code, which amused the residents when it opened in 1984. Along with the proper dress, these places have prices to match that encourage most budget travellers to walk on by. For the most part Alaska is still a land of jeans, hiking boots (or brown rubber boots in Southeast) and woollen shirts, which is the acceptable attire for the vast majority of restaurants, bars and hotels throughout the state. If you are going to backpack around the north on a shoestring, there is no reason to take anything that isn't comfortable, functional in the harsh environment and easy to pack and wash.

There is no need to buy a pair of the brown rubber boots you'll see throughout the Southeast, but you should wax or 'grease' your boots to protect your feet from rain and the wet brush on the trail. It is best to avoid anything with goose-down fillings such as jackets or sleeping bags, as wet feathers tend to clump and lose most of their insulating power. Polyester fibre is the most common filling used by Alaskans.

EMPLOYMENT

Tales of astronomical wages for jobs on the Alaska pipeline and of other high-paying employment opportunities are, unfortunately, either exaggerated or non-existent today. The cold reality is that Alaska has one of the highest unemployment rates in the country, which often reaches 20% during the winter. Many summer travellers arrive thinking they will get work on a fishing boat after hearing of someone earning $10,000 in six weeks by getting a percentage of the catch on a good boat. In the end, if you lack the deck-hand experience necessary for any position on a fishing vessel, you'll probably end up cleaning salmon in a cannery for minimum wages ($3.85 per hour).

Summer employment in Alaska is possible but be realistic about what you will be paid, and look in the right places. Search out tourist-related businesses such as hotels, restaurants, bars and resorts that need additional short-term help to handle the influx of customers. Other places such as the US Forest Service and national parks also hire a large number of temporary workers during the summer. Be aware that these agencies, like many canneries, recruit their workers during the winter and have little (if anything) to offer someone passing through in June or July.

Top: Harbor seals on icebergs in Glacier Bay (JD)
Left: Bald eagle in Southeast Alaska (ADT)
Right: Moose in Interior Alaska (ADT)

Top: Cow moose in Mt. McKinley National Park (DR)
Left: Young mountain goat by the side of the Alcan Highway (DR)
Right: Bear tracks (JD)

Those whose sole interest is working for a summer in Alaska (rather than travelling) should begin looking the winter before. Start by contacting regional offices of the US Forest Service, national parks or the Chambers of Commerce of fishing communities like Petersburg, Juneau, Kodiak or Sitka. You can also get some information from the Alaska State Employment Service, though they tend to do everything they can to discourage outsiders from seeking jobs in Alaska:

Alaska State Employment Service
  Box 3-7000
  Juneau, Alaska 99802
  USA

FILM & PHOTOGRAPHY

The most cherished items you can take home from your trip are pictures and slides of Alaska's powerful scenery. Much of the state is a photographer's dream and your shutter finger will be tempted by mountain and glacier panoramas, bustling waterfronts and the diverse wildlife encountered during paddling and hiking trips. Even if you have never toted a camera before, seriously consider taking one to Alaska.

A small, lightweight 35 mm camera is perfectly suited for a summer of backpacking in the North Country. To photograph wildlife in its natural state a telephoto lens of 135 mm or larger is needed to make the animal the main object in the picture. A two-times converter is also handy in this respect, while a wide-angle lens of 28 to 35 mm adds considerable dimension to scenic views. Keep in mind the rainy weather that will be encountered during any trip; a waterproof camera bag is an excellent investment, especially if a great deal of your time will be spent in the woods.

Most photographers find that Kodachrome ASA 64 is the best all-round film, especially when photographing in areas of glaciers or snow-fields where the reflection off the ice and snow is strong. A few rolls of high-speed film (ASA 200 or 400) are handy for nature photography as the majority of wildlife will be encountered at dusk and dawn, which are periods of low light. Bring all your own film if possible; in the large cities and towns it will be expensive, up to $9 to $10 for a roll of Kodachrome (36 exposures), while in smaller communities you might have a hard time finding the type you want.

ALASKA ON A SHOESTRING

Alaska is a trip in itself. For all the expense and energy you will use in getting there, it should not be a seven-day/six-night fling through five cities. To truly appreciate several regions of the state (or even one), visitors need to take the time to meet the people, hike the trails and view some of nature's most impressive features. You can drive or hitch from Anchorage to Fairbanks in one day, but in your hurry you will miss small and interesting towns like Talkeetna or outdoor opportunities like the canoe routes in the Nancy Lake State Recreational Area.

This is where backpacking has a distinct advantage over taking a package tour; with plenty of time and few obligations, you can slowly make your way through the state, stopping when it pleases you and moving on when it doesn't. Often a quaint little village or seaport will be especially inviting and you can pitch your tent along the beach for a few days or even a few weeks.

Although the state Division of Tourism also promotes visiting Alaska in winter, summer is when the vast majority of travellers choose to come. The heaviest tourist time is late June through to the end of August, though you can visit the state anytime from mid-April to late September and expect reasonably mild weather with only an occasional freak snowfall or cold spell. Many travellers who have less than three weeks to spare spend it entirely in the Southeast, taking the State Marine Ferry out of Seattle. Those who want to see the Southeast and then move further north to Fairbanks, Denali National Park and Anchorage need at least a month and should possibly plan on returning from Anchorage by air. Any less time would be a rush job through a land where you simply cannot afford to hurry.

It's wise to start your trip at the beginning of the summer in case you want to extend your stay another month or even longer. One of the most common stories among residents is how somebody came to visit Alaska for six weeks and ended up staying six years. Once you're there, Alaska is a hard land to leave.

THE BEST OF ALASKA

There is much to do and see in Alaska. The following is my favourite ten attractions, but there are many others. Twenty outstanding wilderness trips are listed in the chapter on The Wilderness.

1 – Riding the shuttle bus along the Denali National Park and Preserve road to view wildlife (Interior chapter).

2 – Taking passage on one of the three special State Marine Ferry runs from Kodiak to Dutch Harbor out on the Alaskan Peninsula (Bush chapter).

3 – Flying into a US Forest Service Cabin for a few days (Wilderness chapter).

4 – Viewing the Northern Lights from the University of Alaska campus in Fairbanks (Fairbanks chapter).

5 – Travelling to Tenakee Springs aboard the State Marine Ferry and soaking in the village's hot springs (Southeast chapter).

6 – Taking the State Marine Ferry across Prince William Sound to view the Columbia Glacier (Southcentral chapter).

7 – Spending the Fourth of July holiday in a small backcountry community such as Gustavus or Seldovia (Southeast and Southcentral chapters).

8 – Having a crab boil at the end of Homer Spit (Southcentral chapter).

9 – Viewing the midnight sun on or near 21 June (summer solstice) from Eagle Summit off the Steese Highway (Fairbanks chapter).

10 – Hiking the West Glacier Trail near Juneau to view Mendenhall Glacier (Southeast chapter).

Getting There

Many travellers from the Lower 48 make the mistake of thinking that a trip to Alaska is like visiting another state. It isn't; getting to the North Country entails as much cost and complication as travelling to a foreign country. Plan ahead and check around for the best possible deal on airline flights or bus tickets.

If you are coming from the US mainland, there are three ways of getting to Alaska: the Alcan Highway, the Inside Passage waterway, or flying in from a number of cities. If you are coming from Asia or Europe, it is also possible to fly direct to Anchorage. Alaska is a crossroads for any airline that flies the polar route. Tokyo and New York are just seven hours away from Anchorage and London is nine. Eight international and four major domestic airlines have services to Anchorage.

THE ALCAN

What began in April 1942 as an unprecedented construction project during the heat of WW II ended eight months later as the first overland link between the Lower 48 and Alaska, known formally as the Alaska-Canada Military Highway and affectionately as the Alcan. Today the Alaska Highway is a road through the vast wilderness of north-west Canada and Alaska; a spectacular drive enjoyed by thousands each summer who take their time to soak up the scenery, wildlife and clear, cold streams which they pass along the way.

For those with the time, the Alaska Highway is a unique way to travel north. The trip is an adventure in itself; the 1520-mile (2450 km) road is a legend among highways and to complete the journey is a feather in any traveller's cap. *Mile 0* of the Alcan is at Dawson Creek in British Columbia while the other end is at Fairbanks. In between is a two-lane road

of pavement and gravel breaks, but with nowhere near the rough conditions it was famous for 10 or 15 years ago. By 1984 almost the entire Alcan had been asphalt-paved, although sections of jarring potholes, frost heaves (rippling effect of the pavement caused by freezing and thawing) and loose gravel still prevail here and there. The era of lashing spare fuel cans to the side of the car and gasoline stations every 250 miles are also gone. Food, petrol and lodging can be found every 20 to 50 miles (32 to 80 km) with a 100-mile (160 km) stretch being the longest between fuel stops.

There are several ways to get to the Alaska Highway: you can begin in either Washington, Idaho or Montana and pass through Edmonton or Jasper in Alberta or Prince George in British Columbia. There are also several ways of travelling the highway: bus, car, a combination of marine ferry and bus or the cheapest of all – hitch-hiking.

Hitching the Alcan

If you are properly prepared and have sufficient time, thumbing the Alcan can be an easy way to see the country, meet the people and save money. Many travellers, myself included, have thumbed from Los Angeles to Anchorage, Fairbanks or Juneau in seven to 10 days for under $100. There are, however, many 'do's', 'don'ts' and 'ifs' to hitching the highway.

The Alcan seems to inspire the pioneer spirit in those who drive it. Drivers are good about picking up hitch-hikers, much better than if you were thumbing across the Lower 48. The only problem is that there aren't as many of them. In some places along the route you may have to wait 30 minutes or longer before a car passes by. During the summer the number of vehicles increases significantly, but if you are attempting the trip in early spring or late fall, be prepared to wait two or three hours or possibly even overnight (like many of the hitch-hikers at Haines Junction).

All hitch-hikers should be self-sufficient with a tent, some food, water, warm clothing and a good book; or maybe two good books. While in many parts of the country a long wait would make you go stir-crazy, along the Alcan it isn't so bad. In fact, if the weather is good, it is enjoyable to sit out in the wide open land, surrounded by mountains and clean air. Hitch-hikers must be patient and not over-anxious to reach their destination. Moving through the US and southern Canada, you will get the usual short and long rides from one city to the next. Once you make it to Dawson Creek, it will probably only take you one or two longer rides to reach your destination.

Any part of the Alcan can be slow, but some sections are notorious. The worst might be Haines Junction, the crossroads in the Yukon where south-bound hitch-hikers occasionally have to stay overnight before catching a ride to Haines in the Southeast. Longer waits will also be needed if you are heading home in late summer or early fall and are thumbing out of Glennallen, Tok or Delta Junction back into Canada and the Lower 48. The same holds true for those trying to hitch north from Dawson Creek in spring and early summer. A sign with your destination on it helps, as does displaying your backpack, which tells drivers you're a summer traveller.

The hardest part of the trip for many can be crossing the US-Canada border. Canadian officials usually pull cars over if the passengers are not of the same nationality as the driver, and they will ask to see proof of sufficient funds. Anybody without pre-arranged transportation is required to have $80 per day to travel through Canada or a total of $200 to $250. The Canadians are not hassling hitch-hikers when they do this, they're just making sure that visitors don't get stuck somewhere for a week because they ran out of money. On the way to Alaska, most travellers will have these funds; on the way back, however, it might be difficult if you are at the end of your trip and your money.

Possible solutions are to catch a ride with someone driving the entire way or with a Canadian willing to tell officials you are a friend visiting. Three places to make contacts for a ride back to the Lower 48 are the Anchorage Youth Hostel; the Wood Centre in the middle of University of Alaska campus in Fairbanks with its notice-board for students offering or needing rides, and the Chamber of Commerce hospitality centre in Tok, where the free coffee pulls in many drivers before they continue into Canada. If you are heading north, the notice-board outside the tourist office in Dawson Creek is worth checking, as it often contains notices of people looking for somebody to help with fuel costs.

With some luck it could take you four days or less to hitch from Seattle to Fairbanks or Anchorage, but to be on the safe side, plan on the trip taking seven to eight days. The best route is from Seattle as it is the most direct and offers the most traffic to Dawson Creek. This combines hitching along the I-5 in Washington to the Canadian border, the Trans-Canada Highway 1 to Cache Creek, and Highway 97 north to Dawson Creek and the Alcan.

An alternative to hitching the entire Alaska Highway is to take the State Marine Ferry to Haines and start from there, cutting the journey in half but still travelling along the highway's most spectacular parts. Haines, however, is a town of about 1000 people and traffic is light on the road to the Alcan at Haines Junction. It is best to hustle off the ferry and begin thumbing immediately while the ferry is unloading its vehicles, so that you can try to catch a driver heading north; or seek out a driver with space while you are still on the boat by taping a notice outside the ship's cafeteria or showers.

A couple more 'do's' and 'don'ts' for those who want to attempt this great adventure in thumbing: taking drugs across the border is risky if you are driving and downright foolish when hitch-hiking as both Canadian and American customs officials make it a habit to search hitch-hikers. With only a backpack, it's tough to hide drugs in a place where they won't look.

It is good to have your Canadian money before leaving southern Canada. Once hitching, it is hard to stop at a bank. Most businesses along the Alcan take American money, but they either give less than the normal 25 to 30% difference on the exchange rate or give none at all.

Discuss your plans with the driver and make sure that he or she doesn't let you off at some deserted corner. This isn't a major problem if you're self-sufficient, but it's still nice to be near a town when waiting for a ride. No matter when you attempt the highway, make sure you have warm clothing, mittens, boots and a woollen hat. Don't underestimate the place's ability to turn freezing cold at any time. Keep in mind that there is a youth hostel at Tok with 10 beds and tent space. Call the Tok Visitors Centre for information on (907) 883-5667. There is also a Youth Hostel (907) 895-4627 further along the Alcan near Delta Junction, just off the highway.

Keep a journal – the main reason the Alaska Highway legend lives on long after it has been paved is because the road and the people you meet are one-of-a-kind.

Bussing the Alcan

Through a combination of bus companies you can take a bus from Seattle to the Alaska Highway and reach Fairbanks for a moderate cost. There are no direct bus services from the Lower 48 to Alaska; travellers have to be patient with services and routes that are much more limited than those in the rest of the country. By doing so, the cost of reaching the heart of Alaska is pennies compared to flying in or taking the State Marine Ferry.

Greyhound In Seattle, you begin by hopping on a Greyhound bus for Vancouver. You can purchase a one-way ticket at the downtown station at 8th and Stewart. There are daily runs to the Canadian city but call (206) 624-3456 for exact times and current fares. You'll end up at the Greyhound Station at 150 Dunsmuir St, Vancouver where you can take a Greyhound Lines of Canada bus to Whitehorse. A one-way ticket costs C$99 and buses depart three times a day for the Yukon capital. Call (604) 683-9277 for the exact times and changes in the schedule.

Norline Coaches & Yukon Stage Lines From Whitehorse you can continue north by taking a Norline bus to Beaver Creek, Yukon followed by an immediate transfer to Yukon Stage Lines to complete the journey to Fairbanks. The summer service, which runs from June to mid-September, departs Tuesdays and Saturdays at 9 am from the Whitehorse Bus Terminal at 3211A Third Avenue (behind the Hudson Bay Company) and arrives at Fairbanks 14 hours later. The one-way fares are C$45 for the Norline ticket to Beaver Creek and US$48 for the Yukon Stage Lines section to Fairbanks. Norline also has three runs weekly (Monday, Wednesday and Friday) to Dawson City from Whitehorse for C$60 and, depending on the demand, a service from Dawson Creek to Tok Junction on Tuesdays and Saturdays for C$55. At Tok Junction you can take a Yukon Stage Line bus to Fairbanks for US$37.

Unless you don't mind spending a few days in Whitehorse, you might want to write or call ahead for the current schedule: Norline Coaches, 3211 Third Avenue, Whitehorse, Yukon, Canada Y1A 1G6; tel (403) 668-3355.

Canadian Coachways The subsidiary of Greyhound Lines of Canada offers scheduled services between Edmonton and northern British Columbia to Whitehorse. They also act as a booking agent for the Norline bus route of Whitehorse to Fairbanks. For schedules and information call or write to Coachways, 3211A 3rd Avenue, Whitehorse, Yukon, Canada Y1A 1G6; tel (403) 667-2223.

White Pass & Yukon Motorcoaches Also departing from the Whitehorse Bus Terminal every Tuesday at 11.30 am is the WP&Y bus to Haines Junction and then on to Tok, Alaska where it stops overnight. On Wednesday the bus continues to Anchorage, reaching the city at 6 pm. One-way fare is C$149 and does not include lodging at Tok. In Whitehorse, call (403) 668-6665 for current information. If you are still in the planning stages of your trip, call the toll-free number of Gray Line of Alaska, 1 (800) 544-2206. This tour company giant runs WP&Y Motorcoaches.

Bus Tours

Other companies with bus services to Alaska sell the transportation as 'tours' and include overnight lodging in the fare. This sends the price out of the reach of most budget travellers. The one exception is Green Tortoise Alternative Travel, the company with recycled buses whose seats have been replaced with foam-covered platforms, sofas and dinettes. When not sleeping on the bus during night drives, Green Tortoise groups use state and federal campgrounds as accommodation and make an effort to include hiking, rafting and other outdoor activities on their itinerary. Food is not included in the fare but the bus groups pool their funds to purchase goods in bulk and then prepare it in group cookouts.

On Green Tortoise tours group interaction is a large part of the experience. Everybody pitches in during mealtime and spontaneous volleyball matches or Frisbee games are frequent activities during rest breaks. Beer and wine are allowed on the bus and people are encouraged to bring musical instruments. Although passengers could be any age, the vast majority range from the 20s to early 30s.

The company runs a four-week tour through Alaska in July and August that can be picked up in San Francisco or Seattle and costs $650 for the entire trip. For more information write to Green Tortoise, Box 24459, San Francisco, California 94124; or you can call a variety of offices around the country, including San Francisco (415) 821-0803, Seattle (206) 324-7433 or New York (212) 431-3348.

THE INSIDE PASSAGE

As an alternative to the Alcan or to avoid doubling back on the highway, you can travel Southeast's Inside Passage, a waterway made up of thousands of islands, fjords and steep-mountain coastlines. To many, Southeast is the most beautiful area in the state and the Alaskan marine ferries are the country's best bargain in public transportation.

The large 'blue canoes' of the state marine highway are equipped with observation decks, food services, bars, lounges and solariums with deck chairs for sunning. You can rent a stateroom for overnight trips but most backpackers head straight for the solarium and sleep in one of the deck chairs or on the floor with a sleeping pad. On long-distance hauls from Seattle they sometimes even pitch their dome tents. With its leisurely pace, travel on the marine ferries is a delightful experience; the midnight sun is warm and apart from the scenery, the possibility of sighting whales, bald eagles or sea lions, keeps most travellers at the side of the ship. This is also an excellent way to meet other backpackers heading for a summer in the North Country.

The ferries are extremely popular during the peak season from June to August. Reservations are needed for cabin or vehicle space and for walk-ons (those without cabin reservation or vehicle space) for departures from Seattle. Space for summer sailings from Seattle is often filled by April, forcing walk-ons to wait stand-by for an available spot. If you plan to sail out of Seattle in June or July, it is best to make reservations. The reservation office of the state ferries will take written requests anytime and telephone requests from the first working day of January for summer sailings. As telephone lines are jammed most of the time after the first day of the year, it is wise to send in a written request as soon as you can figure out your itinerary.

The summer sailing schedule comes out in December and you can obtain one by writing to Alaska Marine Highway, Pouch R, Juneau, Alaska 99811; tel (907) 465-3941. There is now a toll-free telephone number to handle schedule requests and reservations: 1 (800) 544-2251 (from the Lower 48) or 1 (800) 551-7185 (from within Alaska).

The ferries stop first at Prince Rupert (British Columbia) and then continue on to Ketchikan. Most runs then depart for Wrangell, Petersburg, Sitka, Juneau, Haines and Skagway before heading back south. A trip from Seattle to Juneau takes 2½ to four days depending on the route. Most ferry terminals are a few miles out of town and the short in-port time doesn't allow passengers to view the area without making it a stopover. However, walk-ons can make as many stopovers as they wish without additional cost. For example, if you purchase a ticket from Seattle to Haines, you could spend a few days at the fishing village of Petersburg and then catch the next ferry north without having to purchase another ticket or make a reservation. Just make sure that you stop at the purser's office and get a stopover coupon before leaving the boat.

If you intend to use the ferries to view the Southeast, obtain a current schedule and keep it handy at all times. State ferries stop almost every day at larger towns like Juneau, but the smaller villages may have only one every three or four days and most places won't have a service at all.

There are seven ships working Southeast; four of them are larger vessels that sail the entire route from Seattle to Skagway. The *Columbia*, *Malaspina*, *Matanuska* and *Taku* all have cabins, lounges, eating facilities and public showers for both walk-ons and cabin renters. The other three ships are smaller, do not have cabins, and serve out-of-the-way villages from Juneau or Ketchikan. In the summer the *Aurora* sails between Ketchikan, Kake, Hollis, Petersburg and Prince Rupert. The *Le Conte* stops at Juneau, Hoonah, Angoon, Sitka, Kake, Tenakee Springs, Skagway, Haines and Petersburg, and makes a special run to Pelican once a month. The *Chilkat*, the original ship of the fleet, serves Ketchikan and Metlakatla.

If you plan to just pass through the Southeast on your way north, purchase a ticket from Seattle to Haines and make a few stopovers at the places that take your fancy. If you plan to spend a good deal of time or the entire summer in the region, purchase a ticket to Juneau and then use that as your base, taking shorter trips to other towns on the *Le Conte*. The fare for walk-ons from Seattle to Haines is $198 while the ticket to Juneau is $178.

One way to save money is to take a bus or hitch to Prince Rupert in British Columbia where the dramatic mountain scenery begins, and hop on the ferry from there. To Haines the fare from Prince Rupert is $86 and to Juneau $72. Sample fares for travel within the Southeast are: Ketchikan to Juneau $54; Petersburg to Juneau $29; Juneau to Haines $19; Haines to Skagway $9; Juneau to Angoon $21.

The state department of transportation puts out a brochure entitled *Alaska Marine Highway*, but here are a few tips they don't tell you: when boarding in Seattle, it is best to scramble to the solarium and either stake out a lounge chair or at least an area on the floor. The solarium and observation deck are the best places to sleep as the air is clean and the night-time peace is unbroken. The other place to crash out is the indoor lounges, which can be smoky, noisy or both. In 1985 backpackers were still allowed to pitch free-standing tents near the solarium, but discussion has begun among ferry officials to ban this practice. The tents tend to take up more space than two people really need in an already popular and crowded section of the ship.

Food on board is inexpensive compared to what you will pay on shore, but it is cheaper to bring your own grub and eat it in the solarium or the cafeteria. Some backpackers bring their own tea bags, coffee or 'Cup-A-Soup' and then purchase just the cup of hot water for 10c. The pursers, however, do not allow any camp-stoves to be used on board and are very strict about enforcing this. Bringing your own liquor is also prohibited as there is a bar aboard the larger ships, but I have yet to see a cruise where a happy traveller isn't handing out beers from an ice-chest in the solarium.

There is an additional cost if you want to bring a car or motorcycle on the ship, but bicycles and kayaks can be carried on free. A bicycle can be a handy way to see at least part of town without disembarking for a few days, while a summer (or even a lifetime) can be spent using the marine ferry system to hop from one wilderness kayak trip to another.

Above all else, when using the Alaska marine ferry system, check and double-check the departures of vessels once you have arrived in the Southeast. It is worth a phone call to the terminal to find out the actual arrival and departure times; the state ferries are notorious for being late or breaking down and having their sailings cancelled. It's something that happens every summer without fail.

If the Alaska state ferries are filled in Seattle, one alternative is to head north to Port Hardy at the end of Vancouver Island and catch a sailing on the British Columbia Ferry to Prince Rupert. From this Canadian city there is a much better chance to board the Alaska marine ferry because there are five vessels that connect Prince Rupert to Southeast Alaska. Port Hardy can be reached from Victoria on Pacific Coast Lines, which runs a bus once a day to the small town for a one-way fare of C\$37. The bus depot is at 710 Douglas St, behind the Empress Hotel in downtown Victoria.

At Port Hardy the BC Ferry *Queen Of The North* sails to Prince Rupert one day and returns to Vancouver Island the next, maintaining this every-other-day schedule from the first of June to the end of September. One-way fare for walk-ons is C\$50. The same ship also makes a stop once a week along this route at the isolated town of Bella Bella. For more information or the complete schedule of the BC Ferries call or write to BC Ferries, 1045 Howe St, Vancouver, British Columbia, Canada V6Z 2A9; tel (604) 669-1211. In Victoria call (604) 386-3431 and in Seattle call (206) 682-6865 for information and reservations on the Canadian ferry.

AIR

The quickest and easiest (but unfortunately the most expensive) way to reach Alaska is to fly there. Four major domestic carriers offer regular service from the Lower 48 to Alaska, and eight international airlines make stops in Anchorage. They all have special fares and travel promotions and it would be well worth the effort to check out all possibilities before purchasing a ticket. Generally they fall into two groups: regular fares and Advance Purchase Excursion (Apex) or 'Super-savers' that require round-trip tickets to be booked 14 to 30 days in advance and have a maximum number of days you can stay. The domestic airlines also offer a special price to passengers travelling on Tuesday and Wednesday – off-peak days for the airline industry.

Seattle, Washington and Portland (Oregon) are the traditional departure spots within the US for air travel to Alaska, but now you can book a non-stop flight to Anchorage from a number of cities including San Francisco, Chicago, Minneapolis and Honolulu. Flights to Anchorage direct or via Seattle are also offered from places such as Boston, Washington, San Diego, Los Angeles, New Orleans, Houston and Dallas.

Alaska Airlines is by far the largest carrier for travellers to Alaska and offers an Apex return fare between Seattle and Anchorage of $286.50. The requirements are that you book it at least 30 days in advance, travel on a Tuesday or Wednesday and stay no more than 21 days. Similar return fares between Seattle and Juneau are $231 and Seattle to Fairbanks is $309. The price of tickets for stays of longer than 21 days jumps astronomically; an Apex return fare for Seattle-Anchorage that allows you to stay up to 30 days is $489.31.

United Airlines offers an Apex return fare for a non-stop Chicago-Anchorage flight for $455 if you travel on a Tuesday or Wednesday. That is, of course, if you stay 21 days or less. For stays of up to 30 days the price of the same ticket jumps to $689 and a regular return fare costs $1057. The other two domestic carriers are Northwest Airlines and Western Airlines. Alaska Airlines has a toll-free telephone number, 1 (800) 426-0333, as does Western Airlines, 1 (800) 277-6105; these make it possible to get instant schedules and fare information.

In short, air travel is the best way to go if you plan to spend three weeks or less touring Alaska, as most tickets allow you one or two stopovers on each leg of the flight. However, if you are planning to spend a month or the entire summer venturing through the state, economically you are much better off using the State Marine Ferry or jumping on a bus.

The international carriers that make stops in Anchorage are Korean Airlines, Japan Airlines, Air France, British Airways, KLM, Lufthansa, Sabena Belgian World Airlines and SAS Scandinavian Airlines. Most of them offer Apex fares. From Europe, Sabena Belgian traditionally offers the lowest rates to Anchorage. Again it pays to check them out. At times it might be cheaper to take an Apex flight to Seattle or Los Angeles and then purchase a second ticket from there to Alaska with one of the domestic carriers.

Getting Around

Touring Alaska on limited funds means not departing from the roads and not travelling in areas lacking a State Marine Ferry dock. However, budget travellers shouldn't worry because although the roads and the marine highway (the cheapest forms of travel) cover only a quarter of the state, this quarter comprises the most popular regions of Alaska and includes the major attractions, parks and cities.

Even if there is a road to your destination, travel around Alaska is not like travel in any other state in the US. The overwhelming distances between regions and the fledgling system of public transportation makes getting around almost as hard as getting there. Any long visit usually combines transport by car, bus, marine ferry, train and eventually a bush plane for a trek into the wilderness.

RAIL

The Alaska Railroad offers year-round passenger service between Fairbanks and Anchorage and between Anchorage and Whittier on Prince William Sound. It is an inexpensive means of transportation for travellers and the scenery on each route is spectacular. During the summer, four trains make the main run from Anchorage to Fairbanks. Two of them are express trains that stop only at Denali National Park; the other two are local trains which make all stops, including flag-stops for backpackers and mountain climbers who emerge from their treks at the railroad track. The express trains are geared for out-of-state travellers, as they are equipped with viewing-dome cars and full dining and beverage service. They also stick to their schedules more than the local trains.

North-bound express trains from Anchorage to Fairbanks depart during the summer (mid-May to late September)

daily at 8.30 am except Wednesday and Saturday, reaching Denali Park at 2.30 pm and Fairbanks at 6 pm. On Wednesday and Saturday the local train leaves Anchorage at 8.30 am, reaching Fairbanks at 6 pm or a little later. South-bound express trains depart from Fairbanks daily at 10.30 am except Thursday and Sunday, reaching Denali Park at 1.55 am and Anchorage at 8 pm. The south-bound local trains run on Thursday and Sunday, departing Fairbanks at 10.30 am.

From late September to mid-May the schedule changes to one train per week, which departs Anchorage at 9 am on Saturday and then leaves Fairbanks at 10 am on Sunday for the return trip. There is no price advantage in buying a round-trip ticket. The fare is $54.50 from Anchorage to Denali Park and $78.25 to Fairbanks. The fare from Fairbanks to Denali Park is $29.50.

Rail service between Anchorage or Portage and Whittier is timed during the summer to meet the arrivals and departures of the Alaska marine ferry, *MV Bartlett*, which crosses the Prince William Sound to Valdez on a scenic cruise that includes sailing past the Columbia Glacier. The train makes a single departure daily from Anchorage south to Portage; times are 11 am Monday to Friday and 6 am on Saturday and Sunday. At Portage there are several runs daily to the isolated town of Whittier. You have to catch the 1.20 pm from Portage to make the 3.30 pm sailing of the *MV Bartlett*, which departs Whittier on Sunday, Monday, Wednesday, Friday and Saturday. Rail fares are $10.75 one-way from Anchorage to Whittier and $5.25 from Portage to Whittier.

During the summer, reservations are required on the express runs between Anchorage and Fairbanks but are not necessary on the local trains. No reser-

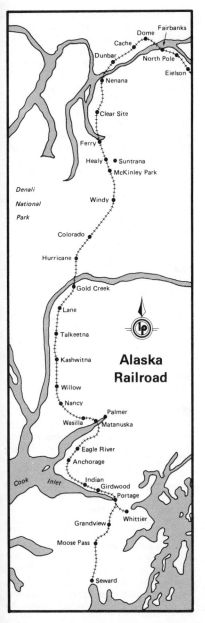

Fairbanks
Dome
Cache
Dunbar
North Pole
Eielson
Nenana
Clear Site
Ferry
Healy · Suntrana
McKinley Park
Denali
National
Park
Windy
Colorado
Hurricane
Gold Creek
Lane
Talkeetna
Kashwitna
Alaska
Railroad
Willow
Nancy
Palmer
Wasilla Matanuska
Eagle River
Anchorage
Indian
Cook Inlet
Girdwood
Portage
Grandview Whittier
Moose Pass
Seward

vations are taken for the rail service between Anchorage and Whittier, but passengers with confirmed ferry tickets have priority on boarding the 1.20 pm run from Portage. For more information, write to the Alaska Railroad, Pouch 7-2111, Anchorage, Alaska 99510. You can also telephone Anchorage at (907) 265-2685, Fairbanks at (907) 456-4155 or Seattle at (206) 442-5416.

The White Pass & Yukon Railroad, a historical narrow-gauge railroad that was built during the Klondike Gold Rush and connected Skagway with Whitehorse, suspended operations in 1982. Every summer there is talk of reviving the rail service but today the cars are still stranded in Skagway while the White Pass & Yukon office in the small Alaskan town has been taken over by the National Park Service. The chances of this train ever returning to the tracks seem remote.

BUS

Regular bus services within Alaska are limited, but between the larger towns and cities motorcoaches are available for independent travellers (as opposed to package tours) with rates that make them the cheapest way to go.

Alaska-Yukon Motorcoaches is the giant among the handful of small bus companies in Alaska as it offers six routes with service both ways. The runs include Anchorage-Fairbanks with a stop at Denali Park for $75; Anchorage-Valdez by highway for $75; Anchorage-Valdez by Prince William Sound for $140; Valdez-Fairbanks for $75; Anchorage or Fairbanks to Haines with two overnight stopovers for $250 (lodging not included). Each route has just one daily morning departure. Exact times and departure points are given in later chapters covering the region. Reservations are not required but are recommended by the company. They will also ship bicycles for an additional $10 fee. For information all year round, write or call Alaska-Yukon Motorcoaches, 349 Wrangell Avenue, Anchorage, Alaska 99501; tel (907) 276-7141.

During the summer you can also contact the bus company in Fairbanks, 900 Noble St, tel (907) 452-8518; or in Haines, c/o Hotel Halsingland, tel (907) 766-2435.

White Pass & Yukon Motorcoaches came to life when the train died in 1982. The bus company provides daily service from Skagway to Whitehorse and on Tuesday has a run from Haines to Skagway and on Sunday from Skagway to Haines. Its other major route is between Haines and Anchorage, with a north-bound run on Tuesday, overnighting at Tok and arriving at Anchorage on Wednesday evening. There is also a run that departs Anchorage on Saturday with connections to Haines, Skagway or Whitehorse that arrive on Sunday. The bus service is offered only during the summer and no lodging is included in the price of the ticket.

A sample of the fares are Skagway-Whitehorse $55, Anchorage-Haines $182, Haines Junction-Haines $54, Haines-Whitehorse $55, and Tok-Anchorage $81. Local passenger boarding points, departure times and phone numbers are given in later chapters. For information or reservations while planning your trip, write to Gray Line of Alaska, 300 Elliott Avenue West, Seattle, Washington 98119; or use the toll-free number 1 (800) 544-2206.

Alaska-Denali Transit is a new company offering the cheapest fares between Anchorage and Denali National Park. There is a daily service with a bus leaving from various points in downtown Anchorage, including the youth hostel, at 8.30 am and reaching Denali at 1.30 pm. There is a return run from Denali the same day, arriving in Anchorage at 7 pm with drop-offs that include the youth hostel; one-way fare is $30.

The company also offers special trips to the Arctic Circle and the Talkeetna Bluegrass Festival, and a tour of the Kenai Peninsula. Tickets and information can be obtained at the Anchorage Youth Hostel, or you can phone or write to Alaska-Denali Transit, 608 West 4th Avenue, Suite 31, Anchorage, Alaska 99501; tel (907) 276-6443.

Valdez-Anchorage Bus Lines offers transportation between Valdez and Anchorage along the Richardson and Glenn Highways with a stop at Glennallen. The bus departs on Tuesday, Friday and Sunday from the Shelton Hotel on the corner of 6th St and Denali in Anchorage and utilises Totem Inn as its drop-off/pick-up point in Valdez. One-way fare for Anchorage-Valdez is $55 while an Anchorage-Glennallen ticket is $34 and Glennallen-Valdez is $21. For more information call (907) 561-5806.

Seward Bus Lines provide services only between Anchorage and Seward and not to any other city in the Kenai Peninsula. The bus connects the two cities twice a day in the summer from the Inlet Inn on 6th Avenue and H St in Anchorage to its terminal at 4th St and Washington in Seward. One-way fare is $20. For more information call (907) 562-0712.

STATE MARINE FERRY

In the Southeast, the State Marine Ferry replaces bus services and operates from Juneau or Ketchikan to Skagway, Haines, Hoonah, Tenakee Springs, Angoon, Sitka, Kake, Petersburg and Hollis, with an occasional special run to the tiny fishing village of Pelican. (See the previous chapter for more details.)

There are also marine ferry services in Southcentral Alaska, where the *MV Bartlett* and the *MV Tustumena* connect towns along the Prince William Sound and the Gulf of Alaska. The Southwest marine ferry does not connect with the Southeast line, but travellers can get around that by picking up an Alaska

of Prince William Sound. Four times during the summer in mid-May, June, July and September, the *MV Tustumena* also makes a special run to Sand Point, King Cove, Cold Bay and Dutch Harbor at the end of the Alaska Peninsula. The cruise takes five days from Kodiak and is the cheapest way to see part of Alaska's stormy arm (see the chapter on the Bush).

Sample fares for marine ferry travel along the Southwest routes for walk-on passengers are: Valdez-Cordova $20, Valdez-Whittier $45, Valdez-Seward $46, Seward-Kodiak $38, Homer-Kodiak $34, Kodiak-Dutch Harbor $137, Homer-Seldovia $9.

Airlines flight from Juneau to Cordova for $120 to continue their ferry trip around the Alaskan coast.

The *MV Bartlett* sails from Cordova and Valdez to Whittier across the Sound, passing the Columbia Glacier along the way. The *MV Tustumena* provides service between Seward, Homer and Seldovia on the Kenai Peninsula; Port Lions and Kodiak on Kodiak Island; and Valdez and Cordova on the eastern shore

SURVIVING THE BUSH PLANE RIDE

I met the classic bush pilot in Yakuta, Alaska. I arrived at the airport on board a sleek Alaska Airlines Boeing 737 and was immediately hustled over to a small

hangar where there was this sputtering machine that appeared to be dripping something and was held together by baling wire. Next to it was 'sourdough' dressed in faded jeans, cowboy boots and a TWA cap, spitting out long streams of tobacco juice. I would have known him anywhere, even without his plane – the famous Alaskan bush pilot, a lovable North Country character who in many ways is the last great adventurer in a frontier that is quickly becoming a regulated piece of real estate.

My group was headed for 10 days of wilderness kayaking in Russell Fjord and he was the only pilot available with a beach-lander. After he proceeded to pack the plane to its roof with gear, somebody asked him what the criterion was to decide how much his plane could safely carry. 'See that wheel in the back,' he said, 'as long as it gets off the ground.' We all squeezed in and took off.

When you want to see more than the roadside attractions, you go to a dirt runway or small airfield outside of town and climb into a bush plane. With 75% of the state not accessible by road, these small, single-engine planes are the backbone of intrastate transportation. They carry residents and supplies to desolated areas of the Bush, take anglers to some of the best fishing spots in the country and drop off backpackers in the middle of prime, untouched wilderness. The person at the controls is a bush pilot, someone who might be fresh out of the Air Force or somebody who arrived in Alaska 'way bee-for statehood' and learned to fly by trial and error. A ticket with him is not only transportation to isolated areas and a scenic overview of the state but sometimes includes an earful of flying tales – some believable, some not.

Don't be alarmed when you hear that Alaska has the highest number of airplane crashes per capita in the country – it also has the greatest percentage of pilots. One out of every 45 residents has a licence, and one out of every 75 owns a plane. Bush pilots are safe flyers who know their territory and its weather patterns. They don't want to go down any more than you do.

A ride in a bush plane is essential if you want to go beyond the common sights and see some of Alaska's most memorable scenery. In the larger cities of Anchorage, Fairbanks, Juneau and Ketchikan it pays to check around before chartering. In most small towns and villages, however, you will be lucky if there is a choice. In the following regional chapters air-taxi services are listed under the town or area out of which they operate.

Bush aircraft include floatplanes that land and take off on water and beachlanders with oversized tyres that can use rough gravel shorelines as air strips. Others are equipped with skis to land on glaciers; sophisticated radar instruments for stormy areas like the Aleutian Islands; or boat racks to carry canoes or hard-shell kayaks.

The fares differ with the type of plane, its size, the number of passengers and the amount of flying time. On the average, a Cessna 206 that can carry three passengers and a limited amount of gear will cost $300 to charter for an hour of flying time; a Beaver, a slightly larger plane that will hold four passengers, will cost around $400. Keep in mind that when chartering a plane to drop you off at an isolated Forest Service cabin or for a wilderness trek, you must pay for both the air time to your drop-off point *and* for the return to the departure point.

As a general rule, if one of the domestic carriers – Alaska Airlines, Western Airlines or the intrastate carrier Mark Air

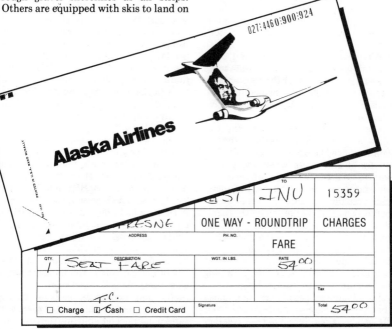

- has a flight to your destination, it will be the cheapest way of flying there. Alaska Airlines provides the most extensive service for travel within Alaska. A sample of their one-way fares for intra-state flights are: Anchorage-Fairbanks $111; Juneau-Cordova $120; Juneau-Anchorage $176; Anchorage-Nome $213; Anchorage-Kodiak $215.

Before chartering your own plane, check out all the possibilities first. Most air-taxi companies have regular scheduled flights to small towns and villages in six to nine-seater aircraft with single-seat fares that are a fraction of the cost of chartering an entire plane. Others offer a 'mail flight' to small villages which are regularly-scheduled flights with one or two seats available to travellers. Even when your destination is a Forest Service cabin or some wilderness spot, check with the local air-taxi companies; it is a common practice to match up a party departing from the cabin with another that's arriving, so that the air charter costs can be split by filling the plane on both runs.

Air travel in Alaska in small bush planes is expensive, but the more passengers, the cheaper the charter. Two people chartering an entire plane, no matter what the distance, is an expensive exercise.

Getting reservations is easy and can often be done the day before or at the last minute if need be. Double-check all pick-up times and spots when flying to a wilderness area. Bush pilots fly over the pick-up point and if you are not there, they usually return, call the Forest Service and still charge you for the flight. When flying in and out of bays, fjords or coastal waterways, check the tides before determining your pick-up time. It is best to schedule pick-ups and drop-offs at high tide or else you may end up tramping half a mile through mud flats.

If a pilot doesn't want to fly, don't push the subject, just re-schedule your charter. He or she is the best judge of weather patterns and can see, or sometimes feel, bad flying conditions when others can't. Always schedule extra days around a charter flight. It's not uncommon to be 'socked in' by weather for a day or even two until a plane can fly in. Don't panic, they know you are there. Think of the high school basketball team in the mid-1960s which flew to King Cove in the Aleutians for a game. They were socked in for a month before they could fly out again.

When travelling to small Bush towns, look for a scheduled flight or mail-run as the cheapest way to go. Don't hesitate to charter a flight to some desolate wilderness spot on your own, though; the best that Alaska has to offer is usually just a short flight away.

CAR RENTAL

Having your own car in Alaska, as in any other place, provides freedom and flexibility that cannot be obtained from mass transportation. As it is elsewhere, car rental is a costly way to travel for one or two people. In Alaska, it isn't the charge per day for the rental but the mileage rate that makes it so expensive. Drivers will find petrol only slightly more expensive than in the rest of the country, but the great distances that you travel in the North Country will skyrocket the cost of car rental.

The Alaska tourist boom over the past five years produced a network of cheap car rental companies that offer rates almost 50% lower than those of the national firms of Avis, Hertz and National Car Rental. The largest of these is Rent-A-Dent, which has offices in a large number of towns including Anchorage, Fairbanks, Kenai, Ketchikan, Petersburg, Wrangell and Sitka. Their rates vary from $15 a day plus 15c a mile up to $20 a day plus 20c a mile in the smaller towns. The cars, though functional, are not pretty and are occasionally stubborn about starting up right away. If there are three or four people splitting the cost, the

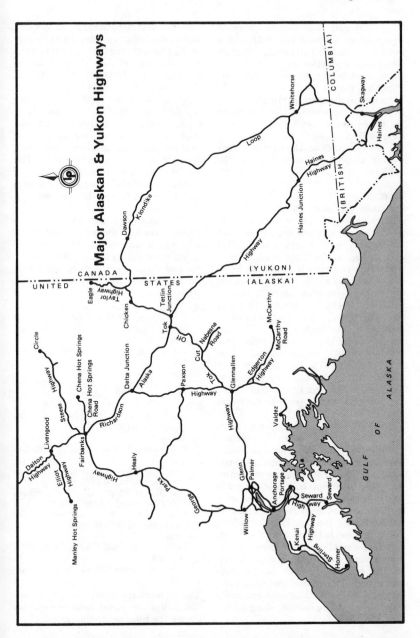

Major Alaskan & Yukon Highways

car rental can often be as cheap or cheaper than taking a bus, with all the freedom of a car. In Fairbanks it is a great way to see the region north of the city where there is no public transport apart from bush planes.

All the used-car rental companies will be listed in the regional chapters under the towns where they maintain offices. Rent-A-Dent, however, maintains a toll-free number for those who want to reserve a car in advance of their trip; it is 1 (800) 426-5243.

BICYCLE

For those who want to bike it, Alaska offers a variety of cycling adventures on paved roads during long days with comfortably cool temperatures. Most cyclists hop on the State Marine Ferry, where they can carry their bike on for no extra charge. The individual communities of Southeast are good places to gear up (and down) for the longer rides that await up north. From Haines you can catch an Alaskan-Yukon Motorcoach to Tok or Anchorage for the price of a ticket plus $10 per bicycle to get immediately to the heart of Alaska. You can also take your bike on Alaska Airlines for a $20 excess baggage fee; it doesn't have to be crated but is merely handed over to the ticket officials at the counter.

Alaska does require some extra precautions to be taken by cyclists planning to spend the summer peddling. There are few towns with comprehensively-equipped bike shops so it is wise to carry not only metric tools but also tube-patch repair kits, brake cables, spokes, brake pads and any other parts that might be needed during the trip. Due to the high rainfall, especially in the Southeast, waterproof saddle bags are useful, as are tyre fenders. Rain gear is a must, and storing gear in zip-lock plastic bags within your side saddles is not being over-cautious. Warm clothing, mittens and a knit hat should be carried, along with a tent and a rain tarp.

Some roads do not have much shoulder – the Seward Highway between Anchorage and Girdwood being the classic example – so cyclists can utilise the long hours of sunlight to pedal when the traffic is light in such areas. It is not necessary to carry a lot of food, as you can easily re-stock every couple of days on all major roads. Most bikers avoid gravel, but biking the Alaska Highway is becoming an increasingly popular trip that involves some short gravel breaks in the paved asphalt. When undertaking gravel roads, figure on making 50 to 70% of your normal distance and take spare tubes – flat tyres will be a daily occurrence.

The following cities and towns in Alaska have bike shops that offer a good selection of spare parts and information on riding in the local area. However, by the end of the summer many are low on (or completely out of) certain spare parts.

Ketchikan
    People Power Bicycles, 435 Dock St, tel (907) 225-2488
Juneau
    Honda Hut, 8602 Teal St, tel (907) 789-0624
Haines
    H N Industries, basement of Gateway Building, tel (907) 766-2249
Sitka
    Southeast Diving & Sport Shop, 203 Lincoln St, tel (907) 747-8279
Anchorage
    REI Co-op, 2710 Spenard Rd, tel (907) 272-4565
    Gary King Sporting Goods, 202 East Northern Lights, tel (907) 279-7454
    The Bicycle Shop, 1035 West Northern Lights Boulevard, tel (907) 272-5219
    Bicycle R&R, West Northern Lights Boulevard, tel (907) 561-5246
Fairbanks
    Beaver Sports, 2400 College Rd, tel (907) 479-2494
    Campbell Sports, Third St, (907) 452-2757

The following are the more common long-distance trips undertaken by cyclists during the summer in Alaska:

Anchorage to Fairbanks The ride can be done comfortably in five to six days along the George Parks Highway. The total distance is 360 miles (580 km) along a road that is flat with scattered sections of rolling hills. Highlights are the impressive views of Mt McKinley and an interesting side-trip into Denali National Park where cyclists can extend their trip with a ride along the gravel park road. Many cyclists take the Alaska Railroad part of the way and then bike the rest. There is an excess baggage charge for carrying your bicycle on the train.

Anchorage to Kenai Peninsula There is an endless number of possible bike trips in the Kenai Peninsula or combinations of biking and hiking adventures. You could also utilise the Southwest runs of the Alaska State Marine Ferry. A common trip here is to bike to Homer, take the ferry to Kodiak, then return to Seward and pedal back to Anchorage. This would be a seven to 12-day trip depending on how much time is spent in Homer and Kodiak. The distance by bike would be 350 miles (560 km) with an additional 400 miles (640 km) by ferry. The bike could also be used to hop from one hiking trail to another in some of Alaska's most pleasant backcountry. Or you can bike to Portage, combine rail service and ferry transport across Prince William Sound to Valdez and then head north.

Fairbanks to Valdez This is perhaps one of the most scenic routes cyclists can undertake and also one of the hardest. The six to seven-day trip follows the Richardson Highway from Delta Junction to Glennallen and then goes on to Valdez for a total of 375 miles (600 km). It includes several hilly sections and tough climbs over Isabel Pass before Paxson, and Thompson Pass at 2771 feet (845 metres), 25 miles (40 km) east of Valdez. New brake pads are a must, along with rain gear and warm clothing, as the long ride downhill from Thompson Pass is often a cold and wet one. From Valdez you can take a ferry across Prince William Sound and back to Anchorage, or back-track to the Glenn Highway and eventually to Anchorage.

North Star Bicycle Route This 3400-mile (5440 km) ride is a summer-long adventure that begins in Missoula (Montana) and ends in Anchorage. Along the way you cross the Canadian Rockies, pick up the Alaska Highway in British Columbia, pedal through Yukon Territory and follow Alaskan highways from Tok to Anchorage.

Although the majority of the Alcan is now paved, this trip should only be considered by the experienced cyclist looking for a grand adventure. The trip can be reduced significantly by either bussing part of the route in Canada (see the Getting There chapter) or by utilising the State Marine Ferry from Seattle. From Haines to Tok it is 446 miles (714 km), while Tok to Anchorage is a 328-mile (525-km) ride that can be done comfortably in five days. Those interested in this route would do well to read *The North Star Bicycle Route* while planning the trip. You can obtain copies of the 24-page booklet by writing to The Bicycle Travel Association, PO Box 8308, Missoula, Montana 59807; tel (406) 721-1776.

The Wilderness

Alaska is many things, but first and foremost it is the great outdoors. You go there for the mountains, the trails, the wildlife, the camping. If retrieving the morning newspaper is all the fresh air you can handle, Alaska can be a dull place. But if you're a camper, hiker, backpacker, or someone who spends a lot of time at scenic turn-offs, the North Country has two things for you – the most wilderness in the United States and the longest days to enjoy it in.

Compared to the cost of getting there, the cost of enjoying most of the backcountry is relatively low. Hiking is free and even the steepest camping fee is pennies compared to what motels will charge. Areas to pitch a tent vary all over the state from places with cozy lounges and heated bathrooms to clearings you might find outside of town.

The different adventures you can undertake in Alaska vary as much. You can take a three-hour hike on a well-maintained trail that begins in downtown Juneau or a week-long trek in Denali National Park where there are no trails at all.

The best way to enter the state's wilderness is to begin with a day hike the minute you step off the State Marine Ferry or depart from the Alcan. Once having experienced a taste of the woods, many travellers forgo the cities and spend the rest of their trip undertaking long-term adventures into the back-country. Make the most of Alaska's immense surroundings.

Local hiking trails and camping spots are covered in the regional chapters. The 20 trips described in this section are popular wilderness excursions that backpackers can undertake on their own if they are equipped properly and have sufficient outdoor experience. For those who don't have the experience or the equipment but still want to venture to the state's most isolated corners, there is a list of guide companies at the end of the chapter that can meet those needs.

The Wilderness Experience

Alaska covers over 550,000 square miles (1,400,000 square km) and is serviced by only 5000 miles (8000 km) of public highway. Most of the recent tourist boom centres around these roads as visitors cling to them and ironically cause the state, with all its space, to have its share of over-crowded parks and campgrounds.

Residents know this and tend to stay away from places like Denali National Park during the middle of the summer. They also know how to escape into the backcountry. Those wearing Sierra Club T-shirts call it a 'wilderness experience'. Others throw a backpack together and say they're 'going out the road for a spell'. It's all the same – a journey into the woods, away from the city, neighbours, television sets and other signs of human existence. That is the greatest enjoyment Alaska can offer anyone; a week of nothing but nature in all its splendour.

You have to be careful on such adventures. In a true wilderness experience, you are completely on your own. However, don't let the lack of communication with the civilised world prevent you from venturing into the woods; that's the best part. On an ideal trip, you won't meet another person outside your party, see a boat or hear the hum of a bush plane. In this perfect tranquility, all worries and pressures of day-to-day living are cast aside. You begin to discover yourself in the natural setting. More enjoyment and satisfaction can be derived from a few days in the wilderness than from a three-week bus tour. Some people, once they enter, never get it out of their blood.

Those with their own equipment and some backpacking experience can undertake on their own any of the 20 trips described in this chapter. They are either maintained trails or natural paddling routes enjoyed by backpackers every year. Some trips cannot provide a true 'wilderness experience', as they are too popular during the summer, but most lie out of the reach of most people and offer a glimpse of pristine backcountry.

Those who didn't come north with the right gear or who lack camping knowledge can still escape into the woods and come back out safely again. There are two ways of doing this: one is to join a guided expedition where equipment, group organisation and knowledge of the area are supplied. Guided expeditions cover any section of the state, range from half a day to three weeks in length and cost between $100 and $125 per person per day.

FOREST SERVICE CABINS

The other way to sample the wilderness without enduring a 20-mile hike or hiring the services of an outfitter is to rent a Forest Service cabin. Built and maintained by the US Forest Service (USFS), the cabins are scattered throughout the Tongass National Forest (practically the entire Southeast), the Chugach National Forest in the Kenai Peninsula, and different islands and bays in Prince William Sound. For the most part, the cabins are rustic log cabins or A-frames with wood-burning stoves, plywood bunks, pit toilets out back and often a rowboat if they are situated on a lake. They are usually located near remote lakes or streams, along coastal beaches or above the timberline.

A few cabins can be reached by hiking, but for most a bush plane or chartered

boat has to drop you off and then return to fetch you. The cabins are an ideal way to sneak into the woods and separate yourself from the world without having to undertake rigorous backcountry travel.

Although there are a few free shelters, the vast majority cost $10 per night to rent but can comfortably hold parties of six or more. You can reserve them 180 days in advance by sending the total payment and the dates you want to the various Forest Service offices which administer them. During the summer the cabins are heavily used by both locals and travellers and have a limit of seven consecutive nights per party. Some are so popular that the Forest Service holds lottery-type drawings among all the reservation requests sent 180 days in advance, in order to determine who will be allowed to occupy them during peak periods of the summer.

The cabins provide excellent shelter from bad weather but you have to bring your own bedding (sleeping bag and ground pad), food and cooking gear, including a small backpacker's stove for when the wood pile is wet. Other items that come in handy are insect repellent, matches, candles and a topographical map of the surrounding area. The USFS also recommends that any water obtained from nearby lakes and streams be boiled first for five minutes or treated with a water filter that is capable of removing giardiasis.

Of the 178 USFS public-use cabins, 142 of them are located in the Southeast and are accessible from Ketchikan, Petersburg, Juneau or Sitka. If you don't make reservations but have a flexible schedule, it is still possible to rent one. During the summer USFS offices in the Southeast maintain lists of the cabins and dates still available. There are always a few cabins available for a couple of days in the middle of the week, although they are most likely the remote ones requiring more flying time (and thus money) to reach. The most accessible ones are usually booked solid by the time June rolls around.

In the regional chapters a description of selected cabins is given under the names of towns they are most accessible from. These cabins are special because either they can be reached in 30 minutes or less by bush plane or have some intriguing feature about them such as natural hot springs or a nearby glacier. For a complete list of cabins, write to the following USFS offices, which will forward a booklet describing each cabin in its district along with details about the surrounding terrain and the best way to travel to it.

Forest Service Information Centre
  Box 1628
  Juneau, Alaska 99802
  tel (907) 586-8751

Chatham Area Supervisor
  204 Siginaka Way
  Sitka, Alaska 99835
  tel (907) 747-6671

Ketchikan Area Supervisor
  Federal Building
  Ketchikan, Alaska 99901
  tel (907) 225-3101

Stikine Area Supervisor
  PO Box 309
  Petersburg, Alaska 99833
  tel (907) 772-3871

The Chugach National Forest in South-central has 36 cabins, including seven along the Resurrection Trail and two on the Russian Lakes Trail. There are also a couple in the Cordova area that can be reached by foot, but the rest are accessible only by air or boat. For a complete list of cabins in each district, write to the USFS office for the district concerned.

Anchorage Ranger District
  2221 East Northern Lights Boulevard, Suite 238
  Anchorage, Alaska 99508
  tel (907) 279-5541

Seward Ranger District
  PO Box 275
  Seward, Alaska 99664
  tel (907) 224-3374

Cordova Ranger District
  PO Box 280
  Cordova, Alaska 99574
  tel (907) 424-7661

WHO CONTROLS WHAT

With almost three-quarters of the state locked up, it's good to know what federal or state agency administers the land you want to hike on. Almost all the recreational areas, parks and forests, including the campgrounds and trails in them, are controlled by one of five agencies.

US Forest Service

This federal bureau handles the Tongass and Chugach national forests which cover practically all of Southeast and Eastern Kenai Peninsula, including Prince William Sound. The USFS can provide information about 178 public-use cabins it maintains, along with campground, trail and other recreational opportunities in its domain. The addresses for the main offices are given above but there are also smaller offices in Craig, Wrangell, Hoonah and Yakutat.

In the Southeast each USFS office has a copy of the *Southeast Alaska Community Opportunity Guide*, which is put together by the Forest Service and contains information about camping, trails, fishing areas and cabins throughout Tongass National Forest. If you plan to spend any amount of time in a Southeast town, it is well worth your effort to venture to the USFS office and thumb through this reference guide.

National Park Service

The National Park Service administers Denali, Glacier Bay and Katmai national parks and preserves, all of which have maintained campgrounds and are accessible by either an Alaska Airlines flight or by road. The seven campgrounds in Denali are scattered across the park, including Morino Campground at the entrance – a free, 'no-thrills' area for backpackers.

There are five other national parks and preserves under National Park Service control, which are accessible only by bush plane or boat and offer no facilities within the park. They are Gates of the Arctic, Kenai Fjords, Kobuk Valley, Lake Clark and Wrangell-St Elias. Most visitors reach them through guide companies who venture into the wilderness areas by raft, kayak or foot.

The Park Service also maintains numerous national preserves, wild rivers, national monuments and national historical parks. For addresses and more information on the individual parks, check the chapters on the regions in which they are located. For general information on all parks, contact the main National Park Service offices:

National Park Service
    2525 Gambell St
    Anchorage, Alaska 99503
    tel (907) 271-4243

National Park Service
    709 West 9th St
    Juneau, Alaska 99801
    tel (907) 586-7137

Bureau of Land Management

The Bureau of Land Management is the federal agency that maintains much of the wilderness around and north of Fairbanks. It has developed 25 camping areas in the Interior and three public-use cabins as well as two popular trails (Pinnell Mountain and White Mountain) both located off the highway north of Fairbanks. Camping is free in BLM campgrounds and is handled on a first-come first-serve basis.

The BLM offices have good publications on Elliott, Steese and Taylor highways – secondary roads that are adventures in themselves. Write to or call:

BLM District Office
    PO Box 13
    Anchorage, Alaska 99513
    tel (907) 267-1200

BLM District Office
    1541 Gaffney
    Fairbanks, Alaska 99703
    tel (907) 356-2025

US Fish & Wildlife Service

This arm of the Department of the Interior administers 16 wildlife refuges in Alaska that total more than 77 million acres (31 million hectares). The largest (the Yukon Delta that surrounds Bethel in western Alaska) is bigger than Connecticut, Hawaii, New Jersey and Massachusetts combined.

The purpose of wildlife refuges is to protect habitats; visitor use and developed recreational activities are strictly an afterthought. Most of them are in remote areas of the Bush, with few, if any, developed facilities. Again, guide companies are the only means by which most travellers visit them. The one exception is Kenai National Wildlife Refuge, which can be reached by road from Anchorage. This preserve offers 15 campgrounds, of which only the Kenai-Russian River Campground has a user's fee, and over 200 miles (320 km) of hiking trails and water routes, including the popular Swanson River Canoe Route.

The Kodiak National Wildlife Refuge, although considerably more remote and expensive to reach than Kenai, does offer nine wilderness cabins along the same lines as USFS cabins. For more information about individual areas, see the regional chapters. For general information contact:

Regional Office
    US Fish & Wildlife Service
    1011 East Tudor Rd
    Anchorage, Alaska 99504
    tel (907) 786-3542

Alaska State Parks
The Alaska Department of Natural Resources controls the 97 units of its Alaska State Parks, which range from 490,000-acre (198,000 hectare) Chugach State Park east of Anchorage to small wayside parks along the highway. The list includes state trails, campgrounds, wilderness parks and historical sites, all maintained by the state.

Among the more popular ones which offer a variety of recreational opportunities are Chugach, Denali State Park south of Mt McKinley, Nancy Lake Recreational Area just south of Willow, Captain Cook State Recreation Area on the Kenai Peninsula, and Chilkat State Park south of Haines. There are no user's fees for state campgrounds and waysides. For more information contact:

State Park Information
  Pouch 7001
  Anchorage, Alaska 99510
  tel (907) 561-2020

Backpacking

Camping, hiking and backpacking in Alaska are the same as in most other places, with one major difference: the danger is greater. The weather is more unpredictable, the climate harsher, the encounters with wildlife a daily occurrence. Unpredictable situations like getting lost, snow storms in the middle of the summer or being socked in by low clouds and fog for days while waiting for a bush plane are not just a good campfire story, but happen annually to hundreds of backpackers in Alaska.

If you're planning to wander beyond the roadside park, don't take your adventure lightly. You must be totally independent in the wilderness - a new experience for most city dwellers. You need the knowledge and equipment to sit out bad weather, endure a possible overturned boat or assist an injured member of your party.

The following information and suggestions are only a guide to backpacking in Alaska and are not the first lesson on surviving the outdoors. For that you should consult a survival manual such as *The Wilderness Handbook* by Paul Petzoldt (W W Norton & Company, New York). Be prepared before you enter the woods so you can make it out later.

DAY-HIKE EQUIPMENT
Too often visitors undertake a day hike with little or no equipment and then, three hours from the trailhead, get caught in bad weather wearing only a flimsy cotton jacket. Worse yet, they suffer a major mishap such as losing the trail and having to spend a long night in the woods without food, matches or warm clothing.

Along with your large, framed backpack, take a soft day pack or rucksack on your journey to Alaska. These small knapsacks are ideal for day hikes and should contain rain gear, woollen mittens and hat, knife, high-energy food (candy), matches, map and compass, metal drinking cup and also insect repellent.

EXPEDITION EQUIPMENT

For longer treks and adventures into the wilderness, backpackers should double-check their equipment before they leave home, as opposed to scurrying around some small Alaska town trying to locate a campstove or a pair of glacier goggles. Most towns in Alaska will have at least one store with a wall full of camping supplies, but by mid to late summer certain items will be out of stock, while anytime during the year prices will be high.

You don't need to arrive with a complete line of the latest Gortex, but then again, that $4.95 plastic rain suit probably won't last more than a few days in the woods. Bring functional and sturdy equipment to Alaska and you will go home after a summer of wilderness adventures with much of it intact.

BOOTS

The traditional footwear is the heavy, leather hiking boot that has been smeared on the outside with half a can of bees wax. More and more backpackers, however, are opting for the new lightweight nylon boots made by sporting-shoe companies like Nike. These are lighter to pack and easier on the feet than leather boots, while providing all the foot protection and ankle support needed on most trails and wilderness trips other than technical mountaineering. Normal tennis shoes are not enough for the trails but are handy to have along as a change of footwear at night or for fording rivers and streams.

CLOTHING

Alaska has traditionally been wool country. The amazing fabric insulates not only against snow and cold but also against the constant drizzle, which is usually one of the main causes of hypothermia. Even when wet, wool will keep you warm, while its drying time is a fraction of cotton's.

However, wool is gradually giving way to the new synthetic pile or spun artificial fibres which possess the same qualities. They may even out-perform wool under severe wet and cold conditions. The drawback is that the jersey of acrylic piling costs twice as much as a good old woollen jacket. Take your pick but avoid cotton items (jacket, socks, blue jeans) and outerwear that contains goose down, as they are useless when wet.

On any trip longer than two days you should have two to three pairs of woollen socks, along with mittens and knitted hat. Woollen pants and shirts are not going too far in this land of sudden weather changes. Dress in layers – or like an artichoke, as residents say – for maximum containment of body heat. Always carry a heavy jersey or jacket for those less-active periods at night. Rain gear, pants and jacket should be on the top of everybody's pack.

TENT

Coming to Alaska without a lightweight tent is like going to Hawaii without a beach towel. It's the biggest cost-cutter you can bring. The tent doesn't have to be fancy, but it should have a rain fly that will double as a shield for those long summer days in the Interior when the sun can remain intense long after you've gone to bed. Make sure the netting around doors and windows is bug proof and won't turn you into a nightly smorgasbord for any mosquito that passes by.

If the tent is five years or older, waterproof the floor and rain fly before departing on your trip.

SLEEPING BAG

This is a good item to bring whether you plan on camping or not, as it is also very useful in youth hostels, on board the State Marine Ferry and in seedy hotels when you're not sure what's crawling in the mattress.

An all-night discussion among backpackers can centre on the qualities of down versus man-made fibres. What can't be argued though is down's quality of clumping when wet. In rainy Southeast and Southcentral Alaska, this means trouble during most wilderness trips. Along with a sleeping bag, bring an insulated foam pad, which will reduce much of the ground chill from below. Often in the Interior you will be sleeping just inches away from permafrost or permanently frozen ground.

CAMPSTOVE
Cooking dinner over a crackling campfire may be a romantic notion while you're planning your trip, but it is an inconvenience and often a major headache when you're actually on the trail. Bring a reliable backpacker's stove and make life simple in the woods. Rain, strong winds and a lack of available wood will hamper your efforts to build a fire, while some preserves like Denali National Park won't even allow campfires in the backcountry. You cannot carry white gas or other campstove fuels on an airline flight.

MAP & COMPASS
Backpackers should not only carry a compass into the wilderness but should have some basic knowledge of how to use it correctly. Along with the invaluable field instrument, you should have the correct US Geological Survey map for the area in which you are planning to travel.

USGS topographical maps come in a variety of scales but hikers and kayakers prefer the smallest scale of 1:63,360, where each inch equals a mile (1.6 km). The free maps of Tongass and Chugach National Forest sent by the USFS will not do for any wilderness adventure, as they cover too much and lack the detail that backpackers rely on. USGS maps cost $2.25 a section and can generally be purchased at bookstores, sports shops or camping stores in the last Alaskan town from which you enter the backcountry.

However, it is not uncommon for the stores to be out of the sections covering popular areas. If you know ahead of time where you want to hike or paddle, order your maps directly from the main USGS office by first writing to them and asking for a free index of maps for Alaska.

USGS Western Distribution Branch
    PO Box 25286 Denver Federal Centre
    Denver, Colorado 80225

SUN PROTECTION
The long hours of sunlight during the Alaskan summers are even more intense when they are reflected off snow or water. All backpackers should bring a cap with a visor on it and a small tube of sun screen to save at least one layer of skin on their nose. If you plan to do any amount of kayaking, canoeing or alpine hiking where you will be around snowfields, you should also plan on bringing a pair of dark sunglasses, known by many locals as 'glacier goggles'.

FOOD
You can buy food in almost any town or village at the start of most trips. If travelling to Glacier Bay, Denali or Katmai National Parks, don't plan on purchasing your main supply of food at the park headquarters; stock up at the last major town you pass through.

Backcountry Living

WHERE TO CAMP
Choosing a spot to pitch a tent in a campground is easy, but in the wilderness the choice is more complicated and should be made carefully to avoid problems in the middle of the night. Through much of Alaska, especially the Interior, river bars are the only place to pitch a tent. Strips of sand or small gravel patches along rivers provide good drainage and a smoother surface on which to pitch a tent

than tussock grass. Take time to check out the area before unpacking your gear. Avoid animal trails (whether the tracks be moose or bear), areas with a concentration of bear scat, and extensive berry patches with ripe fruit. In late summer, it is best to stay away from streams choked with salmon runs.

In Southeast and other coastal areas of Alaska, search out beaches and ridges with southern exposures that provide the driest conditions in these rainy zones. Old glacier and stream out-washes make ideal campsites as long as you stay well above the high-tide line. Look for the last ridge of seaweed and debris on the shore and then pitch your tent another 20 to 30 yards/metres above that to avoid waking up in the middle of the night with salt water flooding your tent. Tidal fluctuations along Alaska's coast are among the largest in the world; up to 30 feet (nine metres) in some places.

DRINKING WATER

Like most western states, Alaska is affected by *giardia lamblia* or 'beaver fever' as it is known among backpackers. The cyst is found in surface water, particularly beaver ponds, and is transmitted between humans and animals. Of the three methods to treat water for giardia, filtering is the easiest, but filters with pore size smaller than the five microns needed to trap the parasite are bulky and expensive. The other two methods consist of boiling the water or using iodine, the only chemical agent that safely destroys the micro-organism. Purifying tablets such as Globaline or Potaline-Aqua are popular among backpackers even though they leave a strong taste in the water.

INSECTS

Alaska is notorious for its biting insects. In the cities and towns you have few problems, but out in the woods you'll have to contend with a variety, including mosquitoes, black flies, white-socks, no-see-ums and deer flies. Coastal areas, with their cool summers, have smaller numbers than the Interior. Generally, camping on a beach where there is some breeze is better than pitching a tent in the woods. In the end, just accept the fact that you will be bitten.

Most bugs appear in early June, peak in late June through July and begin to taper off in mid-August. By late August and early September the plague is over. The best insect repellent has a high percentage of DEET (diethyltoluamide), the active ingredient, but don't be alarmed when that little bottle of Musk Oil or Cutters costs $4 or $5. It's one of the best investments you will make and before you leave the wilderness you will be rubbing it in your scalp as if it was hair tonic. Long-sleeved shirts, socks that will allow you to tuck your pants into them and a snug cap or woollen hat are facts of life in Alaska's backcountry. One other item that comes in handy is an after-bite medication. Most of them rub on and contain ammonia and while it might drive away your tent partner, it does soothe the craving to scratch the assortment of bites on your arms and neck.

WILDLIFE

From the road, most visitors see more wildlife in Alaska than they do in a lifetime elsewhere. From the trail such encounters often become the highlight of the entire trip; you can spot an animal, watch it quietly and marvel at the experience when it moves on leisurely.

During an extended trip, you could view moose which are widespread throughout the state but are frequently sighted along the Alaska Highway, in the Interior and on the Kenai Peninsula. The long-legged animal, which can weigh up to 1600 pounds (720 kg), has been known to invade the city limits of Anchorage during severe winters. Caribou, of which there is an estimated 600,000 living in 13 herds in Alaska, are more difficult to view as they range from the Interior north to

the Arctic Sea. The best bet for seeing caribou is Denali National Park, where they are occasionally seen from the park road.

Other mammals encountered during alpine treks include Dall sheep and the mountain goat in alpine regions of Southeast and Southcentral Alaska. In the lowlands, hikers have a chance to view red fox, beaver, pine marten, snowshoe hare, red squirrel and on rare occasions wolves or even a wolverine.

Marine mammals most commonly spotted include harbour seals, sea otters, sea lions, harbour porpoises and killer whales or Orcas, whose high black-and-white dorsal fin makes them easy to identify from a distance. The two most common whales seen in coastal waters are the humpback with its hump-like dorsal fin and long flippers and the smaller minke whale.

The salmon runs are one of Alaska's most amazing sights and are common throughout much of the state. From late July to mid-September many coastal streams are choked with salmon swimming upstream to spawn. You'll see not just one here and there, but thousands – so many that they have to wait their turn to swim through narrow gaps of shallow water. The salmon are famous for their struggle against the current and their magnificent leaps over waterfalls, and for decorating stream banks with carcasses afterwards.

Equally impressive in Alaska's wilderness is the bald eagle, the majestic and powerful bird that is, rightfully so, the symbol of a nation. While elsewhere the

bird is almost extinct, in Alaska it thrives in strong numbers. The eagle can be sighted almost daily in most of the Southeast and is common in Prince William Sound. It also migrates once a year in a spectacle that exceeds even the salmon runs. Thousands of bald eagles gather along the Chilkat River north of Haines from late October through to December. They come to feed on the late salmon run and create an amazing scene during the bleakness of early winter. Bare trees, without a leaf remaining, support dozens of white-headed eagles, four or five to a branch.

BEARS & BACKPACKERS

You could spend the entire summer in Alaska without ever seeing a bear, or you could be on an early-morning stroll in Juneau and see one scrambling towards the woods a block away from the Governor's Mansion. Too often travellers decide to skip a wilderness trip because they hear a local tell a few bear stories. Your own equipment and outdoor experience should determine whether you take a trek into the woods, not the possibility of meeting a bear on the trail. You have a much better chance of being mugged in Los Angeles than getting mauled by a bear in Alaska.

Some people carry a gun to fend off any bear charges. This is a delicate situation if you are a good marksman, a foolish one if you are not. With a gun, you must drop a charging bear with one or two shots otherwise it will be three times as dangerous if only wounded. Other people attach 'bear bells' all over their backpack, boots and clothing. Bells will alert any bear in the immediate area, but unfortunately will also scare all other wildlife, even the species you want to see. The constant ringing not only eliminates the chances to view animals but blocks out the natural sounds of the woods that ease the mind and fill the soul with wonder.

The best way to avoid bears is to follow

a few commonsense rules. Bears do not roam the backcountry looking for hikers to maul; they only charge when they feel trapped, when a hiker gets between a sow and her cubs or when they are enticed by food. It is a good practice to sing or clap when travelling through thick bush so you don't bump into one. That has happened, and usually the bear feels threatened and has no choice but to defend itself. Don't camp near its food source or in the middle of an obvious bear path. Stay away from thick berry patches, streams choking with salmon or beaches littered with bear scat.

Leave the pet at home; a frightened dog only runs back to its owner and most dogs are no match for a bear. Set up your 'kitchen' – the spot where you will cook and eat – 30 to 50 yards/metres away from your tent. In coastal areas, many backpackers eat in the tidal zone, knowing that when the high tide comes in all evidence of food will be washed away. At night try to place your food sacks 10 feet (three metres) or more off the ground by hanging them in a tree, placing them on top of a tall boulder or putting them on the edge of a rock cliff. In a treeless, flat area, cover up the sacks with rocks. A bear is not going to see the food bags, it's going to smell them. By packaging all food items in zip-lock plastic bags, you greatly reduce the animal's chances of getting a whiff of your next meal.

And please, take no food into the tent at night. Don't even take toothpaste, hand lotion, suntan oils, or anything with a smell. If a bear smells a human, it will leave. Anything else might encourage it to investigate.

If you do meet a bear on the trail, *do not turn and run.* Stop, make no sudden moves and begin talking calmly to it. Bears have extremely poor eyesight and speaking helps it understand that you are there. If it doesn't take off right away, back up slowly before turning around and departing the area. A bear standing on its hind legs is not on the verge of charging, only trying to see you better. When a bear turns sideways or begins a series of woofs, it is only challenging you for space. Just back away slowly and leave.

Most bear charges are bluffs, with the animal veering off at the last minute. Experienced backpackers handle a charge in different ways. Some throw their packs three feet in front of them, as this will often distract the bear long enough for them to back away. Others fire a hand-held signal flare over the bear's head (but never at it) in an attempt to use the noise and sudden light to scare it away. If an encounter is imminent, drop into a foetal position and place your hands behind your neck.

Be extremely careful in bear country, but don't let their reputation keep you out of the woods.

BLUEWATER PADDLING

Bluewater in Alaska refers to the coastal areas of the state that are characterised by extreme tidal fluctuations, cold water temperatures and the possibility of high winds and waves. Throughout Southeast and Southcentral Alaska the open canoe gives way to the kayak, and bluewater paddling is the means of escape into the coastal wilderness. Don't confuse whitewater kayaking with ocean touring. River-running in the light, streamlined kayaks with helmets, wet suits and Eskimo rolls has nothing to do with

paddling coastal Alaska in ocean-touring kayaks. Every year hundreds of backpackers with canoeing experience arrive in the North Country and undertake their first kayak trip in such protected areas as Muir Inlet of Glacier Bay National Park or Tracy Arm Fjord south of Juneau.

Tidal fluctuations are the main concern. Paddlers have to make it a habit to not only pull their boat above the high-tide line but to always secure it by tying a line to a rock or tree. A tide book for the area should be in the same pouch as the topographical map, as paddlers schedule days around the changing tides, travelling with the tidal current or during slack tide for easy paddling. Check with local rangers for the narrow inlets or straits where rip tides or whirlpools might form, and always plan to paddle these areas during slack tides.

Cold coastal water, rarely above 45°F degrees (7°C) in the summer, makes capsizing more than unpleasant. Even with a life-jacket, survival time in the water is less than two hours; without one it is considerably less. Route your trips to run parallel with the shoreline and arrange your schedule so you can sit out rough weather without missing your pick-up date. If you do flip, stay with the boat and attempt to right it and crawl back in. Trying to swim to shore in arctic water is risky at best.

Give wide berth to marine mammals such as sea lions, seals and especially any whales that are sighted during a paddle. Glacial ice should also be treated with respect. It is unwise to approach a glacier face closer than half a mile, as calving icebergs can happen suddenly and create a series of unmanageable waves and swells. Never try to climb onto a floating iceberg as they are extremely unstable and can roll without warning.

Framed backpacks are almost useless in kayaks; gear is better stowed in duffle bags or small day packs. Carry a large supply of assorted plastic bags, including several garbage bags. All gear, especially sleeping bags and clothing, should be stowed in plastic bags, as water tends to seep in even when you seal yourself in with a cockpit skirt. Other equipment that should be taken along on any bluewater paddle are an extra paddle, a large sponge for bailing the boat, sunglasses and sunscreen, extra lines and a repair kit of duct tape and a tube of silicon sealant for fibreglass cracks.

BACKCOUNTRY CONDUCT

It is wise to check in with the USFS office or National Park headquarters before entering the backcountry. By letting them know your intentions, you get peace of mind knowing that someone knows you're out there. If there is no ranger's office in the area, the best place to state your intention is the air charter service responsible for the pick-up of your party.

Do not harass wildlife while travelling in the backcountry. Avoid startling an animal, as most likely it will flee, leaving you with a short and forgettable encounter. If you flush a bird from its nest, leave the area quickly, as an unattended nest leaves the eggs vulnerable to predators. Never attempt to feed wildlife; it is not healthy for you or the animal.

Finally, be thoughtful when in the wilderness, as it is a delicate piece of real estate. Carry in your supplies and carry out your trash, never littering or leaving garbage to smoulder in a fire pit. Always put out your fire and cover it with natural materials. Burn only dead and fallen wood and leave no evidence of your stay.

BOOKS

A great deal of reference material is available that will assist backpackers in finding their way along the trail or will give them a better understanding of the natural world around them. The following books can be found in a good Alaskan bookstore or can be obtained directly from the publisher.

Hiking & Paddling Guides

55 Ways To The Wilderness In Southcentral Alaska (Nancy Simmerman and Helen Nienhueser, Mountaineer-Books, 306 2nd Avenue West, Seattle, Washington 98119, 1985; 176 pp, $9.95). A hiking guide with the most up-to-date information covering popular trails around Kenai Peninsula, the Anchorage area and north from Palmer to Valdez. The text includes maps, distances and estimated times.

Exploring Katmai National Monument (Alaska Natural History Association, 2525 Gambell St, Anchorage, Alaska 99503; 1974, 276 pp, $12). A general though slightly out-dated guide to Katmai National Park. However, little has changed regarding the park's history, geology, wildlife and the 15 backpacking routes described in the book.

Floating Alaskan Rivers (Marilyn Carter, Aladdin Publishing, PO Box 364, Palmer, Alaska 99645; 1982, 114 pp, $6.95). A guide to 34 water trips throughout Alaska, from Bristol Bay and the Arctic Region to Fairbanks and the Kenai Peninsula. The descriptions are short and the maps lack much detail, but all the necessary information is there for most float trips. *Alaska Back Trails* (Marilyn Carter, Aladdin Publishing; 1977, 76 pp, $5.95). A collection of favourite hiking and paddling trips by the author who wrote *Floating Alaska Rivers*. The information about the 43 trips is slightly outdated.

Juneau Trails (US Forest Service, 1983, 60 pp, free). This little green book is a bible for Juneau hikers, as it describes 27 trails around the Capital City – perhaps the best area for hiking in Alaska. The guidebook is free and includes maps, distances, rating of the trails and location of trailheads along with brief descriptions of the route. The book can be obtained at the USFS Information Centre in the Centennial Building on Egan Drive, but you have to ask for it.

Exploring The Yukon River (Archie

Top: Glacier hike in Southeast Alaska (AD)
Left: Backpackers on the outside coast of Glacier Bay (JD)
Right: Hikers on White Thunder Ridge in Glacier Bay (JS)

Top: Hikers on the Chilkoot Trail (DT)
Bottom: Hikers crossing the Chilkoot Pass on the Chilkoot Trail (JS)

Satterfield, Mountaineer-Books; 200 pp, $7.95). A guidebook for paddlers along the Yukon River, beginning with its headwaters and covering the first 500 miles to Dawson City.

The Coastal Kayaker (Randel Washburne, Pacific Search Press, 222 Dexter Avenue North, Seattle, Washington 98109; 1983, 214 pp, $10.95). The book deals mostly with the art of bluewater kayaking and how to survive in the coastal wilderness of British Columbia and Southeast Alaska. It does contain paddling notes and basic maps for seven different areas, including four in Southeast.

A Guide To Alaska's Kenai Fjords (David Miller, Wilderness Images, Anchor Cove, PO Box 1367, Seward, Alaska 99664, 1984). A coastal paddling guide to the Kenai Fjords National Park with route description and maps.

Glacier Bay National Park: Water And Foot Routes (Jim DuFresne, Mountaineer-Books, 1987). The Mountaineer book is due out in spring 1987 and will be the complete guide to Glacier Bay's backcountry. Along with introductory material on the park, the book contains information on kayak rentals, transportation up bay and detailed descriptions of water and land routes in this trail-less park. Maps are included.

Discover Southeast Alaska With Pack And Paddle (Margaret Piggott, Mountaineer-Books, 1987). This long-time guidebook to the water routes and hiking trails of Southeast will reappear as a two-volume set beginning in 1987, after being out of print for several years. The first volume will be an updated version of hiking trails of the area from Ketchikan to Haines. The second book will cover kayak trips in this coastal region of Alaska.

General

A Guide To Alaskan Seabirds (Alaska Natural History Association, 2525 Gambell St, Anchorage, Alaska 99503; 1982, 40 pp, $4.50). A thin guide to the birds that thrive along coastal Alaska. Excellent drawings for easy identification.

Wild Edible And Poisonous Plants Of Alaska (Dr Christine Heller, Alaska Natural History Association, 2525 Gambell St, Anchorage, Alaska 99503; 88 pp, $1.50). The handy little guide is an excellent companion on any hike, as it contains both drawings and colour photos of Alaskan flora, including edible plants and berries and wildflowers.

Mammals Of Denali (Alaska Natural History Association; 1984, 64 pp, $4.50). This guidebook provides information and photos on the wildlife that can be seen in Denali National Park and throughout much of the Interior.

Adventures on Foot

The following trips are along trails and water routes that are popular and well developed. Backpackers still need the proper gear and knowledge but can undertake these adventures on their own without the services of an outfitter. Always check into the offices or park headquarters listed for current trail conditions. A few trails have USFS cabins, but these must be reserved far in advance. Bring a tent on any wilderness trek.

CHILKOOT TRAIL

Denali National Park may be the most popular park in Alaska, but the Chilkoot is unquestionably the most famous trail and often the most used during the summer; 1500 hikers follow it annually. It is the same route used by the Klondike gold-miners in the 1898-1900 gold rush and is not so much a wilderness adventure as a history lesson.

The well-developed and well-marked trail is littered from one end to the other with artefacts of the era – everything from entire ghost towns and huge mining dredges to a lone boot lying next to the

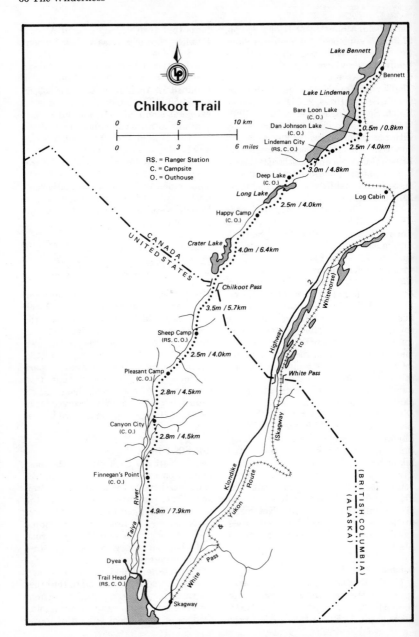

Chilkoot Trail

RS. = Ranger Station
C. = Campsite
O. = Outhouse

trail. The trip is 33 to 35 miles (53 to 56 km) long (depending on where you exit) and includes the Chilkoot Pass – a steep climb up loose rocks to 3550 feet (1082 metres), where most hikers use all fours to scramble over the loose rocks. The trail can be attempted by anyone in good physical condition with the right equipment and enough time. The hike normally takes four to five days, though it can be done in three or even two by experienced trekkers.

Until 1982, one of the popular highlights of the hike was riding the White Pass & Yukon Railroad back to Skagway, but the train has since ceased operations. With the loss of the train, the trail's popularity has dwindled from 2500 hikers in 1981 to less than 1500 four years later.

Getting Started

Most hikers arrive at Skagway to tackle the Chilkoot. The trail can be hiked from either direction, however, and is actually easier from Lake Bennett. From historical Skagway, make your way to Dyea, eight miles (13 km) to the north-west and the site of the trailhead. *Mile 0* of the Chilkoot is just before the Taiya River crossing.

Near the start is the Dyea Camping Area (22 sites, no fee) and a National Park Service Ranger Station. You can reach Dyea by either hitch-hiking or contacting Grayline Motorcoach, tel (907) 983-2500 in Skagway, which charges $7 per passenger for a one-way ride to the trailhead.

Getting Back

At the north end, hikers used to catch the White Pass & Yukon Railroad but the rail service no longer operates. Today there are two ways to leave the trail at the northern end: you can hike six miles (10 km) from Bare Loon Lake Campsites (*Mile 29* of the trail) along the narrow-gauge tracks to the log cabin on Klondike Highway. A White Pass & Yukon Motorcoach stops at the log cabin at 5 pm

on its way south to Skagway daily except Tuesday and Sunday, while a northern bus reaches the warming hut at 11.50 am on its way to Whitehorse. On Tuesday and Sunday the buses reach the log cabin 1½ hours earlier. One-way fare for log cabin-Skagway is $12 and for log cabin-Whitehorse is $30. The bus company can be contacted in Skagway during the summer at (907) 983-2471.

The alternative is the ferry service (which also sprang up after the WP&Y railroad ceased operations) which for $35 will carry hikers from the trail's end across Lake Bennett to Carcoss, where you can catch a bus north or south. Arrangements are made at the Lake Bennett Campground but the service is sporadic at best. The vast majority of hikers walk out to Klondike Highway.

More Information

Stop at the National Park Service visitor centre in the refurbished railroad depot on 2nd Avenue and Broadway, Skagway for current weather and trail conditions as well as exhibits and films on the area's history and hiking maps. It's hard to get lost on the Chilkoot as there seems to be an orange marker every 50 yards. For more information contact the National Park Service at PO Box 517, Skagway, Alaska 99840; tel (907) 983-2921.

Section	miles	km
Dyea to Canyon City	7.7	12.4
Canyon City to Sheep Camp	5.3	8.5
Sheep Camp to Chilkoot Pass	3.5	5.6
Chilkoot Pass to Happy Camp	4.0	6.4
Happy Camp to Deep Lake	2.5	4.0
Deep Lake to Lindeman City	3.0	4.8
Lindeman City to Bare Loon Lake	3.0	4.9
Bare Loon Lake to Log Cabin	6.0	9.6
Bare Loon Lake to Lake Bennett	4.0	6.4

RESURRECTION PASS TRAIL

Located in the Chugach National Forest, the 38-mile (61 km) trail was carved by prospectors in the late 1800s and today is

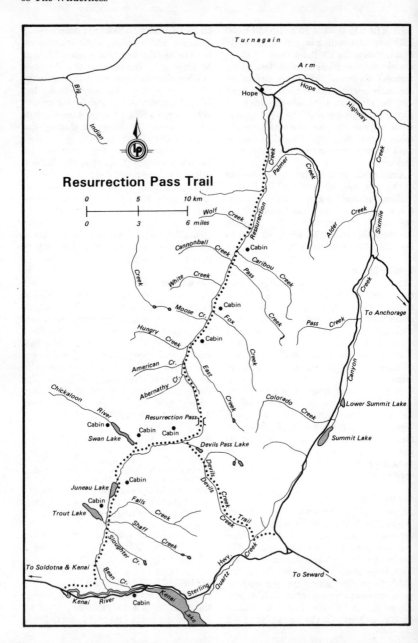

the most popular hiking route in the Kenai Peninsula. The trip could be done in three days by a keen hiker but most people prefer to do it in five to seven days to make the most of the immense beauty of the region and the excellent fishing in Trout, Juneau and Swan lakes.

There is a series of nine USFS cabins along the route that have a $10 per night rental fee. They have to be reserved in advance and, being quite popular, are fully-booked for most of the summer which makes last-minute reservations almost impossible. Inquire at the USFS office in Anchorage about reserving them. Most hikers take a tent and a campstove, as fallen wood can sometimes be scarce during the busy summer.

Getting Started

The northern trailhead is 20 miles (32 km) from the Seward Highway and four miles (6.4 km) south of Hope on Resurrection Creek Rd. Hope, a historical mining community founded in 1896 by gold seekers, is a charming, out-of-the-way place to visit, but Hope Highway is not an easy road to thumb. Patience is the key, as eventually someone will give you a lift.

From Hope Highway you turn south at the posted airport signs onto Resurrection Creek Rd, passing the fork to Palmer Creek Rd. The southern trailhead is on Sterling Highway, 53 miles (85 km) east of Soldotna and 106 miles (171 km) south of Anchorage. Hitch-hiking is easy on the Sterling and Seward highways in either direction. A quarter-mile east of the southern trailhead along Sterling Highway is the Russian River USFS Campground (84 campsites, $6 per night) and the trailhead for the Russian Lakes Trail.

An alternative route that lets you avoid travelling to the remote northern trailhead is the Devils Creek Trail, which is posted at *Mile 39* of Seward Highway (88 miles / 142 km south of Anchorage). The 10-mile (16 km) path leaves the highway and climbs to Devils Pass at 2400 feet (730

metres), where it joins the Resurrection Pass Trail. By using Devils Creek and the lower portion of Resurrection Pass Trail, you can hike from the Seward Highway to the Sterling Highway in two days.

More Information

For more information on the trail or reserving cabins along it, contact the USFS office for the Anchorage District: Chugach National Forest, PO Box 10-469, Anchorage, Alaska 99511; tel (907) 261-2500.

Section	miles	km
Resurrection Pass to Devils Pass Cabin	6.9	11.1
Devils Pass to Swan Lake campsite	4.7	7.6
Fox Creek to East Creek Cabin	2.8	4.5
East Creek to Resurrection Pass	4.9	7.9
Resurrection Pass to Devil's Pass Cabin	2.1	3.4
Devil's Pass to Swan Lake Cabin	4.4	7.1
Swan Lake to Juneau Lake Cabin	3.3	5.3
Juneau Lake to Trout Lake Cabin	2.7	4.3
Trout Lake to Juneau Creek Falls	2.3	3.7
Juneau Creek Falls to Sterling Highway	4.4	7.1

RUSSIAN LAKES TRAIL

The 21 mile (34 km), two-day hike is an ideal alternative for those who do not want to over-extend themselves in the Chugach National Forest. The trail is well travelled, well maintained and well marked during the summer and not too demanding on the legs and feet. Most of the hike is a pleasant forest walk broken up by patches of wildflowers, ripe berries, lakes and streams.

Highlights of the walk are the possibilities of viewing moose or bears, the impressive glaciated mountains across from Upper Russian Lake or, for those who pack in a fishing pole, the chance to catch your own dinner.

If you plan ahead, there are two USFS cabins on the trail that are rented out for $10 per night but need to be reserved in advance. One is on Upper Russian Lake, nine miles (14.4 km) from the Cooper Lake trailhead. The second is at Aspen Flats, another three miles (4.8 km) along the trail or 12 miles (19 km) from the western trailhead.

Getting Started

It is easier to start from the Cooper Lake trailhead, the higher end of the trail. To reach the trailhead, head west on Sterling Highway and turn off at *Mile 47.8* (76.9 km) onto Snug Harbour Rd. The road leads 12 miles (19.3 km) to Cooper Lake and ends at a marked parking lot and the trailhead. The western trailhead is on a side road marked 'Russian River USFS Campground' at *Mile 52.7* (84.7 km) of Sterling Highway. Hike 0.9 mile (1.4 km) to the end of the campground road to reach a parking lot at the beginning of the trail. If you're planning to camp at Russian River the night before starting the trek, keep in mind that the campground is extremely popular during the

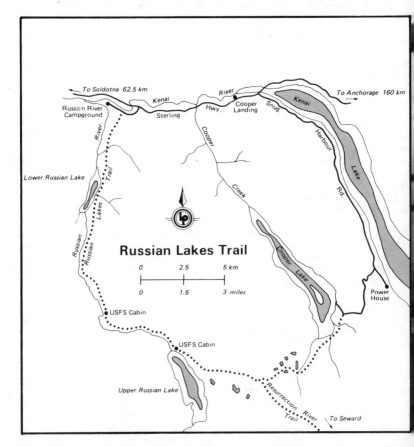

To Soldotna 62.5 km

Russian River Campground

Kenai River

Sterling

Hwy.

Cooper Landing

Snug

Kenai

To Anchorage 160 km

River

Cooper

Lower Russian Lake

Russian River

Russian Lakes Trail

Creek

Cooper Lake

Harbour Rd.

Russian Lakes Trail

| 0 | 2.5 | 5 km |
| 0 | 1.5 | 3 miles |

USFS Cabin

USFS Cabin

Power House

Upper Russian Lake

Resurrection River Trail

To Seward

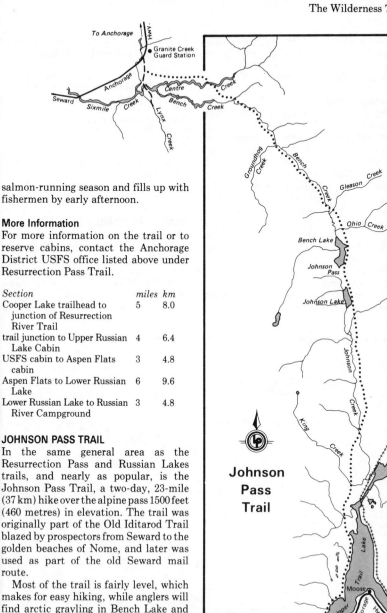

salmon-running season and fills up with fishermen by early afternoon.

More Information

For more information on the trail or to reserve cabins, contact the Anchorage District USFS office listed above under Resurrection Pass Trail.

Section	miles	km
Cooper Lake trailhead to junction of Resurrection River Trail	5	8.0
trail junction to Upper Russian Lake Cabin	4	6.4
USFS cabin to Aspen Flats cabin	3	4.8
Aspen Flats to Lower Russian Lake	6	9.6
Lower Russian Lake to Russian River Campground	3	4.8

JOHNSON PASS TRAIL

In the same general area as the Resurrection Pass and Russian Lakes trails, and nearly as popular, is the Johnson Pass Trail, a two-day, 23-mile (37 km) hike over the alpine pass 1500 feet (460 metres) in elevation. The trail was originally part of the Old Iditarod Trail blazed by prospectors from Seward to the golden beaches of Nome, and later was used as part of the old Seward mail route.

Most of the trail is fairly level, which makes for easy hiking, while anglers will find arctic grayling in Bench Lake and rainbow trout in Johnson Lake. Plan to camp at either Johnson Lake or Johnson

Pass, but keep in mind that these places are above the tree line, making it necessary to carry a small stove. There are no cabins on this trail.

Getting Started

The trail can be hiked from either direction. The northern trailhead is at *Mile 64* (103 km) on Seward Highway or 96 miles (154 km) south of Anchorage. There is a gravel road marked 'Forest Service Trail No 10' that leads a short way to a parking lot and the trail. The trail works its way south over Johnson Pass and then to the shore of Upper Trail Lake before reaching Seward Highway again at *Mile 32.5* (52.3 km). Hitch-hiking to or from either end is easy during the summer.

More Information

Because the trail lies in the Chugach National Forest, contact the USFS office of the Anchorage District for more information and trail conditions.

Section	miles	km
northern trailhead to Bench Creek Bridge	3.8	6.1
Bench Creek to Bench Lake	5.5	8.8
Bench Lake to Johnson Pass	0.7	1.1
Johnson Pass to Johnson Lake	0.6	1.0
Johnson Lake to Johnson Creek Bridge	5.1	8.2
Johnson Creek Bridge to Upper Trail Lake	3.7	5.9
Upper Trail Lake to Seward Highway	3.6	5.8

PINNELL MOUNTAIN TRAIL

The midnight sun is the outstanding sight on the Pinnell Mountain Trail, a 24-mile (39 km) trek 85 miles (137 km) north-east of Fairbanks on Steese Highway. From 18 to 25 June, the sun never sets on the trail, giving hikers 24-hour days. The polar phenomenon of the sun sitting

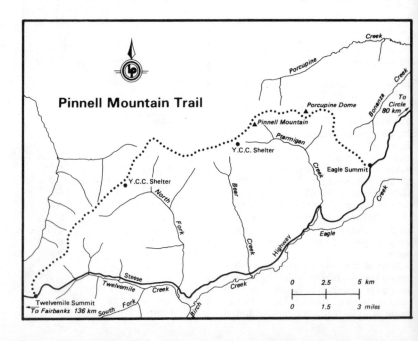

Pinnell Mountain Trail

above the horizon at midnight can be viewed and photographed at several high points on the trail, including the Eagle Summit trailhead.

The route is mostly tundra ridgetops that lie above 3500 feet (1100 metres) and can be steep and rugged at times. The other highlight of the trip is the wildflowers (unmatched in much of the state) which carpet the arctic-alpine tundra slopes, beginning in late May and peaking in mid-June. Hikers may spot small bands of caribou along with grizzly bears, rock rabbits and an occasional wolf or lynx. The views from the ridge tops are spectacular, with the Alaska Range visible to the south and the Yukon Flats to the north.

Getting Started
The trail is a three-day adventure at the rate of eight miles (13 km) a day. Most hikers begin at the Eagle Summit trailhead on *Mile 107.3* (172.6 km) of the Steese Highway, the higher end of the trail. The other end lies at Twelvemile Summit closer to Fairbanks at *Mile 85* (137 km) of the highway. There are two three-sided shelters built by the Youth Conservation Corps and open to use by anyone, without reservations or fees. It is still necessary to bring a tent with good bug netting; use the shelters as your kitchen.

Snow cover can be expected in May and mid-September, with patches remaining through June. These are good sources of water, which unlike in most of Alaska, is scarce on the trail. Bring at least two quarts (two litres) per person and then refill at every opportunity at either snow patches, springs or tundra pools. Boil or filter all standing water from pools and slow-running springs. The winds can be brutal in this barren region, as there are no trees to slow the gusts that can come howling over the ridges. Bring a wind screen for your campstove, otherwise cooking dinner could become a long ordeal.

Traffic on the Steese Highway is light this far out of Fairbanks, but there is a trickle. Hitch-hiking is only possible if you are very patient and prepared to spend a night on the road. Van service is provided by Kak Tours, tel (907) 488-2649, which charges $60 for a round trip to Circle Alaska and will make arrangements to drop off and pick up hikers at the trailheads.

If there are two or more of you, a cheaper alternative is to rent a used car through Rent-A-Wreck of Fairbanks and combine the trip on the trail with a drive to Circle Hot Springs or the bush town of Circle on the Yukon River. There is a gasoline station and restaurant at *Mile 101* (162 km) of the highway, but stock up in Fairbanks.

More Information
For trail conditions or a free trail map, contact the Bureau of Land Management Office in Fairbanks by writing to BLM District Office, 1541 Gaffney St, Fairbanks, Alaska 99701; or telephone (907) 452-4725.

Section	miles	km
Eagle Summit trailhead to Porcupine Dome	5.0	8.0
Porcupine Dome to 1st YCC shelter	4.0	6.4
1st shelter to 2nd YCC shelter	7.0	11.2
2nd shelter to Twelvemile Summit	7.0	11.2

WHITE MOUNTAIN TRAIL
The Bureau of Land Management, which maintains the Pinnell Mountain Trail, also administers another hike – the White Mountain Trail. This 21-mile (34 km), out-and-back route winds through dense spruce forest, traverses scenic alpine ridgetops and arctic tundra and ends at Beaver Creek in the foothills of the majestic White Mountains. On the banks of the creek is the Borealis-Le Fevre Cabin, which should be reserved but is easier to obtain than most USFS units in

White Mountain Trail

Tongass and Chugach National Forest. The rental fee is $5 per night for the cabin and can usually be obtained by calling the BLM district office in Fairbanks two months in advance on (907) 356-2025.

The hike to the cabin is a steady two-day walk from the trailhead at *Mile 28* (45 km) of Elliott Highway, 31 miles (50 km) north of Fairbanks. As on the Pinnell Mountain Trail, you need to bring water, which is scarce in the alpine sections.

Highlights of the trek are the views on top of Wickersham Dome, which include Mt McKinley, the White Mountains and the Alaskan Range.

Getting Started

Don't confuse the White Mountain Summer Trail, which is built for hikers, with the Winter Trail, 4.5 miles (7.2 km) closer to Fairbanks on the Elliott Highway. The Winter Trail was cut for snow machines, cross-country skiing and people using snow shoes, and leads through swampy, muskeg lowlands. The two trails meet up two miles (3.2 km) from the Borealis-Le Fevre Cabin. Stock up with provisions in Fairbanks. The last place to purchase food and gasoline is at Fox, the junction of the Steese and Elliott highways. There is usually more traffic on the Elliott than on back portions of the Steese, but it is still thin for hitch-hiking.

More Information

The BLM District Office in Fairbanks can supply a free map that lacks topographical detail but contains plenty of information on the trail. The office will also have current information on trail conditions and the availability of water, and is the place to reserve the Borealis-Le Fevre Cabin. Contact the BLM District Office at 1541 Gaffney, Fairbanks, Alaska 99701; tel (907) 356-2025.

Section	miles	km
Summer trailhead to Wickersham Creek	2.0	3.2
Wickersham Creek to Wickersham Dome	2.0	3.2
Wickersham Dome to Winter Trail junction	13.0	21.0
trail junction to cabin	2.0	3.2

BOREALIS - LEFEURE
CABIN

MT EIELSON CIRCUIT - DENALI NATIONAL PARK

Denali National Park & Preserve is a paradise for backpackers – especially backpackers on a shoestring. You could spend days or even weeks at the park and only pay for the food you eat.

The reserve is divided into more than 30 sections and only a regulated number of overnight hikers are allowed into each area. In the height of the summer, it may be difficult to get a permit into the section of your choice and other sections will be closed off entirely when the impact of visitors is too great for wildlife. The number of visitors tapers off dramatically in late August. Many people consider the end of August to mid-September as the prime time to see the park as the crowds and bugs are gone and the autumn colours are setting in.

There is an almost endless number of hiking combinations in the park. If time allows, begin by taking the shuttle-bus ride and a day hike to get acquainted with a trail-less park, fording streams and rivers and reading your topographical map accurately, then plan an overnight excursion. The Mt Eielson Circuit is a 14-mile (22.5 km) hike that can make for a leisurely two-day walk – or a three-day one if a day is spent scrambling up any of the nearby peaks. The hike offers an excellent opportunity to view Mt McKinley, Muldrow Glacier or an abundance of wildlife. The route begins and ends at Eielson Visitors Centre and involves climbing 1300 feet (400 metres) through the pass between Mt Eielson and Castle Peak. The most difficult part, however, is crossing Thorofare River, which should be done in tennis shoes with an ice-axe or sturdy pole in hand.

From Eielson Visitors Centre, *Mile 66* (106 km) of the park road, you begin the route by dropping down the steep hill to George Creek, crossing it and continuing south-southeast to Thorofare River. Follow the tundra shelf along the east side of the river until you cross Sunrise Creek, which

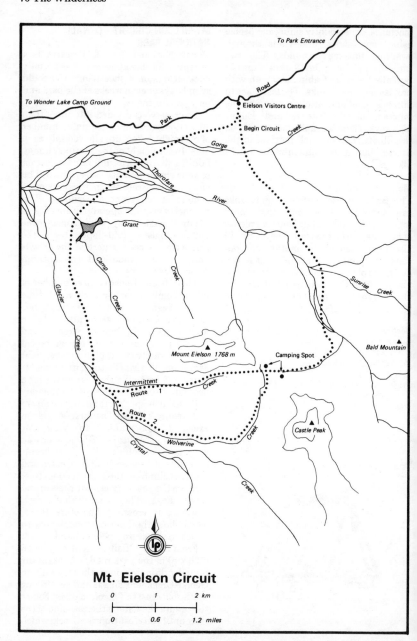

Mt. Eielson Circuit

flows into the Thorofare. The river is next and must be forded with extreme caution. Once on the west bank, continue hiking south until you reach Contract Creek's junction with the Thorofare. The clearwater creek is due west of Bald Mountain Summit and leads up to the pass between Mt Eielson and Castle Peak. The pass, at the elevation of 4700 feet (1400 metres), is a good place to spend the night, as views of Mt McKinley are possible in clear weather.

From the pass, hike west towards Intermittent Creek, where rock cairns point the way. The creek leads to the gravel bars of Granite Creek on the southwest side of Mt Eielson. This section of the river makes for easy hiking or a good campsite for those who want to tackle Mt Eielson from the west side, its most manageable approach. Head north along Glacier Creek until you reach the flood plain with the many braids of Camp Creek and Thorofare River woven across it. Cross the channels and swing to the north-east towards Eielson Visitors Centre.

Getting Started

General information about the park is contained in the chapter on the Interior. There are several ways of getting to the park from either Fairbanks or Anchorage, including a handful of bus companies that have regularly-scheduled runs (see the Getting Around chapter). Alaska-Denali Transit, tel (907) 276-6443, is a cut-rate company that offers one-way transportation from the Anchorage Youth Hostel to the park for $30. Alaska Railroad runs an express train that departs both Anchorage and Fairbanks and goes non-stop to the park headquarters.

Once at the park, most backpackers stay at the free Morino Campground or check into the unofficial Youth Hostel that consists of bunks in old railroad cars and costs $3 per night. The next step is to obtain your backcountry permit from

either Riley Creek Visitors Centre or Eielson Visitors Centre. Both places sell topographical maps; the Mt Eielson Circuit is contained on one section – Mt McKinley B-1. There is a small store within park headquarters that sells food and campstove fuel, but it is best to stock up in Anchorage or Fairbanks.

More Information

For a shoe box full of free information about the park, contact the Denali National Park & Preserve, PO Box 9, Denali Park, Alaska 99755; tel (907) 683-2294. If you are in Anchorage, contact the National Park Service centre for information about Denali or any national park in Alaska at the NPS Information Centre, 2525 Gambell St, Room 107, Anchorage, Alaska 99503; tel (907) 271-4243.

Section*	miles	km
Eielson Visitor Centre to George Creek	1.0	1.6
George Creek to Sunrise-Thorofare junction	2.0	3.2
junction to Contact Creek	1.0	1.6
Contact Creek to Pass Summit	1.2	1.9
Pass Summit to Glacier Creek	3.3	5.3
Glacier Creek to flood plains	2.5	4.0
flood plains to Eielson Visitor Centre	3.0	4.8

*This is a route, not a trail, so all distances are rough estimates only.

DEER MOUNTAIN TRAIL

Located in Ketchikan, Deer Mountain Trail is often the first hike visitors undertake in the North Country. Rarely does it disappoint them, as the trail is a steady but manageable climb to the sharp peak above the city, with incredible views of the Tongass Narrows and surrounding area.

What many visiting backpackers don't realise is that Deer Mountain is only part of an alpine trail system that can be followed for a challenging overnight trip.

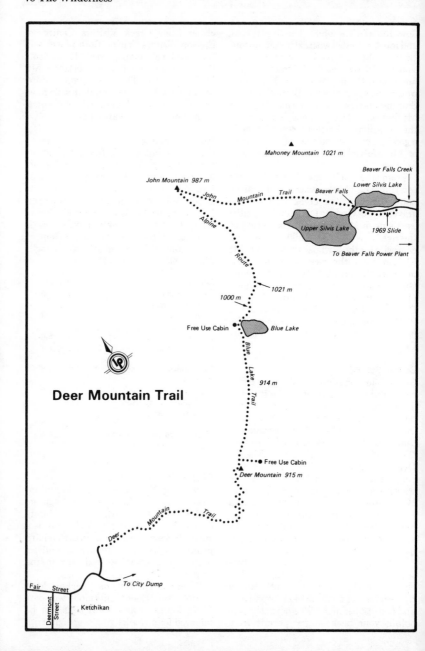

Mahoney Mountain 1021 m

Beaver Falls Creek

John Mountain 987 m

John   Mountain   Trail   Beaver Falls

Lower Silvis Lake

Alpine

Upper Silvis Lake

Route

1969 Slide

To Beaver Falls Power Plant

1021 m

1000 m

Free Use Cabin

Blue Lake

Blue

Lake

Trail

914 m

Free Use Cabin

Deer Mountain 915 m

Deer Mountain Trail

Deer   Mountain   Trail

Fair   Street

To City Dump

Deermont Street

Ketchikan

This 11-mile (17.7 km) trip includes spending the night in a free-use USFS cabin and begins with the three-mile (4.8 km) Deer Mountain Trail which leads into the Blue Lake Trail. The path is a natural route along an alpine ridge extending north four miles (6.4 km) to John Mountain. Here hikers can return to the Ketchikan road system by taking the John Mountain Trail south for two miles (3.2 km) to Upper Silvis Lake and then following an old access road from the hydroplant on Lower Silvis Lake to the parking lot off Beaver Falls Highway.

Deer Mountain is a well-maintained and heavily-used trail during the summer. Even though it climbs steadily, the hike to the summit is not difficult. A quarter-mile before the summit you pass the junction to Blue Lake and the posted side-trail to the Deer Mountain Cabin. The cabin, located above the treeline, sleeps eight and is filled on a first-come first-serve basis. The Blue Lake Trail crosses alpine country with natural but good footing, although in rainy and cloudy weather it may be difficult to follow. The scenery from the trail is spectacular.

Within two miles (3.2 km) from the junction of the Deer Mountain Trail, you arrive at a second free-use USFS cabin on the shore of Blue Lake. The cabin also sleeps eight, and at the elevation of 2700 feet (820 metres) is above the tree line in a scenic setting. John Mountain Trail has grades of 20% the first mile from Upper Silvis Lake and then covers alpine country, marked by a series of steel posts. It is a moderately difficult track to follow and presents hikers with a challenge in reading their topographical maps and choosing the right route.

Getting Started
The trailhead for Deer Mountain can be reached by following the gravel road from the corner of Fair and Deermount Sts, past the new subdivision towards the city dump. Just before reaching the dump, a

trail sign points to a side road to the left and the trailhead and small parking lot are quickly reached.

To get to the start of the John Mountain Trail, hitch 12.9 miles (20.8 km) along South Tongass Highway (also known as Beaver Falls Highway) to its end at the power plant. There is a two-mile (3.2 km) hike along an old access road from the power plant at tidewater to the hydroplant on Lower Silvis Lake. As the road to the upper lake was destroyed by a landslide, some scrambling up the steep hillside is necessary. There are a couple of ways to reach the next lake; one begins on the roof of the lower lake power-house, following an old outlet stream course. John Mountain Trail begins at the old outlet at the west end of the upper lake.

More Information
The cabins and trails are maintained by the US Forest Service, which have their main headquarters and visitors centre in the Federal Building on Stedman St in downtown Ketchikan. You can contact them for trail conditions or for more information write to or call the USFS Office, Federal Building, Ketchikan, Alaska 99901; tel (907) 225-3101.

Section	miles	km
Deer Mountain trailhead to summit	3.1	5.0
summit to Blue Lake Cabin	2.2	3.5
Blue Lake Cabin to John Mountain	2.0	3.2
John Mountain to Upper Silvis Lake	2.0	3.2
Upper Silvis Lake to South Tongass Highway	2.0	3.2

PETERSBURG CREEK TRAIL
A short hop across the Wrangell Narrows from the fishing community of Petersburg is Petersburg Creek and the first of four trails that can be combined into a circular hike connecting two USFS cabins. The entire trail system is due to be re-marked and finished by 1986 and will provide

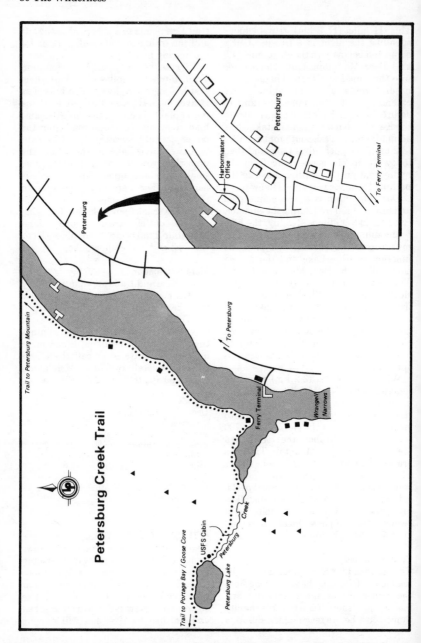

Petersburg Creek Trail

Trail to Petersburg Mountain

Petersburg

Harbormaster's Office

Petersburg

To Ferry Terminal

To Petersburg

Ferry Terminal

Wrangell Narrows

Trail to Portage Bay / Goose Cove

USFS Cabin

Petersburg Creek

Petersburg Lake

backpackers with a wilderness opportunity and access to USFS cabins that doesn't require expensive bush plane travel. Both cabins need to be reserved and have a rental fee of $10 per night.

Petersburg Creek Trail is entirely planked, but those planning to go beyond to Portage Bay or Salt Chuck should consider carrying along a pair of rubber boots or 'Southeast sneakers', as you will encounter wet, muskeg areas. Also bring a fishing pole, as there are good spots in the creek for Dolly Varden and cut-throat trout. In August and early September there are large coho salmon-runs throughout the area that attract the attention of fishermen as well as bears.

The adventure begins on the west side of Wrangell Narrows, across from downtown Petersburg at the Kupreanof Island public dock. From the dock a partial boardwalk leads south for two miles (3.2 km) past a handful of cabins and then turns north-west up the arm of the creek, almost directly across Wrangell Narrows from the ferry terminal.

A well-planked trail goes from the saltwater arm and continues along the side of the freshwater creek, reaching the Petersburg Lake USFS cabin on the eastern end of the lake. From the cabin a second trail continues north to Portage Bay, and though some sections might be hard to follow, most of it is well marked with a series of blue diamond-shaped blazes in the trees.

West of the trail is the beginning of the trail to Salt Chuck. This path leads to the Salt Chuck East Cabin and will be re-marked in 1986. The route is scheduled to be completed in 1986 when the USFS build a a trail around the south side of Portage Mountain from Salt Chuck to Petersburg Lake Cabin.

Getting Started
The only hitch in this trip is getting across Wrangell Narrows to the public dock on Kupreanof Island. The USFS office above the post office provides a list of charter boat operators and places to rent a skiff. This can be expensive; a skiff and motor rental can cost as much as $100. The cheapest and probably easiest way is to hitch a ride with one of the number of boats that cross every day. Go to the skiff float in North Harbor (Old Harbor) near the harbour-master's office on the waterfront and ask around for anybody crossing. A small population lives on the other side so boats are constantly being shuffled across, though at times you might have to wait a bit. Avoid inquiring at the harbour-master's office about rides, as they tend to discourage this practice.

Those who arrive at Petersburg with their own kayak can paddle to the creek during high tide to avoid much of the hike along the tidewater arm. This is one trip when you'll want good rain gear and rubber boots. Bring a tent or plan on reserving the cabins at least two months in advance; or even further ahead if you want to tackle the route in August during the coho runs.

More Information
The Petersburg District USFS office is on the second floor of the post office along Main St. Make sure you contact the office before embarking to double-check on trail conditions and the status of the new trail from Salt Chuck to Petersburg Lake. Contact them at Petersburg Ranger District, PO Box 1328, Petersburg, Alaska 99833; tel (907) 772-3871.

Section	miles	km
Kupreanof Island dock to tidewater arm	2.0	3.2
tidewater arm to Petersburg Creek	3.0	4.8
trail by creek to USFS cabin	6.5	10.4
USFS cabin to Portage Bay	5.5	8.8
Portage Bay to Salt Chuck East Cabin	6.0	9.6
USFS cabin to Petersburg Lake*	10.0	16.0

*Estimated distance of the trail scheduled to be built in 1986.

PERSEVERANCE-MT JUNEAU TRAIL

Juneau is the centre for some of the best hiking in Alaska. There are over 20 trails in the area maintained by the US Forest Service, and many more 'unofficial' ones. Almost all of them offer spectacular scenery as they wind through alpine areas and around glaciers or offer views of the surrounding mountains. Most of them can be undertaken in a day or turned into an overnight escape to the woods.

Within easy walking distance of the Juneau Youth Hostel are several trails, including the Perseverance, the most popular trek in the area. Branching off the Perseverance are the Mt Juneau and Granite Creek trails, and together the system can be combined into a rugged 10-hour walk for hardy hikers or an overnight excursion into the mountains that surround Alaska's capital city.

From the Perseverance Trail it is possible to pick up the Granite Creek Trail and follow the path to the creek's basin with its impressive waterfalls and wildflowers. From here you can gain access to Mt Juneau by climbing the ridge and staying left of Mt Olds, the huge, rocky mountain. Once at the summit of Mt Juneau you can complete the circular trip by descending along the Mt Juneau Trail, which joins the Perseverance Trail a mile from its beginning.

An easier hike would be to turn the adventure into an overnight trip by camping in Granite Creek Basin, a beautiful spot to pitch a tent. The following day, leave the packs behind and scramble up the ridge to Mt Juneau, elevation 3576 feet (1090 metres). The alpine sections of the ridge are peacefully serene on a clear day in the summer, the views outstanding. Return to your campsite that evening and hike out. Beyond the junction to Granite Creek at the end of the Perseverance Trail are some ruins of an old gold mine in Silver Bowl Basin and the steep-sided Glory Hole.

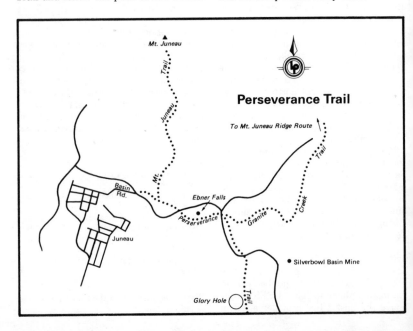

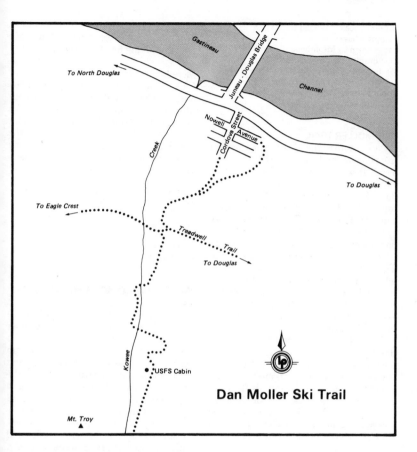

Dan Moller Ski Trail

Getting Started

From the Youth Hostel, take 6th St one block to Gold St and climb the steep road toward Mt Juneau. Gold St will swing right into Basin Rd, a dirt road that curves away from town and into the mountains as it follows Gold Creek. After the Basin Rd bridge over Gold Creek, you come to a fork. The road to the left is marked and leads straight to the Perseverance trailhead. From the beginning of the trail junction to Mt Juneau is 0.5 mile (0.8 km), while Granite Creek is 1.8 miles (2.9 km).

More Information

The USFS maintains an information centre in the Juneau Centennial Hall (tel (907) 586-8751) on 101 Egan Drive one mile (1.6 km) from the Youth Hostel. It's open daily from 8.30 am to 6 pm and can provide information on area trails as well as make USFS cabin reservations. Ask for their green *Juneau Trails* booklet.

Section	miles	km
Perseverance trailhead to Granite Creek	1.8	2.9

Granite Creek trailhead to upper basin	1.5	2.4
upper basin to Mt Juneau summit	3.0	4.8
Mt Juneau summit to Ebner Falls on Perseverance Trail	12.0	19.3
Ebner Falls to Perseverance trailhead	0.5	0.8

DAN MOLLER TRAIL

Located across the Gastineau Channel from downtown Juneau is the Dan Moller Trail. It was originally built during the 1930s for downhill skiers and at one time had three warming huts and two toll ropes placed along it. Today the skiers continue along North Douglas Highway to Eaglecrest Ski Area, while Dan Moller has become a popular access to the alpine meadows in the middle of Douglas Island. The trail is 3.3 miles (5.3 km) and leads to a beautiful alpine bowl where the USFS restored the remaining ski cabin in 1984. As with all USFS cabins, you have to reserve it in advance and there is a $10 per night rental fee.

Even if you can't secure the cabin, don't pass up this trail. Camping in the bowl is superb and an afternoon or an extra day can be spent scrambling up and along the ridge that surrounds the bowl and forms the backbone of Douglas Island. From the ridge there are scenic views of not only Douglas Island but also Admiralty Island and Stephens Passage.

Getting Started

The trailhead lies 1.5 miles (2.4 km) from the Juneau Youth Hostel. You can easily walk it or catch the minibus to Douglas and get off at Cordova St, which leads to a growth of apartments and condominiums known as West Juneau. From Cordova, turn left onto Nowell Avenue and follow it to the end of the pavement. The trail begins between lot Nos 3059 and 3051 on Nowell Avenue. An old jeep track serves as the first part of the trail before it emerges into open muskeg. Most of it is planked, but waterproof boots are a must.

The hike is a steady climb to the alpine bowl but is not overly tiring. Plan on six hours of hiking for the round trip.

More Information

Call or stop at the USFS office in the Juneau Centennial Hall for trail conditions or news on the availability of the Dan Moller Cabin. To reserve the cabin before you depart for Alaska, see the previous section in this chapter covering USFS cabins and write to the Juneau District office.

Section	miles	km
Youth Hostel to Dan Moller trailhead	1.5	2.4
Dan Moller trailhead to junction with Treadwell Ditch Trail	0.8	1.3
trail junction to upper cabin	2.5	4.0

WOLF POINT - GLACIER BAY NATIONAL PARK

Nestled in the northern section of Southeast is Alaska's frozen gem – the Glacier Bay National Park & Preserve. The preserve has spectacular mountain scenery, impressive fjord-like bays and inlets and a long list of wildlife that can be seen including harbour seals, whales and porpoises. However, its major draw-card for visitors and outdoor enthusiasts is its tidewater glaciers – those magnificent frozen rivers that roar, rumble and thunder into the upper reaches of the bay, filling the water with sculptured ice.

Glacier Bay is not just another trailless park in Alaska's wilderness; it should be viewed as a marine park, with the kayak being the most practical way of travelling the backcountry. Every summer, to the dismay of a few uninformed visitors, there are no glaciers near Bartlett Cove (park headquarters) and it is impossible to hike to the nearest one, some 40 miles (64 km) up bay. The most common way to explore the park is to rent a kayak and spend a few days paddling the well-protected inlets.

Backpackers who want nothing to do with small boats, double-bladed paddles and spray skirts still have an opportunity to explore the park and view glaciers. Wolf Point, located in the upper portions of Muir Inlet, is one of the three drop-off points of the tour ship *Thunder Bay*. Here you can climb off the ship onto the rocky shore and spend two to four days exploring on foot. There are no trails in the Wolf Point area, but there are several routes that offer the chance to hike over glacier remnants or to view McBride and Riggs glaciers from a distance.

The cove formed by Wolf Point is a river delta, offering good camping. From here it is an easy 1.2-mile (1.9 km) climb to the 700-foot (213 metre) point of White Thunder Ridge, where there are good views of McBride and Riggs glaciers. The most popular overnight trip from Wolf Point is to hike north across the Muir Glacier Remnant, reaching Muir Inlet again after it curves from north to west. From this spot on Muir Inlet the ice pack is thick and it's interesting to see the mother seals and their pups resting on icebergs.

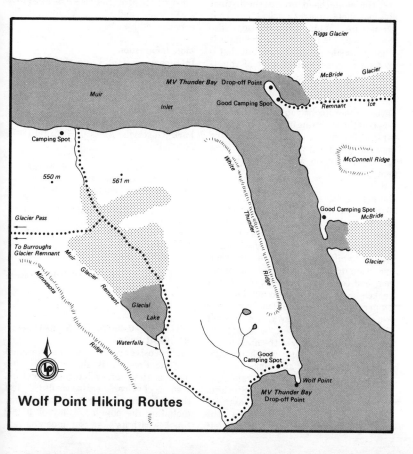

Wolf Point Hiking Routes

To reach Muir Glacier Remnant, hike 0.5 mile (0.8 km) along the shoreline south of Wolf Point to the second river that flows into Muir Inlet. This is the larger of the two and is much too wide and deep to ford. Follow the riverbank for 0.6 miles (1.0 km) and you will approach a large waterfall. At this point you will be forced to hike up the steep bank and into the thick alder around the falls for 0.25 mile (0.4 km), but you will emerge at the stunning sight of Muir Glacier Remnant and the glacial lake in front of it.

After hiking around the lake, climb onto the ice and head towards the distinct 800-foot (244 metre) rock knob that extends from White Thunder Ridge into the ice-field. On the topographic maps it is shown as surrounded by ice, but that is no longer true. Directly west of this is Glacier Pass, while to the north the ice continues towards a pass between a pair of 1800-foot (549-metre) knobs. Once beyond these knobs you follow a stream down to the shoreline of Muir Inlet. This far up Muir Inlet the terrain is bare and very rocky, forcing you to search a little for a flat spot on which to pitch your tent.

Getting Started

Turn to the Glacier Bay section of the Southeast chapter for general information about the park. Once at Bartlett Cove, backpackers can stay in the free campground while they prepare for their excursion up bay. Check in at the visitor centre at the foot of the dock to obtain a backcountry permit and to purchase the proper topographic maps (for Wolf Point you will need two: 'Skagway A-4' and 'Mt Fairweather D-1'), then book passage onto the *Thunder Bay* at the main lodge. A ticket will cost $115, which includes your fees for drop-off and pick-up.

In your pack you must have rain gear, pants, parka and a campstove. Stock up on supplies in Juneau to avoid having to purchase anything in Gustavus, the small settlement just outside Bartlett

Cove. Stagnant glacial remnants are composed of ice with a rough surface, filled with minerals and rocks that offer good footing. Crampons are not needed, though some hikers carry an ice-axe or stout pole with them to check cracks before stepping over them. For the most part, Muir Remnant is a gently sloping, unbroken section of glacier except for around the fringes and a few crevasses here and there. It is best to stay away from such areas when hiking over the ice, and you should always travel in pairs. The overnight trip from Wolf Point to the other side of Muir Inlet is a 6.5-mile (10.4 km) walk and is a challenge for experienced hikers.

More Information

In Juneau the USFS information centre in the Centennial Hall supplies information on Glacier Bay along with maps and handouts. For information before you depart for Alaska, contact the National Park Service at Glacier Bay National Park, Gustavus, Alaska 99826; tel (907) 697-3341.

Section*	miles	km
Wolf Point to Glacial River	0.5	0.8
mouth of river inland to Glacial Lake	0.9	1.5
around Glacial Lake to Muir Remnant	1.2	1.9
across Muir Remnant to 800-ft (244-m) knob	1.1	1.8
knob north to Muir Inlet	2.7	4.3

*This is a route, not a trail, so all distances are rough estimates only.

VALLEY OF 10,000 SMOKES - KATMAI NATIONAL PARK

An expensive side trip, Katmai National Park & Preserve is also an intriguing place for a long-term wilderness adventure. A series of volcanic eruptions in 1912 left the area with unique land formations, including the popular Valley of 10,000 Smokes with its eerie and 'moon barren'

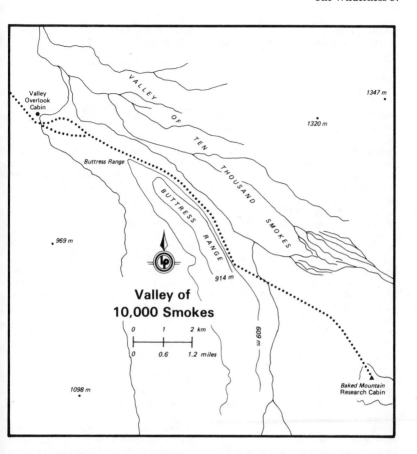

landscape. Hiking in the park is generally considered moderately difficult. Wildlife is plentiful, with the brown bear the most prominent animal. Moose live in most parts and the fishing is often said to be among the best in Alaska, as Katmai is an important spawning area for salmon.

The Valley of 10,000 Smokes is the most popular route for backpacking in Katmai, even though few of the famed '10,000 smokes' are active today. It begins with a short trail from Three Forks Overlook at the end of the park road to Windy Creek on the floor of the valley. A well-defined route then leads 12 miles (19.9 km) south-east across the valley to a research cabin on the side of Baked Mountain. The hike is considered moderately hard and includes some up-and-down trekking along the foothills of Buttress Range, followed by a drop down to the River Lethe, a major fording. From the river you head for the divide between Broken Mountain, 3785 feet (1154 metres), and Baked Mountain, 3695 feet (1126 metres). You then swing south-east to climb the short but steep slope of Baked Mountain to the cabin.

Getting Started

Turn to the chapter on the Bush for travel information on getting to and from Katmai National Park, but be ready to pay around $300 for a round-trip ticket from Anchorage, 290 miles (466 km) away. The only developed facilities in the park, outside of a couple of expensive wilderness lodges, are at Brooks Camp, the summer headquarters of the park. Here there is lodging and a restaurant. A park store sells limited quantities of freeze-dried food, topographic maps and white gas for campstoves, and rents tents, canoes, campstoves and fishing poles among other things. It is best to stock up on food and fishing tackle in Anchorage to avoid emptying your entire money pouch on one side-trip.

Like Denali National Park, Katmai has a shuttle bus that runs the park road almost daily but, unlike Denali's, it is not free. Round-trip fare on the bus is $50 and a spot should be reserved the night before. Hikers who have a week in the park can skip the bus fare by walking the 23 miles (36.8 km) out to Three Forks Overlook from Brooks Camp. The weather can be consistently poor even by Alaskan standards; the skies are clear only 20% of the summer, and from September onwards, strong winds are frequent in the area.

More Information

In Anchorage contact the National Park Visitors Centre (tel (907) 271-4243) on 2525 Gambell St for information about Katmai. If you are planning to visit the park it is best to write ahead for the packet of visitor's information they will send you. The address is Katmai National Park, PO Box 7, King Salmon, Alaska 99613; tel (907) 246-3305.

Section	miles	km
Brooks Camp to Three Forks via Park Rd	23.0	36.7
Three Forks to Windy Creek*	1.0	1.6
Windy Creek to River Lethe via Buttress Range*	7.0	11.2
River Lethe to Baked Mountain Cabin*	4.0	6.4

*Marked distance are rough estimates only.

Adventures by Paddle

MISTY FJORDS

The national monument encompasses 2,294,343 acres (928,491 hectares) of wilderness that lie between two impressive fjords – Behm Canal, 117 miles (188 km) long, and Portland Canal, 72 miles (116 km) in length. The two natural canals give the preserve its trademark of extraordinarily deep and long fjords with sheer granite walls that rise thousands of feet out of the water.

The destination for many kayakers are the smaller but equally-impressive fjords of Walker Cove and Punchbowl Cove in Rudyard Bay, both of which lie off Behm Canal. The vegetation in this monument is dense spruce-hemlock rainforest, while the abundant wildlife includes sea lions, harbour seals, killer whales, brown and black bears, mountain goats, moose and bald eagles.

Ketchikan is the departure point for most trips into Misty Fjord. Several tour boats run day-trips into the area and there are the usual expensive sightseeing flights on small bush planes. Kayakers can either paddle out of the city (a seven to 12-day trip for experienced paddlers only) or utilise one of the tour boats to drop you off deep in Behm Canal near Rudyard Bay and protected water. Those contemplating paddling all the way from Ketchikan have to keep in mind that the currents around Point Alava and Alava Bay are strong and tricky, often flowing in unusual patterns. Rounding the point into Behm Canal should be done at slack tide, which means leaving the city at high tide. The three to four-mile (4.8 to 6.4 km) crossing of Behm Canal also has to be done with caution, as northerly winds

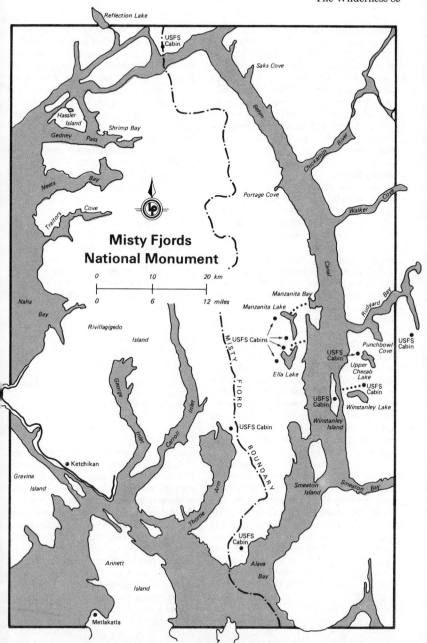

whipping down the waterway can create choppy conditions.

The USFS, which administers the monument, has 15 cabins (reservations needed, $10 rental fee) and 15 miles (24 km) of trails. Two of the cabins, Alava Bay and Winstanley Island, are located right on Behm Canal and allow kayakers to end a day of paddling at the doorstep of a cabin. Many of the others are a short hike inland.

Getting Started

Outdoor Alaska offers the most services for kayakers interested in paddling Misty Fjords. This Ketchikan tour company has a variety of boat/plane trips into the monument and will take kayakers and their boats along at a reduced rate. The company will drop you off and pick you up anywhere in the preserve for $150 and has a boat making runs on Wednesday, Friday and Sunday. This allows inexperienced paddlers to avoid much of the open water of Behm Canal and to experience only the protected and spectacular areas of Rudyard Bay or Walker Cove. For $75 they will place your kayak on their tour boat and fly you out to Manzanita Bay, almost directly across from Rudyard Bay, and then return you to Ketchikan on the tour boat. However, this involves crossing Behm Canal if you want to view the east side. They also have one-way fares for those who want to paddle all the way back to town.

Outdoor Alaska rents single kayaks for $20 per day, but on longer rentals they claim they are 'always ready to make a deal.' You can also rent kayaks from 1025 Water (the store took its name from its street address), which charges $25 per day for single kayaks and $30 for doubles. Both have a limited number of boats and if you can plan ahead it is best to reserve them before the summer. Contact 1025 Water at (907) 225-1736. Outdoor Alaska is at PO Box 7814, Ketchikan, Alaska 99901; tel (907) 225-6044.

You cannot undertake this trip without good rain gear or a backpacker's stove, as wood in the monument is often too wet for campfires. Be prepared for extended periods of rain and have all gear sealed in plastic bags. Either order your maps ahead or hope that the sections you want are in stock at Tongass Trading Company, 203 Dock St in downtown Ketchikan, then take them to the USFS office and have somebody point out the camping spots in the area where you are going to paddle. Since much of the monument is steep-sided fjord, good campsites are scarce in many sections.

More Information

For information or handouts on the monument, either visit the USFS information centre in the Federal Building in downtown Ketchikan or contact the monument office at Misty Fjords National Monument, 1817 North Tongass Highway, Ketchikan, 99901; tel (907) 225-2148.

Section	miles	km
Ketchikan to Thorne Bay	13.0	20.9
Thorne Bay to Point Alava	9.0	14.4
Point Alava to Winstanley Island	21.0	33.8
Winstanley Island to Rudyard Bay	9.0	14.4
Rudyard Bay to Walker Cove	10.0	16.0

TRACY ARM

Tracy Arm is another fjord in Southeast that, like Glacier Bay, features tidewater glaciers rumbling and calving icebergs into the water. Unlike Glacier Bay, this wilderness area is not particularly popular during the summer. It combines steep 2000-foot (600 metre) granite walls rising straight out of the water, with cascading waterfalls and a pair of glaciers at the end that sparkle like diamonds on a ring.

The 30-mile (48 km) arm is no more than half a mile wide at its upper end, which makes for ideal conditions for the novice kayaker. Calm water is the norm for Tracy Arm, as the steep, narrow fjord

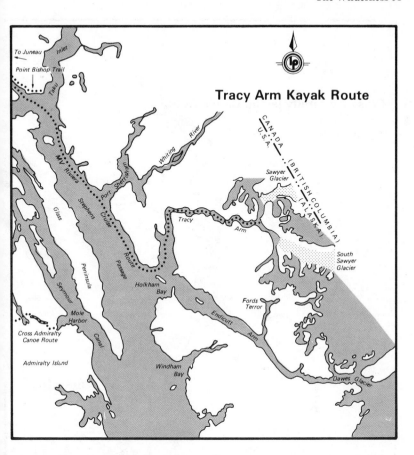

Tracy Arm Kayak Route

walls provide protection from stormy weather and strong winds. Wildlife includes bald eagles, mountain goats, seals and an occasional whale. Even more interesting is the gallery of icebergs that float past you out to sea.

Getting Started

The departure point for Tracy Arm is Juneau. Kayaks can be rented for $25 singles and $30 doubles per day from Alaska Discovery and placed on the tour boat *Riviera*, which offers drop-offs and pick-ups deep in the bay for $75 per person. This makes the trip considerably easier as otherwise it would be a two or three-day paddle in open water to the mouth of the arm. From the end of Tracy Arm where the *Riviera* drops off most kayakers (and the most interesting section), it is a pleasant three-day paddle towards the mouth. Most kayakers camp on the island which faces the two glaciers the first night even though level space for a tent is difficult to find. The only other camping spots in the first half of the arm are two valleys almost across from each other, eight miles (13 km) further down.

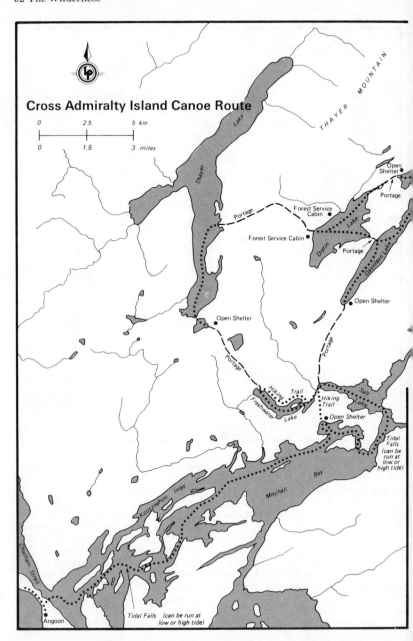

Cross Admiralty Island Canoe Route

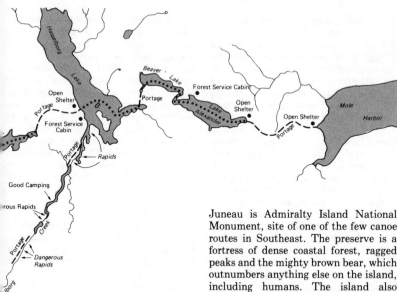

Purchase topographic maps from the Baranof Bookstore in downtown Juneau at 100 North Franklin St, and head south along the street to the Alaska Discovery office at 418 South Franklin for tips on the trip and campsite locations. Also secure a tide book in town and plan your paddles with the tides for an easier trip. To reserve kayaks or passage on the *Riviera* ahead of time contact Alaska Discovery at PO Box 26, Gustavus, Alaska 99826, tel (907) 697-2257; or Riviera Alaska, 14 Marine Way, Juneau, Alaska 99801, tel (907) 586-9888.

More Information

Tracy Arm Wilderness is managed by the US Forest Service, which can be contacted for more information or handouts at USFS Juneau District, PO Box 2097, Juneau, Alaska 99801; tel (907) 789-3111.

CROSS ADMIRALTY ISLAND

Situated 50 miles (80 km) south-west of Juneau is Admiralty Island National Monument, site of one of the few canoe routes in Southeast. The preserve is a fortress of dense coastal forest, ragged peaks and the mighty brown bear, which outnumbers anything else on the island, including humans. The island also supports one of the largest bald-eagle nesting areas, while Sitka black-tail deer can be seen throughout the monument.

The Cross Admiralty Canoe Route is a 32-mile (51 km) water route that spans the centre of the island from the native village of Angoon to Mole Harbor. Although the majority of it consists of calm lakes connected by streams and portages, the 10-mile (16 km) paddle from Angoon to Mitchell Bay is subject to strong tides that challenge even experienced paddlers. Avoid Kootznahoo Inlet as its tidal currents are extremely difficult to negotiate; instead, paddle through the maze of islands south of it. Leave Angoon at low tide, just before slack tide so that the water will push you into Mitchell Bay, and keep a watchful eye out for tidal falls and whirlpools. When paddling to Angoon, leave Salt Lake four hours before the slack period, after high tide.

From the west end of Salt Lake there is a 3.5-mile (5.6 km) portage to Davidson Lake, which is connected to Lake Guerin by a navigable stream. Between Lake

Guerin and Hasselborg Lake is a 1.7-mile (2.7 km) portage followed by a 0.5-mile (0.8 km) portage on the east side of Hasselborg to Beaver Lake. Canoeists can paddle straight from Beaver Lake to the east end of Lake Alexander, where they pick up a 2.5-mile (four km) trail to Mole Harbour. This is the most common route followed, but there are numerous trails in the area, including portages to Thayer Lake and a route along Hasselborg Creek that connects Salt Lake with Hasselborg Lake.

There are good camping spots at Tidal Falls at the beginning of Salt Lake, on the islands at the south end of Hasselborg Lake and at Davidson Lake portage to Distin Lake. The USFS also maintains three-sided shelters (no reservations or rental fee) at the south end of Davidson Lake, at the east end of the Hasselborg Lake portage and at Mole Harbour. Finally, for those who can plan in advance, there are several USFS cabins (reservations needed, $10 per night) along the route, including some on Hasselborg Lake, Lake Alexander and Distin Lake.

Getting Started
Consider Juneau the departure point for the four to seven-day trip even though you will probably pass through the small village of Angoon. The native community is a port-of-call for the state marine highway, which greatly reduces your transportation costs as one-way fare between the two towns is $21. The problem is what to do at Mole Harbor, the east end of the trail. You can charter a bush plane to pick up both your party and the boats, but that is an expensive exercise for those on a tight budget. One alternative is to back-track to Angoon and return on the state ferry, which does not charge for canoes or kayaks that are carried on. This means setting up your trip around the ferry schedule, but the savings would be enormous.

Check with Alaska Discovery in Juneau,

418 S Franklin St, tel (907) 586-1911, about canoe rentals. In Angoon canoes can be rented for $30 per day at the Angoon Trading Company on Kootznahoo Rd, tel (907) 788-3111. The outfitters also have some canoes cached along the route for their guided trips, and during spring and fall canoes may be rented in one place and left on the other side of the island. Purchase your topographic maps in Juneau and then take them to the USFS Information Centre in Centennial Hall or to the Alaska Discovery office to have someone point out where strong tidal currents exist.

More Information
This is a USFS-maintained preserve and information can be obtained from the information centre in the Juneau Centennial Hall or by writing to the Juneau District Office (see Tracy Arm for address). To contact Alaska Discovery during the winter for reservations, write or call Alaska Discovery, PO Box 26, Gustavus, Alaska 99826; tel (907) 697-2257.

Section	miles	km
Angoon to Salt Lake Tidal Falls	10.0	16.0
Tidal Falls to Davidson Lake portage	2.5	4.0
portage to Davidson Lake	3.5	5.6
Davidson Lake to Hasselborg Lake portage	6.0	9.6
portage to Hasselborg Lake	1.7	2.7
Hasselborg to Beaver Lake portage	2.0	3.2
portage to Beaver Lake	0.5	0.8
Beaver Lake to Mole Harbor portage	3.0	4.8
portage to Mole Harbor	2.5	4.0

HOONAH TO TENAKEE SPRINGS
This 40-mile (64 km) paddle follows the shorelines of Port Frederick and Tenakee Inlet between the villages of Hoonah and Tenakee Springs and includes a short portage of a hundred yards /metres or so. You might pass an occasional clearcut,

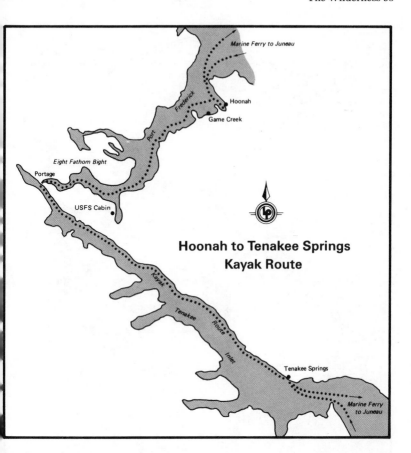

Hoonah to Tenakee Springs Kayak Route

but there are few other signs of human existence along the route once you are beyond the two villages. The area is part of Tongass National Forest and consists of rugged and densely forested terrain populated by brown bears, which you will probably see feeding along the shoreline.

It is important to carry a tide book and to reach the portage at high tide. Boot-sucking mud will be encountered along the portage, but take heart in that it is just a short walk over a low ridge to the next inlet. Highlights of the trip include the scenic south shore of Tenakee Inlet

with its many bays and coves. The village of Tenakee Springs has a public bath house around its natural hot springs that will soothe any sore muscles resulting from the paddle.

Getting Started

This adventure is within the grasp of many backpackers on a budget as there is a state ferry service to both Hoonah and Tenakee Springs from Juneau. One-way fare between the capital city and Hoonah is $14 (to Tenakee Springs $18), with no charge for kayaks. The best way to paddle

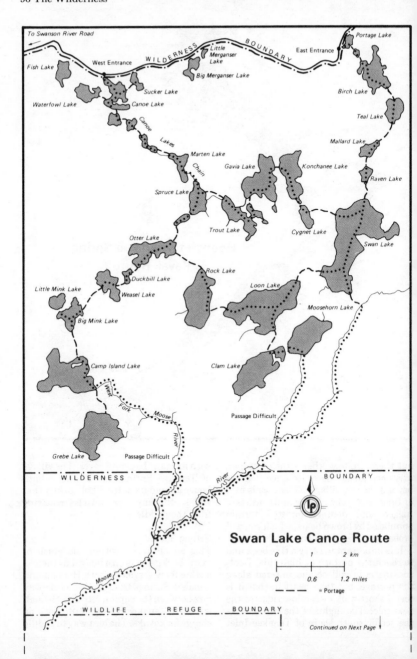

Swan Lake Canoe Route

```
0          1          2 km

0        0.6        1.2 miles

----- = Portage
```

Continued on Next Page ↓

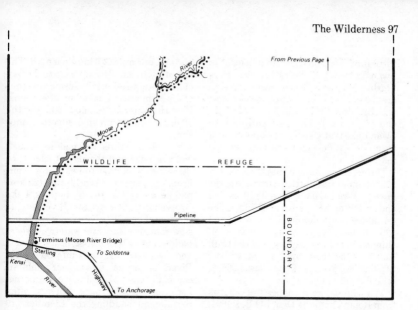

From Previous Page

WILDLIFE   REFUGE

Pipeline

BOUNDARY

Terminus (Moose River Bridge)
Sterling   To Soldotna
Kenai
River   Highway
To Anchorage

the route is from Hoonah to Tenakee Springs in order to end the trip in the charming village. However, that has to be planned carefully, as there is only one ferry every four days to Tenakee Springs. Kayaks can be rented at Alaska Discovery in Juneau (see Tracy Arm trip) for $30 per day for doubles. Plan to purchase all supplies and topographic maps in Juneau, although there is food and lodging in both villages (see the Southeast chapter).

More Information

For more information about the route or the surrounding area, contact the USFS office in Hoonah at the Hoonah Ranger District, PO Box 135, Hoonah, Alaska 99829; tel (907) 945-3631.

SWAN LAKE & SWANSON RIVER

In the northern lowlands of Kenai National Wildlife Refuge there is a chain of rivers, lakes and streams – and portages, of course – that make up the Swanson River and nearby Swan Lake canoe routes. The trips are perfect for novice canoeists as rough water is rarely a problem and the portages do not exceed

0.5 mile (0.8 km) on the Swan Lake system or a mile (1.6 km) in the Swanson River area. Fishing is good in both and wildlife is plentiful. A trip on either could result in sightings of moose, bear, beaver or a variety of waterfowl. Both routes are popular trips among Anchorage canoeists as they are well marked and maintained with open shelters along the way.

The Swanson River system links more than 40 lakes and 46 miles (74 km) of river for a total one-way trip of 80 miles (128 km). The easier Swan Lake route connects 30 lakes with forks of the Moose River for a one-way trip of 60 miles (96 km). A common four-day trip on Swan Lake begins at the west entrance of the canoe route, where you paddle to the Moose River Bridge of Sterling Highway. The most direct route is 20 miles (32 km) long and includes five portages.

Getting Started

To reach either the Swan Lake or Swanson River canoe routes, travel west on Sterling Highway to *Mile 84* (135 km) and turn north on Robinson Lake Rd, just west of Moose River Bridge. Robinson Rd turns into Swanson River Rd and leads to Swan Lake Rd 17 miles (27 km) from Sterling Highway. East on Swan Lake Rd are the entrances to both canoe systems, with Swanson River beginning at the very end of the road. The west entrance for Swan Lake is at Canoe Lake and the east entrance is at Portage Lake; both are well marked.

During the summer Kenai Drifters rent canoes and run a shuttle bus service to the head of Swan Lake Canoe Trail, which ends back at Moose River Bridge. The rental fee is $15 per day for a canoe and $35 to have your boat and yourself shipped to the west entrance of the trail. Contact the company at *Mile 81.7* Sterling Highway, Sterling, Alaska 99672; tel (907) 262-7541.

You can also rent canoes in Soldotna from Roland's Sports Den, PO Box 2861, Soldotna, Alaska 99669, tel (907) 262-7491; or in Anchorage from Hugh Glass Backpacking Company, PO Box 110796, Anchorage, Alaska 99511, tel (907) 243-1922.

More Information
The Kenai National Wildlife Refuge visitor centre is at *Mile 97.9* of Sterling Highway, two miles south of Soldotna. You can also get information before your trip from the Refuge Manager, Kenai National Wildlife Refuge, PO Box 2139, Soldotna, 99669; tel (907) 262-7021.

BAY OF ISLANDS CIRCUIT – KATMAI NATIONAL PARK
This route begins and ends at Brooks Camp (the summer headquarters of Katmai National Park) and takes paddlers into seldom-visited sections of the preserve, offering the ultimate in wilderness adventure. The complete circuit would be an 80-mile (128 km) paddle, requiring seven to 10 days of travel depending on weather and wind conditions. The trip is long but not difficult, as no whitewater is encountered and boats only have to be carried across one portage, one mile (1.6 km) in length. The first stretch from Brooks Camp to the Bay of Islands is an especially scenic area that offers calm water flanked by mountains. Here the water is deep and clear and the offshore islands provide superb campsites.

It is a two to three-day paddle through Naknek Lake and the Bay of Islands to the one-mile portage to Lake Grosvenor. From the portage it is a 14-mile (22 km) paddle along the south shore of Lake Grosvenor to Grosvenor River at its south-east end. The Grosvenor River is a slow-moving clearwater waterway where paddlers often spot moose, bears, beavers and river otters. It flows into Savonoski River, a prime brown-bear habitat, especially when the salmon are running. For this reason, park rangers often recommend paddling the 12 miles (19 km) of the Savonoski in a single day and not camping along the river. Canoeists also have to keep a sharp eye out for sweepers and sand bars that may develop in the river. The last leg is the 20-mile (32 km) paddle along the south shore of the Iliuk Arm back to Brooks Camp.

Getting Started
Turn to the Bush chapter for information on getting to and from Katmai National Park; also check the previous section on the Valley of 10,000 Smokes for the special backcountry needs of the preserve. Paddlers have to remember that Katmai is famous for its sudden and violent storms, some that last for days. Good rain gear cannot be stressed enough, nor the habit of sealing all gear in plastic bags. It is unwise to paddle too far from shore, as it leaves you defenceless when sudden storms or high winds spring upon you.

Getting a canoe or hard-shell kayak into the park can be an expensive exercise for backpackers. Most visitors rent a canoe from the lodge in Brooks Camp for $30 per day. It is a good practice to call a couple weeks before your arrival at Katmai to reserve one. For advance

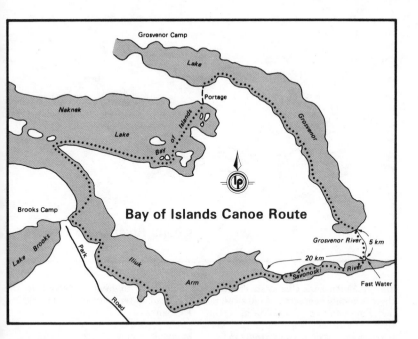

Bay of Islands Canoe Route

reservations or rental information write to Katmailand Inc, 455 H St, Anchorage, Alaska 99501; or use their toll-free number 1 (800) 544-0551.

More Information
For more information about the park or handouts covering backcountry travel, contact the year-round park headquarters at Katmai National Park, PO Box 7, King Salmon, Alaska 99613; tel (907) 246-3305.

Section	miles	km
Brooks Camp to Lake Grosvenor portage	30.0	48.0
portage	1.0	1.6
Lake Grosvenor to Grosvenor River	14.0	22.5
Grosvenor River to Savonoski River	3.0	4.8
Savonoski River to Iliuk Arm	12.0	19.3
along Iliuk Arm to Brooks Camp	20.0	32.0

CHENA RIVER
One of the finest rivers for canoeing in the Fairbanks area and a long-time favourite among local residents, the Chena flows through a landscape of rolling forested hills with access to alpine tundra above 2800 feet (850 metres). The river features no whitewater and paddlers only have to keep an eye out for an occasional sweeper or logjam. Wildlife that may be spotted along the way includes brown bears, moose, red foxes, beavers and river otters, while the fishing is excellent for grayling and northern pike. With the Interior's long, hot summer days, this trip can be an outstanding wilderness adventure.

Getting Started
Chena Hot Springs Rd provides access to the river along points at *Mile 27.9* (44.9 km) out of Fairbanks, *Mile 28.6* (46 km), *Mile 29.4* (47.3 km), *Mile 33.9* (54.6 km) at Fourmile Creek and *Mile 39.6* (63.7

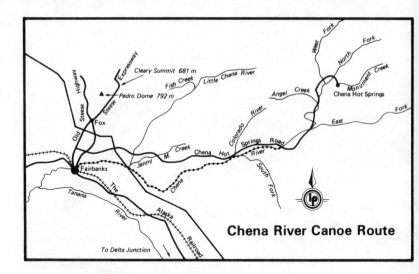

Chena River Canoe Route

km) at North Fork Chena River where there is a state campground (20 sites, no fee). From *Mile 39.6* the paddle along the river to Fairbanks is a 70-mile (113 km) trip that can be done comfortably in four to five days.

Canoes can be rented in Fairbanks from Beaver Sports, 2400 College Rd, Fairbanks, Alaska, tel (907) 479-2494, for $20 to $25 per day (depending on which type), with discounts for longer rental periods. The store is across the road from Noyes Slough, which can be paddled to from the Chena River, solving the problem of your pick-up. Now you just have to worry about getting to the trailhead. Hitch-hiking with a canoe is tough, though I've seen several backpackers try it success-fully. The only bus service to the end of Chena Hot Springs Rd is offered by Tours Unlimited, tel (907) 456-1948, which charges $25 round-trip to the resort and uses vans to carry passengers. You'll have to call them to find out if they can accommodate somebody with a canoe. The other alternative is to rent a used car in Fairbanks (see the Fairbanks chapter) for a single day to drop off the canoe. You

would have to hitch back out to the trailhead after returning the car in Fairbanks.

More Information
Much of the river lies in the Chena River State Recreation Area, which is admin-istered by the Alaska Division of State Parks. Contact the Fairbanks office for more information at the Division of Parks, 4420 Airport Way, Fairbanks, Alaska 99701; tel (907) 479-4136.

Guide Companies

Much of Alaska's wilderness, in fact the majority of it, is not accessible to the first-time visitor. Travellers either don't know about a wilderness area, or if they know about it, don't know how to get to it. That is where guide companies earn their living.

Guides are not only for novice, never-put-on-a-backpack campers. Their clients can also be experienced backpackers who want to explore the far reaches of Alaska ut don't have the time or money to put together an expedition on their own. Guides are organisers who arrange the many details of a large-scale trip into the backcountry – everything from food and equipment to air charter and pick-up. They work on the principle that a group of 10 or 12 can explore an area cheaper than one or two. Most guided trips cost far less than if you made all the arrangements and went on your own.

Trips can range from single-day hikes on top of glaciers to 12-day raft trips or three-week ascents of Mt McKinley. Costs range from $100 to $150 per person per day, depending upon the amount of air charter involved. Expeditions number between five and 12 clients; outfitters are hesitant to take groups any larger because of their environmental impact. The season for outfitters is late May through to September. A select group specialises in winter expeditions of Nordic skiing or dog-sledding.

Guided expeditions cost money, no doubt about that, and most budget travellers choose unguided trips which they can do on their own. However, outfitters are offering an adventure in areas that will be visited by only a few (if any) people each year. There is something inviting about that. Although most outfitters begin taking reservations in April, don't hesitate to call one after you've arrived in Alaska and decide you want to join a guided expedition. Many times you can score a hefty discount of 30 to 50% in the middle of the summer because outfitters will be eager to fill any leftover spots on an already scheduled trip.

The following is a list of recreational guide companies in Alaska. Don't get them confused with hunting or fishing guides whose main interest is to make sure their client gets a trophy to hang on the wall of the family room. Also be careful not to confuse expeditions with fishing camps or wilderness lodges. The camps and lodges are established rustic resorts in the wilderness where you spend a week with many of the comforts of home, but see little beyond the immediate area.

SOUTHEAST

Alaska Discovery, PO Box 26, Gustavus, Alaska 99826; tel (907) 697-3431. One of the oldest and largest guide companies in Alaska, Alaska Discovery operates strictly in the Southeast with kayak trips in Glacier Bay, canoe trips across Admiralty Island and raft trips down the Tatshenshini River being their specialty. Among their expeditions are four-day paddles in Glacier Bay for $534 and a spectacular seven-day Hubbard Glacier adventure for $893. The company also rents kayaks ($30 per day) in Glacier Bay and at their Juneau office, 418 S Franklin St, Juneau, 99801, tel (907) 586-1911. They rent canoes in Juneau and Angoon on Admiralty Island. The Juneau office runs a single-day glacier walk to the top of Mendenhall Glacier.

Chilkat Guides, PO Box G, Haines, Alaska 99827; tel (907) 766-2409 offers a handful of raft trips from its base in Haines, including a four-hour float down the Chilkat River, an area with a large concentration of bald eagles. The trip departs twice-daily during the summer and costs $45 per person. The company also runs the Tsirku and Tatshenshini rivers.

Alaskan Waters, PO Box 1551-B, Petersburg, Alaska 99833 provides access to the wilderness areas that surround Petersburg, including Thomas Bay, LeConte Glacier, Duncan Canal and the Stikine River. It rents kayaks and canoes for $25 per day, as well as camping gear. There's a drop-off and pick-up service aboard their 26-foot (9 metre) launch.

Ice Field Ascents, PO Box 449, Haines, Alaska 99827. This small guide company offers mountaineering trips and treks that allow clients to view the wonders of the Haines-Skagway region and to learn the art of glacier travel and alpine survival. Expeditions of 10 to 14 days include Glacier Bay Boundary Peaks, a Haines-to-Skagway Mountain Trek and the Mendenhall Towers Rock Climbing Adventure, all priced at $500 per person. The company also offers a weekend ice-climbing experience onto Davidson Glacier south of Haines for $130 per person.

Alaska Cross Country Guiding & Rafting, PO Box 124, Haines, Alaska 99827. Based in Haines, this outfitter runs trips centring around the Chilkat Bald Eagle Preserve, including a nine-day trek from the preserve to Glacier Bay National Park.

ANCHORAGE AREA & SOUTHCENTRAL

Kachemak Wilderness Adventures, PO Box 2074, Homer, Alaska 99603; tel (907) 235-6094. Everything from kayaking, rafting and alpine treks to dog sledding, sailing and horse packing is offered by this company. Day trips include Grewingk Glacier hike and raft trip for $80 per person or scaling one of several local peaks for $100. One 14-day trip, called 'Homeric Odyssey,' involves kayaking, rafting, skiing, backpacking and the use of dog sleds and horses across the Kachemak Icefield for $1985. The company also rents kayaks out of Homer.

Alaska Float Trips, PO Box 826, Anchorage, Alaska 99508; tel (907) 333-4442. Utilising rafts or folboats, this company specialises in river trips, including the John and Kobuk rivers in the Brooks Range, Kisaralik and Aniakchak rivers in western Alaska and Swan Lakes and Lake Creek closer to home. Weekend trips to Lake Creek and Swan Lakes cost from $450 to $649 per person.

Hugh Glass Backpacking Co, PO Box 110796, Anchorage, Alaska, 99511; tel (907) 243-1922, is one of the long-established outfitters which offer a wide range of guided trips into areas of Prince William Sound, Kenai Fjord, Arctic National Wildlife Refuge, Katmai, Brooks Range, Wrangell and St Elias Mountains. Trips may include trekking, canoeing, rafting or sea kayaking, or they may be

designed as photo or fishing adventures The company also rents canoes i Anchorage for $15 per day or $75 week.

Alaska Sea Kayaking, PO Box 1386 Palmer, Alaska 99645; tel (907) 745-3487 offers a variety of sea kayaking trip among the many fjords and coves of th western Prince William Sound. The utilise a charter boat out of Whittier t ship kayaks and clients to cut dow paddling time to and from wildernes areas. They offer several two-night/three day adventures that cost from $400 t $500 per person.

Alaska Mountain Adventures, 377 Terrace Drive, Anchorage, Alaska 99502 tel (907) 248-3961. From Anchorage, th company offers a single-day glacier wal along the Matanuska Glacier and a four day hike through the Alaska Range a well as longer nine-day treks in the sam area. The glacier walk, which include transportation to and from Anchorage lunch and the mountaineering gear, cost $75 per person.

Alaskan Wilderness Sailing Safaris, P(Box 701, Whittier, Alaska 99693; tel (907 338-2134. Out of an office in Whittier an Valdez, the company runs a variety of six day sailing trips and overnight cruise throughout Prince William Sound. Fare begin at $500 per person and man specialise in sailing instruction or wildlif photography.

Alaska Treks & Voyages, PO Box 60(Moose Pass, Alaska 99631; tel (907) 288 3610, offers a wide range of adventure including a Ruth Glacier ski tour near M McKinley, sea kayaking in Kenai Fjord National Park, a trail-and-tundra trek i the Kenai Mountains and day-and-a-ha kayak trips out of Seward. They also ren sea kayaks from Seward Boat Harbor fc $130 a week or $70 for the weekend.

Alaska River & Ski Tours, 1831 Kuskokwin St, Anchorage, Alaska 99508; tel (907 276-3418. A year-round outfitter, who i summer offers float trips from a single day outing along Kenai River for $79 pe person to three days of whitewater through Talkeetna Canyon for $595 and five days on Lake Creek south of Mt McKinley for $959. Even longer expeditions take place on the Alagnak River and the Kanektok in the Bristol Bay region.

Yak Treks, Star Route A-Box 37C, Homer, Alaska 99603; tel (907) 235-8302. The Homer-based outfitters run several kayak trips across Kachemak Bay, from a half-day paddle to Gull Island bird rookery to expeditions ranging from three to five days.

Prism Ski Touring, PO Box 136, Girdwood, Alaska 99587. A one-person operation which maintains a custom approach to trips rather than a slick brochure of regularly-scheduled ones. Bill Guide works more as a ski instructor than a guide and will arrange spring ski expeditions and summer glacier skiing for small parties on almost any kind of budget. He must have advance notice, as he is an Alaskan who truly likes to live in the woods.

MT MCKINLEY & INTERIOR

Genet Expeditions, Talkeetna, Alaska 99676; tel (907) 376-5120, specialises in Mt McKinley ascents and ski expeditions. They run mountaineering trips to several other peaks in the Interior. Spring ski trips are priced from $500 to $800 per person for five to 10-day adventures.

Weber-Alyeska Wilderness Guides, PO Box 11663, Anchorage, Alaska 99511; tel (907) 345-2081, runs trips almost state-wide but tends to specialise in trekking and rafting adventures in the shadow of Mt McKinley and floats along the Copper River to Cordova.

St Elias Alpine Guides, PO Box 111241, Anchorage, Alaska 99511; tel (907) 277-5867. Wrangell-St Elias National Park is the site for many of the trips offered by this outfitter who specialises in mountaineering and glacier skiing adventures. They also offer a 14-day float down the Copper River to Cordova for $1400.

Mountain Trip, Box 41161, Anchorage, Alaska 99509; tel (907) 345-6499, offers eight mountaineering adventures on Mt McKinley as well as several ascents of other peaks, all priced at $1950 per person. In the spring, the company runs a Ruth Glacier teleskiing and climbing seminar for $900.

Alaska-Denali Guiding, PO Box 326, Talkeetna, Alaska 99676; tel (907) 733-2649, offers the opportunity (for those who have the desire) to climb the highest mountain in North America. The outfitter runs a handful of Mt McKinley ascents during the summer at a cost of $1900 to $2600 per person and lasting 24 to 30 days. On a slightly lesser scale is the company's tundra trek in Denali National Park and a rafting and hiking trip on the John River in the Brooks Range. Alaska-Denali also rents mountaineering equipment.

Denali Raft Adventures, PO Box 427, Denali Park, Alaska 99755; tel (907) 683-2234, offers a variety of day raft trips down the Nenana River near Denali National Park. Some are mild while others are two hours of whitewater. Prices are from $25 to $42 per person for trips that last two to five hours.

Nova, SRC Box 8337-Chickaloon, Palmer, Alaska 99645; tel (907) 745-5753, specialises in river raft trips. Their most popular is the Nenana River Day Trip near Denali National Park for $42 per person. Other trips include a three-day Talkeetna River float and a 10-day expedition down the Yukon River in Yukon-Charley National Preserve.

FAIRBANKS AREA & BROOKS RANGE

Wilderness Alaska, PO Box 6092, Ketchikan, Alaska 99901, offers a variety of hikes and floats in the Brooks Range, including several expeditions in Gates of the Arctic National Park, one of which is a nine-day trek for $525 per person.

Tundra Treks, SR 20972, Fairbanks, Alaska 99701; tel (907) 479-2754, specialises in raft and kayak outings in the Brooks Range and Lake Clark National

Park. One expedition involves rafting and kayaking the HulaHula River from the Brooks Range to the Arctic Ocean, a two-week adventure that costs $2900 per person.

Alaska Fish & Trails Unlimited, 1177 Shypoke Dr, Fairbanks, Alaska 99701; tel (907) 479-7630. Along with backpacking trips in Gates of the Arctic National Park, this outfitter offers a late-autumn photography trip, spring Nordic ski tours and fishing adventures that include rafting out of the Brooks Range to Bettles.

Caribou Wilderness Outfitters, PO Box 27, Salcha, Alaska 99714; tel (907) 488-4594. Departing from Bettles, this small guide company offers a 10-day Yukon-Charley rivers float for $1500 and a second float down the north branch of the Koyukuk River in Gates of the Arctic National Park for $1250 per person.

Arctic Treks, PO Box 73452, Fairbanks, Alaska 99707; tel (907) 455-6502. This company specialises in treks and floats in Gates of the Arctic National Park and the Arctic National Wildlife Refuge. One trip combines backpacking and rafting in the Gates of the Arctic and runs for 15 days at the cost of $1525 per person.

Sourdough Outfitters, Bettles, Alaska 99726; tel (907) 962-5252, handles canoe, kayak and backpacking trips in Gates of the Arctic National Park, Noatak and Kobuk rivers and other areas. It also provides unguided trips for individuals who have the experience to make an independent journey but want an outfitter to handle the logistics of a major expedition such as trip planning, transportation and canoe or raft rental. Unguided trips take place throughout the Brooks Range and are priced from $300 to $775 per person.

Alaska Wilderness Expeditions, PO Box 73297, Fairbanks, Alaska 99701; tel (907) 452-7715, specialises in float trips in the region surrounding Fairbanks. Their more popular outings are the two-day, one-night run of the Chena or Chatanika rivers for $150 per person, five days on the Gulkana River for $375 and seven days along the Forty-Mile River for $775.

General Bullmoose Canoe Tours, SR 30074, Fairbanks, Alaska 99701; tel (907) 479-4061. This is another one-person operation which takes no more than than five clients on a trip and specialises in two to four-day trips along the Chena River. There is a basic rate of $80 per person per day.

Brooks Range Expeditions, Bettles Field Alaska 99726; tel (907) 692-5333, explores the Brooks Range by canoe, raft, inflatable canoe and foot during the summer. Two expeditions are highly popular because they combine hiking and floating: backpacking in the Gates of the Arctic & North Fork River Float, a 10-day adventure for $1500 per person; and 10 days on the Noatak headwaters with numerous day hikes for $1750. The company also rent canoes for those who want to venture into the Brooks Range on their own.

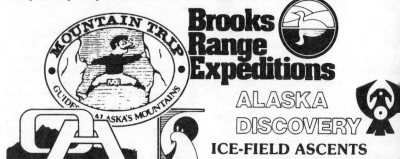

Southeast Alaska

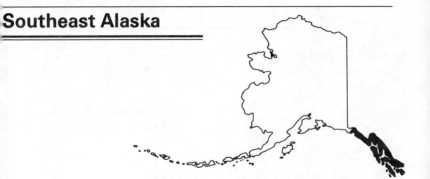

The North Country begins in Southeast Alaska, as do the summer adventures of many visitors to the state, and for good reasons. Southeast is the closest region to Seattle, as Ketchikan is only 90 minutes away by air or two days on the State Marine Ferry.

Southeast has the mildest climate. Everything north of here becomes more extreme. Affected greatly by warm ocean currents, Southeast offers warm summer temperatures averaging 69°F (20°C), with an occasional heat wave that sends the thermometer to 80°F (26°C). The winters are equally mild and sub-zero days are rare. Residents who have learned to live with rainfall of 60 to 200 inches (1500 to 5000 mm) per year across the region call the frequent rain 'liquid sunshine'. The heavy precipitation creates the dense, lush forests and numerous waterfalls most travellers come to cherish.

Travel to and around the Southeast is easy. The Inside Passage connects this road-less area to Seattle, and the Alaska State Marine Ferry system provides the transportation, making it the longest (and many think the best) public ferry system in North America. Relaxing three-day cruises through the maze of islands and coastal mountains that make up Southeast's Alexander Archipelago is a pleasant alternative to the long and often bumpy Alaska Highway.

However, the best reason to begin and end in the Southeast is its scenery. Few places in the world have the spectacular combinations of scenery which are found in the Southeast; rugged snow-capped mountains rising steeply from the water forming sheer-sided fjords and decorated by cascading waterfalls; ice-blue glaciers that begin among the highest peaks and fan out into a valley of dark-green spruce trees; wilderness waters that surround everything and support whales, sea lions, harbour seals and huge salmon-runs.

At one time Southeast was the heart and soul of Alaska and Juneau was not only the capital but the state's major city. However, WW II and the Alcan shifted the growth to Anchorage and Fairbanks. Today most of the region lies sleepily in the Tongass National Forest, the largest in the US at 16 million acres (6.5 million hectares). The state ferry connects 14 ports and services 54,000 residents, of which 75% live in Juneau, Ketchikan, Sitka, Petersburg and Wrangell.

There is room to breathe in the Southeast. The population density is about 2½ people per square mile and will probably stay that way, as a great deal of the region is federal monuments and preserves. Included in this group is the spectacular Glacier Bay National Park & Preserve, Admiralty Island and Misty Fjords national monuments, Klondike National Historical Park, Tracy Arm and Ford's Terror Wilderness.

More than anywhere else in Alaska,

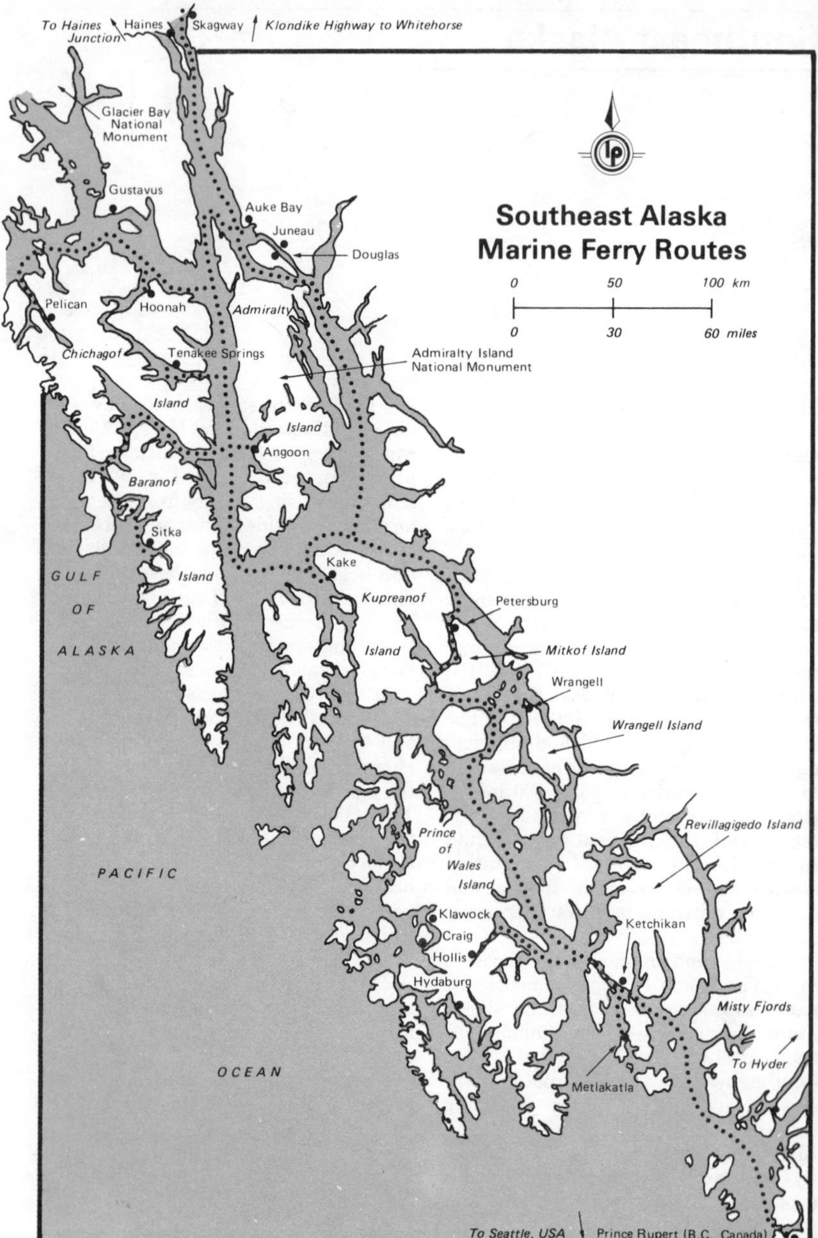

To Haines Junction ← Haines ↘ Skagway ↑ Klondike Highway to Whitehorse

Glacier Bay National Monument

Gustavus

Auke Bay

Juneau

Douglas

Pelican

Hoonah

Admiralty

Chichagof

Tenakee Springs

Admiralty Island National Monument

Island

Island

Angoon

Baranof

Sitka

Island

GULF

OF

ALASKA

Kake

Kupreanof

Petersburg

Island

Mitkof Island

Wrangell

Wrangell Island

Revillagigedo Island

PACIFIC

*Prince
of
Wales
Island*

Klawock

Craig

Hollis

Ketchikan

Hydaburg

Misty Fjords

To Hyder

OCEAN

Metlakatla

To Seattle, USA ↓ Prince Rupert (B.C., Canada)

Southeast Alaska
Marine Ferry Routes

| 0 | 50 | 100 km |
| 0 | 30 | 60 miles |

each community in the Southeast clings to its own character, colour and past. There is Norwegian-accented Petersburg and Russian-tinted Sitka. You can feel the gold fever in Skagway, see lumberjacks and fishermen in Ketchikan or venture to Juneau for a hefty dosage of government, glaciers and uncontrolled growth.

The best way to visit the Southeast is to purchase a ferry ticket from Seattle to Skagway ($198 one way) with no itinerary but plenty of time. Stop at each town, explore it and then hop back on the ferry north to the next one. To rush from the Lower 48 to Juneau and then fly to Anchorage is to miss some of the best things that Alaska has to offer.

Ketchikan

Everything begins with Ketchikan, otherwise known as the First City. This city of 11,500 is located on the south-west side of Revillagigedo (ra-vee-ah-ga-GAY-doh) Island and is only 90 miles (144 km) north of Prince Rupert (British Columbia). It is the first stop the state ferry makes in Alaska, so it's here that tourists pile off the boat for their first look at the North Country. Rarely does Ketchikan disappoint them.

The town grew up around salmon canneries and sawmills. The first cannery was built in 1883, and at one time Ketchikan was proclaimed the 'Salmon Captital of the World', a title which has since slipped away. A sawmill was built in downtown Ketchikan in 1903, and in 1954 the huge Ketchikan Pulp Mill was constructed at Ward Cove. However, the very industries that gave birth to the town nearly deserted it in the 20th century. In the 1970s, over-fishing nearly collapsed the salmon fisheries while strikes began to mar the logging industry. Just when Ketchikan began crawling out from under hard times the downtown spruce

mill was hit by a strike in 1983 that resulted not in a settlement, but in Louisiana-Pacific closing the mill. Two years later the historical downtown mill was razed for a parking lot. In 1984, Louisiana-Pacific shut down the Ward Cove Pulp Mill, the area's major employer, for six months, and the continuing hard times of the early 1980s decreased Ketchikan's population.

The city and the people survive, a credit to their frontier and Alaskan image. Although the First City has shifted its economy slightly to include government and tourism, fish and timber are still its trademark. The industries have given Ketchikan its rough-and-tumble character of being a 'workingman's town', something people would call a redneck haven in Southern California. On a Saturday night Ketchikan bars are full, loud and lively.

If you stay in Ketchikan longer than an hour, chances are good that it will rain at least once, if not several times. On the average it pours 162 inches (4110 mm) a year in the area, but it has been known to rain more than 200 inches (5000 mm). For all that water falling out of the sky, the only people with umbrellas are tourists. First City residents never seem to use them, nor do they let the rain interfere with their daily activities, even outdoor ones, whether it be fishing, hiking or having a softball game. If they stopped every time it drizzled, Ketchikan would cease to exist.

The layout of the city is linear. Never more than 10 blocks wide, it is several miles long and is centred around one road, Tongass Avenue. The road runs along the shores of Tongass Narrows and sometimes over it, supported by pillars. Cross streets appear mostly in the downtown area and the area surrounding the state ferry terminal known as West End. There is only one stop light in Ketchikan, and that came in 1984 despite the objections of many residents. Many businesses and homes are suspended above the water or cling to the hillside with winding staircases or wooden streets leading to their front doors.

On a clear day – and there are a few during the summer – Ketchikan is a bustling community backed by wooded hills and flanked by a waterway that hums with floatplanes, fishing boats, ferries and large cruise ships. It is crowned to the south by the the distinctively shaped Deer Mountain. Whether basked in sunshine or painted with a light drizzle, it can be a very interesting place to start an Alaskan summer.

Information
The Visitors Bureau on the City Dock (tel 225-6166) can supply general information about Ketchikan or the city bus system. The bureau is open Monday to Friday from 8 am to 6 pm, Saturday from 7.30 am to 3.30 pm and Sunday from 12 noon to 6 pm. For information about hiking trails, cabin reservations or other outdoor opportunities, contact the Visitors Information Centre of the USFS office (tel 225-2148) in the Federal Building on Stedman and Mill Sts.

Things to See
The best way to explore Ketchikan is on foot with a three-hour, two-mile (3.2 km) walk around the downtown area. Start at the Visitors Bureau, a brown building on the busy City Dock, and pick up a free city map or a copy of *Ketchikan Daily News Visitors Guide* which has the walking tour in it. Begin by heading south on Front St, which changes to Mill St when it swings sharply east past the site of the Ketchikan Spruce Mill which was demolished in 1985.

Within three blocks at the corner of Mills and Stedman Sts is the distinctive white **Federal Building** where the USFS maintains its Tongass National Forest Visitors Centre on the first floor. The centre is open 8 am to 4.30 pm Monday to Friday and has information and handouts on recreational opportunities in the Ketchikan area and a list of cabins still available during the summer. There is also an interesting slide presentation and other displays.

By turning right on Stedman St you cross Ketchikan Creek and come to **Creek St**, not a street but a boardwalk built on pilings. This was the famed red-light district in Ketchikan for half a century until prostitution became illegal in 1954. During its heyday Creek St became famous as the only spot in the world where 'both fishermen and fish went upstream to spawn'. The first house with its bright red doors and windows is **Dolly's House**, the parlour for the city's most famous madam, Dolly Arthur. The house has since been turned into a museum dedicated to this infamous era and is open 9 am to 4 pm daily except Sunday. For a $2 admission fee you see the cathouse, including its wet bar that was placed over a trapdoor to the creek for quick disposal of bootleg whiskey. There are another 20 buildings on Creek St, consisting of small shops, the Morning Raven Artists Gallery and apartments.

Across from Creek St is **Thomas Basin**, one of three boat harbours in the city. It is impossible to stay in Ketchikan and not spend any time at the waterfront. The lifeblood of this narrow city can be found in its collection of boat harbours, floatplanes and fishing fleets that stretch along the lapping waters of the Tongass Narrows. It is here that the First City makes its living and does business.

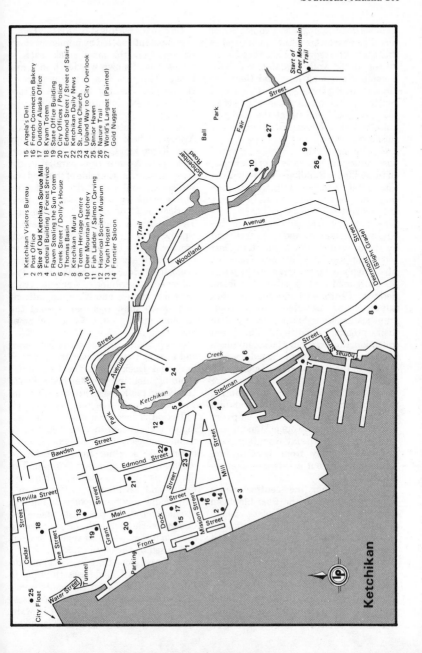

1 Ketchikan Visitors Bureau
2 Post Office
3 Site of Old Ketchikan Spruce Mill
4 Federal Building / Forest Service
5 Raven Stealing the Sun Totem
6 Creek Street / Dolly's House
7 Thomas Basin
8 Ketchikan Mural
9 Totem Heritage Centre
10 Deer Mountain Hatchery
11 Fish Ladder / Salmon Carving
12 Historical Society Museum
13 Youth Hostel
14 Frontier Saloon
15 Angela's Deli
16 French Connection Bakery
17 Outdoor Alaska Office
18 Kyam Totem
19 State Office Building
20 City Offices / Police
21 Edmond Street / Street of Stairs
22 Ketchikan Daily News
23 St. Johns Church
24 Upland Way to City Overlook
25 Senior Haven
26 Nature Trail
27 World's Largest (Painted) Gold Nugget

Ketchikan

Thomas Basin, along with Thomas Street (another boardwalk built on pilings) is the most picturesque. An hour or so spent at the docks will acquaint you with Ketchikan's fishing fleet and the three kinds of fishing boats – gillnetters, power trollers and seiners. Any more time than that and you'll end up at the colourful Potlatch Bar on Thomas St having a brew with a fisherman.

Continuing south on Stedman, you'll pass the large mural, *Return of the Eagle*, on the Robinson Building of the Ketchikan Community College. Turn left (to the east) onto Deermont St. At the beginning of the street is a knee-bending hill, the first of many you will tackle in the Southeast and at the end is the trailhead for the 3.1-mile (5.0 km) climb to Deer Mountain (see the Wilderness chapter). About halfway up the street to the left is the short road that swings to the **Totem Heritage Centre**, where totem poles salvaged from deserted Tlingit communities are brought to be restored to their original condition. The total collection, the largest in Alaska, numbers more than 30, and five of the poles are on display in the central gallery along with native art and artefacts. There are lectures, films and guided tours during the summer, usually scheduled around the times when the large cruise ships are in port. The centre is open Monday and Wednesday to Saturday from 9 am to 5 pm, and Sunday from 1 to 5 pm. Admission is $1 but it is free on Sunday afternoon.

A bridge from the centre crosses Ketchikan Creek to the **Deer Mountain Hatchery**, a fascinating place where biologists raise 150,000 king salmon and an equal number of coho annually and then release them into the nearby stream. Observation platforms, outdoor displays and friendly workers provide an interesting lesson in the life cycle of the salmon. Come in July or later and you'll see not only the salmon fry but returning adults swimming upstream to spawn.

Next to the rearing station is **City Park**, a quiet spot intersected by numerous small streams from the main creek, each, it seems, with its own wooden bridge and bench. The park is a pleasant place to escape the bustling crowds and tour groups that fill downtown when a cruise ship is in.

From the hatchery head down Park Avenue, where you will immediately cross Ketchikan Creek again. In a short spell, Park Avenue runs parallel to the creek and on the other side of the road you will see Upland Way stairs. A climb up the stairs takes you to a viewing platform overlooking downtown Ketchikan, Thomas Basin and Creek St. Beyond Upland Way on Park Avenue you will arrive at another bridge crossing Ketchikan Creek, with a wooden salmon mounted over a fish ladder at the creek's falls. The ladder enables salmon to reach upstream spawning gravels and it's a magnificent sight when these fish leap against the current during the late summer migration.

Park Avenue curves towards downtown and ends at Dock St. Near the corner of Park and Dock Sts is the Centennial Building, housing the **Ketchikan Public Library** and the **Tongass Historical Museum**. The museum is free and has a small collection of local and native artefacts, many of them tied in with Ketchikan's fishing industry. The museum is open during the summer from Monday to Saturday from 8.30 am to 5.30 pm. The library is open Tuesday, Thursday, Friday and Saturday from 12 noon to 6 pm; Wednesday from noon to 9 pm; and Sunday from 1 to 4 pm. Just outside the Centennial Building is the *Raven Stealing the Sun* totem, which was commissioned and raised by the city in 1983.

Head west along Dock St, and alongside the Ketchikan Daily News Building is Edmond St. This is the 'Street of Stairs', as it leads to a system of long staircases. The next cross road on Dock St is Main St, which leads north to the Ketchikan

Youth Hostel on the corner of Grant St and to the huge *Kyan* totem another block beyond that. If you stay on Dock St you will return, full circle, to the City Dock.

Places to Stay

Hostels The Ketchikan *Youth Hostel* is in the basement of the First Methodist Church on the corner of Grant and Main Sts in the downtown area of the city. It's open from Memorial Day (25 May) to Labor Day (7 September) and provides kitchen facilities (50c extra per meal), showers and a space on the floor with a mat to sleep on. The hostel is an interesting one because it always seems filled with travellers heading upstate for a long trip or even for the whole summer. Since Ketchikan is their first Alaskan stop, they fill the recreation room with travel talk and much excitement in the evenings, and often depart from the place with a travelling partner and a warm friendship. The fee is $2.25 per night for AYH members and $5.25 per night for non-members. If you're arriving at night, call the hostel first at 225-3780 to check whether space is available.

One step above the Youth Hostel is the *Rain Forest Inn* (tel 225 9500) at 2311 Hemlock St, 0.7 mile (1.1 km) from the state ferry terminal and half a block from the bus stop at the corner of Tongass Avenue and Jefferson St. The Inn offers dormitory bunks for $15 per night and provides showers, laundry facilities and a guest lounge. There are also eight rooms for rent that accommodate two to four guests; rates vary with size.

Hotels There is a wide range of hotels in Ketchikan, from those catering to cruise ship tourists to the more dilapidated ones that survive on the flood of summer workers. The *Knickerbocker Hotel* (tel 225 3580) at 421 Dock St is one of the latter and offers rooms with shared baths for $25 per night or $104 per week. The *Gilmore Hotel* at 326 Front St used to be another rundown place before undergoing major renovations recently, giving it a historical flavour. They still have studio rooms with shared baths, but the rate is now $38 per night. From here the better hotels jump to $50 per night or more.

Camping There are four public campgrounds in Ketchikan, but the only free one is at *Settler's Cove* (16 sites), 16 miles (26 km) north of the ferry terminal. The other three are on Ward Lake Rd and charge $5 per night. Take North Tongass Highway four miles (6.4 km) north of the ferry terminal to the pulp mill on Ward Cove, then turn right onto Ward Lake Rd. The first campground is *Signal Creek* (25 sites), one mile (1.6 km) up the road. It is followed by *3 C's Campground* (four sites), 0.25 mile (0.4 km) further up. The third one is *Last Chance Campground* (25 sites), another 1.8 miles (2.9 km) along. The entire area is known as Ward Lake Recreational Area and a night spent here is worth all the effort it takes to reach it. Along with the campgrounds there are four lakes and three trails that dip back into the surrounding rainforest.

If you are camping and are in need of a shower in town, you can head to one of Ketchikan's two public pools at Valley Park Elementary School (tel 225-5720) south-east of downtown, or Ketchikan High School (tel 225-2010) on Baranof Rd in the highland area of the West End. Call for the various swimming periods and rates. There are also showers at *Highland Café & Laundromat* (tel 225-5308), 2703 Tongass Avenue. The laundromat closest to the Youth Hostel is *Suds & Duds* at 825 Bawden, just off Park Avenue, which is open daily from 8 am to 9 pm.

Places to Eat

There's a nice choice of places to eat in Ketchikan, but all reflect those Alaskan prices that usually send the newly arrived visitor into a two-day fast. If this is your first Alaskan city, don't fret – it only gets worse from here on up.

For breakfast downtown there is the *Pioneer Pantry* at 124 Front St, where two eggs, potatoes and toast is $4.50. Even better and just as close to the Youth Hostel is *Jackie's*, just north of the tunnel at 834 Water St (Tongass Avenue in the middle of the city). The usual two eggs, potatoes and toast breakfast is $4.95 but the portions are big and the atmosphere is friendly. The specialty is hamburgers (there are 25 kinds on the menu) including some variations with no beef at all. Hamburgers with a big scoop of potato salad are priced from $3.75 to $7. They also serve an incredible strawberry sundae that spills over the sides of a soup bowl. There's beer on tap.

Downtown there are several good spots for a sandwich, including *Angela's Delicatessen* across from the City Dock, an excellent deli with sandwiches priced at $4.35 to $5.50. On equal footing is *Aardvarks'* in the back of the Gilmore Mall on Front St, with soup and a small sandwich for under $5. *The Dawg Shop* on Mission St across from the Federal Building has a variety of hot dogs for $1.29 and up. For a late breakfast there is the *French Connection*, which bills itself as a 'croissantarie'. The small bakery is at 322 Mission St a block off Front St and has good croissants for $1.30 as well as hot croissant sandwiches for $2.99, which can be carried down to the City Dock and enjoyed while watching the busy waterway. During the summer the City Dock itself is the scene of several food vendors serving everything from shish kebabs and clam chowder to halibut sandwiches and crepes; most items are under $5.

The best eatery in town is *Kay's Kitchen* on 2813 Tongass Avenue, overlooking the Bar Boat Harbor. Kay's menu is limited to sandwiches, thick soups and home-made pies that could very well be the best in the Southeast. The small restaurant is 10 minutes south of the ferry terminal but unfortunately it is only open from 11 am to 4 pm Tuesday through Saturday. Ketchikan finally received its *McDonald's* in 1985; it is in Port West Plaza on Tongass Avenue between the ferry terminal and the tunnel. *Pizza Mill* at 808 Water St offers a large pizza and a huge pitcher of beer for under $15.

For a good Alaskan seafood dinner, try the *Gilmore Garden* in the Gilmore Hotel, which offers abalone, prawns, salmon and halibut, fresh from the fleet. Dinners cost from $10 to $16, while in the morning you can order a two-egg breakfast for $3.95 in this quiet and quaint restaurant. If you want to save but still try Alaskan seafood, stop at the *Silver Lining* store at 1705 Tongass Avenue, where you can purchase fresh seafood and then haul it back to the Youth Hostel to cook yourself.

Nightlife

After hiking all day, if you're still raring to go, try the *Frontier Saloon* on 127 Main St downtown. The split-level bar has entertainment and dancing nightly during the summer and can be an exceptionally lively place in the true Ketchikan 'bottoms up' fashion.

Another lively place with dance music but dedicated to fishermen is the *Sourdough Bar* at the north end of the City Dock. The walls of the bar are covered with rows of photos, all of fishing boats, while ship bells, ring floats and other fishing memorabilia hang from the ceiling.

The long-time fishermen's pub is the *Potlatch Bar* on Thomas St just above the Thomas Basin Boat Harbor. Right before you enter the tunnel you'll see the *Arctic Bar*, a quiet little place where you can go for an afternoon brew on a hot summer day. The bar is built on pillars above the water and has an open deck that overlooks Tongass Narrows. Here you can enjoy the sea breeze while watching the floatplanes take off and land, as Taquan Air is located next door and moors its planes at the dock right below the deck.

Events

Ketchikan has three major festivals during the summer, of which the Fourth of July celebration is the biggest and one of the best. The event includes a parade, contests and softball games, an impressive display of fireworks over the channel and a logging show sponsored by the Alaska Loggers Association.

During the third week in August look for the Alaska Seafest, Ketchikan's fishing festival with a parade of local, spruced-up boats in the channel. There is also a community fish feed, boat races, net-setting and skiff-pulling contests, seafood sampling and other activities related to the important fishing industry.

On a smaller scale is the Blueberry Festival that takes place in the lower floor and basement of the state office building towards the end of August. The festival consists of an arts and crafts show, singers and musicians, and food booths that serve blueberries every possible way.

Hiking

There is a variety of hiking adventures in the Ketchikan area, but the majority are located out the road or the trailhead and must be reached by boat. The one exception is Deer Mountain Trail, a 3.1-mile (five km) climb which begins near downtown and provides access to two free-use USFS cabins and two other alpine trails (see the Wilderness chapter).

Ward Lake Nature Walk An easy trail is the nature walk around Ward Lake that begins near the shelters at the far end of the lake. The trail is one mile (1.6 km) of flat terrain and information signs. To reach the lake, follow North Tongass Highway seven miles (11 km) out of the city to the pulp mill on Ward Cove, turn right on Ward Lake Rd and follow it for a mile (1.6 km).

Perseverance Trail This trek is a two-mile (3.2 km) walk from Ward Lake Rd to Perseverance Lake through mature coastal forest and muskeg. The view of the lake with its mountainous backdrop is spectacular, while the hiking is easy as the trail consists mainly of boardwalks and steps. The trailhead is located 1.5 miles (2.4 km) up Ward Lake Rd.

Talbot Lake Trail This trail starts from Connell Lake Rd, which is a gravel road that heads east from three miles (4.8 km) up Ward Lake Rd. The 1.6-mile (2.6 km) trail is a mixture of boardwalk and gravel surface. It leads north from the Connell Lake Dam to Talbot Lake, where it deadends at private property. Future plans call for connecting this path with the Perseverance Trail.

Paddling

The short and long-term kayak trips that begin in Ketchikan are numerous and range in difficulty from an easy paddle in well-protected waters to a two-week trip to Misty Fjords and back. Kayaks can be rented from the 1025 Water Shop (tel 225-1736), which picks up its name from its address, 1025 Water St. The shop is open from 10 am to 6 pm daily during the summer and rents out single kayaks for $15 from morning to evening or $25 for a 24-hour period. The shop also rents double kayaks for $30 per day and will make drop-offs and pick-ups at the end of the roads for an additional fee. Before any trip, purchase the map that covers the area from Tongass Trading Company at the north end of City Dock.

Naha River Trail From the road's end at North Tongass Highway, it is an eight-mile (13 km) paddle to the trailhead of the Naha River Trail, a 6.5-mile (10.4 km) path that follows the river and leads to three USFS cabins and two lakes. The trailhead is located in Naha Bay, a body of water that leads into Roosevelt Lagoon through a narrow outlet. Kayakers trying to paddle into the lagoon must enter it at high slack, as the narrow constriction becomes a frothy, roaring chute when the tide is moving in or out. The trail is a combination of boardwalk, swing bridges and uphill walking as it leads to Naha River, Jordan and Heckman Lake cabins. All three cabins ($10 per night) must be reserved in advance at the USFS office in Ketchikan.

Wolf Creek Trail An even easier paddle is the five-mile (eight km) trip to the trailhead of Wolf Lake Trail at Moser Bay from the end of North Tongass Highway. The 2.5-mile (four km) trail passes through timber slopes and over muskeg to a three-sided shelter (no reservation or rental fee) at the outlet of Wolf Lake. A steep hill is encountered near the salt-water but should not discourage the average hiker.

George-Carroll Inlets At the end of South Tongass Highway past Herring Bay, you are already in George Inlet, which makes this three to four-day paddle an easy one in water that is calm most of the time. North winds do occasionally whip down George Inlet but both waterways are protected from south-westerlies, the prevailing winds in the Ketchikan area.

While not on the same dramatic scale as Misty Fjords, the two inlets are scenic and are an easy way to explore some of Ketchikan's backcountry. Round trip to the end of George Inlet would be a 25-mile (40 km) paddle from Herring Bay.

USFS Cabins
There are 30 cabins in the Ketchikan area. The majority need to be reserved in advance and cost $10 per day. The following have been noted because of their close proximity to the city, which reduces air charter time, the biggest cost factor in using them. There are numerous bush plane operators in Ketchikan; two of the more reliable ones are Tyee Air, Box 8331, Ketchikan, Alaska 99901, tel 225-9810; and Revilla Flying Service, 1427 Tongass Avenue, Ketchikan, Alaska 99901, tel 225-4379.

Alava Bay Cabin is situated at one end of Behm Canal. It provides ample opportunity for hiking and beachcombing along the coast as well as freshwater fishing and viewing such wildlife as black bear and Sitka deer. The cabin is 20 air miles (32 km) from the city.

Fish Creek Cabin A short trail connects Thorne Bay with the Fish Creek Cabin. You can either paddle to it (a three to four-day trip) or fly in, as it is only 18 air miles (29 km) from Ketchikan. There is a trail to nearby Low Lake, while fishing for cut-throat, rainbow trout and Dolly Varden is possible in the creek.

Patching Lake Cabins Two cabins are situated on this lake, 20 air miles (32 km) from Ketchikan. At either one there is good fishing for cut-throat trout and grayling.

Other cabins in the area include the three on the Naha River Trail (see Paddling section) and the two free-use cabins on the Deer Mountain and Blue Lake trails that require no reservations (see the Wilderness chapter).

Getting There
Air Alaska Airlines (tel 225-2141) services Ketchikan with stops at the other major communities of the Southeast as well as Anchorage and Seattle. There are several flights between Ketchikan and Juneau, including one that locals call the 'milk run', as it stops at Petersburg, Wrangell and Sitka and is little more than a series of take-offs and landings. One-way fares to Juneau and Sitka are $90 and Petersburg $76. Western Airlines (tel 225-6697) has one north-bound flight per day to Juneau and one south-bound to Seattle.

Boat It's an exceptional day when there isn't a ferry departing from Ketchikan for the rest of the Southeast or Seattle. Fares from the First City to Wrangell are $23, Petersburg $30, Juneau and Sitka $54 and Haines $67.

The state ferry *Chilkat* services

Metlakatla from Ketchikan on Wednesday to Saturday, leaving the First City at 6.30 am, 10 am and 3 pm for the 1½-hour cruise. The one-way fare is $9 and makes an interesting day trip. The ship *Aurora* makes several runs each week between Ketchikan and Hollis, giving cheap access to Prince of Wales Island. One-way fare to Hollis is $13.

For exact sailing times while in Ketchikan, call the Ferry Terminal at 225-6181.

Getting Around

Airport If you fly to Ketchikan, you'll quickly discover that you're on one side of Tongass Narrows and the city is on the other. Years ago there was talk of building a bridge from the airport across the channel to town. That was only talk; today you hop on the airport ferry that leaves the airport every half hour and departs from next to the state ferry terminal on the quarter hour. The fare is $2 one way or round trip if you travel both ways in a single day. Small white-and-yellow Air Porter buses will take you from the airport to major hotels at the rip-off price of $7. It's cheaper to take the ferry yourself and catch the city bus.

Bus The city bus system consists of small buses that hold up to 30 passengers and follow a circular route from the ferry terminal in the west end of town to the area south of Thomas Basin, circling back by the Totem Heritage Centre and the trailhead to Deer Mountain. The route does not include Saxman Totem Park or anything north of the state ferry terminal. Buses return to a stop every hour; the fare is $1. The drivers are exceptionally friendly and can often be coaxed into pointing out the town's highlights and giving you tidbits of Alaskan lore. In the end, buses can be a cheap alternative to the expensive Grayline Bus Tours of the city.

Bicycle Another way to get around the city

– an alternative to hitching – is to rent a bicycle at People Power Bike Shop, tel 225-2488, at 435 Dock St. Then there is always Rent-A-Dent Car Rental, which rents used vehicles for $19 a day plus 19c per mile. The company operates two offices, one in the airport, tel 225-4515, and one downtown, tel 225-5123.

AROUND KETCHIKAN

For the best view of totem poles, head 2.3 miles (3.7 km) south of Ketchikan on South Tongass Highway to **Saxman Totem Park**, the world's largest standing collection. The 25 poles were bought here from abandoned villages around Southeast and were restored or re-carved in the 1930s. At the entrance is the impressive *Sun and Raven* totem, probably the most photographed one in Alaska, while the rest of the park is located uphill from there. Among the collection is a replica of the *Lincoln Pole*; the original is in the Alaska State Museum in Juneau. This pole was carved in 1883 to commemorate the first sighting of white people, using a picture of Abraham Lincoln.

If you head north of Ketchikan along North Tongass Highway, you will pass the **Ward Creek Recreation Area** (see Places to Stay section) seven miles (11 km) out, and then in another 2.5 miles (four km), **Mud Bight**. This community of float houses is an interesting spot as the dwellings rise and fall with the water to the extent that they are left high on the mud at low tide.

Totem Bight is 10 miles (16 km) north of Ketchikan and is a state historical park (no entry fee) that contains 14 restored or re-carved totems and a colourful community house. Just as impressive as the totems are the park's wooded setting and the coastline. A viewing deck overlooks the Tongass Narrows. The road ends 18 miles (29 km) north of Ketchikan at **Settler's Cove** State Campground (see the Places to Stay section), another scenic coastal area with a lush rainforest bordering a gravel beach and rocky coastline.

Around Ketchikan

Talbot Lake

Revillagigedo

Island

To Settler's Cove Campground

Last Chance Campground

Totem Bight
State Park

Connell Lake

Ward Lake

Pump Mill

CCC
Camp
ground

Signal
Creek
Campground

Perserverance
Lake

John Mountain

Ketchikan Lakes

Gravina

Blue Lake

Island

Main Post Office
Ferry Terminal

Free Use Forest Service Cabin

Ketchikan

Tongass

Deer Mountain

Whitman Lake

0   2.5   5 km

0   1.5   3 miles

Saxman Totem Park

Narrows

Misty Fjords

This spectacular national monument that begins just 22 miles (35 km) east of Ketchikan is best noted for its sea cliffs, steep-sided fjords and rock walls that jut 3000 feet (900 metres) straight out of the ocean. Walker Cove and Rudyard Bay with Punchbowl Cove, are the most picturesque areas of the preserve and are reached via the Behm Canal, the long, deep inlet of the Pacific Ocean that separates Revillagigedo Island from the Coastal Mountains of the mainland.

Possible on any trip to Misty Fjords are sightings of brown or black bears, mountain goats, Sitka deer, bald eagles and a variety of marine mammals. As the name suggests, the monument can be a drizzly place with an average of 150 inches (3810 mm) of rain annually, but many people think the real beauty of Misty Fjords lies in the granite walls and tumbling waterfalls wrapped in a veil of fog and mist.

The preserve is the destination of many kayak expeditions (see the Wilderness chapter), while less adventurous visitors view it on day cruises or 'flight-seeing' tours. Viewing Misty Fjords from a charter plane costs $110 for an hour or so with either Tyee Airlines (tel 225-9810) or Temsco Air Service (tel 225-9810). The time spent actually viewing the monument is short and the area's peaceful setting is lost when the pilot has to yell to you over the roar of his bush plane.

Tour ships offer a more dramatic perspective of the preserve while letting you view it at a more leisurely pace. Outdoor Alaska (tel 247-8444) offers a 12-hour cruise for $120 that departs from its office at 501 Water St at 9.15 am every Sunday, Wednesday and Friday. A shorter eight-hour trip in which you return aboard a bush plane costs $159. If you can plan ahead, the best way to experience Misty Fjords is to rent one of the 15 USFS cabins (reservations needed, $10 per night) in the area.

Metlakatla

An interesting day trip out of Ketchikan is to take the state ferry *Chilkat* to this small native community on the west side of Annette Island Indian Reservation, the only reservation in Alaska. The village of 1400 bustles during the summer as its boat harbour overflows with fishing vessels and its cold-storage/cannery, which has been operating continuously since 1901, is busy handling the catch of the fleet. While on board the *Chilkat*, you might view one of the community's four fish traps, a large collection of logs and wire with a small hut off to one side. The fish traps, illegal everywhere else in Alaska, catch salmon by guiding the fish through a series of funnels, keeping them alive until ready to harvest.

Other sights in town include Father Duncan's Cottage, the home (now a museum) of the missionary who founded the village in 1887; and the traditional Tribal Loghouse down by the small boat harbour. The Loghouse features displays of log carvings and native art and is the site of the community salmon bake. The cannery is open for tours too.

The hike to Yellow Hill provides good views of the west side of the island. To reach Yellow Hill, walk south along Airport Rd for 1.5 miles (2.4 km) and look for the boardwalk on the right. Another hike in the area is the three-mile (4.8 km) Purple Lake Trail, 1.8 miles (2.9 km) down Purple Mountain Rd. You can reach Purple Mountain Rd by travelling south 2.7 miles (4.3 km) on Airport Rd. Walking the trail involves a steep climb to the mountainous lake area.

The *Chilkat* makes three round trips to Metlakatla per day from Wednesday to Saturday, with the first departing Ketchikan at 6.30 am and the last one leaving the native community at 4.45 pm; one-way fare is $9. You can also fly over Metlakatla; Tyee Airlines and Temsco provide daily, regularly-scheduled flights for $15 one way and $25 round trip. There is accommodation at the *Taquan Inn* (tel 886-7090) and a small café overlooking the cannery, but it is better and much cheaper to bring your own lunch and plan on spending the night back in Ketchikan.

Prince Of Wales Island

For most visitors the days are too precious to spend any time touring the native villages and logging camps of Prince of Wales Island, but if time is no problem and out-of-the-way places or different life-styles intrigue you, this accessible island can be an interesting jaunt. You can take the state ferry from Ketchikan to Hollis; from this village of 450 there is a 500-mile (800 km) network of rough dirt roads, the most extensive in Southeast, connecting remote backcountry with the villages of Craig, Klawock, Throne Bay and Hydaburg.

Craig (population 900), 31 miles (50 km) from Hollis, is the most interesting community to visit, and on a Saturday night you can rub elbows with loggers and fishermen in lively Alaskan fashion at the *Craig Inn*. There are hotels, grocery stores and four restaurants. *Abel's Confectionery Café* is known for its incredible home-made donuts.

Camping is permitted in the city park overlooking the ocean. The park is a short hike from town and can be reached by asking any local for directions to the ball field.

Klawock (population 430), a Tlingit village 24 miles (39 km) from Hollis, is noted for its collection of 21 totem poles in a park overlooking the town.

Within town there are three grocery stores, a restaurant, a city-operated campground (12 sites, fee) and Log Cabin Sports Rentals (tel 755-2205) that rents out canoes, bicycles, tents and other equipment.

Thorne Bay (population 350) is an old logging camp in a picturesque setting 59 miles (95 km) from Hollis.

The small settlement has a restaurant, grocery store, gas station and USFS ranger station.

Getting There & Around The state ferry *Aurora* makes five Ketchikan-Hollis runs per week and a longer trip that continues from Hollis north to Petersburg. The one-way fare for Ketchikan-Hollis is $13 and the fare for Hollis-Petersburg is $30. Once at Hollis, where there are few visitor facilities and no stores or restaurants, getting around the island is a little more difficult. A mini-van runs between the community and Craig and carries passengers for $15 one way. Ask the ticket agent at the state ferry terminal as soon as you arrive for information on when and where it departs. You can always hitchhike as there is a small amount of traffic to Craig and Klawock after the arrival and departure of each ferry.

If there are four or more of you, the best way to get around is to rent a used car at Ketchikan's Rent-A-Dent (see previous section) and take it over on the state ferry for an additional $15. This would allow you to explore the far reaches of the island and to fish the highly productive streams (accessible from the road system) for cutthroat trout, Dolly Varden and salmon. Two USFS cabins (reservations needed, $10 rental fee) can be reached from the road – Stanley Creek Cabin and Red Bay Lake Cabin; check with the USFS Information Centre in the Ketchikan Federal Building for availability.

Wrangell

The next major town north along the state ferry route is Wrangell – a cluster of canneries, shipping docks, lumber mills and logging tugs. The community's claim to history is that it is the only Alaskan fort to have existed under three flags – Russian, British and American. Its strategic location near the mouth of the Stikine River has given it a long and colourful history.

The Russians founded the town when they arrived in 1834 and built a stockade they called Redoubt St Dionysius. In 1840 they leased it to the British, who renamed it Fort Stikine. The Americans gained control of the centre when they purchased Alaska, and in 1868 changed the name to Fort Wrangell. Wrangell thrived as an important supply point for fur traders and later for gold-miners, who used the Stikine River to reach gold rushes in both British Columbia and the Klondike fields in the Yukon.

Today the town is still considered colourful by Southeast residents, but for different reasons. Wrangell is a proud, traditional and sometimes stubborn community that clings to age-old Alaskan beliefs of independence from excess government and of using the land and natural resources to earn a living. As the rest of the state is pushed into the 21st century with heavy regulations on

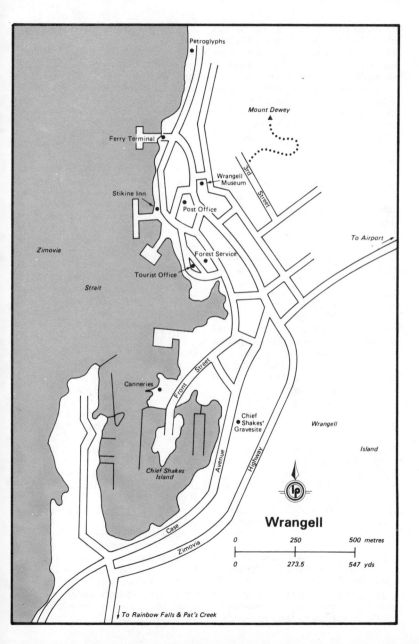

Petroglyphs

Mount Dewey

Ferry Terminal

Wrangell
Museum

Stikine Inn

3rd Street

Post Office

Zimovia

To Airport

Forest Service

Tourist Office

Strait

Canneries

Front Street

Chief
Shakes'
Gravesite

Wrangell

Island

*Chief Shakes
Island*

Avenue

Zimovia Highway

Case

Wrangell

0	250	500 metres
0	273.5	547 yds

To Rainbow Falls & Pat's Creek

industries such as mining, logging and fishing, Wrangell often finds itself lagging behind economically while resisting the new ideas of preserving and setting aside the wilderness. It's not that the town lynches environmentalists every Saturday night, but the issues surrounding the Alaska Lands Bill or 'd-2' were not easy ones for Wrangell residents to accept.

The Wrangell economy is still based heavily on a lumber mill six miles (9.6 km) south of town and on a fishing fleet that supports a cannery and a cold-storage plant along the waterfront. The boat harbour in town is busy during the summer, but is nowhere as large as those in Ketchikan or Petersburg.

Information

The Visitors Information Centre is an A-frame hut on Outer Drive in front of City Hall. It is open on a part-time basis that usually coincides with the cruise ship schedule. The phone number for the centre is 874-3901. Nearby is the Wrangell Sentinel on Lynch St, which published the free *Wrangell Visitors Guide*, the best source of information for the area.

The USFS office (tel 874-2323), upstairs in the Yamaskai Mall, is open from 8 am to 5 pm Monday through Friday. It is the source of information about USFS cabins, trails and campgrounds in the area.

Things to See

Wrangell is one of the few places in Southeast where the ferry terminal is in the heart of town. If you're not planning to spend a night here, you can still disembark for a quick look around. To get a good view of Wrangell, including a stroll out to the petroglyphs along the shoreline, you need two hours or more of walking time.

Beginning at the state ferry terminal, you can reach the **Wrangell Museum** by going straight from the dock up 2nd St and ascending the road to the large white building on the left. The museum is housed in the town's first schoolhouse,

built in 1906 and later used as a morgue and city hall, among other things. The collection features native artefacts, petroglyphs, local relics and photographs from Wrangell's past. There is also a room devoted to the town's artists. The museum is open Monday to Saturday from 1 to 4 pm and on Sundays when a cruise ship is in port; it charges $1 for admission. Next door is the **Wrangell Public Library** with several totem poles in front of it, while diagonally opposite the museum is the US Customs & Post Office. There is a good view of Zimovia Strait from the post office lawn, which features another totem.

By heading down the hill at the post office, you come to Front St and the beginning of Wrangell's business district. The uphill side of Front St is the historical section, each building featuring its distinctive false front. The other side of the street is a land-fill area, as a fire ravaged the downtown area in 1952, destroying docks and buildings originally built on pilings over the water.

Just off Front St, on Lynch and Outer Drive, is the A-frame **Visitors Centre**, a source of local information about Wrangell. There's also a small **city park** with picnic tables and a totem pole.

Continue along Front St and you will pass the former mill site of the Alaska Pulp Company. The mill still stands but operations have been moved to another mill six miles (9.6 km) out along the Zimovia Highway. At the old mill, Front St flows into Shakes St, which ends with the cannery and freezing factory of Wrangell Fisheries Inc and Wrangell Fresh Seafood. No tours are available at either place.

Across from the cannery is the bridge to **Chief Shakes Island**, Wrangell's most interesting attraction, about a mile (1.6 km) from the ferry terminal. Located in the town's Inner Boat Harbor, the island features an impressive collection of totem poles (duplicates of the originals that were carved in the late 1930s) and the

Shakes Community House. The community house is an excellent example of a high-caste tribal house and contains tools, native blankets and other cultural items. It is open on a varying schedule to accommodate the cruise ships in town and there is a $1 donation to see it. Call 874-3770 to find out the opening times of a particular day. Just as impressive as the tribal house is the view from the island of bustling Wrangell Harbor.

From Shakes St you can swing to the right on to Case Avenue and follow it two blocks to Hansen's Boat Shop. Across the street on the hillside is **Chief Shakes' gravesite**, enclosed by a Russian-style picket fence topped by two killer-whale totems.

Places to Stay

Hotels There is no Youth Hostel and only two hotels in town, of which the cheaper is the *Thunderbird Hotel* (tel 874 3322) at 223 Font St that offers singles and doubles for $52.

Bed & Breakfast If staying in a private home interests you, there is *Clarke Bed & Breakfast* at 732 Case Avenue. A bed and a meal in the morning costs $35 for singles and $45 for doubles. You should call ahead (day 874-2125, evening 874-3863), as their rooms are limited.

Camping The nearest campground is the *City Park*, located 1.8 miles (2.9 km) south of the ferry terminal on Zimovia Highway. The waterfront part is immediately south of the cemetery and city ball field and provides picnic tables, shelters and rest rooms. Camping is free but there is a two-day limit.

Further out is *Shoemaker Bay Recreation Area*, 4.7 miles (7.5 km) south of the ferry terminal on Zimovia Highway and across from the Rainbow Falls Trailhead. Tent camping is provided in a wooded area near a creek and there are no fees or time limit.

Still further is *Pat's Creek* at *Mile 10.8*

(17 km) of Zimovia Highway where it becomes a narrow Forest Service road. There are two dirt roads heading off to the left; the first is to the lake and the second is to the campground, basically just a clear spot that is no longer maintained by the USFS. Near the campground there is a trail along the creek that leads back to Pat's Lake. You'll find good fishing for cut-throat trout and Dolly Varden.

Places to Eat

The cheapest place for a meal is *The Wharf* on Front St, across from the laundromat. The restaurant is open daily and has the usual fare of eggs, sandwiches and hamburgers. Nearer to the ferry terminal and open later at night is *J & W's* at the City Dock, which sells hamburgers and hotdogs. The same menu can be found at the *Snack Shack* on Front St.

The town's best dining, featuring local shrimp and other seafood, is at the *Dockside Restaurant* in the Stikine Inn, with its excellent view of the boat harbour. Dinners are from $12 to $17. *Benjamin's*, on Outer Drive in town, is the largest supermarket and carries ready-to-eat items in its deli. Also, fishermen often sell their catch to residents and visitors down at the boat harbours. Shrimp and salmon are the delicacy of the Wrangell fleet.

Nightlife

It is often at the bar that the true spirit of Wrangell comes shining through. Intermingle with locals at the *Totem Bar* on Front St or with fishermen at the *Marine Bar* on Shakes St near Shakes Island. During a night run on the ferry, you have time to get off for a beer at the *Stikine Inn Lounge*, which has live music and the only dance floor in Wrangell.

Events

The only major event during the summer, other than the local salmon derby, is the Fourth of July celebration. Like most small Alaskan communities, all of Wrangell, gets involved in the festival, which features a parade, fireworks, logging show, street games, food booths and a salmon bake in town.

Hiking

Petroglyphs An interesting afternoon can be spent looking for petroglyphs – primitive rock carvings believed to be 8000 years old. The best set lies 0.75 mile (1.2 km) from the ferry terminal and can be reached by heading north on Evergreen Rd or, as it is called by locals, Old Airport Rd. Walk past Stough's Trailer Court and proceed a little farther to a marked wooden walkway on the right (seaward side). Follow the boardwalk to the beach and then turn right and start walking north toward the end of the island. With your back to the water, look for the carving on the large rocks.

Many of the petroglyphs are spirals and faces and there are about 20 in the area but most are submerged during high tide. Check a tide book before you head out and remember that the entire walk takes one to two hours, too long for the short in-port time of the state ferry. Several gift shops in town sell 'rubbing kits' that allow you to take images of the carvings home on paper.

Mt Dewey Trail The 0.5-mile (0.8 km) trail winds its way up a hill to an observation point overlooking Wrangell and the surrounding waterways. From Mission St, walk a block and turn left at the first corner, Third St. Follow the street past a brown and red A-frame home with a white balcony. The trail, marked by a white sign, begins 50 yards (45 metres) past the home on the right. Once you're at the trailhead, the hike is a short one – 15 minutes or so to the top – but is often muddy.

Rainbow Falls Trail The old trail was rebuilt and extended in 1985 by the USFS. From the trailhead it is a one-mile

(1.6 km) hike to the waterfalls and then another 2.5 miles (four km) to an observation point overlooking Shoemaker Bay on Institute Ridge, where the USFS has built a three-sided shelter. The lower section can be soggy at times so it is best hiked in rubber boots, while upper sections are steep. The views are worth the hike and a pleasant evening could be spent on the ridge.

The trailhead is sign-posted and is 4.7 miles (7.5 km) south of the ferry terminal on the uplands of Zimovia Highway. The trail begins directly across from the Shoemaker Bay Recreation Area and just before the Wrangell Institute Complex. Round trip to the ridge requires four to six hours of hiking.

Thomas Lake Trail At the end of the paved Zimovia Highway is the start of a dirt road known officially as Forest Road number 6290 that extends 30 miles (48 km) south along Wrangell Island. On this road, 23 miles (37 km) south of town, is Thomas Lake Trail, which leads 1.2 miles (1.9 km) to a USFS cabin (reservations needed, $10 per night) and a skiff on the lake. Inquire at the USFS office in Wrangell about the availability of the cabin and ways to get out to the trailhead.

Long Lake Trail Another seven miles (11 km) beyond Thomas Lake is the trailhead for Long Lake, a one-mile planked trail to a picnic shelter and skiff on the shores of the lake.

Paddling

The beautiful and wild Stikine River is characterised by its narrow and rugged shoreline and the mountains and hanging glaciers that surround it. It is the fastest navigable river in North America and is highlighted by its Grand Canyon, a steep-walled enclosure of the waterway where churning whitewater makes river travel impossible. Trips from below the canyon are common among rafters and kayakers;

they begin with a charter flight to Telegraph Creek in British Columbia and end with a 160-mile (256 km) float back to Wrangell.

Those who arrive at Wrangell with their own kayak but not enough funds for the expensive charter of a bush plane can undertake a trip from the town's harbour, across the Stikine Flats and up one of the three arms of the river. By keeping close to shore and taking advantage of eddies and sloughs, experienced paddlers can make their way up the Stikine but you must know how to line a boat upstream.

The USFS office in Wrangell can provide information on the Stikine, including a very helpful brochure/map entitled *Stikine River Canoe and Kayak Trips*. There are also several USFS cabins in the Stikine Flats that can be paddled to. There are no places in Wrangell to rent a canoe or kayak. If you are without a boat but are still intrigued by the Stikine, plan to rent one in Petersburg.

Two companies offer trips along the Stikine. Alaska Discovery (tel 697-2257) offers a seven-day kayak or raft float from Telegraph Creek to Wrangell. The trip begins in Juneau and ends in Wrangell, and includes the air drop-off into British Columbia. The cost is $975 per person. Stikine River Adventures (tel 874-2027) offers day trips out of Wrangell aboard a 25-foot (7.5 metre) power boat that allows parties of six to travel upriver and then float downstream.

USFS Cabins

There are 23 USFS cabins in the Wrangell Ranger District that normally do not have the same high usage as those around Juneau or Ketchikan. Six of them (Binkley Slough, Koknuk, Little Dry Island, Sergief Island and two on Gut Island) lie in the Stikine River Tideflats, 12 to 15 miles (19 to 24 km) from Wrangell. They can either be paddled to or are a 30-minute flight on a charter bush plane.

The most interesting cabin in the area,

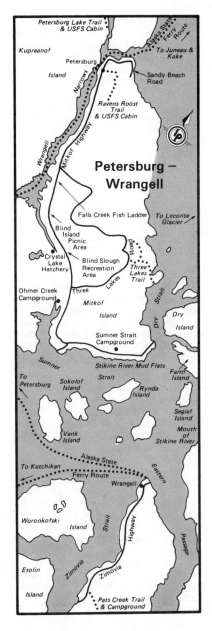

however, is on the mainland at Anan Bay, 28 air miles (45 km) from Wrangell. Near the Anan Bay Cabin is a one-mile (1.6 km) trail that leads to a bear observation/photography platform. The observatory is on the creek from Anan Lake and in July and August can be used to safely watch black bears feeding on the salmon runs. The cabin is a 50-minute flight from Wrangell or a 31-mile (50 km) paddle.

Getting There

Air Alaska Airlines (tel 874-3308) provides a year-round jet service in Wrangell, with a daily north-bound and south-bound flight. Many claim that the flight north to Petersburg is the 'world's shortest jet flight', since the 11-minute trip is little more than a take-off and landing with the huge aircraft seemingly skimming the waterway.

Boat There is an almost daily north-bound and south-bound ferry service in the summer out of Wrangell. The next stop north is Petersburg via the exciting Wrangell Narrows. The ferry terminal is open 1½ hours before each ferry arrival and from 2 to 5 pm on weekdays. There is also a recorded message (tel 874-3711) for 24-hour ferry information.

Petersburg

When the state ferry heads north from Wrangell, it begins one of the most scenic and exciting sections of the Inside Passage. After crossing over from Wrangell Island to Mitkof, the ferry begins a 22-mile (27 km) stretch known as the Wrangell Narrows, where the boat threads its way through 46 turns in this narrow channel that in places is only 300 feet (91 metres) wide and 19 feet (six metres) deep. At one point the sides of the ship are so close to the shore you can almost gather firewood for the evening.

The breath-taking journey is only

fitting as at the other end of the Narrows lies Petersburg, one of the hidden gems of Southeast Alaska. This busy little town of 3200 is an active fishing port during the summer and is decorated by weathered boathouses on the waterfront, freshly painted homes along Main St and the distinctive Devil's Thumb peak and other snow-capped mountains on the horizon.

Peter Buschmann arrived in the area in 1897 and found a fine harbour, abundant fish and a ready supply of ice from nearby LeConte Glacier. He built a cannery and enticed his Norwegian friends to follow him there and the resulting town was named after Buschmann. Today a peek into the local phone book will reveal evidence of the strong Norwegian heritage which unifies Petersburg.

Petersburg is the youngest community in the Southeast but boasts of having the largest home-based halibut fleet in Alaska, and some say the world. The economy has blossomed on fishing and on the town's canneries and cold-storage plants, which pulled in summer workers from the Lower 48.

Naturally the waterfront is the prominent part of Petersburg and one of the busiest in Southeast. It has several canneries sitting above the water on pilings, boat harbours bulging with vessels and a constant flow of barges, ferries and sea planes. Even at night you can see small boats trolling the nearby waters for somebody's dinner.

Information

For general information about Petersburg, go to the Chamber of Commerce office (tel 772-3646) in the Harbormaster's Building at the head of North Boat Harbor on the waterfront. The office doubles up as the Visitor Information Centre and among other handouts has free maps of Petersburg. Summer hours are 9 am to noon on weekdays.

For anything dealing with hiking, paddling, camping or reserving cabins,

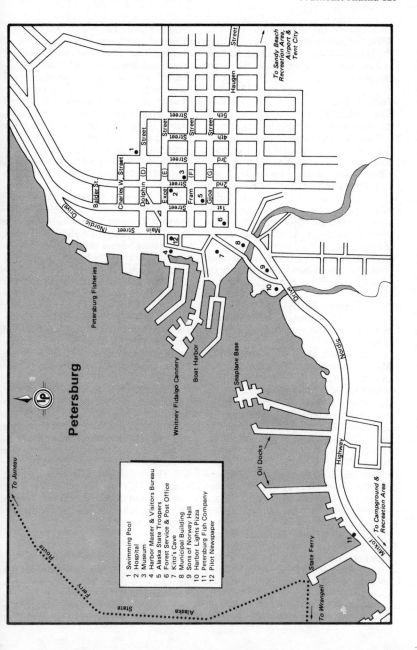

Petersburg

1 Swimming Pool
2 Hospital
3 Museum
4 Harbor Master & Visitors Bureau
5 Alaska State Troopers
6 Forest Service & Post Office
7 Kito's Cave
8 Municipal Building
9 Sons of Norway Hall
10 Harbor Lights Pizza
11 Petersburg Fish Company
12 Pilot Newspaper

head over to the USFS office (tel 722-3871) upstairs in the post office on Main St. The office is open weekdays from 8 am to 5 pm and the entrance is at the rear of the building.

Things to See

The city has recently changed many of its street names from simple letter names to full names that represent fishing boats of the past. Both names will be given here, with the new one appearing in parentheses. Information and city maps can be picked up at the Chamber of Commerce office in the Harbormaster Building on Harbor Way down by the waterfront. Across the street from the building is the office of the Petersburg Pilot, which publishes the free *Viking Visitor Guide* every summer.

The Harbormaster Office sits on top of the ramp to **North Boat Harbor**, also known as the Old Harbor or Small Boat Harbor. Hikers attempting to cross to Kupreanof Island to tackle Petersburg Mountain and Petersburg Lake trails should seek a ride at the Skiff Float near the end of these docks.

To the north along the waterfront on Main St is **Petersburg Fisheries**, founded in 1900 by Peter Buschmann and today a subsidiary of Icicle Seafoods of Seattle. To the south along Harbor Way, at the end of G St (Gjoa St), is the long pier that leads out to **Chatham Strait Seafoods**. The canneries, backbone of the Petersburg economy, are not open to the public and do not offer tours.

Continuing south, Harbor Way passes Middle Boat Harbor next and then swings into **Sing Lee Alley** (Indian St), a wooden street. This was the centre of old Petersburg, with much of the street is built on pilings over Hammer Slough. The **Sons of Norway Hall**, begun by Buschmann in 1897 and finished in 1912, is the predominant large white building with the colourful rosemaling, a flowery Norwegian art form.

Hammer Slough provides photographers with the most colourful images of Petersburg. Both Sing Lee Alley (Indian St) and Birch St follow the tidal area west of Nordic Drive. They wind past clusters of weathered homes and boathouses suspended on pillars above a shoreline of old boats, nets and crab pots. Sing Lee Alley (Indian St) crosses Hammer Slough and then joins Nordic Drive. To the right, Nordic Drive turns into Mitkof Highway and heads out past the state ferry terminal. To the left, it heads back into downtown Petersburg, first passing Birch St along the tidal area and then becoming Main St.

Turn west at the corner of Main and F St (Fram St) to reach the **Clausen Memorial Museum** in two blocks. Outside the museum is the *The Fisk*, the 11-foot (3.3 metre) bronze sculpture commemorating the town's life by the sea. Inside is an interesting collection of local artefacts and relics, most tied in with the history of fishing in Petersburg. Included in the back room is the largest king salmon ever caught, at 126 lb (57 kg). You'll also see the giant lens from the old Cape Decision Lighthouse. The museum is open daily during the summer from 1 to 4 pm. There is no admission but donations are welcome.

The museum is on the corner of F St (Fram St) and 2nd St. Follow 2nd St north for three blocks to reach the Petersburg High School. Within the same complex is the **Roundtree Swimming Pool**, a large white building attached to the rear of Stedmen Elementary School up the hill. The pool offers a variety of swimming times for $1.50 per person, or use of the showers and locker room for 75c. A swimming schedule can be obtained by calling 772-3392.

Places to Stay

Petersburg likes its tourist dollars but, unlike other Southeast towns, does not actively seek them. The community is a hard-working fishing town that concentrates on the present rather than on trying to package its past for a ship full of visitors. This explains why budget accommodation is non-existent here.

There is no Youth Hostel in Petersburg, although the town desperately needs one, and the one cheap hotel recently underwent major renovation and hiked its prices. *Scandi House* (tel 772-4281) on Main St in the downtown area now has a 'European' style to it and charges $42 for a single without a bath and $48 for a double. From here the rates for the rest of the town's hotels soar upwards.

Camping It is difficult to even camp near town. Petersburg offers *Tent City* on Haugen Drive, 0.5 mile (0.8 km) or a 10-minute walk north-west of the airport. The city-operated campground provides wooden pads, each holding three to five tents, to avoid the wet muskeg. However, the facility was designed primarily for young cannery workers who arrive in early summer and occupy an entire pad by building plastic shelters around them. By the time you come along, there are few, if any, spaces available to pitch a tent. If you can stake out an area, head down to the police station in the Municipal Building on Main St and pay the officer in charge your user fee. The cost is $3 per night plus a $25 deposit, although the last few summers city officials have been rather loose about collecting the deposit.

The other organised campgrounds are designed for RVers/camper vans and are located out the road. At *Mile 22* (35 km) of the Mitkof Highway is the *Ohmer Creek Campground* (15 sites, no fee) with a 14-day limit; and at *Mile 26.8* (43 km) is *Sumner Strait Campground* (no fee), an unimproved area for campers.

Backpackers have a couple of ways to get around the lack of budget accommodation in Petersburg. There is no camping within the city limits, and if you pitch a tent at the Sandy Beach Recreation Area, on the corner of Sandy Beach Rd and Haugen Drive three miles (4.8 km) north of town, local police will most likely kick you out in the middle of the night. However, by hiking half a mile beyond the picnic area and shelter along the shoreline, you can get away with camping on the scenic beach. Bring drinking water and camp above the high-tide line. You can also hike up the Ravens Roost trail that begins near the airport to camp, but you will have to walk more than a mile uphill before finding a suitable spot that isn't muskeg.

Another way to get around a $50 room for the night is to rent a used car at Rent-A-Dent and then drive out the road to a campground. The agent for this state-wide car rental company is in the Bottle Shop across from the ferry terminal, but during the summer it pays to call ahead (tel 772-4424) to reserve a vehicle. Rates are $20 per day and 20c per mile.

Places to Eat

Even if you're trying to survive the summer on a bag of rice and a bottle of soy sauce, splurge for a seafood dinner in the town that makes a living from what it catches. Just about every eatery in Petersburg serves seafood, but the best by far is the *Petersburg Fish Company* just north of the ferry terminal on Nordic Drive, a 15-minute walk from downtown. Dinners of halibut, clams, oysters, salmon or stuffed prawns range from $5.25 to $9.25 while a big bowl of clam chowder and bread is $2.75. There are half a dozen tables inside and a few more outside where, if it isn't raining, you can enjoy your meal while watching floatplanes take off and land. Petersburg Fish Company also sells fresh seafood, including cooked crab that you crack yourself for $2/lb ($4.40/kg).

For breakfast there's *Irene's* and *Homestead Café*, a pair of long-time favourites, both downtown on Main St. A plate of eggs, potatoes and toast costs $5 while hamburgers are $4 and up. *Harbor Lights Pizza* is diagonally opposite the Sons of Norway Hall on Sing Lee Alley (Indian St) and offers pizza, beer and wine along with a good view of the busy boat harbour below it and a few tables outside. *Beach Boy*, the snack shack of Petersburg, is downtown on Main St but it's limited to a few tables outside. Hamburgers cost between $2.50 and $5.

Two more interesting places in town are *Helse Health Foods* and *Tantes Kitchen*, both near the beginning of Sing Lee Alley (Indian St). Helse is a health-food store and restaurant, and a pleasant place for tea during a rainy afternoon if the place is open. Hours tend to be irregular. Tantes (closed Mondays) is a bakery that sells fresh pastries, cookies and croissants. It's in the rear of Bibliomania Bookstore, one of Petersburg's more interesting shops.

Nightlife

To listen to the fisherman's woes or to meet cannery workers, there is the *Harbor Bar* on Main St. For something a little livelier try *Kito's Kave* on Sing Lee Alley (Indian St). This bar and liquor store has live music and dancing most nights after 9 pm and when the boats are in it can be a rowdy place that hops until 2 or 3 am.

Events

Petersburg puts on its own Fourth of July celebration with the usual small-town festivities. The community's best event, and one that is famous around the Southeast, is the Little Norway Festival, held on the weekend closest to Norwegian Independence Day on May 17 and usually before most tourists arrive. If you are even near the area, plan to hop over to Petersburg for it. The locals dress in old costumes, Main St is turned into a string of booths and games and several dances are held in local halls. The best part is the fish feed, when the town's residents put together a pot-luck feast.

Hiking

Raven's Roost Trail The three-mile (4.8 km) trail begins at the water tower on the south-east side of the airport, accessible from Haugen Drive. The start is boardwalk across muskeg areas while much of the route is a climb to beautiful open alpine areas at 2013 feet (610 metres). Some of it is steep and requires a little scrambling. A USFS cabin (reservations needed, $10 per night) is located above the treeline in an area that provides good summer hiking and spectacular views of Petersburg, Frederick Sound and Wrangell Narrows.

Petersburg Mountain Trail Located on Kupreanof Island, this trail climbs 2.5 miles (four km) from Wrangell Narrows behind Sasby Island to the top of Petersburg Mountain. There are outstanding views from here – the best in the area – of Petersburg, coastal mountains, glaciers and Wrangell Narrows. Plan on three hours to the top and two for the return. To get across the channel, go to the skiff float at the North Boat Harbor (Old Boat Harbor) and hitch a ride with somebody who lives on Kupreanof Island. From the Kupreanof Public Dock, head to the right on the overgrown road towards Sasby Island.

Petersburg Lake Trail This 6.5-mile (10.5 km) trail is just one of a system in the Petersburg Creek-Duncan Salt Chuck Wilderness on Kupreanof Island and leads to a USFS cabin (reservations needed, $10 per night). See the Wilderness chapter for details.

Three Lakes Trails Four short trails that connect three lakes and Ideal Cove are located off Three Lakes Rd, a Forest Service road that loops off Mitkof Highway at *Mile 13.6* (22 km) and returns at *Mile 23.8* (38 km). Beginning at *Mile 14.7* (23.5 km) of Three Lakes Rd and lying within a mile of each other are three marked baranof to Sand, Crane and Hill lakes, known for their good trout fishing. All the baranof are 0.5 mile (0.8 km) or less in length, while even shorter trails

Top: Cruise ship pulling into downtown Juneau (ADT)
Left: Commercial fishing boat in Petersburg (ADT)
Right: Creek Street in Ketchikan (ADT)

Top: The village of Angoon in Southeast Alaska (ADT)
Left: Totem pole in Haines (ADT)
Right: Totem poles in Sitka National Historical Park (ADT)

connect the lakes to each other. From Sand Lake Trail there is a 1.5-mile (2.4 km) trail to Ideal Cove on Frederick Sound. There is a free-use shelter on Sand Lake.

Paddling

There is a variety of interesting water trips in the Petersburg area, most of which are bluewater paddles and require a week or more to undertake. Alaskan Waters rents single kayaks and canoes for $25 per day and provides drop-off and pick-up services for paddlers aboard their charter boat. The outfitters have a very limited number of boats for rent, so it is best to contact them before your trip by writing to Alaskan Waters, PO Box 1551, Petersburg, Alaska 99833. While in town you can leave messages for them through Viking Travel (tel 772-3818). You can purchase topographic maps in Petersburg at Lapeyri's on Main St, but their stock is badly depleted and it is far better to order your maps or purchase them in Ketchikan or Juneau.

LeConte Glacier The most spectacular paddle is LeConte Glacier, the southernmost tidewater glacier in North America 25 miles (40 km) east of Petersburg. From town, it would take three to four days to reach the frozen monument, which would include crossing Frederick Sound north of Coney Island. The crossing should be done at slack tide, as winds and tides can cause choppy conditions. If the tides are judged right, it is possible to paddle far enough into LeConte Bay to camp within view of the glacier.

Thomas Bay Almost as impressive is Thomas Bay, north of LeConte Bay on the east side of Frederick Sound and 20 miles (32 km) from Petersburg. The bay features a pair of glaciers at the end of its arms, including Baird Glacier, on which many paddlers spend a day hiking. The mountain scenery surrounding the bay is spectacular and there are three USFS

cabins (reservations needed, $10 per night): Swan Lake Cabin, Spurt Cove Cabin and Cascade Creek Cabin. Consult the local USFS office about crossing Frederick Sound and availability of cabins. Paddlers need four to seven days for the round trip out of Petersburg.

Kake to Petersburg This trip is made possible by the state ferries, which backpackers can take to the native village of Kake, paddling back to Petersburg. The 90-mile (144 km) route follows the west side of Kupreanof Island through Keku Strait, Sumner Strait and up Wrangell Narrows to Petersburg. The highlight is Rocky Pass, a remote and narrow winding waterway in Keku Strait that has almost no boat traffic other than an occasional kayaker. Caution has to be used in Sumner Strait, which lies only 40 miles (64 km) away from open ocean and has its share of winds and waves. Plan on seven to 10 days for the trip.

Getting There

Air Alaska Airlines' milk run through the Southeast provides a daily flight northbound and south-bound out of Petersburg. The airport is one mile from the post office on Airport Rd (or Haugen St, as it is called in town). The airline office can be reached by calling 772-4255.

Boat The State Marine Ferry terminal (tel 772-3855) is about a mile off Nordic Drive on the south edge of town. There is usually one north-bound ferry arriving daily. Those travellers continuing on to Juneau should consider taking the *Le Conte* if it fits into their schedule. This ship sails from Petersburg to Juneau but stops at Kake, Sitka, Angoon, Tenakee and Hoonah along the way; one-way fare is $29.

AROUND PETERSBURG

Out the road there are a few sights, although it's debatable whether it's worth the hassle of getting out to see them. The **Crystal Lake Fish Hatchery** at *Mile 17.5* (28 km) of the Mitkof Highway is a $2.2-million facility used to stock coho, king salmon and trout throughout the Southeast. No formal tours are offered, but hatchery personnel are pleasant and informative. Hours are weekdays from 8 am to 12 noon and 12.30 to 4 pm.

On the way back to town, stop at the **Falls Creek Fish Ladder** at *Mile 13.7* (22 km) of the Mitkof, an impressive sight in August when coho and pink salmon leap along its steps. At *Mile 9* (14 km) of the highway is the **Heintzleman Nursery** operated by the USFS, which includes six greenhouses that produce a million seedlings of Sitka spruce per year. It is open to the public on an informal basis on weekdays from 8 am to 4.30 pm. Like the hatchery, it does not charge admission.

KAKE

Kake is a native beachfront community of 700 on the north-west corner of Kupreanof Island. It is the traditional home of the Kake tribe of the Tlingit Indians and today maintains subsistence rights while also turning to commercial fishing, fish processing and logging to round out its economy. It's known for having the tallest totem pole in Alaska, a 124-foot (38 metre) carving above town that was first raised at Alaska's pavilion in the 1970 World's Fair in Osaka, Japan.

The community is a port-of-call for the state ferry, as the *Le Conte* and *Aurora* stop once a week, usually on the same day, one heading north and the other south. Within town, 1.5 miles (2.4 km) from the ferry terminal, are two grocery stores, *Jackson's Coffee Shop* and *New Town Inn*, where rooms begin at $50 for singles. Rough logging roads lead south from town and eventually reach scenic Hamilton Bay, 20 miles (32 km) from Kake.

Paddling
Tebenkof Bay Wilderness Kake serves as the departure point for bluewater trips into Tebenkof Bay Wilderness, a remote bay system composed of hundreds of islands, small inner bays and coves. The round-trip paddle is a scenic 10-day adventure that can lead to many sightings of bald eagles, black bears, signs of wolves and a variety of marine mammals. Paddlers should have experience in ocean touring and be prepared to handle a number of portages. Kayaks can be rented in either Juneau or Petersburg and then carried on board the state ferry to Kake.

The most common route is to paddle from Kake south through Keku Strait into Port Camden, where at its western end there is a 1.3-mile (two km) portage trail to the Bay of Pillars. From the Bay of Pillars you encounter the only stretch of open water as you paddle three miles (4.8 km) around Point Ellis into Tebenkof Bay. The return east follows Alecks Creek from the bay into Alecks Lake, where there is a 2.3-mile (3.7 km) portage trail to No Name Bay. From here paddlers can reach Keku Strait and paddle the waterway, including its scenic Rocky Pass section, north to Kake.

Sitka

For a region of Alaska strong in colour and history, Sitka is the gem in a beautiful setting. Facing the Pacific Ocean, the city of 8500 is overshadowed to the west by Mt Edgecumbe, the extinct volcano with a cone duplicating Japan's Mt Fuji. The waters offshore are broken up by a myriad of small, forested islands that are ragged silhouettes during sunsets, while to the east the town is flanked by snow-capped mountains and sharp granite peaks. On a clear day Sitka rivals Juneau for the sheer beauty of its surroundings.

Along with its natural beauty, Sitka is

steeped in history. It became the first non-native settlement in Southeast when Alexander Baranov established a Russian fort near the present ferry terminal in 1799. Three years later, Tlingit Indians, armed with guns from British and American traders, overwhelmed the fort, burned it to the ground and killed most of its inhabitants. Baranov returned in 1804 and after destroying the Tlingit fort, established a settlement called New Archangel at the present site of Sitka, making it the headquarters of the Russian-American Company. On the strength of the fur trade, Sitka flourished both economically and culturally and enjoyed its golden era as the 'Paris of the Pacific'.

In 1867, Sitka picked up its present name after the United States took control of the town following the purchase of Alaska. After the territorial capital was transferred to Juneau in 1900, the city fell upon some hard times but boomed again during WW II when a military base was built on nearby Japonski Island. At one time during the war, Sitka boasted a population of 37,000 military and civilian residents. Today the city is supported by a pulp mill, fishing fleet, cold-storage plants and several federal agencies that have offices in the area.

However, the town clings to its strong Russian heritage and prides itself on being the cultural centre of Southeast, if not all of Alaska. It seemed only natural to those living in Sitka that when author James Michener decided to write an epic novel on Alaska he chose their town as his home base to conduct research.

When arriving in Sitka by state ferry, you will sail through the Sergius Narrows, a tight waterway that ships must follow at slack tide. Any other period is too hazardous for vessels to negotiate the fierce currents caused by the changing of the tides. This often forces the state ferry to take a three-hour stop at Sitka while waiting for the tide and allows travellers a quick view of the city even if they are not disembarking. The ferry terminal is seven miles (11 km) from town, too far to see anything on foot, but Sitka Tours does run a bus tour for those waiting for the ferry to depart. The tour covers briefly the major sites of Sitka National Historical Park, St Michael's Cathedral and Sheldon Jackson College. The cost is $8 per person.

Information
The Sitka Visitors Bureau (tel 747-8604) is in the Centennial Building downtown on Harbor Drive and is open daily from 9 am to 5 pm. The USFS Office – the place to go to for trail information, cabin reservations and handouts about enjoying the wilderness – is in a three-storey red building on the corner of Siginaka and Katlian Sts, across from Thomas Boat Harbor. The office (tel 747-6671) is open on weekdays from 8 am to 5 pm. Sitka has three state recreation areas; information about their use or any Alaskan state park can be obtained from the Division of Parks Office at Old Airport Turnaround on Halibut Point Rd. The office (tel 747-6249) is open from 8 am to 5 pm on weekdays.

 Sitka Visitors Bureau

Things to See
The Sitka Visitors Bureau is in the Centennial Building downtown off Harbor Drive next to Crescent Boat Harbor. Among their handouts is a map of the city listing the points of interest. Also inside the building is the **Sitka Historical Society** and its collection of relics from the past, along with a model of the town as it appeared in 1867. Outside is the hand-carved Tlingit canoe made from a single log. The Centennial Building is open daily, 8 am to 5 pm and 7 to 10 pm.

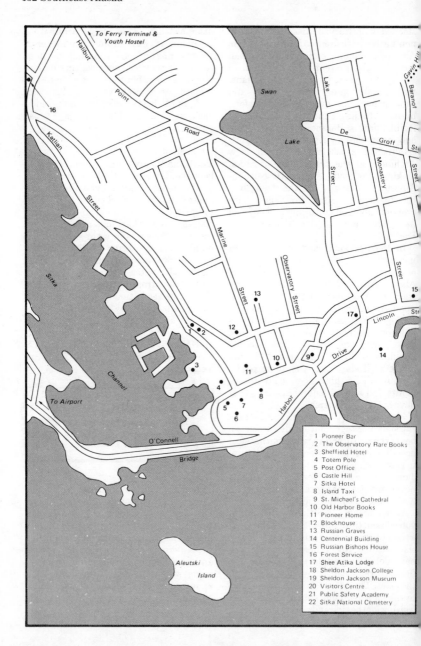

1 Pioneer Bar
2 The Observatory Rare Books
3 Sheffield Hotel
4 Totem Pole
5 Post Office
6 Castle Hill
7 Sitka Hotel
8 Island Taxi
9 St. Michael's Cathedral
10 Old Harbor Books
11 Pioneer Home
12 Blockhouse
13 Russian Graves
14 Centennial Building
15 Russian Bishops House
16 Forest Service
17 Shee Atika Lodge
18 Sheldon Jackson College
19 Sheldon Jackson Museum
20 Visitors Centre
21 Public Safety Academy
22 Sitka National Cemetery

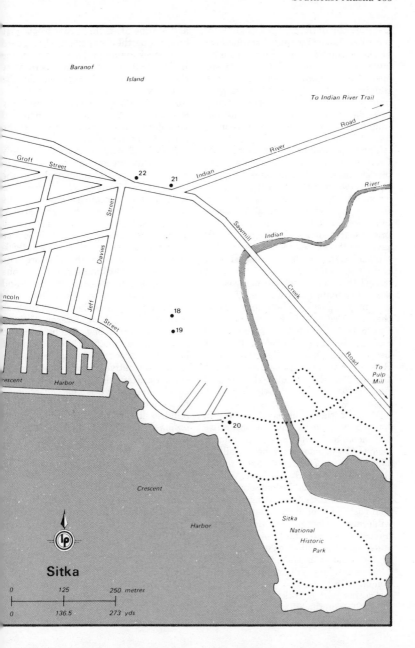

If it's early in the day, you might want to head up Lake St to the fire station a few blocks on the left, where you can store a bulky backpack until the Youth Hostel opens. Next door to the Centennial Building is the city's **Public Library**, an impressive facility that is open Monday to Friday from 10 am to 9 pm, Saturday from 10 am to 5 pm and Sunday from 1 to 5 pm.

The heart of downtown is **St Michael's Cathedral**, in the centre of Lincoln St two blocks away from the Centennial Building. Built between 1844 and 1848, the church stood for over 100 years as the finest Russian Orthodox cathedral in Alaska until fire destroyed it in 1966. The priceless treasures and icons inside were saved by Sitka residents, who built a replica of the original cathedral. The church is open from noon to 4 pm daily during the summer for visitors, who are asked to donate $1 upon entering.

Continuing west on Lincoln St next to the post office is the walkway that leads to Castle Hill, the site of a succession of Russian buildings including **Baranof's Castle**, which housed the governor of Russian America. It was here on 18 October 1967 that the official transfer of Alaska from Russia to the US took place.

More Russian cannons can be seen in **Totem Square** across from the post office on Lincoln St. Next to it is the prominent yellow **Alaska Pioneers Home**. Built in 1934 on the old Russian Parade Ground, the home is for elderly Alaskans. Visitors are welcome to meet the 'old sourdoughs' and listen to their fascinating stories of gold-rush days or homesteading in the wilderness. The 13-foot (four metre) bronze Prospector statue in front of the state home was dedicated on Alaska Day in 1949 and is modelled on long-time Alaskan resident William 'Skagway Bill' Fonda.

Another part of Sitka's Russian past can be seen on the hill west of the Alaska Pioneer Home. On the corner of Kogwanton and Marine Sts is the replica **blockhouse** of the type the Russians used to guard their stockade and separate it from the Indian village. Originally there were three on a wall that kept the Tlingits restricted to an area along Katlian St Adjacent to the wooden blockhouse is the **Russian Cemetery**. There are more old headstones and Orthodox crosses at the end of Observatory St.

Russian Bishop's House, the only original Russian building still standing in Sitka, is the first of many sights at the east end of downtown. The soft-yellow structure is on Lincoln St across from the west end of Crescent Harbor and is a prime example of Russian colonial architecture. The National Park Service purchased the building in the early 1980s and has been restoring the structure to its 1853 setting. The building, which at one time has been used as a church, office and school, was opened to tours in 1985.

Further along Lincoln St, past the boat harbour, is **Sheldon Jackson College**, which includes among other buildings an octagonal museum. It's the oldest cement building in Alaska and today houses one of the best native culture collections in the state. Hanging from the ceiling and equally impressive is the collection of boats and sleds used in Alaska – from reindeer sleds and dog sleds to kayaks and *umiaks*. The Sheldon Jackson Museum is open daily from 8 am to 5 pm; admission is $1.

Sitka's most noted attraction lies further east at the end of Lincoln St, where the National Park Service maintains the **Sitka National Historical Park**. The 107-acre (43 hectare) park, 0.5 mile (0.8 km) from downtown, features a trail that winds past 15 totem poles in a beautiful forest setting next to the sea. The park is at the mouth of the Indian River, where the Tlingit Indians were finally defeated by the Russians in 1804 after defending the spot for over a week. Begin at the Visitors Centre, where there are displays of Russian and native artefacts and where carvers demonstrate traditional arts. Admission is free and the centre (tel 747-6281) is open daily from 8 am to 6 pm in the summer.

Also at the east end and a place of interest mostly to history buffs is the **Sitka National Cemetery**. The plot is off Sawmill Creek Rd, just before the Public Safety Academy, and can be reached from Sheldon Jackson College along Jeff Davis Rd. The area was designated a national cemetery by past president Calvin Coolidge and includes headstones for Civil War veterans, members of the Aleutian Campaign in WW II and many notable Alaskans.

For a lot of visitors, Sitka's most colourful section is **Katlian St**, which begins off Lincoln St at the west end of town next to the Sheffield Hotel. The road is a classic mixture of weather-beaten houses, docks and canneries where there always seems to be fishing boats unloading their catch. Katlian St portrays the sights, sounds and hum of the busy Southeast fishing industry. Even the vacant yards along it reflect dependence on the sea, as they are sites of discarded fishing nets or stacks of crab pots. The buildings have that slanted, coastal look to them, with paint peeling in corners and a little grass growing out of clogged eaves troughs. In short, it is a colourful, bustling place and a photographer's haven.

Places to Stay

Youth Hostel The Sitka *Youth Hostel* (tel 747-8775) is in the basement of the Methodist Church at 303 Kimsham Rd. Follow Halibut Point Rd out from downtown and then turn right onto Peterson Rd, 0.25 mile (0.4 km) past Lakeside Grocery Store. Once on Peterson you immediately veer left onto Kimsham. Registration is from 6 to 11 pm and checkout time is 8 am. There are no kitchen facilities, but there is an eating area. The cost is $4 for AYH members and $5.50 for non-members.

Hotels There are four hotels in Sitka. The cheapest is the *Sitka Hotel* (tel 747-3288), downtown at 118 Lincoln St. Single rooms with no bath cost $33 per night and the establishment offers showers for $3.

Camping There are two USFS campgrounds in the Sitka area. Both are free but neither is close to downtown. *Starrigavan Campground* is a 0.7-mile (1.1 km) walk north of the ferry terminal on *Mile 7.8* (12.4 km) of Halibut Point Rd. The campground (26 sites) is in a scenic setting and adjacent to a saltwater beach and hiking trails. On your way to the area you'll pass Old Sitka State Park, which features lighted trails and interpretive displays dedicated to the site of the original Russian settlement.

Sawmill Creek Campground (seven sites) is six miles (9.6 km) east of Sitka on Blue Lake Rd off Sawmill Creek Rd and past the pulp mill. Although the area is no longer maintained by the USFS, it provides mountain scenery with an interesting trail to Blue Lake.

Showers in town can be obtained for $1.25 per person at the *Sitka Public Pool* (tel 747-5677) in Riatchley Junior High School on Halibut Point Rd, which has varying opening hours. You can also get a shower for a $1.50 at *Homestead Laundromat*, 621 Katlian St.

Places to Eat

Sitka has a restaurant for anybody's budget and desire. The breakfast places downtown are *Lory's Sitka Café* at 166 Lincoln St and *Revard's* at 324 Lincoln, two restaurants that have been pouring the morning coffee for locals for years. Both have eggs, potatoes and toast for around $3. The Sitka Café's best bargain is its huge bowl of home-made clam chowder for $2. For just coffee in the morning there is the *Coffee Express* on Lake Rd next door to the fire station. It has limited seating inside and opens at 7 am on weekdays but a choice selection of coffees and teas is offered.

For dinner, *Casa Blanc* on Lake St across from the Shee Akita Lodge offers Mexican meals that cost between $5 and $9 and include large portions of chips, salad, rice and beans with the entree. The *Bayview*, upstairs in the Bayview Trading Centre across from Crescent Harbor, has the best hamburgers in Sitka. Although the service can be slow at times, their menu lists 26 varieties of hamburgers ranging from $5 to $7. The eatery also serves beer and wine in a setting which offers every table a view of the boat harbour across the street.

Along Katlian St there is *Twin Dragon* and *Sitka Sound Seafood*. Twin Dragon is a Chinese restaurant with greasy decor but good food, especially their fried beef in hot sauce and Mongolian beef. Complete dinners run from $10 to $12 and a-la-carte entrees begin at $6. Sitka Sound Seafood sells smoked salmon and fresh halibut, prawns and crab as well as seafood dinners from $5 to $9.

For those who like to make an evening out of their meal, there is the *Strawberry Patch* on Siginaka Way, a short walk down from the junction with Katlian St, where the USFS office is located. The restaurant offers great views of the Sitka coastline and Thomsen Harbor and specialises in freshly baked breads and pastries and has a good salad bar. The *Shee Atika Lodge* has a fine restaurant where dinners cost from $10 to $15. The hotel serves a good breakfast so you can sip your coffee while watching the sunrise over Crescent Boat Harbor.

Nightlife

Sitka's most interesting night spot is the *Pioneer Bar*, the classic fishermen's pub on Katlian St down by the waterfront. The walls are covered with photos of fishing boats and the score board for the pool table often has 'help wanted' messages scrawled across it from fishermen looking for black-cod crewmen or from somebody seeking work on a troller. Above the long wooden bar is a large brass bell, but put off the urge to ring it unless you want to buy a round of drinks for the house. Just as crowded after work but with a different clientele is the lounge in the *Shee Atika Lodge*, which draws professionals and office workers for music, dancing and drinking.

Another option at night is to book passage on the 2½-hour night cruise offered by Silver Bay Harbor Tours (tel 747-8941). Their boat departs from Crescent Harbor daily at 7 pm for a view of Sitka and its waterfront at night. The fare is $18 per person.

Events

Extending its reputation as the cultural centre of Southeast, the city sponsors the Sitka Summer Music Festival during three weeks in June at the Centennial Building. The emphasis of the festival is on chamber music and brings together professional musicians for concerts and workshops. The highly-acclaimed event is popular so it can be hard to obtain tickets to the twice-weekly evening concerts. However, rehearsals are open to the public, are easier to attend and are usually free.

Sitka highlights its Fourth of July celebration with the All-Alaska Logging Championships. The event brings loggers from around the state and the Pacific Northwest to compete in a variety of contests, including axe-throwing and tree-topping.

On 16-18 October the city holds its Alaska Day Festival by re-enacting the transfer of the state from Russia to the US with costumes (and even beards) of the 1860s. A parade highlights the three-day event.

Hiking

Sitka offers superb hiking in the beautiful but tangled forest that surrounds the city. Second only to Juneau for variety and number of trails that can be reached on foot, Sitka has 10 trails that start from its road system and total over 40 miles (64 km) through the woods and up mountains. Already mentioned is the 1.8-mile (2.9 km) path in the Sitka National Historical Park at the east end of Lincoln St.

Indian River Trail This easy trail is a 5.5-mile (8.8 km) walk along a clear salmon stream to the Indian River Falls and its 80-foot (24 metre) drop at the base of the Sister Mountains. The hike takes you through a typical Southeast rainforest and offers the opportunity to view black bears, deer and bald eagles. The trailhead, a short walk from downtown, is off Sawmill Creek Rd just past the National Cemetery. Pass the driveway leading to the Public Safety Academy parking lot and turn up the dirt road with a gate across it. This leads back to the city water plant where the trail begins left of the pump house. Plan on four to five hours for a round trip to the falls.

Galvin Hill Trail Also close to downtown is Galvin Hill Trail, which climbs three miles (4.8 km) and 2500 feet (762 metres) to the alpine summit of this hill. The trail provides excellent views of Sitka and the

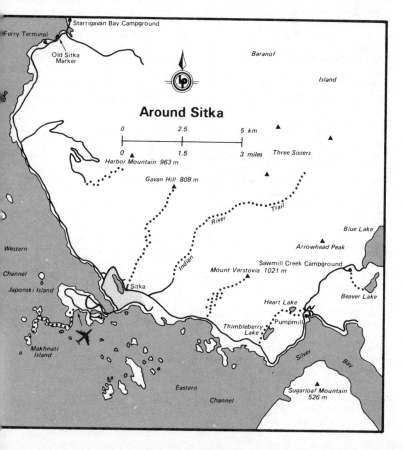

Around Sitka

surrounding area. From the end the adventurous hiker can continue to the peaks of the Three Sisters Mountains. From Lincoln St downtown head up Baranof St for six blocks to the house at 508 Baranof past Merrill St. The trail begins just beyond the house and heads to the north-east, reaching Cross Trail within 0.74 miles (1.2 km). There is good camping in the alpine regions of the trail, but bring water and a campstove, as wood and drinking water are not available above the tree line. Plan on three to four hours to hike the trail one way.

Airport Causeway Hike This hike begins downtown with a 1.8-mile (2.9 km) walk across O'Connell Bridge and past the boat harbours on Japonski Island to the airport. From the high arch of the bridge, you get some of the best views of downtown Sitka and the mountains that flank it to the east. At the airport the hike continues along the airport causeway and extends 1.5 miles (2.4 km) into Sitka Sound, where there is fascinating beach-combing for shells and driftwood and interesting tidal pools to investigate. You can also view the underground bunkers, personnel quarters and gun emplacements on Makhnati Island that are left over from Sitka's military build-up during WW II.

When you get to the airport you must contact the airport manager during work hours for an escort across the runway to the causeway. Simply scampering across the runway is illegal. Plan on two to three hours for the round trip.

Mt Verstovia Trail This 2.5-mile (four km) trail is a challenging climb of 2550 feet (777 metres) to the 'shoulder', a small summit that is the most common stopping point. It is possible to climb to 3300 feet (1006 metres), the actual peak of Mt Verstovia. The view from the shoulder on clear days is spectacular – undoubtedly the best in the area. The trailhead is two miles (3.2 km) east of Sitka along

Sawmill Creek Rd. Once you reach the Kiksadi Club on the left, look for the trailhead marked 'Mount Verstovia Trail'. The Russian charcoal pits (posted) are reached within 0.25 mile (0.4 km) and shortly after that the trail begins climbing with a series of switchbacks. From the 'shoulder' the true peak lies to the north along a ridge that connects the two. To hike the ridge, allow an extra hour each way. Plan on a four-hour round trip to the shoulder.

Harbor Mountain Trail The trail is reached from Harbor Mountain Rd, the only road in Southeast that provides access to a sub-alpine area. Head four miles (6.4 km) north-west from Sitka on Halibut Point Rd to reach the junction with Harbor Mountain Rd. It is 4.5 miles (7.2 km) up the rough dirt road to a parking area and nearby picnic shelter. After another 0.5 mile (0.8 km) you reach the parking area at the end of the road and an unmarked trail begins on the east side of the lot. The trail climbs 1.5 miles (2.4 km) to the alpine meadows, knobs and ridges above the road from where the views are spectacular. Plan on spending two to four hours scrambling through alpine area – or better yet, camp up there.

Beaver Lake Hike This short trail is in Sawmill Creek Campground, which is reached from Sawmill Creek Rd 5.5 miles (8.8 km) east of Sitka. Across from the pulp mill, turn left on Blue Lake Rd for the campground; on its south side is the trailhead. Although steep at the beginning, the 0.8-mile (1.3 km) trail levels out and ends up as a scenic walk through open forest and along muskeg and marsh areas to the lake that is surrounded by mountains. Vandals have made the skiff at the lake unsafe to use. Plan on an hour hike for the round trip.

Mt Edgecumbe Trail The 6.7-mile (11 km) trail begins at Fred's Creek Cabin, a USFS structure (reservations needed,

$10 per night), and climbs to the top of the summit crater of this extinct volcano. Needless to say, the views from the summit are spectacular on a clear day. About three miles (4.8 km) up the trail is a free-use shelter that does not require reservations.

Mt Edgecumbe lies on Kruzof Island, 10 miles (16 km) west of Sitka, and can be reached only by boat because of large swells from the ocean that prevent floatplanes from landing. Explore Alaska Charters (tel 747-3465) is a booking agency for charter boats in town and can arrange a drop-off and pick-up for hikers at the cost of $60 one way per party. Actual hiking time is five to six hours one way, but by securing Fred's Creek Cabin you can turn the adventure into a pleasant three-day trip with nights spent in two shelters.

Paddling

Sitka also serves as the departure point for numerous bluewater trips along the protected shorelines of Baranof and Chichagof Islands. Baidarka Boats, owned and managed by Larry Edwards, rents kayaks in town, including folding doubles and rigid singles and doubles. Contacting Edwards ahead of time is a must, as he seems to spend little time in town, leaving you a recorded phone message. Write to PO Box 2158, Sitka, Alaska 99835; or call 747-8996. You can purchase topographic maps at Old Harbor Books (tel 747-8808) at 201 Lincoln St downtown.

Katlian Bay This 45-mile (72 km) loop trip, beginning from Sitka Harbor and ending at scenic Katlian Bay on the north end of Kruzof Island, is one of the most popular paddles in the area. The route follows narrow straits and well-protected shorelines which are marine traffic channels, making it an ideal trip for less experienced bluewater paddlers who will never be far from help. A fish buyer is usually anchored in Katlian Bay and has limited groceries for sale. A scenic side-trip is to hike the sandy beach from the bay around Cape Georgiana to Sea Lion Cove on the Pacific Ocean. Catch the tides to paddle Olga and Neva Straits on the way north and return along Sukoi Inlet, spending a night at the USFS cabin on Brent's Beach if you can reserve it. Plan on four to six days for the paddle.

Shelikof Bay You can combine a 10-mile (16 km) paddle to Kruzof Island with a six-mile hike across it along an old logging road and trail from Mud Bay to Shelikof Bay. Once on the Pacific Ocean side you find a beautiful sandy beach, providing lots of beachcombing with the use of the USFS Shelikof Cabin (reservations needed, $10 per night).

West Chichagof The western shoreline of Chichagof Island is one of the best bluewater trips in Southeast Alaska for experienced kayakers. Unfortunately the trip involves a floatplane charter, as few paddlers have the experience to paddle the open ocean around Khaz Peninsula that forms a barrier between the north end of Kruzof Island and Slocum Arm. The arm is the southern end of a series of straits, coves and protected waterways that shield paddlers from the ocean's swells and extend 30 miles plus (48 km) north to Lisianski Strait.

With all its hidden coves and inlets, the trip makes for a good two-week paddle. Those with even more time and a little adventure in their hearts could continue another 25 miles (40 km) through Lisianski Strait to reach the fishing village of Pelican, where the state ferry stops twice a month in the summer. Such an expedition would require at least two to three weeks but would keep air charter down to a 30-minute flight to Slocum Arm.

USFS Cabins

There are a number of USFS cabins close to Sitka which require less than 30 minutes of air time to reach. All the following should be reserved ahead of time through the USFS office in town and cost $10 per night for the entire cabin:

Already mentioned above have been *Fred's Cabin, Brent's Beach Cabin* and *Shelikof Cabin* on Kruzof Island, the site of Mt Edgecumbe. Local air service operators who can handle chartering requests are Bell Air at 475 Katlian St, tel 747-8636; and Mountain Aviation in the airport terminal, tel 966-2288.

Redoubt Lake Cabin is an A-frame at the north end of Redoubt Lake, a narrow body of water south of Sitka on Baranof Island. The cabin is a 20-minute flight from Sitka. You could also reach it by paddling to the head of Silver Bay from town and then hiking a five-mile (eight km) trail south to the cabin.

Baranof Lake Cabin is a favourite among locals, as it has a scenic, mountainous setting on the east side of Baranof Island with a one-mile (1.6 km) trail to Warm Springs Bay. At the bay there is a bath house constructed around the natural hot springs which costs $2.50 to use. The cabin is a 20-minute flight from Sitka.

Lake Eva Cabin, a pan abode on Baranof Island, provides a skiff with oars and an outdoor fire pit as well as a wood stove inside. A trail from the outlet of the lake (which can be fished for Dolly Varden, cut-throat trout and salmon in late summer) leads down to the ocean. The cabin is a 20-minute flight from Sitka.

White Sulphur Springs Cabin requires a 45-minute flight to the western shore of Chichagof Island, but the spot is another popular one with Southeasterners because of the hot springs bath house in front of it. The free hot springs are used by cabin renters as well as fishermen and kayakers passing through.

Getting There
Air Sitka is served by Alaska Airlines (tel 966-2266) with flights to Juneau and Anchorage. It is part of the milk-run that connects the city to Wrangell, Petersburg and Ketchikan. The airport is on Japonski

Island, 1.8 miles (2.9 km) from downtown. On a nice day it can be a scenic 20-minute walk from the airport terminal, over the O'Connell Bridge to the heart of Sitka. Otherwise, the white Airporter mini-bus of Sitka Tours meets all jet flights and charges $2.50 for a ride to the downtown hotels; it does not go to the Youth Hostel.

Regularly scheduled flights among the small air charter companies include Sitka-Pelican for $75 one way with Bellair (tel 747-8636) at 475 Katlian St. Mountain Aviation (tel 966-2288), in the airport terminal, offers a one-way fare of $35 for Sitka-Tenakee Springs.

Boat The State Marine Ferry terminal is seven miles (11.2 km) from downtown on Halibut Point Rd and there are departures almost daily by state ferries, either north-bound or south-bound. This does not always apply, however, so it's a good idea to call the terminal (tel 747-3300) or to read your schedule carefully when planning your departure from the city. Passage from Sitka-Juneau is $29, Sitka-Angoon $18, Sitka-Petersburg $29 and Sitka-Tenakee Springs $20. The Airporter mini-bus meets all ferries and for $2.50 will take you downtown. You can also catch the bus out to the ferry terminal by being at a major hotel (Shee Atika Lodge, Sheffield House) when it makes its run to pick up hotel guests.

Car Rental Rent-A-Dent (tel 966-2552) has a handful of used cars they'll let you use for $20 a day and 20c per mile. The dealer is adjacent to the airport terminal.

TENAKEE SPRINGS
What began in the late 1800s as a winter retreat for fishermen and prospectors on the east side of Tenakee Inlet has evolved today into a rustic village known for its exceptionally slow and relaxed pace. Tenakee Springs, a community of 150,

has no roads, cars or running water and consists mainly of a ferry dock, a row of houses and cabins on pilings and the dirt path behind them.

The reason for its existence is the natural hot springs that sends 106°F (41°C) water bubbling out of the ground. The alternative life-style is centred around the public bath house at the end of the ferry dock. The building there encloses the principal spring which flows through the concrete bath at a rate of seven gallons (27 litres) per minute. There are posted bath hours separating men from women, and they are strictly followed. Most locals take at least one good soak per day if not two.

The waterfront of Tenakee Springs was hit full force by the Thanksgiving Storm of 1984 which demolished a dozen of the buildings on pilings and damaged even more. The community has since patched itself up and the relaxed atmosphere has returned to this quaint hamlet on Chichagof Island. The spot makes for an interesting side trip and an inexpensive one as well if you can spare three to four days to arrive and leave on the state ferry.

There is good fishing in the local streams for trout, salmon and Dolly Varden, and there are day hikes that begin at each end of town. The dirt path, dubbed Tenakee Avenue, extends six miles (9.6 km) to the east and five miles (eight km) to the west, passing a few cabins in either direction.

Places to Stay, Eat & Drink

Opposite the bath house at the foot of the ferry dock is Snyder Mercantile Company, where the town's first phone was installed in 1976. The store sells limited supplies and groceries and also rents cabins that hold two to four people for $25 per night. To be sure of getting a cabin, you have to reserve in advance (PO Box 505, Tenakee Springs, Alaska 99841; tel 736-2205) and check-in during the store hours of 9 am to 5 pm Monday to Saturday. If your ferry arrives in the middle of the night, plan on camping out the first night.

Since much of the land around town was purchased through the Alaska Lands Lottery in the late 1970s, you have to hike out a way before finding an available spot to camp. An unofficial campground exists two miles east of town at the mouth of Indian River and is the best place to pitch a tent if you are planning to stay a few days. The town's restaurant is the *Blue Moon Café*. Further down the path towards the boat harbour is *Tenakee Tavern*, the spot to have a brew after your evening soak.

HOONAH

As you head north on board the state ferry *Le Conte*, the next stop after Tenakee Springs before reaching Juneau is Hoonah. It is the largest Tlingit village in Southeast, with a population of almost 900. Hoonah lacks the charm and friendliness – as well as the public bath house – of Tenakee Springs, but it does offer spectacular scenery in the surrounding mountains. Its population is predominantly native and the life-style is mainly subsistence.

The town serves as the beginning of the kayak trip down Port Frederick to Tenakee Inlet (see the Wilderness chapter). The most photogenic area lies one mile (1.6 km) north-west of Hoonah, where the faded red buildings of the old Hoonah Packing Cannery serenely guard Port Frederick. There is good fishing for Dolly Varden from this point.

In town, or actually on a hill overlooking Front St, is the Cultural Centre & Museum that displays native art and artefacts. The centre is open Monday to Friday from 9 am to 3 pm.

Places to Stay & Eat

There are three small grocery stores in Hoonah. On occasion you can purchase fresh seafood directly from the Cold Storage Plant. *Dliet Toos Café & Inn* is a coffee shop half a mile (0.8 km) from the ferry terminal on Front St which has rooms at $45 for singles and $55 for doubles. There are no official campgrounds but backpackers do not have to walk far out the road to find a suitable spot to pitch a tent.

Hiking & Paddling

Hoonah lies south-east of Glacier Bay National Park across Icy Strait, but the paddle to the preserve is an extremely challenging trip for advanced kayakers only. A trickle of paddlers arrive in the fishing town each summer and then take a boat across the waterway to Glacier Bay. This is perhaps the only reasonable way to get a rigid kayak into the park.

An overnight kayak trip can be made to the Salt Lake Bay Cabin, a USFS structure 14 miles (22.4 km) from Hoonah on Port Frederick. The cabin is rented out for $10 per night and needs to be reserved, but is not heavily used. For more information about paddling or hiking in the area, contact the USFS office at PO Box 135, Hoonah, Alaska 99829; tel 945-3631.

Spassky Trail This 3.3-mile (5.2 km) trail begins 3.5 miles east of town and winds to Spassky Bay on Ice Strait.

Juneau

First appearances are often misleading, and Juneau is a case in point. Over half the north-bound state ferries arrive in the Capital City between midnight and 6 am at the Auke Bay Terminal, 14 miles (22 km) from downtown, leaving disgruntled backpackers to sleepily hunt for transportation and lodging. At this point you might be unappreciative of Alaska's capital, but give it a second chance. Few cities in the US and none in Alaska are as beautiful as Juneau, claimed by its residents to be the most scenic capital in the country, while others describe it as a 'little San Francisco'.

The downtown section, hugging the side of Mt Juneau, consists of a score of narrow streets running past a mixture of new structures, old storefronts and slanted houses, all held together by a network of staircases. The bustling waterfront in front of this section features cruise ships, tankers, fishing boats, a few kayakers and a dozen floatplanes buzzing in and out like flies. Overhead are the snow-capped peaks of Mt Juneau and Mt Roberts, which provide just a small part of the superb hiking found in the area.

The city of 27,500 was born in the 1880s when gold was found in a local stream, and today Juneau still holds much of its frontier appearance. Joe Juneau and Dick Harris, two vagabond prospectors, stumbled onto the precious metal in Gold Creek in 1880 and almost overnight a tent city appeared. The post office was established two years later and the capital of Alaska was moved to Juneau in 1900 after whaling and the fur trade reduced the importance of Sitka. Almost 75 years later, Alaskans voted to move the capital again in 1974, this time to a small highway junction called Willow that lay in Anchorage's strong sphere of influence. The so-called 'capital move' issue hung over Juneau like a dark cloud, restricting its growth and threatening to turn the place into a ghost town, as 65% of the residents work for the state government.

The issue became a political tug-of-war between Anchorage and Southeast until the voters, faced with a billion-dollar price tag to reconstruct a capital at Willow, defeated the funding in 1982. Although the conflict will probably never go away, the state-wide vote gave Juneau new life and the town boomed in typical Alaskan fashion, literally bursting at its seams. McDonald's and Wendy's fast-food chains appeared, new office buildings sprang up and apartments and condominiums mushroomed. The sudden growth was too much too soon for many of the residents, who were disgusted at the sight of wooded hillsides being bulldozed.

Travellers will find Juneau to be a fine city offering a variety of accommodation, good restaurants and transport services. It also serves as the departure point for several wilderness attractions, including Glacier Bay National Park and Admiralty Island National Monument.

While downtown clings to a mountainside, the rest of the city sprawls over 3100 square miles (5000 km). There are five areas to Juneau, with downtown being the busiest and most popular among visitors during the summer. From here, Egan Drive – the only four-lane highway in Southeast – heads north and leads to Mendenhall Valley. Known to locals as simply 'The Valley', this area contains a growing residential section, much of Juneau's business district and the world-famous Mendenhall Glacier. In The Valley, Egan Drive turns into Glacier Highway, a two-lane road that takes you to Auke Bay, the site of the State Marine Ferry terminal and more boat harbours and the last spot to purchase food or gas to the end of the road at Echo Cove.

Across the channel is Douglas, a small town south of Juneau that at one time was the major city of the area. Follow the road out of the sleepy little town and you will be on Douglas Highway travelling north around Douglas Island to the fifth area known to locals as North Douglas. Located here are the Eagle Crest Ski Area, many scenic turn-offs and a lot of cabins and homes half-hidden in the trees and owned by those who work in Juneau but don't want to live in its hustle-bustle atmosphere.

Information

The main visitors information centre is the Davis Log Cabin at 134 Third St (tel 586-2201), open 8.30 am to 5 pm Monday to Friday and 10 am to 4 pm Saturday and Sunday. There are also smaller visitors booths at the Juneau Airport terminal out in The Valley, and at Marine Park on the downtown waterfront.

For information about cabin rentals,

hiking trails, Glacier Bay, Admiralty Island or any outdoor activity in the Tongass National Forest, stop at the Information Centre in the Centennial Building at 101 Egan Drive. The centre (tel 586-8751) is staffed by both USFS and National Park personnel and is open 8.30 am to 6 pm daily in the summer. For current fishing conditions and local hot spots the Alaska Fish & Game Department has a fishing hotline at 465-4116. The Alaska Division of State Parks also has an office in Juneau (tel 465-4563) at 500 Willoughby Avenue and is open 8 am to 4.30 pm Monday to Friday.

Things to See

Much of your sightseeing time will be spent downtown, where nothing more than a good pair of walking shoes is needed. Start at the **Marine Park**, a delightful waterfront park across from the Sealaska Building at the south end of Egan Drive, where there is an information kiosk, open daily from 9 am to 6 pm. Among the handouts they offer is a walking-tour map.

The tour leads you from the park along Ferry Way to **South Franklin St** where you begin ascending the street to the north. South Franklin St is now a historical district and underwent major renovation in 1985. The buildings along this stretch, many dating back to the early 1900s, have since been turned into bars, gift shops and restaurants and are stormed by mobs of visitors every time a cruise ship pulls in. In the next two blocks you will pass the two excellent book stores Heartside and Baranof. Both are good sources of Alaskan literature and material.

At the Baranof Hotel, the tour swings

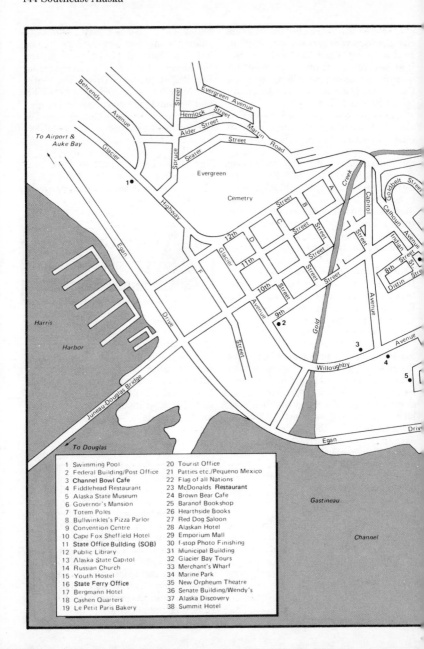

1 Swimming Pool
2 Federal Building/Post Office
3 **Channel Bowl Cafe**
4 Fiddlehead Restaurant
5 Alaska State Museum
6 Governor's Mansion
7 Totem Poles
8 Bullwinkles's Pizza Parlor
9 Convention Centre
10 Cape Fox Sheffield Hotel
11 **State Office Building (SOB)**
12 Public Library
13 Alaska State Capitol
14 Russian Church
15 Youth Hostel
16 **State Ferry Office**
17 Bergmann Hotel
18 Cashen Quarters
19 Le Petit Paris Bakery
20 Tourist Office
21 Patties etc./Pequeno Mexico
22 Flag of all Nations
23 McDonalds **Restaurant**
24 Brown Bear Cafe
25 Baranof Bookshop
26 Hearthside Books
27 Red Dog Saloon
28 Alaskan Hotel
29 Emporium Mall
30 f-stop Photo Finishing
31 Municipal Building
32 Glacier Bay Tours
33 Merchant's Wharf
34 Marine Park
35 New Orpheum Theatre
36 Senate Building/Wendy's
37 Alaska Discovery
38 Summit Hotel

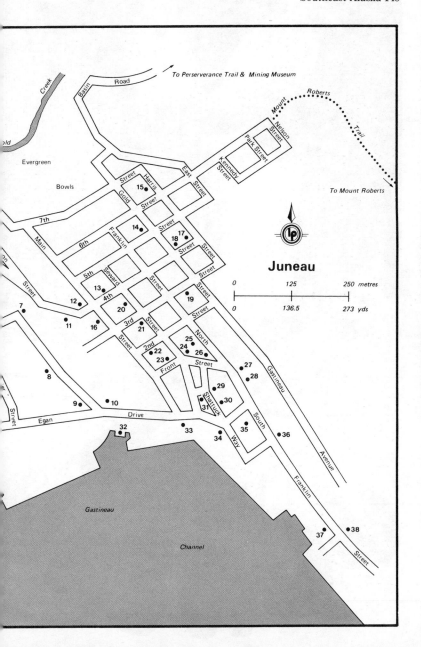

To Perserverance Trail & Mining Museum

Creek

Basin Road

Roberts

Mount

Trail

To Mount Roberts

Evergreen

Bowls

old

Nelson Street

Park Street

Kennedy Street

East Street

Harris Street

Gold Street

15

7th

Main

6th

Franklin

Street

14

Street

18 17

Street

Street

5th

Seward

Street

Street

13

12 4th

20

3rd

19

Street

North Street

Gastineau

Juneau

0   125   250 metres

0   136.5   273 yds

7

11

16

Street

21

2nd 22

23

Front Street

25

24 26

27

28

29

30

Shattuck

31

35

South Way

36

Franklin Avenue

8

9 10

Egan   Drive

32

33

34

37 38

Street

Gastineau

Channel

JUNEAU

left onto 2nd St and then quickly right onto Seward, where it passes the **Davis Log Cabin**, a replica of the first church in Juneau. The cabin is another visitor information centre that houses a small collection of local historical relics and objects. The next building up Seward St is the **Court Building**; here you swing a block to the east and then a block to the north, putting you at the corner of North Franklin and 5th Sts. Just down 5th St to the east is the **St Nicholas Russian Orthodox Church**, probably the most photographed structure in Juneau. The church was built in 1894, making it the oldest one in Southeast, and accepts a $1 donation for viewing the religious relics inside.

Heading back west on 5th St, descend Seward St and then turn west on 4th St to pass between the Court Building and the **State Capitol**, though you might not recognise it at first. The capitol looks more like an old junior high school in Brooklyn, New York than the seat of government in Alaska. Inside are the legislative chambers, the governor's office and offices for the hundreds of staff members who arrive in Juneau for the winter legislative session. Within the lobby is a visitors desk where free tours of the building are offered daily during the summer. The 45-minute tours start every 1½ hours or so from 8.30 am to 5 pm.

Continue a block west along 4th St and you'll reach the **Juneau Memorial Library**. Across from it is the **State Office Building** or the SOB as it is known locally. Inside the SOB on the eighth floor is the grand court which features a century-old totem pole and a restored 1928 Kimball organ played for office workers and visitors each Friday at noon. The **Alaska State Library** is also off the grand court. Most impressive is the panoramic view of Juneau's waterfront and Douglas Island from the adjoining outdoor balcony, an excellent place to have lunch on a sunny day.

At the SOB, 4th St curves north and becomes Calhoun Avenue; in a block it reaches the six-pillar **Governor's Mansion**. Built and furnished in 1912 at the cost of $44,000, the structure has a New England appearance but is accented by a totem pole, carved in 1940 by Tlingit Indians and presented to the governor as a gift. There are no regularly scheduled tours of the mansion. Cut behind the building on Indian St and follow it as it curves sharply down and to the left into 9th St. Following 9th St to the west leads you to the **Federal Building**, where on the first floor is the main post office. The Federal Building sits on the junction of 9th St and Glacier Avenue, a major bus stop where you can pick up buses to The Valley or to Douglas. By following Glacier Avenue back towards town you will arrive at a bridge over Gold Creek where a memorial plaque has been placed to honor Joe Juneau and Dick Harris, who stumbled upon gold in the icy stream.

Glacier Avenue curves east and becomes Willoughby Avenue. In a few blocks you reach Whittier St. Turn right on Whittier St and head halfway down to the **Alaska State Museum**, an impressive white building. The outstanding museum provides Alaskans with a showcase of their past, including artefacts from all four native groups: Athapaskan, Aleut, Eskimo and those on the Northwest Coast. There are also displays relating to the Russian period, major gold strikes in the state and the Alaska pipeline. By far the most impressive sight is the full-size, two-storey eagle nest where a circular staircase allows you to view it from all angles. The museum is open Monday to Friday from 9 am to 7 pm and Saturday and Sunday from 11 am to 7 pm, admission is free.

From Whittier St you can turn left onto Egan Drive and follow it east to the **Centennial Hall**, where there is a USFS Information Centre (tel 586-8751). The centre is open daily from 8.30 am to 5.30 pm and has handouts and information on hiking trails, USFS cabins and campgrounds in the area. The National Park

Service also staffs the centre and can provide information on Glacier Bay, while during the summer a variety of films and slide presentations is given in its adjoining theatre.

Continue on Egan Drive, and just before reaching Marine Park you come to the **Sealaska Building**, housing the headquarters for one of the state's most successful native corporations. Step inside the first floor lobby to view a Haida canoe, Chilkat blankets or the beautiful tapestry in the Bank of the North that was designed by Rie Munoz, a well-known Juneau artist.

Another attraction in the downtown area is at the top of Main St. After you have climbed the steep street, catch your breath and turn right on 7th St to arrive at the **House of Wickersham**, the historical home of Judge James Wickersham, the pioneer judge and statesman of Alaska. The home was taken over by the state in 1985 and tours were suspended due to renovation. Call the Alaska Division of Parks at tel 465-4563 concerning time and details of group tours, which were to resume in 1986.

Gold & Glaciers

Gold fever and gold mines built Juneau. Today there are several interesting and free places to view from what must have been an incredible era in Alaska's history.

The **Last Chance Mining Museum** is at the end of Basin Rd, a two-mile (3.2 km) walk from downtown. The museum was originally the old compressor house for the A-J Mine on Gastineau Channel and today houses tools, machinery, ore samples, mine cars and other relics of the golden past. To reach the museum, follow North Franklin St up the hill to its end and turn right on 6th St. Turn immediately left on Gold St, which will curve into Basin Rd. The museum is 0.5 mile (0.8 km) down the scenic road and is open from 2 to 8 pm daily. Admission is free.

At the end of nearby Perseverance Trail is the **Glory Hole**, a caved-in mine shaft that was connected to the A-J Mine, along with the remains of the **Silver Bowl Basin Mine** (see the Wilderness chapter for trail notes).

Perhaps the most interesting areas to explore are the old mining ruins across the channel near Douglas. From the turnaround for the Capital Transit bus in Douglas, continue south and swing down towards the **Sand Beach Recreation Area**, past the softball fields and Douglas Boat Harbor. The beach was made from the tailings of the Treadwell Mine, and the old pilings from its shipping dock still stand. Take one of the staircases from the beach to St Ann's St right above it and follow the street further south to Old Treadwell Rd. The dirt road leads to old foundations, the shells of boarding houses and the mine shaft – another Glory Hole – of the **Treadwell Mining Community**. The operation closed down in 1922 after a 1917 cave-in caused the financial collapse of the company. During its heyday at the turn of the century, the mine made Douglas the major city on the channel with a population of 15,000.

Across the channel from the Treadwell is the **Alaska-Juneau Mine** on the side of Mt Roberts. The mine closed down in 1944 after producing more than $80 million in gold when it was valued at $20 to $35 an ounce.

Juneau is also known as the 'Gateway to the Glaciers'. There are several in the area that can be viewed, including the **Mendenhall**, Alaska's famous drive-in glacier. The flow of ice is 13 miles (21 km) from downtown at the end of Glacier Spur Rd. Head out Egan Drive and at *Mile 9* (14.4 km) turn right onto Mendenhall Loop Rd, staying on Glacier Spur Rd when the loop curves north to head back to Auke Bay.

Today the Mendenhall flows 12 miles (19 km) from its source, the Juneau Icefield, and has a 1.5-mile (2.4 km) face. On a sunny day it's beautiful, with blue skies and snow-capped mountains in the background. On a cloudy and drizzly afternoon it can be even more impressive, as the ice turns different shades of deep blue. There is an interesting visitors centre with large relief map of the icefield and glaciers, audio-visual room with slide presentations and films, and an information desk. Within the area you can try one of several hiking trails, including a 0.5-mile (0.8 km) nature trail the East Glacier or Nugget Creek Trail (see Hiking section).

The cheapest way to see the glacier is to hop on a Capital Transit bus downtown and get off at the corner of Mendenhall Loop and Glacier Spur. The fare is 75c and buses depart from the State Capitol and the Federal Building every half hour or so. From the Loop Rd it is another mile (1.6 km) to the visitors centre. Then there is always hitch-hiking, a relatively easy method of travel in Juneau.

On your way out to Mendenhall Valley, look to your right high in the mountains when you pass Lemon Creek to see the remains of the **Lemon Creek Glacier**. By hiking you can get a close and uncrowded look at **Herbert Glacier** on *Mile 27.5* (43 km) or **Eagles Glacier** at *Mile 28.4* (45 km) of Glacier Highway (see Hiking section). One way to see all the glaciers and the icefield is to splurge on a flight-seeing charter. With four passengers, a 15 to 20-minute flight costs $40 to $60 per person and provides a spectacular overview of the icefield. All the air charter companies run them. LAB Flying Service (tel 789-9160) offers the scenic flights during the summer that depart from near the Marine Park at the downtown waterfront.

The most awe-inspiring way to view the Mendenhall Glacier is to walk on top of it. Alaska Discovery (tel 586-1911) offers a single-day guided walk that begins at their office at 418 South Franklin St at 8 am and lasts until 6 pm. The trip includes training in the use of crampons, ropes and ice-axes and involves hiking across the glacier to the first ice fall. No experience in mountaineering is needed and all

transportation, gear and lunch are provided. The cost is $90 per person for parties of two or three and $75 for groups of four or more.

Places to Stay

Hostels In the autumn of 1985, the Juneau *Youth Hostel* went from being just another church basement to being one of the best units in the Alaska AYH Council. The large yellow house is on the corner of Harris and 6th Sts in the colourful Starr Hill neighbourhood of downtown. Its location is ideal – five blocks from the State Capitol, four blocks from the Mt Roberts Trail, and two blocks from Basin Rd and the beginning of the scenic Gold Creek area. Inside are cooking facilities, showers and a common-room with a fireplace. Check-in time is 5 to 11 pm, check-out is 9 am and reservations are accepted if accompanied by the first night's fee and sent with a self-addressed, stamped envelope. Fees are $6.50 for AYH members and $8.50 for non-members. For reservations contact the Juneau Youth Hostel, PO Box 1543, Juneau, Alaska 99802; tel 586-9559.

Hotels Most hotels, especially the downtown ones, tend to be heavily booked during the summer tourist season. The cheapest hotel is the *Summit* (tel 586-2050), a small hotel across from the cold-storage plant on South Franklin St and it's the traditional dive in town. The owners recently redecorated the rooms, but it would still be wise to look before you rent. Singles cost $36 and doubles $39 with the bath down the hall.

Cashen Quarters (tel 586-9863) is a small hotel at 303 Gold St with only four rooms to rent. Each room has a three-quarters bath and cost $35 single.

Next door to the Red Dog Saloon on South Franklin St is the *Alaskan Hotel* (tel 586-1000), with its charming historical decor in both its lobby and rooms dating back to 1913 when it was first opened. Singles without baths are $36 a night and the hotel features private sauna rooms and an interesting bar in the back. Out the road there is the *Tides Motel* (tel 780-4622) on Glacier Highway in the Lemon Creek area, with singles for under $40.

Camping There are some fine campgrounds beyond The Valley and a dozen unofficial ones near downtown. One of the most beautiful USFS campgrounds in Alaska is *Mendenhall Lake*, 13 miles (21 km) from downtown and five miles (eight km) south from the Auke Bay ferry terminal. The campground (60 sites) is on Montana Creek Rd, a dirt road that runs off the back side of Mendenhall Loop Rd. The tent sites are alongside a lake and many have spectacular views of the nearby glacier. There is a 14-day limit and the nightly fee is $5 per site.

The other USFS campground is *Auke Village*, two miles (3.2 km) north of the ferry terminal on Glacier Highway. The area (11 sites) provides shelters, tables, wood and an interesting beach to walk along. The fee is also $5 per night with a 14-day limit.

Many backpackers prefer to stay close to the downtown area and end up hiking along Basin Rd. Where the road crosses Gold Creek there are some flat areas in the bush that serve as good spots to pitch a tent. If you have some time, it is even better to hike the Perseverance Trail off Basin Rd to Granite Creek trail and camp in the bowl at the end of this footpath (see the Wilderness chapter). Glacier Highway ends 41 miles (66 km) north of Juneau at a pleasant spot called *Echo Cove*. There are no developed facilities here, but it's a nice spot to camp for a while and a favourite among locals. There is usually good offshore salmon fishing in August. Other scenic but undeveloped areas are Eagle Beach out the road on Glacier Highway, and Fish Creek on North Douglas Highway.

Places to Eat

Juneau's size allows it to have an excellent cross-section of restaurants that no other Southeast town could possibly support. The best bargain for a full dinner during the summer is the *Gold Creek Salmon Bake*, near the Last Chance Mining Museum on Basin Rd and close to the Youth Hostel. The salmon bake costs $16 for an all-you-can-eat affair that includes salad, bread, your first beer and salmon that is cooked outside with a tangy brown sugar sauce. At the outdoor tables you can enjoy the spectacular mountain scenery.

Downtown The cheapest place for breakfast or lunch is the *Federal Building Cafeteria* on the second floor, which also provides a nice view of the Gastineau Channel for its diners. Open from 7 am to 3.30 pm, the restaurant offers eggs, potatoes, toast and bacon for $2.25, hamburgers for $1.80 and sandwiches for $1.10. Nearby is *Channel Bowl Café*, a local hangout on Willoughby Avenue across from Foodland Supermarket. Their portions are unbeatable for breakfast, as the blueberry pancakes for $3.75 literally hang over the plate, almost dragging on the floor. Try the 'Mt Jubo' breakfast for $4.50 if you've been out in the woods for a week.

McDonald's and *Wendy's*, two fast-food chains that also serve breakfast, are near each other. McDonald's is at the corner of 2nd and Seward Sts diagonally opposite the Sealaska Building, while Wendy's is in the Senate Building just over on South Franklin St.

Closer to the Youth Hostel at 299 North Franklin St is *Le Petit Paris*, which offers excellent croissants for 90c apiece and croissant sandwiches for $2.75 and up. The small corner bakery has very limited seating inside and is open from 7.15 am to 6 pm.

Cheap dinners of pizza or sandwiches can be obtained at *Bullwinkles' Pizza Parlor* across from the State Office

Building on Willoughby Avenue. Good-sized sandwiches cost between $3 and $6, while nine-inch pizzas begin at $4. There is also wine, a large selection of imported beer and silent movies on the back wall at night.

The best Mexican restaurant downtown is *El Sombrero* at 157 South Franklin St, where you can fill up on its huge tostada compuesta for $6.50. Almost across the street on the first floor of the Emporium Mall is *Bei Sing Chinese Restaurant* with its interesting interior, including pillow seats. Lunches are $5 to $6 and dinners begin at $10. Also in the Emporium is the *Heritage Coffee Co & Café*, a good spot for an afternoon break, as it serves various coffees, cappuccino, steamed milk and croissants (80c).

Another spot for afternoon tea is *Big City Books* on South Franklin St, across from the new parking structure, where you can enjoy your hot tea while checking out its large selection of travel books.

For a complete dinner, if you're not worrying about paying for your ferry ticket to Haines, try the *Fiddlehead Restaurant* on Willoughby Avenue. The food is excellent but dinners are priced from $13 to $20. The place is another good spot for afternoon tea and freshly baked foods. They occasionally have live folk music at night.

Bellezza Ristorante is Juneau's finest Italian restaurant, where entrees alone cost from $8 to $12. It is at 240 Main St in the Court Plaza Building, better known throughout town as the 'Spam Can' Building where the Alaska state ferry has a ticket office.

The *Summit Hotel Restaurant*, unlike its hotel counterpart upstairs, has a menu of gourmet dishes from $12 to $20 which are served in a tiny dining room that holds perhaps 15 people. It's an interesting little restaurant, but you have to call ahead (tel 586-2050) to reserve a table.

Douglas The best restaurant in Douglas is *Beauty & the Feast* next to the Billiken Bar at 916 Third St. The pub-like restaurant has excellent salads and omelettes. Sandwiches cost between $4 and $8.

The Valley A second *McDonald's* is on the corner of Egan Drive and Old Glacier Highway across from the Nugget Mall. In the shopping centre are several other restaurants, including *Pizzazz* which offers pizza for $7 to $12. In the Mendenhall Mall, on Mendenhall Loop Rd a short way from the Egan Drive junction, is another *Bullwinkle's Pizza Parlor* which has a lunch buffet with all the pizza and salad you can eat for $5.

On Old Glacier Highway near the side road to the airport is *Fernando's*, a good Mexican restaurant with dinners priced from $9 to $15. Diagonally opposite the Mexican eatery is Airport Mall, where *Trapper's In & Out* is the cheapest place in The Valley for breakfast after McDonald's.

Seafood Juneau's fishing fleet is nowhere near the size of those in Ketchikan or Petersburg, but there are still a number of places to obtain Alaska's delicacies from the sea. Downtown, *Foodland Supermarket* on Willoughby Avenue across from the Federal Building has a good selection of local seafood, including salmon, halibut, prawns and crab legs.

Out in The Valley, *Jerry's Meats* across from McDonald's also has a fine selection, with probably the best prices in the area. The *Great Alaska Fish Company* at 285 South Franklin St specialises in shipping seafood home with visitors; they serve a good halibut sandwich for $5 and a large steaming bowl of seafood chowder. The seating inside is limited.

Finally, as you are strolling around town, look for the occasional fishermen selling prawns, crabs and halibut from their boats at several spots along the waterfront, including the City Dock on South Franklin St and the Auke Bay Harbor out the road.

Nightlife

With a population that is larger, younger and a little more cultured than that of most other Southeast towns, Juneau is able to support a great deal more nightlife. The most famous nightspot is the *Red Dog Saloon*, more of a tourist attraction than a place to have a beer. Next door to the Alaskan Hotel on South Franklin St, the saloon is mentioned in every travel brochure and is the final destination of every tour bus. The bar is interesting, with its sawdust floor and relics covering the walls, but the Red Dog is not a place to spend an entire evening drinking unless you can put up with instamatic cameras flashing at the stuffed bear. The best time to go is after 11 pm.

South Franklin as a whole is Juneau's drinking section. Many places are local hangouts that will undoubtedly turn you off – which is fine with those leaning against the bar inside. The *Triangle Club*, however, is a pleasant little spot on the corner of Front and South Franklin Sts. Though there is limited seating inside, the bar offers wide-screen television and a good hot-dog to go along with a mug of beer.

Hidden in the back of the *Alaskan Hotel* is a unique bar with an interior and cash register that match the rest of the hotel's historical setting. Just down the street at the top of the Senate Building where Wendy's is, you'll find *The Penthouse*. The bar, which was the first in Juneau to enforce a dress code after 7 pm, has music, dancing and a huge video screen. Many locals beat the code and high prices by going during 'happy hour' to enjoy a drink and the fine views of downtown Juneau.

A little quieter and at the other end of downtown is the *Breakwater Inn* on Glacier Avenue past the high school. The bar is on the second floor and overlooks the Aurora Basin Boat Harbor, an active place in the summer. On the other side of the channel in Douglas, there are two bars across the street from each other and

similar in atmosphere. *Billikens* and *Louie's* on Douglas Highway are favourites with locals, especially softball players who hold their games at nearby Sandy Beach Recreational Area.

Juneau also supports a unique movie theatre which on nice summer days doubles as an outdoor café. The *New Orpheum Theatre & Café* is off Marine Way across from the south end of Marine Park and specialises in classic movies in a small, 30-seat theatre. The other half of the place is a café and local artist gallery that stays open until midnight and serves cappuccino and espresso coffee along with pastries, ice-cream pies, salads and soups. Every week the owners hold a 'Tightwad Tuesday' when movie admission is lowered to $4 per person.

Another way to spend an evening is soaking in a hot tub or breaking a sweat in a sauna, a favourite activity among all Alaskans. The *Augustus Brown Pool* on Glacier Avenue next to the high school has a large 20-person sauna along with a pool and exercise area. There is a variety of swimming periods, including one at night from Monday to Thursday. Admission ranges from 75c to $3 per session. For a more private evening, rent out one of the hot-tub rooms at the Alaskan Hotel, designed for two or three persons and including sauna and shower. The cost is $10 per person per hour and you should call ahead to reserve it (tel 586-1000). The Summit Hotel also has saunas.

Events

Juneau's main festival during the summer is the Fourth of July, when the celebration includes a parade, a carnival, fireworks over the channel and a lot of outdoor feeds from Sandy Beach in Douglas to downtown Juneau. If you happen to be there early enough, in mid-April there is the week-long Alaska Folk Festival.

Hiking

Few cities, if any, in Alaska have the

many diverse hiking trails Juneau has. To spend time here without taking at least a one-day hike is to miss the area's top attraction. The USFS maintains 20 trails which are described in its booklet *Juneau Trails*, available from the information centre in the Centennial Building.

For those who don't feel up to taking a trail on their own, Juneau Parks & Recreation holds adult hikes every Wednesday and family hikes along easier trails every Saturday. The hikes begin at the trailhead at 10 am; on Wednesday there is often car-pooling to the spot, with hikers meeting at Cope Park downtown, a short walk from the Youth Hostel. For more information call Parks & Recreation at 586-5226.

Perseverance Trail This trail system on Basin Rd is the most popular one in Juneau and includes the trails of Perseverance, Mt Juneau and Granite Creek. For more information turn to the Wilderness chapter.

Mt Roberts Trail This is the other hike next door to the Youth Hostel and it climbs four miles (6.4 km) to the mountain above the city. The trail begins at a marked wooden staircase at the end of 6th St and consists of a series of switchbacks with good resting spots. When you break out of the trees at Gastineau Peak you come across a wooden cross and good views of Juneau, Douglas and the entire Gastineau Channel. The Mt Roberts summit is a steep climb through the alpine brush to the north.

Dan Moller Trail The 3.3-mile (5.3-km) trail leads to an alpine area at the crest of Douglas Island where there is a USFS cabin (reservations needed, $10 per night). For trail notes turn to the Wilderness chapter.

Treadwell Ditch Trail Also in Douglas, this trail can be picked up either one mile (1.6 km) up the Dan Moller Trail or just above

D St in downtown Douglas. The trail stretches 12 miles (19 km) from Douglas north to Eaglecrest, although most people hike only the five miles (eight km) to the Dan Moller Trail and then return to the road. The path is rated easy and provides views of the Gastineau Channel while winding through scenic muskeg meadows.

Mt Bradley Trail The 2.6-mile (4.2-km) trail begins in Douglas through a vacant lot behind the 300 section of 5th St and is a much harder climb than hikes up either Mt Roberts or Mt Juneau. Both rubber boots and sturdy hiking boots are needed, as the trail can be muddy in the lower sections before you reach the beautiful alpine areas above the treeline. The climb to the 3337-foot (1017-metre) peak should only be attempted by experienced hikers.

Cropley Lake Trail One other trail on Douglas Island is the 1.5-mile (2.4-km) route to Cropley Lake. The trail was built primarily for Nordic skiing but in the summer it can be hiked to the alpine lake, which provides good scenery and camping possibilities. The start is up Fish Creek Rd, a short way past the Eaglecrest Ski Lodge in a creek gully to the right. An easier way to reach the lake is to take the chairlift up during the summer. Round-trip fare is $10 per person.

Sheep Creek Trail South of Juneau along Thane Rd is the very scenic Sheep Creek Trail, a three-mile (4.8-km) walk into the valley south of Mt Roberts where there are many historical mining relics. The trailhead is four miles (6.4 km) south of Juneau at a staircase on the gravel spur to a substation of the Snettisham power plant. The trail is relatively level in the valley, from where you scramble up forested hillsides to the alpine zone. Many hikers follow the power-line once they are above the treeline to reach the ridge to Sheep Mountain. It is possible to continue from Sheep Mountain over Mt

Roberts and return to Juneau along the Mt Roberts Trail. This would be a very long 10 to 12-hour day if attempted.

Point Bishop Trail At the end of Thane Rd, 7.5 miles (12 km) south of Juneau, is this eight-mile (13-km) trail to Point Bishop, a scenic spot that overlooks the junction between Stephens Passage and Taku Inlet. The trail is level but can be wet in many spots, making waterproof boots the preferred footwear. The hike makes for an ideal overnight trip, as there is good camping at Point Bishop.

East Glacier Trail The first of several trails near the Mendenhall Glacier is this three-mile (4.8-km) round trip that provides good views of the glacier from a scenic overlook at the halfway point. The trail begins off the half-mile nature walk near the Mendenhall Glacier Visitor Centre and then returns to it at Steep Creek.

Nugget Creek Trail Just beyond East Glacier Trail's scenic overlook is the start of the 2.5-mile (four-km) Nugget Creek Trail to the Vista Creek Shelter, a free-use shelter that doesn't require reservations. The total round trip to the shelter from the Visitor Centre is eight miles (13 km). Those who plan to spend the night at the shelter can continue along the creek towards Nugget Glacier, though the route is bushy and hard to follow at times.

West Glacier Trail This is easily one of the most spectacular trails in the Juneau area. The 3.4-mile (5.4-km) trail begins at the end of Montana Creek Rd past Mendenhall Lake Campground and hugs the mountainside along the glacier, providing exceptional views of the ice-falls and other glacial features. It ends at a rocky outcrop but a rough route continues from here to the summit of Mt McGinnis, another two miles (3.2 km) away. Plan on four to five hours for the West Glacier Trail, an easy hike that can

be done in tennis shoes; or plan on a long day if you who want to tackle the difficult Mt McGinnis route.

Montana Creek-Windfall Lake Trails These two trails connect at Windfall Lake and can be combined for an interesting overnight trip of 13 miles (21 km). It is easier to begin at Montana Creek and follow the Windfall Lake Trail out to Glacier Highway.

The 9.5-mile (15.3-km) Montana Creek Trail, known for its high concentration of bears, begins near the end of Montana Creek Rd near a rifle range. The 3.5-mile (5.6-km) Windfall Lake Trail begins off a gravel spur that leaves the Glacier Highway just before it crosses Herbert River, 27 miles (43 km) north of downtown Juneau. Wear rubber boots as either trail can be muddy during the summer although the worst parts are planked.

Spaulding Trail This trail's primary use is in the winter for Nordic skiing, but it can be hiked in the summer if you are prepared for some muddy sections. The three-mile (4.8-km) trail provides access to the Auke Nu Trail that leads to the John Muir USFS Cabin (reservations needed, $10 per night). The Spaulding trailhead is at Glacier Highway just past and opposite the Auke Bay Post Office, 12.3 miles (20 km) from Juneau. Check at the information centre in the Centennial Building about the availability of the cabin.

Peterson Lake Trail Further out the road is this four-mile trail that provides access to good Dolly Varden fishing in both Peterson Creek and Peterson Lake. The trailhead has been moved to avoid private property and is now located 20 feet (six metres) before the *Mile 24* marker on Glacier Highway, north of the Shrine of St Terese. Wear rubber boots, as it can be muddy during the summer.

Herbert Glacier Trail This level trail extends 4.6 miles (7.4 km) along Herbert River to Herbert Glacier at its end. The trail is easy, though wet in some places, and the round trip takes four to five hours. The trail begins just past the bridge over Herbert River at *Mile 28* (45 km) of Glacier Highway in a small parking lot to the left.

Amalga Trail Also known as Eagle Glacier Trail, this level route winds 5.5 miles (8.8 km) one way to the lake formed by Eagle Glacier, 0.8 mile (1.3 km) from its face. The trailhead is just beyond the Glacier Highway bridge across Eagle River, 0.4 mile (0.6 km) past the trailhead to Herbert Glacier Trail. Plan on a round trip of seven to eight hours to reach the impressive glacier.

Paddling

Both day-trips and extended paddles of three to five days are possible out of Juneau in sea-touring kayaks. Boats can be rented from Alaska Discovery (tel 586-1911) on the waterfront at 418 South Franklin St – $30 for doubles and $25 for singles per day, or $5 per hour. A common afternoon trip is to depart from the dock below the Alaska Discovery office and paddle to downtown Douglas and back.

Topographic maps can be obtained downtown from either Foggy Mountain Shop (tel 586-6780) in the Emporium Mall off Shattuck Way, or Baranof Books (tel 586-2130) on 100 North Franklin St. The bulletin boards at Foggy Mountain and Alaska Discovery are good places to check for used kayaks or canoes for sale. If you have the funds, purchasing and reselling the boat in Juneau is a cheap alternative to renting one for long-term paddles.

Taku Inlet This waterway is an excellent four to five-day trip highlighted by close views of Taku Glacier. Total paddling distance would be 30 to 40 miles (48 to 64 km) depending on how far you travel up

the inlet. It does not require any major crossing, though rounding Point Bishop can be rough at times. There are camping possibilities at Point Bishop and along the grassy area south-west of the glacier, where brown bears are occasionally spotted.

Berners Bay At the end of the road, 40 miles (64 km) from Juneau, is Echo Cove where kayakers put in for paddles into the protected waters of Berners Bay. The bay extends 12 miles (19 km) north to the outlets of Antler, Lace and Berners rivers and is ideal for an overnight trip or longer excursions up Berners River.

Oliver Inlet At the north-east corner of Admiralty Island is Oliver Inlet, where a 0.8-mile (1.3-km) portage trail connects it to scenic Seymour Canal. The paddle to the inlet is 18 miles (29 km) and involves crossing Stephens Passage, a challenging open-water crossing for experienced kayakers only. At the south end of the portage trail from Oliver Inlet is the USFS Seymour Cabin (reservations needed, $10 per night).

USFS Cabins

From Juneau, numerous USFS cabins are accessible but all are heavily used, requiring reservations as much as 180 days in advance. If you're just passing through, however, check the USFS information centre in the Centennial Building, where staff members maintain a cabin update listing that shows which units are still available and when.

Already mentioned above have been John Muir and Dan Moller cabins, accessible by foot trail from the Juneau road system, and Seymour Canal Cabin at the south end of the portage from Oliver Inlet. The following are the cabins within 30-minutes flying time from Juneau, for which the charter cost would run to $150 to $200 per person for both drop-off and pick-up. Both Channel Flying (tel 586-3331) and LAB Flying

Service (tel 789-9160) can provide air service on limited notice.

West Turner One of the most scenic and by far the most popular cabin in the Juneau area, the unit is 30 minutes air time from the Capital City on the west end of Turner Lake, where there is good fishing for trout, Dolly Varden and salmon. A skiff is provided.

Admiralty Cove A new cabin was built on this scenic bay in 1983. It has access to Young Lake along a very rough 4.5-mile (seven-km) trail. The unit is 30 minutes from Juneau in a tidal area where floatplanes can land only during high tide. Brown bears frequent the area.

Young Lake At each end of the lake is a USFS cabin, both provided with a skiff. The lake offers good fishing for cut-throat trout and land-locked salmon. An over-grown trail connects North Young Lake Cabin with Admiralty Cove. There is no trail between South Young Lake Cabin and the unit at the north end.

Tours

Tracy Arm is a steep-sided fjord, highlighted by a pair of tidewater glaciers at its end and a gallery of icebergs that float down the length of it. Located 50 miles (80 km) south-east of Juneau, the fjord makes an interesting day trip. Alaska Riviera (tel 586-9888) offers day cruises to the end of the arm five days a week, Tuesday to Saturday. The 10-hour trip departs at 8 am and costs $129 per person. The company also offers a kayaker's special for those who want to be dropped off for a few days for some scenic paddling (see the Wilderness chapter).

A number of companies offer city tours through Juneau and the surrounding area for those travellers with limited time. All cost around $20 per person. Perhaps the best of them is by Midnight Sun Discovery (tel 586-8155), which offers a three-hour city-and-glacier tour. This company takes small groups around in vans rather than herding large groups around in buses. The tour, which includes Auke Bay, a salmon hatchery and the Mendenhall Wetlands, departs daily from the Alaskan, Baranof and Cape Fox hotels.

Alaska Up Close (tel 789-9544) offers an ArtAlaska Tour in which visitors are taken into the private studios and galleries of Juneau artists. The 2½-hour tour costs $20 per person. The company also runs group tours to the Eaglecrest alpine area via the chairlift on a four-hour adventure for $30 per person.

Getting There & Around

Airport & Ferry Terminal Transportation could be a problem when you're arriving in Juneau at either the airport or the Auke Bay Ferry Terminal. Late-night arrivals who want to head downtown are best off hopping on the Capital ConnX'n vans and buses that meet all airport and ferry arrivals. Fares to downtown, per person, are $5 from the airport and $6 from Auke Bay. For more information about pick-up points in the downtown area, call 780-4677.

During the day travellers have more of an option. Hitch-hiking is easy in the area, as along as you are not rushed to make a ferry and if you avoid thumbing along four-lane Egan Drive. It is also possible to walk to the nearest public bus stop for a 75c ride into town. From the ferry terminal, walk south along the Glacier Highway for a little over a mile (1.6 km) to Dehart's Grocery Store near the Auke Bay Terminal. From the airport, just stroll from the terminal to Airport Mall on Old Glacier Highway.

Air Alaska Airlines (tel 789-0600) has scheduled services to Seattle, all major Southeast communities, Glacier Bay and Anchorage, and Cordova daily during the summer. One-way fare from Juneau north to Anchorage is $176; even better is Juneau-Cordova for $120. This would allow you to continue travelling on the state ferries to Valdez, Seward, Homer and Kodiak. Western Airlines (tel 789-4140) has daily scheduled flights out of Juneau to Anchorage, Fairbanks and Seattle. Both airlines have a ticket office in the Baranof Hotel downtown on South Franklin St.

The smaller air service companies have a number of scheduled flights to small communities in the area that would be considerably cheaper than chartering a plane there. LAB (tel 789-9160) flies to Hoonah for $47 one way and $70 round trip. Channel Flying (tel 586-3331) offers a $45-per-seat flight to Tenakee Springs, $68 to Pelican and $57 to Angoon. On Friday, Tuesday and Sunday evenings Skagway Air (tel 789-2006) flies to Skagway for $45 one way, only $16 over the price of the ferry ticket.

Boat The state ferry no longer uses the downtown terminal, but makes all its arrivals and departures at the Auke Bay Terminal. This is a hassle for budget travellers but it made the downtown businesses happy as it opened up another dock to large 'Love Boat' cruise ships, the real money spenders.

There are daily departures during the summer from Juneau with passage to Sitka and Petersburg $29, Ketchikan $54, Haines $19 and Skagway $24. The smaller *Le Conte* connects Juneau to Hoonah, Angoon and Tenakee Springs. The downtown ferry ticket office is on the ground floor of the silver Court Plaza Building on Main St near the State Office Building. You can either call that office (465-3941) or the Auke Bay terminal (465-3940) for information.

Bus Capital Transit, Juneau's public bus system, runs every half hour during the week with alternating local and express service from 7.30 am until 6 pm. After 6 pm and on Saturdays, only local service is available every hour. The main route circles downtown, stopping at the City Dock Ferry Terminal, Capitol Building and the Federal Building, and then heads out to The Valley and Auke Bay Boat Harbour via the Mendenhall Loop Rd, where it comes close to the Mendenhall Lake Campground. There is also a mini-bus that runs every hour from the downtown stops to Douglas. Fares are 50c per zone and 75c for two zones.

In 1984, Capital Transit began a free downtown shuttle bus to help reduce heavy traffic congestion. The Downtown Shuttle buses run every 12 minutes or so during weekdays and every half hour at night and on Saturday. The route includes Franklin St, Main St, Willoughby Avenue and Glacier Avenue past the high school. For more information call 789-6901.

Car Rental There are several used-car rental places in Juneau for those needing a vehicle. Used cars cost $20 per day and 20c per mile and can be obtained from Rent-A-Dent (tel 789-9000), Rent-A-Wreck (tel 789-4111) and Ugly Duckling Rentals (tel 789-1939). Holiday Payless (tel 780-4ll8) rents cars for $25 per day with no mileage fee.

Bicycle Another good way to get around during a day of sightseeing is to rent a bicycle at Alaska Discovery on 419 South Franklin St. The three, five and ten-speed bikes rent for $2 an hour or $12 overnight. Juneau has an excellent system of bike paths, including ones that parallel Glacier Highway and Egan Drive out to The Valley and the Mendenhall Loop Rd.

AROUND JUNEAU
Eaglecrest is Juneau's superb downhill ski area, 12 miles (19.2 km) from downtown off North Douglas Rd. The mile-long chairlift, which takes you 3000 feet (915 metres) above sea level to a scenic alpine area on top of Douglas Island, continues to run during the summer. The views are great and there are boardwalk trails to follow for a close look at the alpine terrain. The lift is open daily at 11 am and the ride is $10 per person. Either hitch-

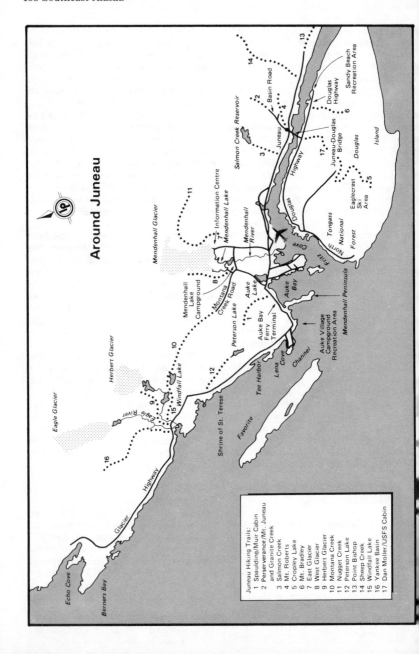

Around Juneau

Juneau Hiking Trails:
1 Spaulding/Muir Cabin
2 Perseverance/Mt. Juneau
  and Granite Creek
3 Salmon Creek
4 Mt. Roberts
5 Cropley Lake
6 Mt. Bradley
7 East Glacier
8 West Glacier
9 Herbert Glacier
10 Montana Creek
11 Nugget Creek
12 Peterson Lake
13 Point Bishop
14 Sheep Creek
15 Windfall Lake
16 Yankee Basin
17 Dan Moller/USFS Cabin

hike out North Douglas Rd to Fish Creek Rd, which climbs to the Eaglecrest, or call Gray Line Sightseeing (tel 586-6464) which run a tour to the area.

Other sights that lie 'out the road' include the **Auke Bay Marine Lab**, 12.5 miles (20 km) north of downtown or one mile (1.6 km) south of the State Marine Ferry terminal. The research facility has a self-guided tour of displays and salt-water tanks and is open from 8 am to 4.30 pm on weekdays. South of the lab on the shores of Auke Lake is the **University of Alaska** – Juneau campus, a small college in a beautiful setting. Among the many classroom buildings are a student union and a bookstore.

At *Mile 23.3* (37 km) of Glacier Highway is the **shrine of St Terese**, a natural stone chapel on its own island that is connected to the shore by a stone causeway. As well as being the site of numerous weddings, the island is situated along the Breadline, a well-known salmon fishing area in Juneau. This is perhaps the best place to fish for salmon from the shore.

Scenic viewing points include North Douglas Rd for a look at Fritz Cove and Mendenhall Glacier from afar, and **Eagle Beach Recreation Area** at *Mile 28.6* (46 km) of Glacier Highway for stunning views of the Chilkat Mountains and Lynn Canal. Bird enthusiasts should stop at the scenic look-out at *Mile 6* (9.6 km) of Egan Drive, which overlooks the **Mendenhall Wetlands & Refuge**. A viewing platform is located there with sign-boards that explain the natural history of the refuge.

If the temperatures soar above 80°F (26.6°C), head over to **Sandy Beach** and watch the pale locals cram in as much suntanning as they can under the midnight sun.

ANGOON

The lone settlement on Admiralty Island is Angoon, a predominantly Tlingit community of 560 residents. Tlingit tribes occupied the site for centuries, but the original village was wiped out in 1882 when the US Navy, sailing out of Sitka, bombarded the natives after they staged an uprising against a local whaling company. Today the economy is a mixture of commercial fishing and subsistence, while in town the strong native heritage is evident in the painted fronts of the 15 tribal community houses. The old life-style is still apparent in this remote community, and time in Angoon is spent observing and understanding someone else's culture rather than enjoying your own. Tourism seems to be tolerated only because the village is a port-of-call for the state ferry.

Angoon has a total of three miles (4.8 km) of road. The village itself is at one end, perched on a strip of land between Chatham Strait on the west coast of Admiralty Island, and turbulent Kootz-nahoo Inlet that leads into the interior of the national monument. The community serves as the final departure point for many kayak and canoe trips into the heart of the monument, including the 32-mile (51-km) Cross Admiralty Canoe Route to Mole Harbour (see the Wilderness chapter).

Many people are content to just spend a few days paddling and fishing Mitchell Bay and Salt Lake. Alaska Discovery rents canoes for $30 a day in Angoon at the Angoon Trading Company (tel 788-3111) on Kootznahoo Rd. Before undertaking such an adventure, stop at the USFS office (tel 788-3166) in the City Office Building on Flagstaff Rd for information on the tides in Kootznahoo Inlet and Mitchell Bay. The tides here are among the strongest in the world. The walk between the airport and the town allows you to view the boiling waters at mid-tide.

There are approximately two south-bound ferries and two north-bound ones stopping at Angoon every week during the summer. Channel Flying also has daily flights to Juneau for $57 per person. In Angoon contact the air service outfit at 788-3641.

Places to Stay & Eat

By far the best place to stay in Angoon is the *Favorite Bay Inn* (tel 788-3123) in Dick Powers' large, rambling home two miles (3.2 km) from the ferry terminal. A bed and a hearty breakfast cost $25 per person.

Angoon is a dry community and the only café in town is *The Surf Deli*, a hangout for teenagers at night. Groceries and limited supplies can be picked up at the Angoon Trading Company or the Seaside Store on Chatham St.

GLACIER BAY & GUSTAVUS

Sixteen tidewater glaciers spilling out of the mountains and filling the sea with icebergs of all shapes, sizes and shades of blue have made Glacier Bay National Park & Preserve an icy wilderness renowned throughout the world. When Captain George Vancouver sailed through the ice-choked waters of Icy Strait in 1774, Glacier Bay was little more than a dent in a mountain of ice. Less than a century later John Muir had made his legendary discovery of Glacier Bay and found that the end had retreated 20 miles (32 km) up bay. Today the glacier that bears his name is 60 miles (96 km) from Icy Strait and in its rapid retreat has revealed plants and animals which have fascinated naturalists since 1916.

Apart from having the world's largest concentration of tidewater glaciers, Glacier Bay is the habitat for a variety of marine life, including whales. The park supports three types of the warm-blooded mammal, with the humpbacks being by far the most impressive and acrobatic as they heave their massive bodies out of the water in leaps known as breaching. Adult

Top: Freight barge on the Yukon River at Circle, Alaska (PZ)
Bottom: Fish wheel on the banks of the Yukon River (JD)

Top: Rafters in Alsek Bay with iceberg in background (AD)
Bottom: Salmon roast on the outside coast of Glacier Bay (JD)

humpbacks can often reach lengths of 40 to 50 feet (12 to 15 metres) and weigh up to nine tons. Other marine life includes harbour seals, porpoises, killer whales and sea otters, while on land, brown and black bears roam along with wolves, moose and over 200 species of birds.

Glacier Bay is a park of contrasts. It is lush spruce/hemlock forests and bare shores recently exposed by glaciers; steep fjords up bay; and the flat terrain around Gustavus, an inlet full of icebergs set aglow by a fiery sunset.

The park is many things to many people, but to nobody is it a cheap side trip. Of the 130,000 annual visitors, over 100,000 of them arrive aboard a cruise ship and never leave the boat. The rest are a mixture of tour-group members who head straight for the lodge and back-packers who wander towards the free campground. Plan on spending at least $200 for a trip to Glacier Bay out of Juneau, but remember that the cost per day of visiting the area drops quickly after you've arrived.

Gustavus

The park is serviced by a small settlement called Gustavus, an interesting back-country community of 150 residents. Among the citizens of Gustavus are a mixture of professional people – doctors, lawyers, former government workers and artists – who decided to drop out of the rat race of city life and live on their own in the middle of the woods. Electricity only arrived in the area in the early 1980s, and in most homes you still have to pump the water at the sink or build a fire before you can have a hot shower.

There is no 'downtown' section in Gustavus; the town is merely an airstrip left over from the military build-up of WW II, and a road from it to Bartlett Cove, known to locals as 'The Road'. They refer to every other road and dirt path in the area as 'The Other Road' regardless of which one they are talking about. Along The Road there is little to see, as most cabins and homes are tucked away behind a shield of trees. The heart of Gustavus is the bridge over the Salmon River; near it is the town's park, the

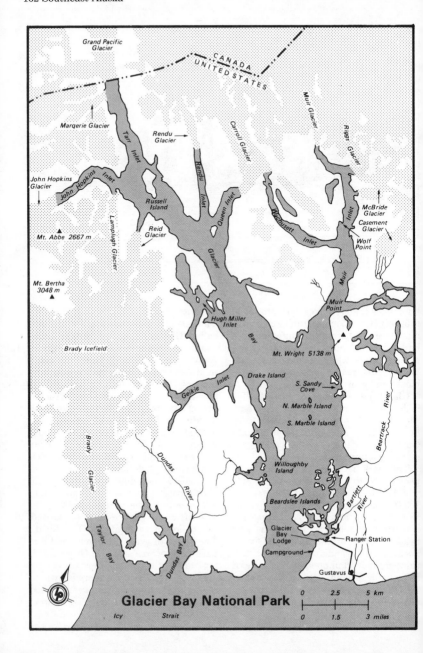

Glacier Bay National Park

Gustavus Inn and the only grocery store in the area.

Places to Stay & Eat *The Gustavus Inn* (tel 697-2254) is a charming, family homestead lodge with space for 20 people in 10 rooms. The inn is mentioned in every travel book and brochure on Alaska and rooms are hard to obtain at the last minute. Nightly rates are $70 per person and include meals. The inn is really known for its gourmet dinners, served family style and including home-grown vegetables and entrees of local seafood such as salmon, crab, halibut and trout. Dinners cost $20 per person and you have to call ahead for a space at the table. Just north of the Salmon River bridge is the dirt road that leads east to the *Hitching Post*, the only other eatery in Gustavus. It offers a limited menu of hamburgers and sandwiches.

An alternative for lodging in Gustavus is *Salmon River Cabins* (tel 697-2245), on another The Other Road that heads east just before you cross the bridge. Cabins rent for $40 per night and can accommodate up to four people. Each has a wood-burning stove and a gas campstove for cooking. The place rents bicycles for $5 per day. There is also a *Gustavus Bed & Breakfast Association* (tel 697-3441) which offers half a dozen cabins, rooms or just a loft for rent. Nightly rates range from $30 to $45 and include breakfast.

Bartlett Cove

Bartlett Cove is the park headquarters and includes the Glacier Bay Lodge, a restaurant, a visitors information centre, a campground and the main dock where the tour boats depart for excursions up bay. The cove lies within the park but is still some 40 miles (65 km) south and another high-priced trip away from the nearest glacier. The campground is free and always seems to have space. It is 0.25 mile (0.4 km) south of the lodge in a lush forest just off the shoreline. It provides a bear cache, eating shelter and pleasant surroundings in which to pitch a tent. At the foot of the dock is the park's visitors centre where you can obtain backcountry permits, seek out information or purchase a variety of books or topographic maps that cover the park. Showers are available in the park at $2.50 a turn, but there is no place that sells groceries or camping supplies.

From Bartlett Cove there are two ways to venture up bay without having to paddle. The tour boat *Thunder Bay* departs every morning from the dock for a day trip up the East Arm to Muir Inlet. The cost is $99.50 and includes viewing three glaciers and usually a variety of wildlife and birdlife. The *Glacier Bay Explorer* also departs daily but stops overnight in Tarr Inlet within sight of two glaciers in the spectacular West Arm. The fare is $150 and includes a berth and meals.

At night in Bartlett Cove there is a crackling fire in the lodge's huge stone fireplace while the adjoining bar usually hums with an interesting mixture of park employees, visitors, backpackers and locals from Gustavus. Nightly slide presentations, ranger talks and movies held upstairs cover the natural history of the park.

Hiking

Glacier Bay is a trail-less park, and in the backcountry foot travel is done along riverbanks, on ridges or across ice remnants of glaciers. The only developed trails are in Bartlett Cove.

Forest Trail This one-mile (1.6-km) nature walk begins and ends near the dock and winds through the pond-studded spruce/hemlock forest near the campground. There are daily ranger-led walks along this trail; inquire at the lodge.

Bartlett River Trail This 1.5-mile (3.2-km) trail begins just up the road to Gustavus – where there is a posted trailhead – and ends at the Bartlett River estuary. Along the way it meanders along a tidal lagoon and passes through a few wet spots. Plan on two to four hours for the round trip of three miles (4.8 km).

Point Gustavus Beach Walk The shoreline south of Bartlett Cove to Point Gustavus and beyond to the community of Gustavus provides the only overnight possibility from the park headquarters. The total distance is 12 miles (19 km) while the walk to Point Gustavus, an excellent spot to camp, is six miles (9.6 km). Plan on hiking the stretch from the point to Gustavus at low tide, which will allow you to ford the Salmon River as opposed to swimming across it. Point Gustavus is an excellent place to sight killer whales in Icy Strait.

Up Bay It is still possible for backpackers to explore the park's backcountry without getting in a kayak. The *Thunder Bay* drops off and picks up hikers at three points within the East Arm for the fare of $115, which includes an extra charge for letting you off. Two of them are suitable for pitching a tent and spending some time undertaking day hikes from. The first is at Wolf Point (see the Wilderness chapter) and the other is further up bay at Riggs Glacier. Here you can unroll your sleeping bag in front of the calving Riggs Glacier and spend a day hiking along the black ice of the McBride remnant or scaling McDonnell Ridge to the south.

Paddling

Glacier Bay offers an excellent opportunity for paddlers still developing their kayaking skills. By utilising the tour boats it is possible to skip the long and open paddle up bay and enjoy only the well-protected arms and inlets where the glaciers are located. Kayaks with skirts, paddles, life vests and foot-controlled rudders can be rented from Alaska Discovery (tel 697-2257), but reservations are strongly recommended for trips in July and August. The rigid doubles rent

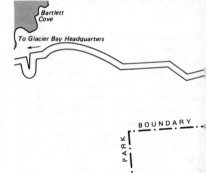

for $30 per day. The drop-offs and pick-ups in the East Arm are made by the *Thunder Bay*, which charges $115 for a round-trip ticket. Most paddlers disembark at Riggs Glacier and spend three or four days paddling up to Muir Glacier or down to Wolf Point, where they board the *Thunder Bay* for a return trip to Bartlett Cove.

The *Glacier Bay Explorer* will drop off and pick up kayakers near Lamplugh Glacier in the spectacular West Arm for a round-trip fare of $149. This would allow kayakers to paddle into John Hopkins and Tarr Inlets, the ice-choked waterways that best symbolise Glacier Bay. If you have two weeks to spare, the best trip and the cheapest way up bay is to purchase a drop-off only on the *Glacier Bay Explorer* for $64 and then paddle back to Bartlett Cove after exploring the West Arm. This requires two major open-water crossings and should only be attempted by experienced kayakers.

For those who want to avoid the tour boat fares but still long for a mild kayak adventure, there are the Breadslee Islands.

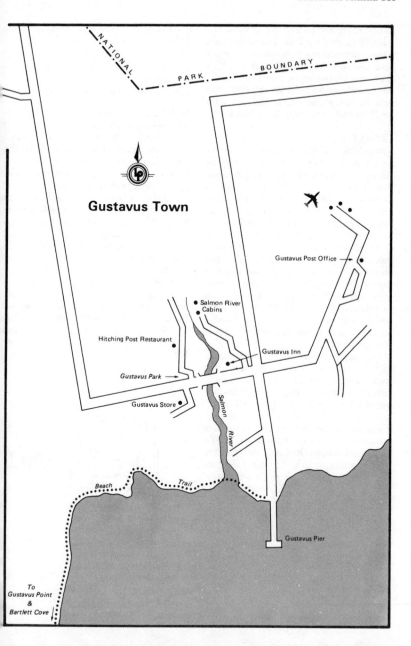

While there are no glaciers to view, the islands (a day's paddle out of Bartlett Cove) offer calm water, protected channels and pleasant beach camping. Wildlife includes black bears, seals and bald eagles, while the tidal pools burst with activity at low tide. The islands make for an ideal and easy three-day paddle.

Getting There

From Juneau the quickest way to arrive at the park is to book passage onto the Alaska Airlines flight that departs daily around 5 pm for a 15-minute trip to Gustavus; one-way fare is $49. The cheapest way to travel to Gustavus, the service centre outside the park, is to board the *Glacier Expres* that departs from downtown Juneau. Exploration Holidays (tel 586-6883) operate the cruise ship which sails daily during the summer except Tuesday. Check-in time is 7.30 am for the three-hour trip, and a round-trip ticket costs $90. Glacier Bay Airways (tel 697-2249 in Gustavus, 789-9009 in Juneau) also flies daily to the Bay and the fare is $54 one way.

Once at Gustavus Airport, you are still 10 miles (16 km) from Bartlett Cove, the park headquarters. Glacier Bay Transportation Company has a bus service that meets all airline flights, but at $10 a seat but you might consider hitch-hiking. Thumbing along the road is easy as there is always a small stream of traffic shuffling between Gustavus and the park headquarters, even if it means riding on the back of somebody's three-wheeler.

The other way to reach Glacier Bay is to book a total package tour out of Juneau, which usually includes round-trip air fare and boat passage up bay to view the glaciers. These are offered by Exploration Holidays (tel 586-6883) and Glacier Bay Yacht Tours (tel 586-6835), but tend to be expensive for the short time you are in the park. Glacier Bay Yacht Tours offers a two-day excursion to the park which includes sleeping on board their boat, *Glacier Seal*, for $279 per person and a three-day trip into the West Arm for $379.

Haines

In the upper reaches of the Inside Passage lies Haines, a town of 1100 residents and an important access point to the Yukon Territory and Interior Alaska. While the town itself may lack the charming makeup of a Sitka or a Petersburg, the surrounding scenery is stunning. Those who arrive on the state ferry will see Lynn Canal, the longest and deepest fjord in North America, close in on them, and then there's a mad scramble to the left side of the vessel when the USFS guide on board announces the approach of Davidson and Rainbow glaciers to the west.

Once in town, mountains seem to surround you on all sides. To the west, looming over Fort Seward, are the jagged Cathedral Peaks of the Chilkat Mountains; to the east is the Chilkoot Range; and standing guard behind Haines is Mt Ripinsky.

Haines is 75 miles (120 km) north of Juneau on a wooded peninsula between the Chilkat and Chilkoot inlets. Originally it was a stronghold of the wealthy Chilkat Tlingit Indians who called the settlement 'Dtehshuh'. Missionaries and a trickle of white settlers arrived in the late 1870s and eventually, of course, the gold prospectors stampeded through.

In 1897, Jack Dalton, a gun-toting businessman, turned an old Indian trade route to the interior into a toll road for miners seeking an easier way to reach the Klondike. He charged $2 per head of cattle. The 'Dalton Trail' quickly became a heavily-used pack route to mining districts north of Whitehorse. He reaped the profits until the White Pass & Yukon Railroad in Skagway put him out of business in 1900. The army established Alaska's first permanent post in 1903 and named it Fort William H Seward after the secretary of state who negotiated the purchase of the state. The fort was used as a rest camp during WW II and was then closed in 1946.

WW II also led to the construction of the Haines Highway, the 159-mile (254 km) link between the Southeast and the Alaska Highway. For years Haines had the single road to the Outside, and today it is still the only one open year-round.

Logging and fishing have been the traditional activities of Haines, but in the 1970s the town became economically depressed because the lumber industry fell on hard times. The town's remaining sawmill filed for bankruptcy in 1984, but by then Haines residents had already begun to swing their economy towards tourism. Haines survived and will probably become a major recreational destination of the Southeast in the future, as it combines spectacular scenery with comparatively dry weather and a road that isn't a dead end.

Information

The Haines Visitors Bureau (tel 766-2202) is on 2nd Avenue and Willard St in downtown Haines and is open from 8 am to 5 pm daily in the summer. The centre has racks of free information, along with restrooms, a small message board and a used-book exchange. For information on the town's three state parks, head to the Alaska Division of State Parks office (tel 766-2292) on Main St above Helen's Shop. The office is open Monday to Friday from 8 am to 4.30 pm.

Things to See

The **Sheldon Museum** is near the waterfront at the foot of Main St just off Front

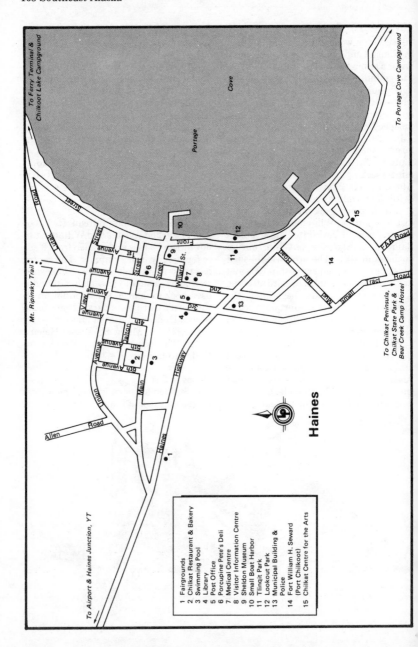

Haines

To Airport & Haines Junction, YT

Allen Road

Union Street

Mt. Ripinsky Trail

To Ferry Terminal & Chilkoot Lake Campground

Lutak Street

1st Avenue
2nd Avenue
3rd Avenue
4th Avenue
5th Avenue
6th Avenue

Main Street
Union Street

Haines Highway

Portage Cove

Front Street

Willard St.

2nd Street
3rd Street

ZAA Road

FAA Road

Mud Bay Road

Small Tract Road

To Chilkat Peninsula, Chilkat State Park & Bear Creek Camp Hostel

To Portage Cove Campground

1 Fairgrounds
2 Chilkat Restaurant & Bakery
3 Swimming Pool
4 Library
5 Post Office
6 Porcupine Pete's Deli
7 Medical Centre
8 Visitor Information Centre
9 Sheldon Museum
10 Small Boat Harbor
11 Tlinqit Park
12 Lookout Park
13 Municipal Building & Police
14 Fort William H. Seward (Port Chilkoot)
15 Chilkat Centre for the Arts

St. It features a collection of native artefacts and relics from Haines' pioneer and gold-rush days, including the sawn-off shotgun Jack Dalton used to convince travellers to pay his toll. The centre also shows *Last Stronghold of the Eagles*, an excellent movie by Juneau film-maker Joel Bennett about the annual gathering of bald eagles, twice a day at 1.30 and 3.30 pm. Admission is $2 and the centre is open 9.30 am to noon and 1 to 5 pm Friday and Saturday, and 1 to 5 pm Sunday.

Across Front St from the museum is the **Small Boat Harbor** that bustles during the summer with fishermen and pleasure boats. A walk up Main St will take you through the heart of Haines' business district. A block north of Main St on 2nd Avenue is **The Gutenberg Dump**, an unusual bookstore in a large rambling house where the owner lives upstairs. The hours are 10 am to 6 pm Monday through Saturday, but a sign on the door says: 'If you need something, knock.' Another block along Main St and two blocks south along Third Avenue is the post office, and across the street is the public library, open Monday to Friday from 11 am to 4.30 pm and Saturday 1 to 4 pm.

Follow 3rd Avenue and turn left on the first road for two blocks to reach **Tlingit Park** near Portage Cove. Between the park and Front St is an old **cemetery** with many of the headstones dating back to the 1880s, marking the graves of Haines' pioneers. Across Front St along the shoreline is **Lookout Park**, a vantage point where you can get good views of the boat harbour to the left, Port Chilkoot Dock to the right and the Coastal Mountains all around. A display points out the various peaks that loom above Haines.

Follow Front St as it curves around Portage Cove, and cut uphill at the Port Chilkoot Dock to reach **Fort Seward**. The old army fort was designated a National Historical Site in 1972 and is slowly being renovated. In the centre of the fort are the parade grounds, while to the north is Building No 53, formerly the Commanding

Officers' quarters and today the Hotel Halsingland. A walking-tour map of the fort is available in the lobby of the hotel. In the centre of the parade ground is **Totem Village**, which although not part of the original fort, provides an interesting view of a tribal house, totem poles and a Yukon trapper's cabin. Also in Fort Seward are the **Alaskan Indian Arts Skill Centre** in the former post hospital and the **Chilkat Centre for the Performing Arts** – a refurbished cannery building and site of the nightly productions of the Chilkat Dancers and Lynn Canal Community Players.

Art Galleries In the past few years Haines has slowly become a commune for artists in the same way that Homer attracts the creative-minded souls of Southcentral Alaska. With Haines' spectacular surroundings, it is not hard to understand why. The *Haines Sentinel* publishes an annual visitors guide which includes descriptions of 30 local artists and a handful of small galleries that display and sell their work.

In the middle of Fort Seward's parade ground is Sea Wolf Art Studio, which features the work of Tresham Gregg, one of Haines' better-known native artists who is involved mostly in wood-carving and prints of Tlingit designs. Nearby on Beach Rd is the Art Shop, the small red gallery that holds an impressive display of work. These include the prints of John Svenson, known throughout the Northwest as Alaska's foremost mountain illustrator. Other galleries worth stopping at are The Enchanted Door in the alley behind the First National Bank on Main St, and the Whale Rider Gallery on 2nd Avenue and Willard St. Right across from it is the Northern Arts Gallery.

Places to Stay

Hostels *Bear Creek Camp & Hostel* (tel 766-2259) is 2.5 miles (four km) south of town. From the post office, follow 3rd Avenue, which turns into Mud Bay Rd near Fort Seward. After 0.5 mile (0.8 km) you veer to the left onto Small Tract Rd and follow it for 1.5 miles (2.4 km) to the hostel. There is room for 20 in dorms at the rate of $7 for AYH members and $10 for non-members per night. There are also tent sites and cabins that hold up to four persons and are rented for $25 per night. Open year-round, the camp has a sauna, wood-stoves and cooking facilities.

Hotels In town there are eight hotels and bed & breakfast establishments. The cheapest is the *Town House Motel* (tel 766-2353) at Main St and 3rd Avenue. The motel has six rooms that cost $30 for singles and $35 for doubles. Everything else begins at $45 and climbs steadily.

Camping Haines has several free-use state campgrounds; the closest to town is *Portage Cove* (nine sites). The scenic beach campground, 0.5 mile (0.8 km) beyond Fort Seward, is designated for tents only and offers no facilities besides water and pit toilets. Follow Front St, which becomes Beach Rd as it curves around the cove near Fort Seward, and the campground is at the end of the gravel road. Five miles (eight km) north of the ferry terminal on Lutak Rd is *Chilkoot Lake State Park* (32 sites). The campground is on Chilkoot Lake, a turquoise-blue lake surrounded by mountain peaks, and offers picnic shelters and good fishing close at hand for Dolly Varden.

If you have a spare day in Haines, spend the night at *Chilkat State Park* (32 sites), seven miles (11.2 km) south-east of Haines on Mud Bay Rd. The park, situated towards the end of the Chilkat Peninsula, has good views of Lynn Canal and of the Davidson and Rainbow glaciers that spill out of the mountains into it. There are hiking trails and fishing opportunities nearby. Within town, you can set your tent up at *Port Chilkoot Camper Park* (tel 766-2755) for $2.50 a night. The private campground is in Fort Seward behind the Hotel Halsingland.

For a shower in town, head to *Susie Q's Laundromat* near the foot of Main St by the boat harbour; showers cost $1.50. There is also the *Haines public pool* (tel 766-2666) with a variety of swimming periods, including early-bird swims that begin at 6.30 am and late-night sessions from 7 to 9 pm. Cost per session is $1.50.

Places to Eat

The popular place in the morning among locals is *Chilkat Restaurant & Bakery* on the corner of Main St and 5th Avenue, which opens at 7 am. A plate of eggs, potatoes and toast is $4.50, and you can get coffee and a warm muffin for around $1 or a loaf of freshly-baked bread for $2. The *Commander's Room* in Fort Seward's Hotel Halsingland provides a historical setting in which to eat, with a nice view of the surrounding mountains. Breakfast is priced the same and the portions are filling. At night the restaurant serves a variety of seafood including prawns, scallops and salmon, with dinners running from $16 to $19. The best breakfast value is at the *Bamboo Room* on the corner of 2nd Avenue and Main St, where a plate of pancakes and coffee costs $3.50.

For deli-type sandwiches try *Porcupine Pete's* across from the Bamboo Room on 2nd Avenue. Sandwiches cost from $3 to $7 and pizza is sold by the slice for $2. The best pizza in town is at the *Pizza Cutter* within the Fogcutter Bar near the foot of Main St. Whole pizzas are $13 to $18; a slice is $2.25.

Locally-caught seafood ends up on a variety of menus in Haines. The town's salmon bake, *Port Chilkoot Potlatch*, takes place nightly from 5 to 8 pm at Totem Village in the centre of Fort Seward. For $16 per person you can enjoy all the grilled salmon, salad and baked beans you can handle in one sitting.

Also within Fort Seward is the *Post Exchange Seafood Restaurant*, just off Beach Rd on Mud Bay Rd. It offers salmon, halibut and prawn dinners for

$10 to $13 and live entertainment twice a week. Haines' most unique restaurant is the *Catalyst* at the heart of Main St. The small eatery has limited seating, so parties of more than four should call 766-2670 for reservations. The food is excellent, and along with seafood selections the restaurant offers a salad bar and freshly baked pastries and desserts.

To take some salmon or crab back to the campsite, go to *Howsers Supermarket*, the distinctive storefront with the large moose antlers on Main St. The food market, which is open daily, usually has a good selection of whatever is being caught. Dungeness crab costs around $3.25/lb ($7.15/kg), salmon $4/lb ($8.80/kg) and prawns (large shrimp) $7/lb ($15.40/kg).

Nightlife
For beer on tap, and to rub elbows with the locals, stop in at the *Fogcutter* on Main St or the *Pioneer Bar* next to the Bamboo Room on the corner of 2nd Avenue and Main St. Both spots can get lively and full at night, as Haines is a hard-drinking town. For someplace a little quieter where you can watch the traffic in the bay, there is the *Harbor Bar* next to the Small Boat Harbor at the foot of Main St.

Other activities at night include performances by the Chilkat Dancers in full Tlingit costume at the Chilkat Centre for the Arts in Fort Seward. The performances are at 7.30 and 8.30 pm on Monday, Thursday and Saturday and at 9 pm on Wednesday; admission is $5. On Friday and Sunday at 8.30 pm you can see the melodrama *Lust For Dust*, performed by the Lynn Canal Community Players during the summer; tickets are $5. There is also a free wildlife/Alaska film series at the Centre, presented by the Haines Visitors Centre, every Wednesday at 7 pm.

Events
Like every other Alaska town, Haines has a Fourth of July celebration, but its biggest festival is the Southeast Alaska State Fair. Held in mid-August, the event includes parades, dances, livestock shows and exhibits that draw participants from all Southeast communities. If you are heading home in late October or November on the state ferry, keep in mind the bald eagle gathering that takes place in Haines annually. The eagles arrive to feed on the salmon-runs in the Chilkat River, as natural hot springs keep it from freezing over. Over 3500 eagles gather in the valley north of Haines, allowing photographers to take incredible close-ups from the road.

Hiking
There are two major trail systems near Haines: south of town are the trails on Chilkat Peninsula, which include the climb to Mt Riley; north of Haines is the path to the summit of Mt Ripinsky. For those who want to venture into the remote mountainous regions that surround Haines, Ice Field Ascents (PO Box 449, Haines, Alaska 99827) runs a weekend Davidson Glacier ice-climbing expedition for $130 per person. The trip provides transportation across Lynn Canal, equipment and instructions in ice-climbing techniques.

Mt Ripinsky Trail The trip to the 3610-foot (5776-metre) summit of Mt Ripinsky is an all-day hike of six to eight hours that rewards you with a sweeping, uninterrupted view almost from Juneau to Skagway. To reach the trailhead, follow 2nd Avenue north as it turns into Young St. At the end of the street, follow the pipeline right-of-way from which the trail heads off, 1.3 miles (two km) from town. From the right-of-way it is a one-way hike of 3.6 miles (5.8 km) to the north-east peak, where there is a trail register.

Battery Point Trail The 2.4-mile (3.8-km) trail is a level walk along the shore to Kelgaya Point, where there are camping possibilities. At the point you can cut across to a pebble beach and follow it to Battery Point. The trail begins 0.25 mile (0.4 km) beyond Portage Cove Campground at the end of Beach Rd.

Mt Riley Trails This is a considerably easier alpine climb to a 1760-foot (537-metre) summit than the one to Mt Ripinsky, but it still provides good views in all directions, including Rainbow and Davidson glaciers. One trail up the mountain begins at a junction almost two miles (3.2 km) up the Battery Point Trail out of Portage Cove Campground. From here you hike 5.5 miles (8.8 km) over Half Dome and up Mt Riley.

Another route close to town begins at the end of the FAA road that runs behind the Officers' Row in Fort Seward. From the road follow the water supply access route for two miles (3.2 km) to a short spur that branches off to the right and connects with the trail from Mud Bay Rd. One-way distance is 3.8 miles (six km) and prevents you from having to find a ride three miles (4.8 km) out Mud Bay Rd, the site of the third trailhead to Mt Riley. Plan on five to six hours for a round-trip hike to the summit.

Rafting

Haines is also the departure point for numerous raft trips in the area. Chilkat Guides (tel 766-2409) offer a four-hour float down the Chilkat River that provides plenty of opportunity to view bald eagles and possibly brown bears, but little whitewater. The outfitters run the trip twice daily at 9 am and 2 pm beginning at the Art Shop on Beach Rd in Fort Seward. The cost is $45 per person.

On a much greater scale of adventure is the 11-day float down the Tatshenshini/Alsek River system from Yukon Territory to the outside coast of Glacier Bay. Haines serves as the departure point for this river trip that is unmatched by any other Alaskan float for its scenic mix of rugged mountain ranges and dozens of glaciers. Both Chilkat Guides and Alaska

Discovery (tel 697-2257) run the trip, priced at around $1300 to $1400 per person.

Getting There & Around

Ferry Terminal The Haines Street Car, a large blue bus, meets all state ferry arrivals and for $3 will take you the four miles (6.4 km) into town. The bus also departs town 30 minutes before each ferry arrival and stops at Hotel Halsingland and the Art Shop in Fort Seward and the Whale Rider Gallery in town before heading out to the ferry terminal.

Air There is no jet service out of Haines, but several charter companies run regularly scheduled service to points both north and south. The cheapest is Haines Airways (tel 766-2646), which will fly you to Juneau for $49 and Skagway for $30. They need a minimum of two persons to fly but will match up individual travellers with already-scheduled flights.

Wings Of Alaska (tel 766-2468) has four daily flights to Juneau for $60, and four flights to Skagway for $35. Either one will arrange a flight-seeing trip over Glacier Bay, as the park is only a 10-minute flight from Haines.

Boat There are arrivals and departures of the state ferry almost everyday from the terminal (tel 766-2111) in Lutak Inlet north of town. One-way fare north to Skagway is $9 and south to Juneau $19.

Bus From Haines you can catch buses north to Whitehorse, Anchorage or Fairbanks. White Pass & Yukon Motorcoaches (tel 766-2468) has a bus that departs every Tuesday at 8.30 am, arriving in Haines Junction at 1.30 pm. From there you can continue on to Anchorage, reaching the city on Wednesday at 6 pm. The fare from Haines to Anchorage is $135, to Haines Junction $40 and to Dezadeash Lodge (one end of a popular trail in Kluane National Park) $30. The passenger boarding point for the bus in

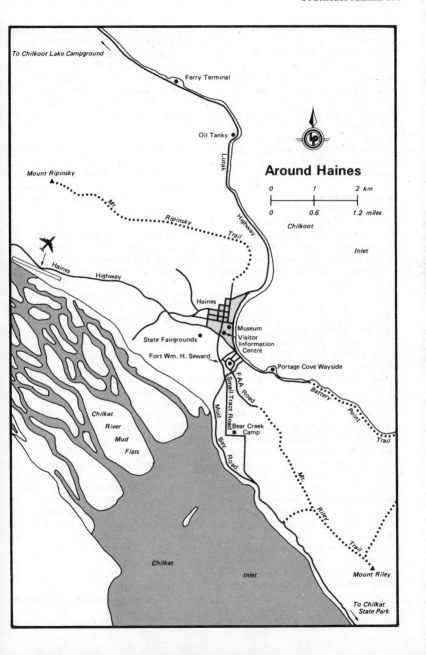

To Chilkoot Lake Campground

Ferry Terminal

Oil Tanks

Lutak Highway

Mount Ripinsky

Mt. Ripinsky Trail

Haines Highway

Haines

State Fairgrounds

Fort Wm. H. Seward

Museum
Visitor
Information
Centre

FAA Road

Small Tract Road

Mud Bay Road

Bear Creek Camp

Portage Cove Wayside

Battery Point Trail

Mt. Riley Trail

Mount Riley

Chilkat River Mud Flats

Chilkat Inlet

To Chilkat State Park

Around Haines

| 0 | 1 | 2 km |

| 0 | 0.6 | 1.2 miles |

Chilkoot Inlet

Haines is the Wings of Alaska office at 277 Main St.

Alaska-Yukon Motorcoaches (tel 766-2435) has a bus that departs every Wednesday at 9 am and arrives in Anchorage at 3.30 pm Friday with two overnight stops. Another bus departs Sunday at 9 am and arrives at Fairbanks on Tuesday at 5 pm. One-way fare for each is $250 and does not include accommodation. The boarding point in Haines is Hotel Halsingland in Fort Seward.

AROUND HAINES
Kluane National Park
Situated 120 miles (192 km) north of Haines is Kluane National Park, one of Canada's newest and most spectacular parks. The preserve encompasses 8649 square miles (22,000 square km) of rugged coastal mountains in the south-western corner of Yukon Territory. There are no roads in this wilderness park but the Haines Highway runs along its eastern edge, providing easy access to the area. The 150-mile (240-km) Haines Highway, which follows Jack Dalton's gold-rush toll road, was recently paved and now makes for an extremely scenic and smooth drive ending at the Alaska Highway in Haines Junction.

Amid the lofty mountains of Kluane lies Mt Logan, Canada's highest peak at 19,636 feet (5950 metres), and the most extensive non-polar ice-field in the world from which glaciers spill out onto the valley floors. Wildlife is plentiful and includes Dall sheep, brown bears, moose, mountain goats and caribou. The park's visitors centre, in Haines Junction on the Alaska Highway, is open from 9 am to 9 pm daily in the summer. Along with displays and a free slide show covering the area's natural history, the centre can provide you with information, back-country permits and topographic maps for overnight hikes into the park.

The main activity in Kluane is hiking, and trails consist primarily of old mining roads, animal trails or natural routes along river beds or ridges. The trailheads for eight routes are located along the Haines and Alaska Highways. For those who want to view the park but not hike it, Burwash Lodge near the north end of Kluane Lake offers one-hour flight-seeing trips for groups of four at $55 per person.

Alsek Pass Trail This 15-mile (24-km) route is a level walk along an old abandoned mining road most of the way. It begins six miles (9.6 km) west of Haines Junction at Mackintosh Lodge and ends at Sugden Creek.

Auriol Trail The 12-mile (19 km) loop begins 3.8 miles (six km) south of Haines Junction and makes for a good day hike. The trail passes several vantage points which provide sweeping views of the area. A primitive campground along the way could be used to turn the walk into an overnight excursion.

Cottonwood Trail The 53-mile (85 km) loop begins at the Kathleen Lake Campground, 12 miles (19 km) south of Haines Junction. It ends at Dezadeash Lodge off the Haines Highway. In between is a route of old mining roads that require some climbing and fording of streams. Wildlife, especially the brown bear, is plentiful on this four-day hike.

Slims River Trail The 16-mile (25.5 km) trail is one of the most scenic in the park, as it passes old mining relics and ends at Observation Mountain, which you can scramble up for a view of spectacular Kaskawulsh Glacier. The trailhead is 40 miles (64 km) west of Haines Junction near a park information centre.

Skagway

A place of many names, much history and

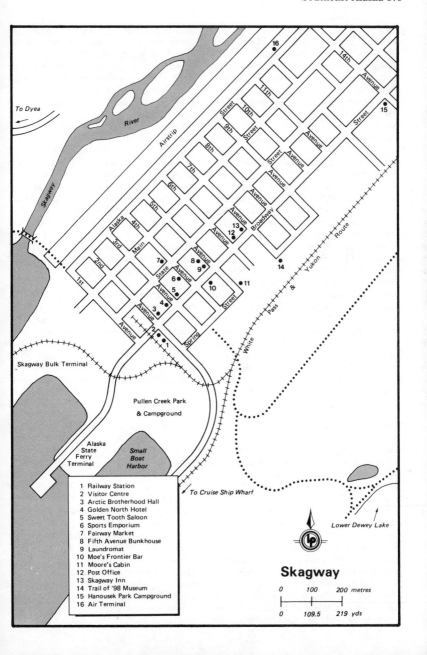

To Dyea

River

Airstrip

Skagway

Alaska State Ferry Terminal

Skagway Bulk Terminal

Pullen Creek Park & Campground

Small Boat Harbor

To Cruise Ship Wharf

11th Street
14th Avenue
10th Street
9th Street
8th Street
7th
6th
5th
4th
3rd
2nd
1st
Main
State
Alaska
Avenue
Broadway
Spring Street
White Pass & Yukon Route

15
16
13
12
8
9
7
6
5
3
2
1
10
11
14

1 Railway Station
2 Visitor Centre
3 Arctic Brotherhood Hall
4 Golden North Hotel
5 Sweet Tooth Saloon
6 Sports Emporium
7 Fairway Market
8 Fifth Avenue Bunkhouse
9 Laundromat
10 Moe's Frontier Bar
11 Moore's Cabin
12 Post Office
13 Skagway Inn
14 Trail of '98 Museum
15 Hanousek Park Campground
16 Air Terminal

Lower Dewey Lake

Skagway

0   100   200 metres
0   109.5   219 yds

little rain is Skagway, the northern terminus of the state ferry. The town of 700 lies in the narrow plain of the Skagway River at the head of the Lynn Canal and at one time or another has been called Skaguay, Shkagway and Gateway to the Golden Interior. It is also known as the 'Home of the North Wind' and residents tell visitors that it blows so much here you never breathe the same air twice.

However, Skagway is also one of the driest places in what can often be a soggy Southeast. While Petersburg averages over 100 inches (over 2500 mm) a year and Ketchikan a drenching 154 inches (3910 mm), Skagway gets only 26 inches (660 mm) of rain annually.

Much of Skagway lies within the Klondike Gold Rush National Historical Park which extends from Seattle to Dawson, Yukon. The National Park Service is constantly restoring the old storefronts and buildings so the result is a town that looks like the boom town it was in the 1890s when the gold rush gave birth to Skagway. The town and nearby ghost town of Dyea were the staging points for over 40,000 stampeders who headed to the Yukon by way of either the Chilkoot Trail or the White Pass Trail. The Chilkoot that started from Dyea was the favourite as it was several miles shorter. The White Pass Trail, which began in Skagway and was advertised as a 'horse trail', was brutal. In the winter of 1897-98, some 3000 pack animals were driven to death by over-anxious owners and the White Pass picked up its name of 'Dead Horse Trail'.

In 1887, the population of the town was two; ten years later there were 20,000 people and the gold-rush town was Alaska's largest city and the centre of saloons, hotels and dance halls. Skagway became infamous for its lawlessness. For a spell the town was held under the tight control of Jefferson R 'Soapy' Smith and his gang that conned and swindled naive newcomers out of their money and stampeders out of their gold dust. Soapy Smith was finally removed from power by a mob of angry citizens in a gunfight between him and city engineer Frank Reid. Both men died from the shooting and Smith's reign as the 'uncrowned prince of Skagway' ended, having lasted nine months.

In the height of the gold rush, Michael J Heney, an Irish contractor, convinced a group of English investors that he could build a railroad over the White Pass Trail to Whitehorse. Construction began in 1898 with little more than picks, shovels and blasting powder, and the narrow-gauge railroad reached the Yukon capital in July 1900. The White Pass & Yukon Railroad was nothing short of a super-human feat, and when the last traces of the rush were gone by 1906, the rail line remained to give Skagway a sense of stability.

Today Skagway doubles its population in the summer, when the town bustles with cruise ships and bus tours. The White Pass & Yukon Railroad, the focal point of the town's economy after the gold rush and during the military build-up of WW II, shut down in 1982. While rumours continue to swirl about restarting the rail service, the fact remains that Skagway is almost entirely dependent on tourism. The town continues to survive, however, as more and more 'Love Boat' cruise ships make the lively little town a port of call. In 1985, over 200 ships stopped at Skagway, setting a new record for the town.

Things to See

Unlike most Southeast towns, Skagway is a delightful place to arrive at aboard the state ferry. The dock and terminal are at the foot of **Broadway St**, the main avenue in town. You can step off the ferry right into a bustling town where half the people are dressed as if they are trying to relive the gold rush days while the other half are obviously tourists off the luxury liners.

Just up the dock at the corner of Broadway and 2nd Avenue is the **National Park Service** office and visitors centre in the old White Pass & Yukon railroad depot. The centre is open from 8 am to 9 pm daily and features displays, slide shows and the movie *Days of Adventure, Dreams of Gold*, shown every hour. The 30-minute movie is narrated by Hal Holbrook and is the best way to slip back into the gold rush days; evening programmes begin at 7 pm. The centre also has walking tours of historical downtown daily at 10 am, noon and 2 pm.

A seven-block corridor along Broadway St is part of the Historical Park and contains the restored buildings, false fronts and wooden sidewalks of Skagway's golden era. A block up Broadway and on the other side of the street from the NPS headquarters is the **Arctic Brotherhood Hall**, the site of the Skagway visitors centre. The hall is hard to miss as there are perhaps 20,000 pieces of driftwood tacked to the front of it, making it one of the most distinctive buildings in Alaska. Three more blocks up Broadway and a block east on 5th Avenue is **Moore's Cabin**, the oldest building in Skagway. Captain William Moore and his son built it in 1888 when they staked out their homestead as the founders of the town.

A block east of Broadway on 7th Avenue is the town's **City Hall**, while upstairs is the **Trail of '98 Museum**. Both are in a granite building that was built in 1900 as McCabe College and later served as a US Court until the city obtained it in 1956. The museum is open daily in the summer from 9 am to 9 pm and charges $2 for admission. The money is well spent, however, as the upstairs is jammed with gold-rush relics, including many items devoted to the town's two leading characters, Soapy Smith and Frank Reid. You can purchase a copy of the 15 July 1898 *Skagway News* that described all the details surrounding the colourful shootout.

For those who become as infatuated as the locals over Smith and Reid, there is the walk out to **Gold Rush Cemetery**. From the ferry terminal it is a two-mile (3.2 km) stroll out to the graveyard along State St, a block west of Broadway. Follow State St until it curves into 23rd Avenue and look for the sign pointing the way to Soapy's grave across the railroad tracks. A wooden bridge along the tracks leads to the main part of the cemetery, the site of many stampeders' graves as well as the plots of Reid and Smith. From Reid's gravestone, it is a short hike uphill to the lovely **Reid Falls** which cascade 300 feet (90 metres) from the mountainside.

Dyea In 1898, Skagway's rival city was Dyea, located at the foot of the Chilkoot Trail, the shortest route to Lake Bennett where stampeders began their float to Dawson City. After the White Pass & Yukon Railroad was completed in 1900, Dyea quickly evaporated and today is little more than a few old cabins and Slide Cemetery, where 47 men and women were buried after perishing in an avalanche on the Chilkoot Trail in April 1898.

Dyea Rd winds nine miles (14.4 km) from Skagway to the ghost town and is a scenic drive but is filled with hairpin turns that are a headache for drivers of recreational vehicles. At *Mile 1* (1.6 km) there is a turnoff with wooden benches that offers an excellent view of downtown Skagway, its waterfront and the peaks above the town. Just before crossing the bridge over the Taiya River you pass the Dyea Camping Area (22 sites), a free campground where a NPS ranger is stationed in the summer to assist hikers on the Chilkoot Trail. The trailhead for the famous trail is near the campground.

Places to Stay
There is no Youth Hostel in Skagway but there is the *5th Avenue Bunkhouse* (tel 983-2468) at the corner of Broadway and 5th Avenue. Gold-rush-style bunks, where you pull a curtain across your bed to turn

in for the night, are available for $10 per person. The place also has a red cedar sauna for $5 per person per hour and coin-operated showers. The proprietors fill the place on a first-come first-serve basis but rarely turn anybody away.

There are also seven hotels in town, with *Irene's Inn* (tel 983-2520) on Broadway at 6th Avenue the cheapest; rooms start at $25. Getting a hotel room in Skagway during the summer is extremely difficult without advance reservations.

Camping The city manages two campgrounds that serve both RVers and backpackers. On Broadway and 14th Avenue is *Hanousek Park*, that provides tables, pit toilets and hot showers for $5 per tent site. Near the ferry terminal is *Pullen Creek Park Campground* (33 sites) on the waterfront by the Small Boat Harbor. Designed primarily for RVers, sites without electricity are $8 per night. Nine miles (14.4 km) outside of Skagway is the free *Dyea Camping Area* (22 sites). Two miles (3.2 km) north of town on the Klondike Highway is *Liarsville Park*, also with free camping.

Places to Eat
For breakfast and sandwiches there is the *Northern Lights Café* on Broadway between 4th and 5th Avenues, and the *Sweet Tooth Saloon* closer to the ferry terminal on Broadway. A full breakfast at either would range from $5 to $7. The Sweet Tooth is the place to go for coffee and a fresh donut. The best spot for dinner on Broadway is *Irene's Place*, where a meal in the gambling-parlour/dining-room costs from $12 to $20.

The cheapest way to go, however, is to buy your grub at the *Fairway Market* on Fourth Avenue and State St and cook it over a fire at your campsite. The *Skagway Sports Emporium* on 4th Avenue between Broadway and State St sells freeze-dried food for hiking trips along with topographic maps and limited camping equipment.

Nightlife
For a town with only 700 permanent residents, there's a lot to do in Skagway at night. On Broadway and 2nd Avenue is the town's most unique bar, the *Red Onion Saloon*, that frequently features folk music. The historical establishment doubles as a gold-rush saloon, with the decor and an upstairs brothel museum. The place really hops when cruise ships are in, as the ships' bands often hold a jam session for locals in the bar.

Moe's Frontier Bar down the street can be a lively spot, especially late at night, as can the *Golden North Hotel Lounge*, where a pitcher of beer is a bargain at $6. For something quieter there is the *Bonanza Lounge* in the Klondike Hotel.

Skagway boasts the best melodrama in the Southeast. Gambling for prizes and drinking begins in the back room of the *Eagle's Hall* on Broadway and 6th Avenue every night at 8 pm. This is followed at 9 pm by the lively production of *Skagway In The Days Of '98*, which covers the gold rush days of the town and the full story of Soapy Smith in a truly entertaining manner. The admission is $8 for both the play and pre-show entertainment.

Events
Skagway's Fourth of July features a foot race, parade and fish feed. The town holds an equally-entertaining Solstice Party of 21 June, highlighted by a street dance on Broadway.

The town also holds a couple of celebrations all its own. On 8 July is Soapy Smith's Wake, when a party is held at the Gold Rush Cemetery in honour of the con man, who now seems to be loved by everybody in Skagway. The event is highlighted by a champagne toast that is sent up every year by Soapy's grandson in California. Held on the last Saturday in August is the Hug And Kisses Road Run from Dyea to Skagway. It ends with each finisher receiving a hug, a kiss and a T-shirt.

Hiking

The Chilkoot Trail (see the Wilderness chapter) is probably the most popular hike in Alaska, but there are other good treks around Skagway. There is no USFS office in Skagway, so for trail conditions and other information contact the National Park Visitors Centre (tel 983-2921) at the corner of Broadway and 2nd Avenue.

Dewey Lake Trail System This series of trails leads east of Skagway to a handful of alpine and sub-alpine lakes, waterfalls and historical sites. From Broadway follow 3rd Avenue east past the Klondike Hotel to the railroad tracks. On the other side of the tracks are the trailhead and signs that point the way to Lower Dewey Lake, 0.7 mile (1.1 km); Icy Lake, 2.5 miles (four km); Upper Reid Falls, 3.5 miles (5.6 km); and Sturgill's Landing, 4.5 miles (7.2 km). Plan on an hour for a round-trip hike to Lower Dewey Lake, where there are picnic tables, camping spots and a trail that circles the lake. At the north end of the lake is the alpine trail that climbs steeply to Upper Dewey Lake, 3.5 miles (5.6 km) from town, and Devil's Punchbowl another 0.7 mile (1.1 km) beyond the upper lake. The hike to Devil's Punchbowl makes for an all-day trip or an ideal overnight excursion, as the views are excellent and there is a free-use USFS shelter that does not require reservations.

A B Mountain Trail Also known as the Skyline Trail, this route climbs 5.5 miles (8.8 km) to the 5100-foot (1555-metre) summit of A B Mountain, named for the A B that appears on its south side in the form of a snow-melt every spring. The trailhead is on Dyea Rd about a mile from Skagway via the Skagway River footbridge off the west end of 1st Avenue. The trail is steep and requires a full day to complete.

Denver Glacier Trail This trail takes you along the right-of-way of the White Pass & Yukon Railroad for three miles (4.8 km) before turning onto a marked Denver Glacier Trail for another two miles (3.2 km) to the glacier itself. Near the glacier is an old, rustic hunter's cabin that can be slept in.

Laughton Glacier Trail An even more strenuous hike along the railroad tracks is to continue nine miles (14.4 km) past Denver Glacier Trail to Glacier Station. Here at the old rail depot is the start of a two-mile (3.2-km) trail to Laughton Glacier, where there is a USFS cabin (reservations needed, $10 per night). The cabin is easy to reserve at the last minute because of the suspension of rail services along the line. The alpine setting around the cabin is extremely scenic, with the impressive glacier nearby.

Getting There & Around

There is cab and bus service out to Dyea and the Chilkoot trailhead (see the Wilderness chapter), or you can thumb it, a possibility because of the stream of hikers that go out there daily in the summer.

Air There are regularly-scheduled flights from Skagway to Juneau, with LAB Flying Service (tel 983-2471), Wings Of Alaska (tel 983-2442 and Skagway Air (tel 983-2218, which generally offers the cheapest fares as well as a $45 flight-seeing tour of nearby Glacier Bay.

Boat The state ferry (tel 983-2229) makes daily departures during the summer from its terminal and dock at the foot of Broadway.

Bus North-bound travellers will find that scheduled bus service is the cheapest way to go. White Pass & Yukon Motorcoaches (tel 983-2934) provides daily service from Skagway to Whitehorse as well as a two-day run on Tuesday from Skagway to Anchorage. The bus departs from the Klondike Hotel at 10 am on Monday and

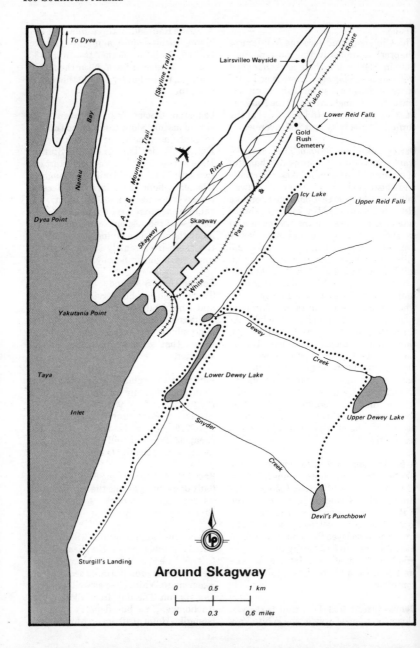

Around Skagway

0   0.5   1 km

0   0.3   0.6 miles

Wednesday to Saturday, reaching White-horse at 2 pm. On Tuesday and Sunday the bus departs at 7.30 am, arriving in Whitehorse at 11.45 am. One-way fare between the two cities is $41. The fare from Skagway to Anchorage is $196. At Whitehorse you can make connections to other Alaskan towns as well (see the Getting There chapter).

Hitch-hiking The cheapest form of transportation is possible along the Klondike Highway if you are patient and are thumbing when a state ferry pulls in. Backpackers contemplating hitching north would do better, however, if they fork out $9 for a ferry ticket to Haines and thumb Haines Highway instead, as it has considerably more traffic.

Southcentral Alaska

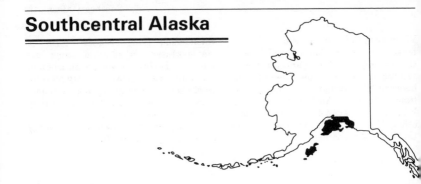

Upon reaching Haines, most independent travellers continue their Alaskan adventure by heading north through Canada's Yukon Territory to the Alaska Highway. They drive, thumb or bus (see the Getting Around chapter) the famous highway to the state's Interior, viewing Denali National Park or possibly Fairbanks before heading south towards towards Anchorage.

For those who were enchanted by the Southeast and charmed by the Alaska Marine Highway and want to avoid the long days on the Alcan, there is a pleasant and cheaper alternative that begins with back-tracking to Juneau. For less than the cost of a Haines-Anchorage motor-coach ticket, you can fly Alaska Airlines from Juneau to Cordova for $120. This puts you in another remote coastal town where fishing and life by the sea are the main threads woven through the community.

Best of all, from Cordova you can jump on the south-west system of the Alaska marine ferry to explore the rest of Southcentral Alaska to the west. Known by many as the Gulf Coast Region, this area is really a continuation of Alaska's rugged coastal playground that begins in Ketchikan. Both Southeast and Southcentral boast spectacular scenery accented by glaciers, fjords and mountain ranges half buried by ice-fields and covered at the base by lush forest and both are affected by the Japanese Current for a wet but mild climate. Fishing is an important industry and the state ferry is one of the main modes of transportation.

However, Southcentral (the region wrapped around Prince William Sound and the Gulf of Alaska) has one important feature that the Panhandle doesn't – roads and traffic between many of the towns. This alone makes the area one of the most accessible and cheap to visit in the state. It also makes it one of the most popular. With half of the state's population just to the north in Anchorage, the Kenai Peninsula of Southcentral can often be a haven for RVers, fishermen and tour groups. There are dozens of trails and water routes throughout the peninsula, but because of its accessibility you might have to hike a little longer or climb a little higher to achieve the wilderness solitude so easily obtained in Southeast.

Southcentral can be divided into three main areas. Prince William Sound and its communities of Cordova, Valdez and Whittier are trademarked by the area's towering mountains that surround the sound, glaciers that spill into it and the abundance of marine wildlife that makes a home there. To the west is the Kenai Peninsula and the towns of Seward, Kenai, Soldotna and Homer. This great forested plateau, bounded by the Kenai Mountains and the Harding Icefield to the east, is broken up by hundreds of lakes, rivers and streams, making it an outdoor paradise for hikers, canoeists and fishermen. To the south-west is Kodiak Island and the city of Kodiak, the home of the largest fishing fleet in Alaska. Though often caught in the rainy and foggy weather created on the Gulf of Alaska, Kodiak offers its own rugged beauty and isolated wilderness areas few visitors make an effort to venture into.

YAKUTAT

On the flight to Cordova there is a stopover at Yakutat, the most northern community of Southeast. The town of 450 is isolated from the State Marine Ferry because of the turbulent nature of the Gulf of Alaska. For those on a tight schedule, there is no reason to stop over in Yakutat but travellers who do so will find the scenic setting of the Tlingit village stunning even if the visitors facilities are limited and expensive.

The town is surrounded by lofty peaks, including Mt Elias at 18,114 feet (5489 metres) to the west and Mt Fairweather at 15,388 feet (4663 metres) to the east. Visible north-west of the community is the Malaspina Glacier, an ice floe larger than the state of Rhode Island.

Yakutat has two lodges, including one at the airport, a handful of restaurants and cafés in town and two grocery stores. Camping is possible at *Cannon Beach*, a picnic area near town that is administered by the USFS. The main attraction is the Malaspina Glacier, which can be viewed from flight-seeing trips offered through Gulf Air Taxi (tel 784-3240), the local air charter operator based at the airport. Others come to beachcomb the miles of sandy beach that surround the area, searching for Japanese glass balls blown onshore by the violent Pacific storms.

USFS Cabins

The USFS, which maintains an office at the Yakutat airport, administers 11 cabins in the area along with the Russell Fjord Wilderness to the east. None of the cabins are actually located on the fjord or near Hubbard Glacier, the advancing ice floe that is threatening to seal off the north end of Russell Fjord and turn it into a freshwater lake. Other than a quick flight-seeing tour, the only way to witness the glacier and the amazing scene of it calving during mid-tides is through an Alaska Discovery guided expedition.

Of the 11 cabins, five of them can be reached from Forest Highway 10 that extends east from Yakutat. Cars can be rented through Marlis Korochi (tel 784-3432) or drop-off and pick-up service can be arranged from Yakutat Cab Service (tel 784-3351). It is best to rent the cabins from the USFS office in the Juneau Centennial Hall when you are passing through the Capital City. Rental information can also be obtained in the Yakutat office in the Flight Service Building of the airport or by contacting USFS, PO Box 327, Yakutat, Alaska 99689; tel 784-3359.

Situk Lake The cabin is on the forested south-eastern shore of the lake and provides excellent fishing opportunities for salmon and steelhead trout as well as viewing of brown bears, moose, otters and bald eagles. It can be reached by a five-mile (eight km) trail that begins east of the bridge at *Mile 9* (14.4 km) of Forest Highway 10.

Situk Weir Rafters who float down the the Situk River end up at Situk Landing, a large parking lot eight miles (12.8 km) from town along Lost River Rd. A 0.25-mile (0.4 km) trail leads from the parking area to the Situk Weir Cabin. The unit provides excellent fishing for salmon, Dolly Varden and trout in the mouth of the Situk River. For some excellent beachcombing the beaches along the Gulf of Alaska can be reached by a two-mile (3.2 km) path.

Harlequin Lake This cabin is reached by a 30-mile (48 km) drive along Forest Highway 10. The unit offers excellent fishing and views of Harlequin Lake and its massive icebergs from Yakutat Glacier. A trail leads south four miles (6.4 km)

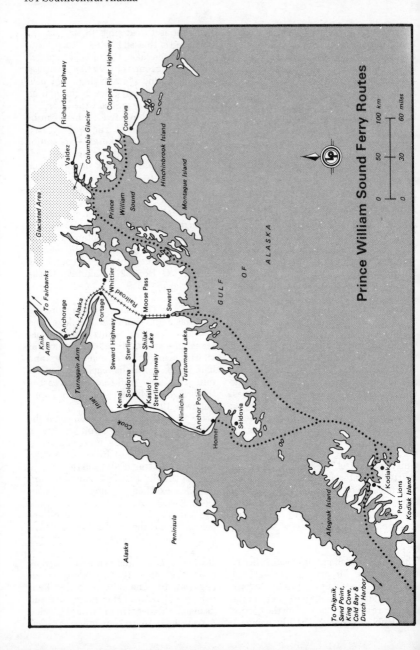

from the cabin to Middle Dangerous Cabin.

PRINCE WILLIAM SOUND
Rivalling Southeast for the steepest fjords, most spectacular coastline and all-inspiring glacier is Prince William Sound, the northern extent of the Gulf of Alaska. The Sound is a marvellous wilderness of islands, inlets, fjords, lush rainforests and towering mountains. Flanked to the west by the Kenai Mountains and to the north and east by the Chugach Mountains, the Sound covers 15,000 square miles (38,000 square km) and is the home of an abundance of wildlife, including whales, sea lions, harbour seals, otters, eagles, Dall sheep, mountain goats and, of course, bears.

One other trait the Sound shares with the Southeast is rain – lots of rain. Most of the Sound averages well over 100 inches (2500 mm) of precipitation per year, with the fishing town of Cordova receiving 167 inches (4240 mm) annually. Summer temperatures range from 54°F (12°C) to a high of 70°F (21°C).

Centre stage of Prince William Sound is Columbia Glacier. The bluish wall of ice, named after New York's Columbia University, is one of the most spectacular tidewater glaciers on the Alaska coast, as it covers 440 square miles (144 square km) or an area six times the size of Washington DC. Its face is four miles (6.4 km) wide and in some places 262 feet (80 metres) high. The stunning scene you are treated to when passing it on a boat includes hundreds of seals sunning on the ice pack, a backdrop of mountains and usually the thunder of ice calving off its face – sometimes induced by the ship's captain who sounds his horn in front of it. When Columbia Glacier sends its icebergs into the sea, it is an explosion of ice and water that few onlookers ever forget.

Those who take the Alaska Airlines jet to Cordova can continue their journey across the Sound by way of the Alaska Marine Ferry. At Valdez you have the option of returning to the road, but most travellers elect to stay on the state ferry to Whittier on the west side of the Sound, as this segment of the marine highway includes passing the Columbia Glacier. From Whittier there is a rail service to Anchorage (see the Getting Around chapter). From Valdez you can reach the city by motorcoach.

CORDOVA
Nestled between Orca Inlet and Lake Eyak and overshadowed by Mt Eccles, Cordova is a beautiful little fishing town on the south-east end of Prince William Sound and a place worth taking the extra time and expense to visit. The community has 2500 permanent residents but doubles its population during the summer with fishermen and cannery workers, as its economy is centred around its fleet and fish-processing plants. The area is also an outdoor paradise and the jumping-off point to 14 USFS cabins, some good alpine hiking and the Cooper River Delta, a staging and nesting area for millions of birds each year.

Modern-day Cordova was born when Michael J Heney, the builder of the White Pass & Yukon Railroad from Skagway to Whitehorse, arrived in 1906 and decided to transform the summer cannery site into the railroad terminus for his line from the Kennicott Copper Mines near McCarthy. Construction of the Copper River & Northwestern Railroad began that year and was completed in 1911 – another amazing engineering feat by the 'Irish Prince' that cost $23 million to build.

Within five years Cordova was a booming town where more than $32 million worth of copper ore passed over its docks. The railroad and town prospered until 1938, when labour strikes and the declining price of copper permanently closed the Kennicott mines. The railroad ceased operations and Cordova turned to fishing, its main economic base today.

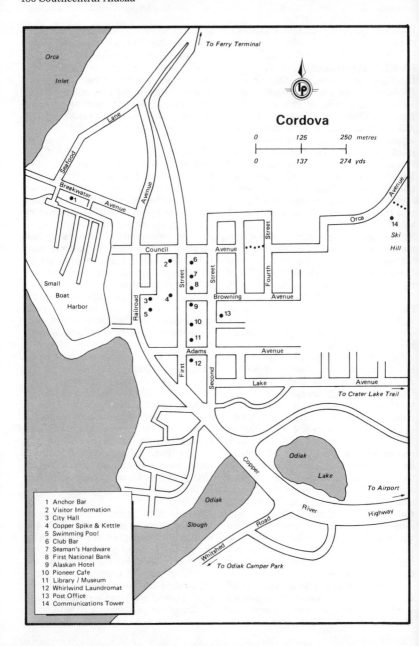

Cordova

1 Anchor Bar
2 Visitor Information
3 City Hall
4 Copper Spike & Kettle
5 Swimming Pool
6 Club Bar
7 Seaman's Hardware
8 First National Bank
9 Alaskan Hotel
10 Pioneer Cafe
11 Library / Museum
12 Whirlwind Laundromat
13 Post Office
14 Communications Tower

Things to See

General information about Cordova can be obtained from the Chamber of Commerce (tel 424-7260) on First St next to the National Bank of Alaska, open Tuesday and Thursday from 1 to 4 pm.

Down the street on the corner of Adams Avenue is the **Cordova Museum & Library** in the Centennial Building. The small but interesting museum has displays on marine life, including a rare leatherback turtle taken nearby, relics from the town's early history, Russian artefacts and a three-seater bidarka (kayak-type boat). When the state ferry is in port, they show an excellent film on the history of the town. There is also a visitors information centre at the entrance of the museum. Admission is free and it is open Tuesday and Thursday from 1 to 9 pm, Monday and Friday 1 to 5 pm and varying hours on Saturday.

First St merges into Railroad Avenue, and by following the avenue north you will reach the **city swimming pool** in a brown building next to City Hall. Built in 1974, the Olympic-size pool is open to the public during a variety of swim periods. For a list of the sessions and activities call 424-7200.

Railroad Avenue continues north and leads past the **Small Boat Harbor**, the real centre of activity in Cordova during the summer. Doubled in size in 1983, the harbour hums with boats and fishermen between season openings and when the fleet is in town on the weekends. Cordova's fleet is composed primarily of salmon seiners and gillnetters.

Places to Stay

Hotels There is no Youth Hostel in Cordova, and of the four hotels in town the *Alaskan Hotel & Bar* (tel 424-3288) on First St is the cheapest. A single with a shared bath costs $30 a night, while singles with a bathroom jump to $40. The Alaskan, like all hotels in Cordova, is booked solid through most of the summer.

Camping The closest campground is the *Odiak Camper Park*, 0.5 mile (0.8 km) from downtown on Whitshed Rd next to the recently-covered and landscaped dump site. The gravel campground is primarily for RVs and charges $5 per night, but showers, restrooms and water are available. Unofficial spots for pitching a tent are on the bluffs across from the ferry terminal or up Sixth St at the ski hill.

Places to Eat

The locals eat at the *Pioneer Café* on First St just up from the museum, open all day but especially crowded at breakfast. The *Ambrosia*, also on First St, specialises in pizza and Italian food, while a little way from downtown at *Mile 1.5* of the Copper River Highway is *The Powder House*, a bar that serves sandwiches, soups and local seafood.

Places to pick up your own supplies are *Davis Super Foods*, a full supermarket on First St; *Hometown Bakery* on Second St for fresh bread and pastries; and *St Elias Ocean Products* on Seafood Lane near the Small Boat Harbor for seafood.

Nightlife

The Powder House Bar, which earns its name because it lies on the site of the original Copper River & Northwestern Railroad powder house, is a fun place that features folk, bluegrass and country music at night. If you happen to be there on a rare evening when it isn't raining, there is a deck outside overlooking Eyak Lake.

In town, there is the *Club Bar* on First St with music nightly; or the *Anchor Bar* on Breakwater Avenue across from the Small Boat Harbor, for those who want to mingle with the fishermen.

Events

Because of the economic importance of the fishing season, no events or festivals are planned during the summer in Cordova other than a small Fourth of July celebration. The town's biggest event is its Iceworm Festival in mid-February, when there is little else to do.

Hiking & USFS Cabins

There are a number of hikes and cabins (reservations needed, $10 per day) accessible from the Cordova road system. Before venturing into the surrounding area, hikers should first stop at the USFS office (tel 424-7661) on the third floor of the Cordova post office on the corner of Browning Avenue and Second St to pick up an assortment of free trail maps. Seaman's Hardware on First St sells topographic maps of the area.

Carter Lake Trail This 2.5-mile (four-km) hike begins on Lake Eyak, about 0.5 mile (0.8 km) beyond the Municipal Airfield on Eyak Lake Rd. The trail climbs steeply but is easy to follow as it winds through lush forest. At the top it offers panoramic views of both the Copper River Delta and Prince William Sound. Plan on two to four hours round trip from the road to open country around Carter Lake.

Mt Eyak Ski Hill A quick hike from town is to scramble up the ski hill at the end of Sixth Avenue. Hardy hikers can spend a day climbing from here to the top of Mt Eyak and down the other side to Carter Lake.

Lydic Slough Trail & Eyak River Cabin At Mile 7.1 (11.4 km) of Copper River Highway is Lydic Slough Trail, which leads three miles (4.8 km) along Copper River Flats to a cabin on Eyak River. The Eyak River offers excellent trout and salmon fishing as well as opportunities to view moose, brown bear and a wide range of waterfowl.

McKinley Lake Trail The 2.5-mile (four km) McKinley Lake Trail begins at Mile 21.6 (34.8 km) of Copper River Highway and leads to the head of the lake and the remains of the Lucky Strike Gold Mine. Two cabins, McKinley Lake and McKinley Trail, are located on this path, making them accessible by foot from the highway.

Pipeline Loop Trail At Mile 21 (33.6 km) of Copper River Highway is this two-mile (3.2-km) trail past several small lakes. The trail provides access to good fishing holes for grayling and trout and merges into the McKinley Trail.

Getting There & Around

Airport All jets use the Cordova Airport, 12 miles (19.4 km) from town on Copper River Highway. The Airporter Bus greets all arrivals and charges $8 for the trip back into town. You can also pick up the bus at the major hotels in town for a ride out to the airport.

Air Alaska Airlines (tel 424-7151) makes a daily stop at Cordova on its run from Seattle to Anchorage. One-way fare for the short flight to Anchorage is $70. Chisum Flying Service (tel 424-7671) provides two daily flights from Cordova to Valdez as well as the usual flight-seeing tours and transportation to USFS cabins. The air taxi company flies out of the city airfield and off Eyak Lake for its floatplanes.

Boat During the summer the MV Bartlett stops twice a week at Cordova and the MV Tustumena once, providing marine ferry service to Valdez and then on to Whittier, Seward, Homer and Kodiak. The fare from Cordova to Valdez is $16, Whittier $33 and Seward $34. The ferry terminal (tel 424-7333) is north of town on Railroad Avenue.

AROUND CORDOVA

There is more than 50 miles (80 km) of road extending out from Cordova, most of it centred around Copper River Highway. Built on the old railroad bed to the Kennicott mines, the road was originally going to connect Cordova with Richardson

Highway and the rest of Alaska. Construction was halted in 1964 after the Good Friday earthquake damaged the existing roadbeds and bridges, knocking out the fourth span of the famous Million Dollar Bridge in front of Childs Glacier.

Today the highway provides access to the **Copper River Delta**, a huge area of tidal marshes and outwashes and a birdwatcher's paradise. Millions of birds and water fowl use it as a nesting and staging area during the summer, including arctic terns, dusty Canada geese, trumpeter swans, great blue herons and bald eagles. A drive along the highway at dawn or dusk could provide views of moose, brown bears, beavers and porcupines, while on a rare occasion a lynx or wolverine will be seen from the roadside.

The highway also provides access to a handful of glaciers that flow out of the Chugach Mountains. The first is **Sheridan Glacier**, which you can view from the bridge over Sheridan River 15 miles (24 km) from town or three miles (4.8 km) beyond the Cordova Airport. One mile (1.6 km) before the bridge, the Sheridan Glacier access road leads 4.3 miles (6.9 km) to the north, ending at a picnic table with a partial view of the ice floe. From here there is a one-mile trail to the dirt-covered glacial moraine.

Several other glaciers are seen spilling out of the mountains; by far the most impressive is **Childs Glacier** to the west of the Million Dollar Bridge, 48 miles (77 km) from town. A short side road leads from the highway to within 200 yards of the spectacular glacier's face whose periodical calving almost stops Copper River's downstream momentum. From the Million Dollar Bridge you can view Childs Glacier, less than a mile (1.6 km) downstream, or **Miles Glacier**, five miles (eight km) upstream.

Hitching Copper Highway would be slow going, and those with only a spare day or afternoon would do best to rent a car. Reluctant Fisherman Hotel (tel 424-3272) rents cars for $55 per day and 50c a mile, making a single-day journey to Childs Glacier a $105 affair, worth it if there are three or more sharing the expense.

VALDEZ

In the heart of Prince William Sound and less than 25 miles (40 km) west of Columbia Glacier is Valdez, the most northerly ice-free port in the western hemisphere and the southern terminus of the Alaska pipeline. The town and port were named by Spanish explorer Don Salvador Fidalgo in 1790 after a Spanish naval officer. Valdez boomed at the turn of the century when thousands of gold-seekers stampeded through on their way to Alaska's Interior and the Klondike fields. They followed the Valdez Trail, a route that included a trek over the Valdez Glacier where hundreds of lives were lost due to falls in crevasses, snowblindness and hypothermia. After the town lost the copper railroad in a bitter rivalry to Cordova, the old gold-rush trail was re-routed and improved into a wagon trail and in the 1920s was paved to become the Richardson Highway.

In 1964, Valdez lost its edge as the main cargo route to Interior Alaska. In four short minutes, the Good Friday earthquake demolished a town and reset the historical clocks of those living there. All of Valdez's history is dated either before or after the devastating catastrophe, as the city was one of the worst hit in Alaska. The earthquake caused the land to ripple like water and sent massive tidal waves that destroyed most of the harbour and left few buildings undamaged. Afterwards the residents voted to rebuild their city at a new site on more stable ground. The old town site lies four miles (6.4 km) east on Richardson Highway, but all that remains today is a vacant field and a plaque dedicated to those who lost their lives during the frightful event.

Valdez regained its gateway role for the Interior when it was chosen as the terminus of the Trans-Alaska pipeline.

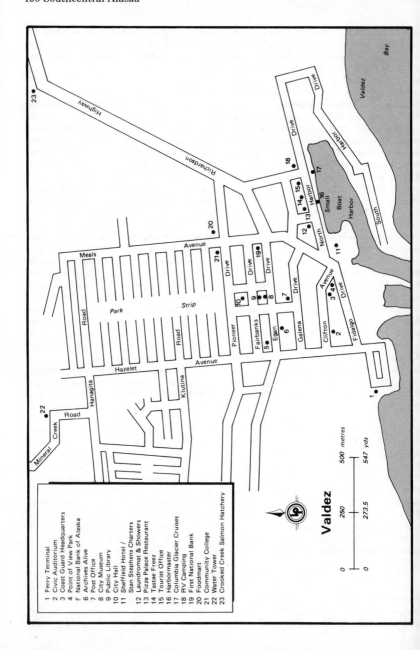

Valdez

1 Ferry Terminal
2 Civic Auditorium
3 Coast Guard Headquarters
4 Point of View Park
6 National Bank of Alaska
6 Archives Alive
7 Post Office
8 City Museum
9 Public Library
10 City Hall
11 Sheffield Hotel /
   Stan Stephens Charters
12 Laundromat & Showers
13 Pizza Palace Restaurant
14 Tastee Freez
15 Tourist Office
16 Harbormaster
17 Columbia Glacier Cruises
18 RV Camping
19 First National Bank
20 Foodmart
21 Community College
22 Water Tower
23 Crooked Creek Salmon Hatchery

Work began in 1974 and the $9 billion project was completed in 1977, when the first tanker was filled with the black gold on 1 August. Today the city's economy depends heavily on oil and the taxes the oil company has paid out. Fishing and tourism also contribute, but oil has clearly made Valdez a rich city. Major projects completed in the early 1980s include a $50 million container terminal to enhance the city's reputation as the 'Gateway To The North' and a $7 million Civic Centre. With oil money, a beautiful backdrop of the Chugach Mountains and an ideal location in the middle of the Prince William Sound playground, Valdez and its 3700 residents seem to have all a city could want.

Things to See

The **Visitors Information Centre** (tel 835-2330) is at 245 East North Harbor Drive across from the Small Boat Harbor and is open daily from 9 am to 9 pm in the summer. Along with the usual handouts and city maps, the centre houses the first barrel of oil from the Alaska Pipeline and a cross-section of the pipeline. They also rent out bicycles for a $10 deposit.

Across the street is Valdez's bustling **Small Boat Harbor**, while just to the west North Harbor Drive dead-ends opposite the corner of Fidalgo Drive and Clifton Court, where **Point of View Park** is located. The observation platform on the knoll is a good spot to view the old town site to the east, the pipeline terminal to the south and Valdez Narrows to the west. Next door is the **US Coast Guard Headquarters**, which offers free tours of its Vessel Traffic Centre and daily slide presentation every 30 minutes from 9.30 to 11 am and 1.30 to 3 pm. West of the Coast Guard is the **Civic Centre** and more panoramas of the area.

From the Civic Centre head two blocks north on Robe River Drive and turn right onto Egan Drive for **Archives Alive** in the Royal Centre. Operated by the Valdez Historical Society, the archives contain a collection of books, photographs and historical relics from Valdez's past. The society also shows a film daily at 7 pm that focuses on the town's history and ends with scenes from the Good Friday earthquake. Admission is free into both the archives and the film.

Continue east along Egan Drive for more history at the **Valdez Heritage Centre**. The museum houses numerous items, including a trapper's cabin, an early 19th-century lighthouse lens and the community's 1907 steam fire engine. There is also a collection of photographs covering the Good Friday earthquake. The museum is free and open daily in the summer from 10 am to 9 pm. Diagonally opposite the Heritage Centre is the **Valdez Library**, which among other things runs a book-and-magazine swap for travellers.

To reach **Prince William Sound Community College,** follow Chenega Avenue north from the Heritage Centre and turn right on Pioneer Drive. The small campus, a division of the University of Alaska, is accented by huge wooden carvings that are part of Peter Toth's collection of 50 sculptures dedicated to the American Indian.

Pioneer Drive runs east into Richardson Highway, where 0.5 mile (0.8 km) to the north is the **Salmon Spawning View Point** on Crooked Creek. The wooden platform, the site of the old hatchery, is a good spot to watch salmon spawn in July and August.

Valdez Convention & Visitors Bureau

Places to Stay

Hotels Valdez, the city of wealth and beauty, desperately lacks cheap accommodations for backpackers. Of the seven motel/hotels, rates range from $65 a night for singles in the *Valdez Motel* (tel 835-4444) at 112 Egan Drive to $98 a night at the nearby *Lamplighter Hotel*.

The lone exception is the *Camp Kennedy Inn* (tel 835-4897), which offers a limited number of rooms with shared baths for $40 a night but is located on Airport Rd almost five miles (eight km) out of town.

Camping Good public campgrounds are also scarce downtown. The nearest one is *Valdez Glacier Campground* (101 sites) almost six miles (9.6 km) from town past the airport on Airport Rd. Though the facility is free and scenic and offers outhouses and water, it is hardly convenient for those on foot.

While there are only expensive private campgrounds catering to RVers in town, Valdez does not have any ordinances restricting camping within the city. It is a common and accepted practice for backpackers to pitch their tents in a number of places around downtown, including across Chitna St from the Visitor Centre on the hill overlooking the waterfront, along Mineral Creek Rd (see the Hiking section) and down by the city dock, especially when waiting for an early-morning state ferry.

Places to Eat

For those at Valdez Glacier Campground, *Hangar 9* in the airport has reasonable breakfasts and a 'cook your own steak' special at night. In town, the *Tastee-Freez* on North Harbor Drive across from the Small Boat Harbor is a fast-food place for hamburgers and fries, and even has a salad bar. Another fast-food place downtown is *MacMurray's* on Meals Avenue and Pioneer Drive across from Village Inn, which offers good hamburgers and local halibut-and-chip dinners.

A little classier than the local hamburger joint is *Pizza Palace* on North Harbor Drive, with views of the harbour from its bar. The place specialises in pasta and local seafood and dinners cost $12 to $17.

On the other end of the eating spectrum is *Foodmart* on Pioneer Drive and Meals Avenue, which has the cheapest supermarket prices in town and its own bakery. At *Valdez Market* on Egan Drive you can buy ready-made sandwiches from its deli inside, along with groceries. Also in town is *Community Foods*, a natural-foods store in the Keystone Mall which serves soup and sandwiches.

Nightlife

Among the places you might want to try are *Sugarloaf Saloon* at the Village Inn on the corner of Meals Avenue and Richardson Highway, or the *Harbor Club Bar* in the Pizza Palace, where you can view the pipeline terminal while ordering your brew.

For those out at the Valdez Glacier Campground, *Hangar 9* has live music nightly and *Donna's Can Can Palace* at the Camp Kennedy Inn features dancing and readings of Robert Service poetry.

During the summer the Civic Centre is the site of numerous activities, including plays performed by local groups and the University of Alaska-Anchorage theatre group, which frequently tours the state. Stop in the centre for a list of current events, or call 835-4440.

Events

Valdez has both a Fourth of July Celebration and an end-of-summer festival called 'Gold Rush Days'. The five-day festival takes place in mid-August and includes a parade, bed races, dances, a free fish feed and a portable jailhouse that is pulled throughout town by locals who go about arresting people without beards and other innocent bystanders.

Top: Downtown Juneau (DT)
Left: Walking at the top of Mendenhall Glacier near Juneau (JD)
Right: One of the many staircases in Juneau (JD)

Top: Kayak in front of iceberg in Tracy Arm Fjord (JS)
Left: Rafting on the Alsek River (JD)
Right: Kayak on Russell Fjord in the Southeast (JD)

Hiking

In an area surrounded by mountains and glaciers, you would think there would be good hiking in every direction, but this is not the case for Valdez. There are few developed trails in the area (though many are now being proposed), so reaching much of the surrounding alpine country requires considerable bush-whacking through thick bush. There is no USFS office in Valdez and no nearby cabins.

Mineral Creek Trail The best walk away from town is the old road along Mineral Creek and the one-mile (1.6-km) trail from its end to the old Smith stamping mill. The road is no longer maintained and is in poor condition, suitable only for those on foot or in a four-wheel-drive vehicle.

To reach the beginning, follow Egan Drive to its end and turn left on Hazelet Avenue for 10 blocks. Turn left on Hanagita and then right on Mineral Creek Rd. The road bumps along for 5.5 miles and from there turns into a trail for a mile to the old stamping mill. Following the trail beyond the mill at Brevier Creek also requires considerable bush-whacking. If you are hiking the entire road, the trip up the lush green canyon can be a pleasant all-day adventure.

Solomon Gulch Trail A newer trail is located across from the Solomon Gulch Fish Hatchery on Dayville Rd. The one-mile trail is a steep, uphill hike that quickly leads to splendid views of the Valdez Port and the city below. It ends at Solomon Lake.

Rafting

Lowe River, a glacial river that cuts through the impressive Keystone Canyon, is a few miles outside of Valdez and has become a popular float trip during the summer. Keystone Raft & Kayak (tel 835-2606) offers day trips on the river, carrying passengers six miles through whitewater and past the cascading water-

falls that have made the canyon famous. The outfitters run the 1½-hour trip five times daily and charge $20 per person for the scenic adventure.

Columbia Glacier

Most travellers view this magnificent tidewater glacier while crossing the Prince William Sound to or from Valdez. The State Marine Ferry is the cheapest way to sail between Whittier and Valdez but stays a good two to three miles (3.2 to 4.8 km) from the face, giving its passengers a wider view of the glacier as it winds back into the Chugach Mountains.

Privately run cruise ships sail considerably closer to the face after threading their way through almost three miles (4.8 km) of icebergs, where you can often observe seals basking under the sun. At one time the private tour boats were able to get within 0.25 mile (0.4 km) of the face, but that is difficult today as the glacier has begun receding rapidly, discharging much more ice. Tour boats can still get within half a mile to a mile at most times, and from this close the ongoing show of ice calving into the Sound is an awesome sight and a photographer's delight.

The *Glacier Spirit* and *Vince Peede*, operated by Stan Stephens Charters (tel 835-4731), depart daily at 9 am and 1 pm respectively from the dock in front of the Sheffield Hotel for a six-hour cruise to the glacier and back. The fare is $50 per person. The *Columbia Queen* departs at 7.30 am from slip B-1 of the Small Boat Harbor for a daily cruise past the glacier to Whittier and back. The fare is $69 for the trip across the Sound and reservations can be made by calling Valdez Charter Service (tel 835-4461). One other way to view the glacier from a different perspective is to join the three-day raft trips offered by Alaska Waterways (tel 835-5151) throughout the summer.

Getting There & Around

Air Alaska Airlines, through its contract

carrier ERA (tel 835-2636), provides two daily flights between Valdez and Anchorage from the Valdez Airport, five miles (eight km) from town on Airport Rd; one-way fare between the cities is $79.

Boat The Alaska marine ferry is by the far the cheapest way to view the Columbia Glacier; a one-way Valdez-Whittier ticket is $45. The state ferry also connects Valdez to Cordova ($20), Seward ($46), Homer ($93) and Kodiak ($70), since both the *MV Bartlett* and *MV Tustumena* call here. Between the two ships there are runs to Whittier five times a week, three weekly sailings to Cordova and a weekly run to Seward, Homer and Kodiak. The ferry terminal (tel 835-4436) is downtown at the end of Hazelet Avenue and reservations for these popular runs are strongly recommended.

Bus Alaska-Yukon Motorcoaches provides a daily run to Fairbanks that departs the Village Inn at 7.30 pm. The fare is $30 to Glennallen and $75 to Fairbanks. The Valdez-Anchorage Bus Line (tel 835-5299) departs from the Totem Inn on the Richardson Highway at 8 am Tuesday and Friday, and Sunday at 9 am for the nine-hour trip to Anchorage. The fare to Glennallen is $21 and to Anchorage $55.

Bicycle The ideal way to get around Valdez is to check out a bicycle from the Visitor Centre. The centre has three bikes for free use, the only requirement being that you leave a $10 deposit and some identification.

AROUND VALDEZ

The **oil pipeline terminal**, the heart and soul of Valdez, lies across the bay on Dayville Rd, eight miles (13 km) from town along Richardson Highway. Dayville Rd is an interesting road as it branches off the highway and hugs the mountainside passing several eagle nests and scenic **Solomon Gulch**.

The **Copper Valley hydro project**, which

supplies power for both Valdez and Glennallen, was recently completed at the Gulch. Across the road is the new **Solomon Gulch Hatchery**, open to visitors from 8 am to 5 pm daily. Dayville Rd ends at the terminal visitors centre and bronze monument dedicated to the construction workers who built the pipeline.

The terminal is nothing short of remarkable, as it contains over 15 miles (24 km) of pipeline, 18 oil storage tanks and four tanker berths. Oil is pumped out of Prudhoe Bay on the Beaufort Sea and travels 800 miles (1300 km) south through the pipeline to the terminal, where it is either stored or loaded into tankers. It is estimated that there are 9.6 billion barrels of oil under the North Slope, of which 1.7 million barrels flow out of the pipeline into tankers every day at the terminal. For most visitors, it is enough to stare at the facility from the visitor centre at the entrance gate, wonder about human dependency on oil and then head back. If you want a closer look at the place, a Gray Line bus departs from the Sheffield Hotel at 10 am and 7 pm for two-hour tour. You never leave the bus except for one viewpoint above the terminal, and the fare is $13 per person. Call 835-2357 for more information or seat on the bus.

RICHARDSON HIGHWAY TO GLENNALLEN

This section of Richardson Highway is an incredibly scenic route that includes canyons, mountain passes, glaciers and access to the massive Wrangell-St Elias National Park. Hitch-hiking is fairly easy during the summer, making it convenient to stop often and enjoy the sights and campgrounds along the way.

The highway begins in downtown Valdez, but *Mile 0* is near the site of old Valdez, as the mileposts were erected before the Good Friday earthquake and were never changed. The junction to Dayville Rd and the pipeline terminal is reached 6.9 miles (11.1 km) from down town, and at this point Richardson

Highway swings north. At *Mile 13* (21 km) you reach Keystone Canyon with its many waterfalls and unusual rock formations high above the road. In the next mile (1.6 km) two magnificent waterfalls appear, first Horsetail and then Bridal Veil 0.5 mile (0.8 km) down the highway. The canyon wall is so sheer that the waterfalls appear to be cascading straight down and actually spray the road with mist. At *Mile 14.8* (23.8 km), the north end of the canyon, there is an abandoned hand-drilled tunnel that residents of Valdez began but never finished when they were competing with Cordova for the railroad to the Kennicott Mines. A historical marker points it out.

The trans-Alaska pipeline can be seen at *Mile 20.4* (32.8 km). The short loop road to the first camping area, Blueberry Lake Wayside, is reached at *Mile 24* (38.4 km). The state recreational area offers nine sites and four covered picnic shelters in a beautiful alpine setting with lofty peaks surrounding it. There's good fishing in the nearby lakes, but beware if you are spending the night here because the site is above the treeline and can get windy and foul at times. The highway continues to rise until it reaches Thompson Pass at *Mile 26* (41.8 km). There are several scenic turnoffs near the pass, elevation 2771 feet (845 metres), which in early summer is covered by wildflowers. This spot also holds most of Alaska's snowfall records, including 62 inches of snow in a 24-hour period in December 1955.

Mile 28.6 (46 km) is the turnoff to Worthington Glacier, where it is possible to drive to the face on a short access road. Within this state recreation area are outhouses, picnic tables and a large covered viewing area. A one-mile (1.6-km) trail begins at the crest of the moraine on the left side of the glacier from the parking lot. It follows the edge of the glacier for a scenic hike but should be done with caution. Never hike on the glacier itself. Thompson Pass and the surrounding area above the treeline are ideal for tramping, as hikers will have few problems climbing through the heather.

The pipeline continues to pop into view as you travel north on Richardson Highway, and at one point passes beneath the road. The next campground, Little Tonsina River State Wayside (eight sites, free) appears at *Mile 65* (104 km). Squirrel Creek State Campground (14 sites, free) is at *Mile 79.4* (127.8 km) and offers a scenic little camping area on the banks of the creek. There is good fishing for grayling and rainbow trout in Squirrel Creek. The junction to Edgerton Highway that leads to the heart of the Wrangell-St Elias National Park (see following section) is passed in three miles (4.8 km). Willow Lake appears at *Mile 87.6* (141 km). This lookout can be stunning on a clear day, with the water reflecting the Wrangell Mountains, the 100-mile (160-km) chain that includes 11 peaks over 10,000 feet (3048 metres) in elevation. The two most prominent peaks visible from the lookout are Mt Drum, 28 miles (45 km) to the north-east, and Mt Wrangell, Alaska's largest active volcano, to the east of it. Mt Wrangell stands at 14,163 feet (4317 metres) and on most days a plume of steam is visible from its crater.

At *Mile 91* (145.6 km) a gravel road leads east and intersects Edgerton Highway. Copper Centre, population 150, is reached at *Mile 101* (161.6 km). At the turn of the century the town was an important mining camp for the thousands of prospectors eyeing the gold-fields in the Yukon and later in Fairbanks. Near the bridge over the Klutina River is the Copper Centre Lodge, which began in 1897 as the Blix Roadhouse and was the first lodge built north of Valdez. It still serves as a roadhouse today and a place where you can get a delicious plate of sourdough pancakes. Just north of the town on Richardson Highway is the Chapel On The Hill, built in 1942. During the summer the log chapel features a slide show on the history of the Copper River Basin area; admission is free.

At *Mile 115* (185 km) is the major junction between Glenn and Richardson highways. The Richardson continues north to Delta Junction and eventually Fairbanks (see the Interior chapter). Glenn Highway heads west to Glennallen a short distance away and later reaches Anchorage (see the Interior chapter).

WRANGELL-ST ELIAS NATIONAL PARK

This national park, created in 1980, stretches north 170 miles (270 km) from the Gulf of Alaska to encompass 12.4 million acres (five million hectares) of mountains and forelands bounded by the Copper River on the west and Canada's Kluane National Park to the east. Together Kluane and Wrangell-St Elias make up 19 million acres (7.7 million hectares) and the greatest expanse of valleys, canyons and towering mountains in North America, including the continent's second and third highest peaks. Expansive icefields and over 100 major glaciers – some of the largest and most active in the world – are found in these two great wilderness preserves.

Wildlife in Wrangell-St Elias is more diverse and plentiful than in any other Alaska park. Species making a home in the preserve include moose, black and brown bears, Dall sheep, mountain goats, wolves, wolverines, beavers and three of Alaska's 11 caribou herds.

Richardson Highway borders the northwest corner of the park and two rough dirt roads lead into its interior. However, Wrangell-St Elias is a true wilderness park with few visitor facilities or services beyond the highway. An adventure into this preserve requires time and patience rather than money, but would lead to a once-in-a-lifetime experience.

Information

The park's main headquarters is at *Mile 105* (168 km) of Richardson Highway, 10 miles (16 km) before the junction with Glenn Highway. The office (tel 822-5234) is open daily during the summer and rangers can answer questions about the park as well as supply various handouts and rough maps of the area. They also schedule daily tours and interpretive programmes. During the summer rangers are stationed in Chitina at the end of Edgerton Highway.

Getting There

Edgerton Highway and McCarthy Rd combine to provide a 92-mile (147-km) route into the heart of the park, ending at the mountainous hamlet of McCarthy near the ruins of the famous Kennicott Copper Mines.

The 32-mile (51 km) Edgerton Highway, partly paved and partly gravel, begins at *Mile 82.6* (133 km) of Richardson Highway and ends at Chitina. The town of 42 permanent residents is the last place to purchase food or gas. Backpackers can camp along the three-mile (4.8-km) road south to O'Brien Creek or beside Trout Lake within Chitina. Those staying overnight in this small village on a Saturday or Sunday should stop in at the Chitina Saloon for a brew and some foot-stomping music.

From Chitina, McCarthy Rd – a rough dirt road that is not regularly maintained – takes over and leads 60 miles (96 km) further east to the two forks of the Kennicott River. To continue the final mile to McCarthy you have to use the hand-pulled trams erected by locals. The two trams are open platforms large enough to carry two persons and their backpacks. Use gloves and make sure you have enough strength to pull your load several hundred feet to the other side of the river. Once you're across, follow the road up a small rise to the McCarthy Museum, an old railroad depot, and take the right fork into McCarthy, an extremely scenic village of 16 or so residents.

The cheapest accommodation in McCarthy is *Sally's Place*, though it's not always open. Owner Sally Gibert has turned the 1911 McCarthy General Store into an unofficial hostel that sleeps 15.

The price of lodging covers bunk, breakfast and dinner. There is also the *McCarthy Lodge*, full of mining relics and photographs of the era and is a place to get a bed, meal, shower or ride to the Kennicott mines. There is no grocery store in the area so bring your own food.

If you're driving, allow four hours to cover McCarthy Rd. If you're hitch-hiking, plan on a day of waiting for that one ride to come along. Those who want to see McCarthy and the Kennicott Mines but want to skip the hitch-hike can take the Tuesday mail plane out of Glennallen. Ellis Air Taxi (tel 822-3368) makes the mail flight and usually has one or two seats available for passengers.

Hiking

From McCarthy it is an 18-mile (29-km) round trip to the Kennicott mine ruins. This makes a long day-hike or a pleasant overnight excursion. Begin at the McCarthy Museum and take the left fork, a gravel road that leads five miles (eight km) to Kennicott. After crossing a ridge over National Creek in Kennicott, you turn right onto a gravel road that parallels the creek and soon begins climbing the final four miles (6.4 km). The road splits after 1.5 miles (2.4 km); to the left an overgrown trail leads to the remains of Jumbo Mine at 5800 feet (1758 metres); to the right the main road continues toward Bonanza Mine where there are good alpine views but no ruins. Good camping exists where the Jumbo Mine Trail crosses Bonanza Creek.

Another overnight hike begins in the O'Brien Creek Campground, three miles (4.8 km) south of Chitina. The scenic trail follows the old bed of the Copper River & Northwestern Railroad five miles (eight km) through Woods Canyon to Haley Creek. Just before reaching Haley Creek you pass through a tunnel. The creek offers superb camping on a sandy strip with a roaring waterfall nearby.

Outfitters

St Elias Alpine Guides (tel 277-6867) based in Anchorage run the most extensive trips into the national park. They offer a three-day exploration trip for $550 per person that begins and ends in Anchorage and includes all transportation and lodging to McCarthy and the Kennicott ruins. They also run several backpacking and mountaineering expeditions in the park during the summer, as well as a 14-day float down the Copper River that begins in McCarthy, ends in Cordova and costs $1400 per person.

WHITTIER

On the day the military was cutting the ribbon that marked the completion of the Alaska Highway, the army was also having a 'holing through' ceremony outside of Whittier. WW II and the Japanese invasion of the Aleutian Islands brought the US military searching for a second warm-water port in Southcentral Alaska, one that would serve as a secret port. Whittier was chosen because it was well hidden between the high walls of the Passage Canal Fjord in which it lies, and for the consistently bad weather that hangs over it.

Work began immediately on two tunnels through the Chugach Mountains that would connect the port to the main line of the Alaska Railroad. The tunnels, though overshadowed by the Alcan, were another amazing feat of engineering. The first was drilled through almost one mile (1.6 km) of solid rock while the second, begun simultaneously from the other side of the mountain, required carving a route 2.5 miles (four km) long. When General Simon Buckner blasted open the second tunnel during the 'holing through' in 1942, the two tunnels missed perfect alignment by an eighth of an inch (0.3 cm).

Whittier owes both its existence and its skyscraper appearance to the military. After WW II, the port became a permanent base, and tall concrete buildings

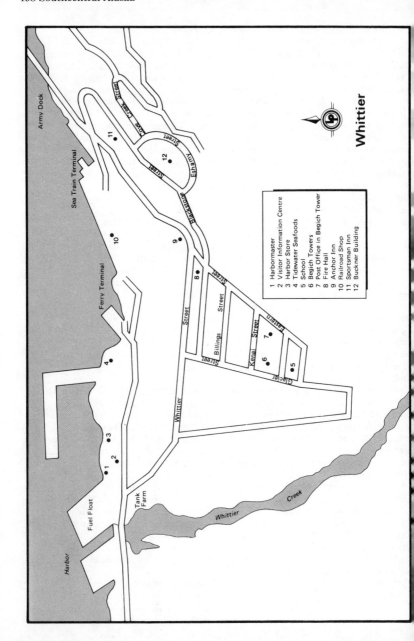

Whittier

1 Harbormaster
2 Visitor Information Centre
3 Harbor Store
4 Tidewater Seafoods
5 School
6 Begich Towers
7 Post Office in Begich Tower
8 Fire Hall
9 Anchor Inn
10 Railroad Shop
11 Sportsman Inn
12 Buckner Building

Army Dock

Sea Train Terminal

Ferry Terminal

Harbor

Fuel Float

Tank Farm

Whittier Creek

Whittier Street

Billings Street

Kenai Street

Glacier Street

Eastern Street

Blackstop

Eastern

Depot Street

were constructed to house and service the men. One, the Begich Towers, is 14 storeys tall. Nearby, the massive Buckner Building once housed 1000 men and had a bowling alley, a theatre, cafés, a hospital and a jail. Today the Begich Towers have been converted into condominiums where 60% of Whittier's 211 residents live. Military and government activities ceased in 1963 but the small town continues to exist on fishing and tourism and as a port of call for both the Alaska marine ferry and the Alaska Railroad.

Things to See

The vast majority of travellers stay in Whittier only long enough to board the train to Anchorage or the ferry to Valdez. However, the small village is one of the more interesting towns in Alaska and on a clear day is a beautiful spot to be. The town is nestled at the base of the mountains that line Passage Canal, and the surrounding peaks are capped with snow for much of the year. To the west a glacier spills out of the mountains and ends hanging above the town.

As soon as you disembark from the train, you will spot the new **Visitor Information Centre**, housed in a railcar donated by the Alaska Railroad. Due north is the **Small Boat Harbor** that contains fishing boats, private craft and the numerous tour vessels that work the Columbia Glacier route between Whittier and Valdez.

There is also a small museum in town on the first floor of the Begich Tower, down the hall from the post office. Open from 2 to 6 pm daily except Tuesday and Thursday, the **Whittier Historical & Fine Arts Museum** contains strips of sperm-whale bone, ivory carvings, and displays on Prince William Sound marine life and the 1964 earthquake which killed 13 people in town but did little damage to the concrete building or nearby tunnels; donations are accepted.

Also in the Begich Towers is the **Whittier Library**, open afternoons from Monday to Friday and featuring a small collection of books and local memorabilia. From the south-west corner of the Begich Towers a track leads west to **Whittier Stream**, while above it, falling from the ridge of a glacial cirque, is picturesque **Horsetail Falls**.

Places to Stay & Eat

There are two hotels in Whittier. The *Sportsman Inn* (tel 472-2352) is the cheapest at $37 a night for a single and $45 for a double. The inn, east of the Buckner Building, also sells groceries and liquor and has a dining room, bar and a three-person sauna which is rented out for $10 an hour.

The best place to camp is First Salmon Run (see the Hiking section), a scenic spot with a shelter, picnic tables and out-houses, or you can pitch a tent just about anywhere near town by walking into the bush and away from the road.

For hamburgers there is *Hobo Bay Trading Company* or *Burger Buggy*, which also serves prawns and fish & chips. Both are right off the Small Boat Harbor. You could also purchase the day's catch from *Tidewater Seafoods* next to the ferry dock. Groceries are available at either of the hotels.

Hiking

Portage Pass Trail This trail makes a superb afternoon hike as it provides good views of Portage Glacier, Passage Canal and the surrounding mountains and glaciers. Even better is to hike up in late afternoon and spend the evening camping at Divide Lake. To pick up the trailhead, walk along the gravel road from the train platform as it parallels the tracks to the west. Follow it 1.3 miles (two km) to the tank farm and the tunnel at Maynard Mountain, and turn left on a road that crosses the tracks. Follow the right fork as it begins to climb steeply along the flank of the mountain, until it goes through a small pond. Here you can climb a promontory, elevation 750 feet (229 metres), for views of Portage Glacier or Passage Canal to the east.

Divided Lake is another half mile along and by travelling left around it you can head down the slope to the glacier. Plan on two hours to reach Divide Lake. The round trip to the glacier and back to Whittier is an eight-mile (12.8 km) hike.

Smitty's Cove From the front of the Sportsman's Inn, Smitty's Cove lies 0.25 mile (0.4 km) down the road to the right. At low tide you can beachcomb all of the cove to the point east of it. Smitty's Cove is a favourite haunt of Alaska scuba divers and is occasionally referred to as Diver's Cove.

First Salmon Run It is a 0.8-mile (1.3 km) walk along a dirt road to the First Salmon Run Picnic Area, so named because of the large king and silver salmon runs that take place in the creek in June and late August. From the north-east corner of the Buckner Building behind the Sportsman's Inn, follow the road that leads up the mountain, staying to the right at the first fork and to the left at the second fork. The road leads into the picnic area, where you can cross a bridge over the stream and continue another three miles (4.8 km) to Second Salmon Run. This walk, along what is known as Shotgun Cove Rd, is exceptionally scenic as you can see Billings Glacier most of the way.

Getting There

There are two ways of getting out of Whittier and neither one is by road. To go west you take the Alaska Railroad; to head east you take a boat.

There are three trains departing on weekdays and five on Saturday and Sunday, but only the final one at 7.50 pm takes you all the way to Anchorage. One-way fare for Whittier-Anchorage is $10.75 and Whittier-Portage is $5.25. If arriving by ferry, you have a 5½-hour wait before departing for Anchorage – enough time to

tackle the Portage Pass Trail (see the Hiking section).

The state ferry *MV Bartlett* goes east five times a week at 3 pm from the ferry dock. All departures go to Valdez and cruise pass the impressive Columbia Glacier; one-way fare from Whittier to Valdez is $45.

The other alternative is the charter vessels that depart from the Small Boat Harbor and usually include lunch and a closer view of the glacier than the state ferry provides. The *Columbia Queen* charges $69 and the *Glacier Seas* costs $90; both make the run daily during the summer. To book passage, search out the boats in the harbour before 3 pm and purchase a ticket from the captain.

Kenai Peninsula

Because of its diverse terrain, easy accessibility and close proximity to Alaska's largest city, the Kenai Peninsula has become the state's top recreational area. It is well serviced, well developed and, unfortunately, well used during the summer. Though some trails are very popular all summer and many camp-grounds are always filled near capacity, if you hike a little further or climb a little higher you can find a tent space with only nature camped next to you.

The area is criss-crossed by two major highways and one minor one. Seward Highway goes from Anchorage, follows the Turnagain Arm where it is carved out of mountains and then turns south at Portage to the picturesque community of Seward on Resurrection Bay. Sterling Highway heads west from the Seward Highway 90 miles (144 km) out of Anchorage at Tern Lake Junction. When it reaches the crossroad town of Soldotna, near Cook Inlet, it turns south, follows the coast past some great clam-digging beaches and ends up at Homer, the most delightful town in the Peninsula. The third road is Hope Highway, which heads north from Seward Highway, 70 miles (113 km) out of Anchorage, for the small historical mining community of Hope, 16 miles (26 km) at the end.

Traffic is heavy on the main highways, making hitch-hiking an easy form of travel during the summer. The area is connected to the rest of Prince William Sound by the state ferry; the *MV Tustumena* makes a run from Cordova and Valdez across the Sound to Seward, over to Homer and then down to Kodiak. Alaska Airlines through its contract carrier also provides regularly scheduled service between Anchorage and Kenai, Homer and Kodiak.

SEWARD HIGHWAY

Those travelling from Whittier should think twice before purchasing a train ticket to Anchorage. For half the fare you can get off at Portage, where there is easy hitching down Seward Highway and into the heart of the Kenai Peninsula, Alaska's outdoor playground. The highway stretches 127 miles (204 km) and is another scenic gem in the state's fledgling system of roads.

The first section from Anchorage, *Mile 127*, to Portage Glacier, *Mile 79* (127 km), is covered in the Anchorage chapter. When heading south, keep in mind that the mileposts along Seward Highway show distances beginning in Seward, *Mile 0*, to Anchorage, *Mile 127*.

Near *Mile 68* (109 km) the highway begins climbing into the alpine region of Turnagain Pass, where there is a wayside with litter barrels and toilets. In early summer this area is a kaleidoscope of wildflowers that range from purple violets to reds. Just past *Mile 64* (103 km) is the USFS sign pointing to the north trailhead of Johnson Pass Trail (see the Wilderness chapter), a 23-mile (37-km) route over the alpine pass. The USFS Granite Creek Campground (19 sites, $5 fee) is reached at *Mile 63* (101.4 km) and provides tables, water and a place to camp for hikers

coming off Johnson Pass Trail at its north end.

The junction to Hope Highway (see following section) is reached at *Mile 56.7* (91 km). From here the paved road heads 18 miles (28.8 km) north to one mile (1.6 km) past the small hamlet of Hope. Seward Highway continues south, and at *Mile 46* (73.6 km) you cross the Colorado Creek Bridge and the short side road to the USFS Tenderfoot Creek Campground (27 sites, $5 fee). The scenic campground lies on the shores of Upper Summit Lake and provides good fishing opportunities in the spring and fall for landlocked Dolly Varden.

Devils Pass Trail (see the Wilderness chapter), a 10-mile (16 km) route over a 2400-foot (732-metre) gap to Resurrection Pass Trail, is reached at *Mile 39.4* (63.4 km), while Tern Lake Junction, the beginning of Sterling Highway (see following section), is at *Mile 37* (59.5 km). By driving 0.5 mile (0.8 km) west from the junction you will reach USFS Tern Lake Campground (33 sites, $5 fee).

Carter Lake Trail

This 2.3-mile (3.7 km) trail is reached at *Mile 33* (53 km) of Seward Highway. The path, an old jeep trail, starts from a parking area on the west side of the highway and climbs steeply almost 1000 feet (305 metres) to Carter Lake. From the lake a foot trail continues another mile around the west side of the lake to Crescent Lake. There is good camping at the end of Carter Lake. Half a mile south of the Carter Lake trailhead on the other side of the highway is the southern trailhead to Johnson Pass Trail (see the Wilderness chapter).

The highway continues south and at *Mile 29.4* (47.3) passes through the village of Moose Pass (population 200). The small town has a general store, post office and two restaurants and sponsors the Moose Pass Summer Festival on the weekend nearest the summer solstice on 21 June. At *Mile 25* (40 km) is an obscure

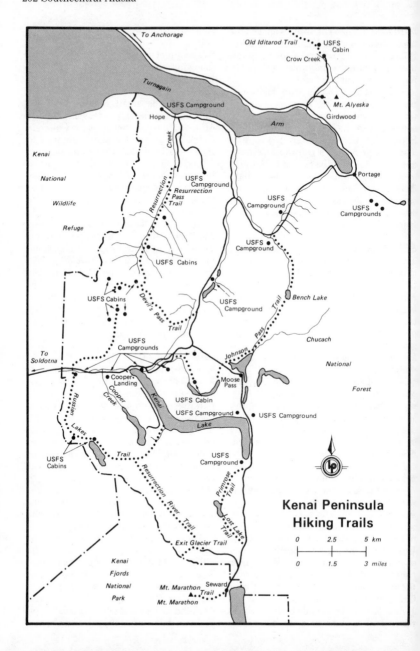

Kenai Peninsula
Hiking Trails

dirt road that leads west to the USFS Trail River Campground (63 sites, $5 fee), featuring many campsites right on Kenai Lake and Lower Trail River.

Ptarmigan Creek Trail

Ptarmigan Creek Bridge is reached at *Mile 23* (37 km). Right before it on the east side of the highway is the entrance to the USFS Ptarmigan Creek Campground (26 sites, $5 fee). The 3.5-mile (5.6-km) trail to Ptarmigan Lake begins in the campground and ends at this beautiful body of water that reflects the mountains surrounding it. A four-mile (6.4 km) trail continues around the north side of the lake, which offers good fishing for Dolly Varden at its outlet to the creek. Plan on five hours for a round-trip hike to the lake, as some parts of the trail are steep.

Victor Creek Trail

At *Mile 19.7* (31.7 km), on the east side of the highway, is the trailhead for the path that climbs two miles (3.2 km) for good views of the surrounding mountains.

After crossing the bridge over South Fork Snow River at *Mile 17.2* (27.7 km), look to the west for the road that leads one mile (1.6 km) to the USFS Primrose Campground (10 sites, $5 fee). The scenic campground is on the east end of beautiful Kenai Lake and contains the trailhead to Primrose Trail (see Lost Lake Trail in the Seward hiking section).

Grayling Lake Trail

This 1.6-mile (2.6 km) trail leads to Grayling Lake. Side trails connect it to Meridian and Leech lakes, a beautiful spot with good views of Snow River Valley. The trailhead is in a paved parking lot at *Mile 13.2* (21.2 km) on the west side of the highway.

SEWARD

The only town on the eastern side of the Kenai Peninsula is a pretty little one flanked by rugged mountains on one side and the salmon-filled Resurrection Bay on the other. Seward, with an area population of 2500, was founded in 1903 by Alaska Railroad surveyors who needed an ice-free port to serve as the ocean terminal for the rail line. The first spike was driven in in 1904 and the line was completed in 1923. During that time Seward prospered, as it served as the beginning of the Iditarod Trail to Nome and saw thousands of prospectors stampeding their way through. Dog teams were used to haul supplies, mail and gold along this 958-mile (1533 km) route.

Like most towns in Southcentral Alaska, Seward began a new era of history in 1964 because the Good Friday earthquake (or Black Friday as Alaskans call it) caused fires and tidal waves that destroyed 90% of the town. Today the only reminder of the natural disaster is at the public library (tel 224-3646) on Fifth and Adams Sts across from City Hall, where the slide show 'Seward Is Burning' is given from Monday to Saturday at 2 pm and covers the earthquake through the eyes of residents who witnessed it.

Otherwise, the town has completely rebuilt its fine Small Boat Harbor and waterfront facilities with a $10 million dock designed to be earthquake proof. Most of the area's residents work at Seward Fisheries, the largest halibut receiving station on the US west coast; or they are fishermen; or they are connected with Seward Marine Centre – a ship-repair facility – and the town's growing maritime industry.

Things to See

First stop in Seward should be the **Seward Railroad Car** at Third and Jefferson Sts. At one time the Pullman dining car carried President Warren G Harding to the place where he drove in the golden spike that completed the Alaska Railroad. Today it houses the Chamber of Commerce Information Cache (tel 224-3046), where you can pick up maps, information or a

walking-tour map of the city. The centre is open daily in the summer from 9 am to 5 pm.

The tour begins north on Third Avenue, where the houses on the left are known as **Millionaires Row**. They were built around 1905 by railroad officials and bankers who had just arrived in the newly-created town.

From Third Avenue and Madison St the tour heads west to First Avenue and follows it south for two blocks, where you pass Lowell St and the start of the **Mt Marathon Trail** (see the Hiking section). The walk swings onto Adams St, where at the corner of Second Avenue is **St Peter's Episcopal Church**, built in 1906. Inside is the famous mural of the Resurrection by Dutch artist Jan Van Emple, who used Alaskan models and the nearby bay as the backdrop.

Head south on Third Avenue to Rail Avenue to view the **Seward Marine Centre**, operated by the University of Alaska. The centre is open to the public Monday to Friday from 1 to 5 pm and has marine displays, films and tours of the facility. The tour continues north on Fourth Avenue where many of the businesses have restored the pioneer look to their buildings. It swings onto Fifth Avenue at Jefferson St and then south to the corner

of Adams St, to the **Seward Library** and **City Hall**. In the basement of City Hall is the **Resurrection Bay Historical Museum**, open daily from 11 am to 4 pm. The museum features artefacts and photographs of the 1964 earthquake, including a clock that stopped the instant the disaster struck; admission is 50c.

Not on the tour but equally interesting is the **Small Boat Harbor** at the north end of Fourth Avenue. The place hums during the summer with fishing boats, charter vessels and a large number of sailboats. Often it is possible to view sea otters in the surrounding waters. Nearby is the visitor information centre for the Kenai Fjords National Park. At the Harbormaster Office you can get a shower for $1.

Places to Stay

Youth Hostel The newest Alaska Youth Hostel opened in 1986 and is 16 miles (25.6 km) north of Seward. The *Snow River Youth Hostel* (no phone) is off Seward Highway near Primrose State Campground and has a beautiful wooded setting. The hostel provides two buildings with 16 beds plus a homesteader's cabin with four additional bunks. There are showers, laundry facilities and a kitchen. Nightly fees are $7.50 for members and $9.50 for non-members. Reservations can be made in advance by writing to the hostel at PO Box 8, Moose Pass, Alaska 99631. The hostel is ideally located for hikers coming off the Lost Lake-Primrose Trail circuit.

Hotels Of the five hotels, the cheapest ones are conveniently located downtown. The *Van Guilder Hotel* (tel 224-3079), which was built in 1916 and has been operating as a hotel since 1921, is at 307 Adams St and charges $36 for singles and $39 for doubles, all with shared baths. The *New Seward Hotel* (tel 224-5211), near Fifth Avenue and Adams St has singles with shared baths for $36 and doubles for $47.

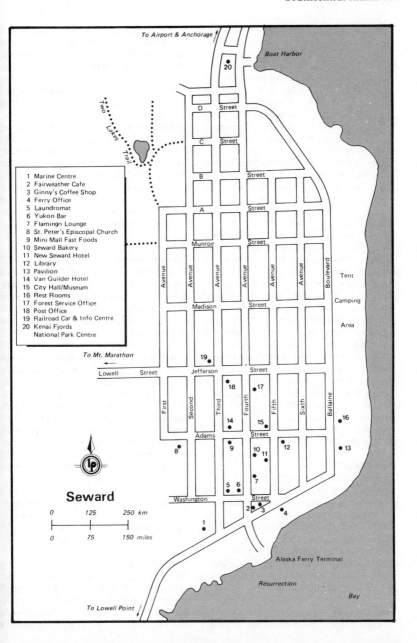

1 Marine Centre
2 Fairweather Cafe
3 Ginny's Coffee Shop
4 Ferry Office
5 Laundromat
6 Yukon Bar
7 Flamingo Lounge
8 St. Peter's Episcopal Church
9 Mini Mall Fast Foods
10 Seward Bakery
11 New Seward Hotel
12 Library
13 Pavilion
14 Van Guilder Hotel
15 City Hall/Museum
16 Rest Rooms
17 Forest Service Office
18 Post Office
19 Railroad Car & Info Centre
20 Kenai Fjords
    National Park Centre

Seward

0   125   250 km
0   75   150 miles

To Airport & Anchorage

Boat Harbor

Two Lakes Trail

D Street
C Street
B Street
A Street
Street
Street

Munroe Avenue
Madison Street

Avenue
Avenue
Avenue
Avenue
Avenue
Avenue
Boulevard

Tent

Camping

Area

To Mt. Marathon

Lowell Street

Jefferson Street

First
Second
Third
Fourth
Fifth
Sixth
Ballaine

Adams Street

Washington Street

To Lowell Point

Alaska Ferry Terminal

Resurrection Bay

Camping There are two city campgrounds in the Seward area and both are free-use areas. In town, you can camp on the shore of the bay along Seventh Avenue (also known as Ballaine Boulevard) from the Small Boat Harbor south to the State Marine Ferry office. Referred to as the *Seventh Avenue Greenbelt Campground*, it has out-houses along the strip and a picnic pavilion at the corner of Railway and Seventh Avenues. *Forest Acres Campground* is two miles (3.2 km) north of town on the west side of Seward Highway. Camping is not allowed in the small city park near the ferry terminal.

Places to Eat

For sandwiches there is the *Shamrock Deli* within Murphy's Motel on the corner of Fourth Avenue and D St at the north end of town. Downtown on Fourth Avenue near the ferry dock is *Fairweather Café*, one of Seward's best places with good prices for soups, sandwiches and quiches or Sunday brunch. The *Peaking Chinese Restaurant* is at the corner of Fourth and Jefferson St and is open until 10.30 pm daily. For breakfast there is *Seward Bakery* at Fourth and Adams St downtown; or if you are camping near the Small Boat Harbor try the *Breeze Inn Restaurant*. The *Captain's Table* next door to the Breeze Inn Motel is good for local seafood but plan on spending $12 to $17 for dinner.

Nightlife

Seward's oldest drinking hole, the *Pioneer Bar* on Fifth and Washington, is a fun place where someone is usually bashing on the honky-tonk piano. *Niko's Night Club*, near the ferry dock downtown, features live music and a rosewood bar that the owner claims is 120 years old. There are also lounges in the *Van Guilder Hotel* and the *Breeze Inn* overlooking the Small Boat Harbor.

Events

Seward holds three events each summer that have become popular with Alaskans throughout Southcentral: the first is the Spring Into Summer Festival on Memorial Day weekend, a four-day event of kayak and foot races, dances, photo and art shows and 'Honky Tonk Night' at the local Elks' Club; the Fourth of July celebration is also a big event in Seward, highlighted by the annual Mt Marathon Race, which pulls runners from around the state; the city's most famous event, however, is its Silver Salmon Derby on the second Saturday of August. First prize is $10,000 for the largest salmon caught. Other events on derby weekend include the Silver Salmon Run and softball tournaments.

Hiking

For information on the hikes in and around the Seward area, stop at the USFS office (tel 224-3374) on Fourth Avenue between Adams and Jefferson Sts. The office is also the place to check out the availability of cabins in the Seward area.

Race Point The most popular trail near downtown is the trek towards the top of Mt Marathon, the mountain that sits behind the city. The route is well known throughout Alaska. In 1909, two sourdough miners wagered how long it would take to run to the top and back and then dashed off for the peak. After that it became an official event at the Seward Fourth of July and today attracts hundreds of runners with an equal number of spectators who line the streets to watch them take off and return. The fastest time is 44 minutes and 11 seconds, set in 1974. Most runners come down the mountain in less than 10 minutes, usually by sliding halfway on their butts.

Hikers can take their time and enjoy the spectacular views of Seward and Resurrection Bay. The hiker's trail begins at the end of Monroe St but is overgrown and hard to find at times. The runner's trail begins at the west end of Jefferson St (also known as Lowell St) up the Lowell Canyon. The trailhead is marked and is in a small gravel pit just past a pair of water tanks. Scramble up the ridge to the right of the gully; for fun, return through the gully's scree. You never really reach Mt Marathon's summit, though you do reach a high point of 3022 feet (921 metres) known as Race Point on the broad east shoulder. Plan on three to four hours for the three-mile round trip.

Two Lakes Trail This easy one-mile (1.6-km) loop goes through a wooded area and passes two small lakes at the base of Mt Marathon. Begin near the first lake behind the Alaska Vocational & Training Centre on Second Avenue and B St. Near the start is a scenic waterfall.

Resurrection River Trail This 16-mile (25.6-km) trail, built in 1984, is the last link in a 70-mile (112-km) system across the Kenai Peninsula from Seward to Hope. This continuous trail is broken only by Sterling Highway and provides the best long-term wilderness adventure on the Peninsula, leading the hiker through a diversity of streams, rivers, lakes, wooded lowlands and alpine areas.

The southern trailhead of Resurrection River Trail is eight miles (12.8 km) up the Exit Glacier access road that leaves the Seward Highway at *Mile 3.7* (six km) (see Kenai Fjords below). The northern trailhead joins Russian Lakes Trail (see the Wilderness chapter), five miles (eight km) from Cooper Lake or 16 miles (25.6 km) from Russian River Campground off Sterling Highway. The hike from Seward Highway to Sterling Highway is a 40-mile (64-km) trip, including walking up Exit Glacier Rd.

Two USFS cabins (reservations needed, $10 per night) are situated along the trail; the Resurrection River unit is 6.5 miles (10.4 km) from the southern trailhead and the Fox Creek cabin is another 1.5 miles beyond it. Check with the USFS office in Seward about availability of the cabins and the best places to camp along the trail, as good sites are scarce.

Lost Lake Trail At *Mile 5.2* (8.4) of Seward Highway is the seven-mile (11.2 km) trail to the alpine lake and one of the most scenic hikes the Kenai Peninsula has to offer in mid-summer. The trailhead is marked in a parking area west of the highway and the beginning is a rough logging road. At 1.5 miles (2.4 km), a winter trail, designed primarily for snowmobiles, branches off to the right. The final two miles of the trail are above the tree line and the lake is a glorious place to spend a night.

An option to returning is to continue around the east side of Lost Lake to Primrose Trail, another USFS-maintained route. This eight-mile (12.8 km) trail leads through alpine country and ends in Primrose Campground at *Mile 17.2* (27.7 km) of Seward Highway. Plan on seven to 10 hours round trip for Lost Lake Trail and bring a campstove because there is no wood near the lake.

Getting There
Rail The Alaska Railroad resumed passenger service to Seward in 1987 for the first time since the 1950s and now makes a daily run to the city from Anchorage. Trains leave Seward at 1 pm and reach Anchorage at 5 pm; one-way fare is $18.

Boat The state ferry terminal (tel 224-5485) is on the waterfront off Fifth Avenue and Railroad St downtown. Ferries arrive twice a week from Kodiak or Valdez and depart for the same communities before continuing on to other Southcentral ports. The fare to Valdez is $46, to Kodiak $38 and to Homer $68. The trip to Valdez includes the Columbia Glacier. The sail to Kodiak Island passes the Stellar Sea Lions on the Chiswell Islands near the mouth of Resurrection Bay and nearby Bear Glacier.

Bus Seward Bus Lines (tel 562-0712) provides daily service to Anchorage during the summer, with a bus departing its terminal at Fourth Avenue and Washington St at 9 am Monday to Saturday. The bus departs Anchorage at 4 pm for a return trip to Seward; one-way fare is $20.

KENAI FJORDS NATIONAL PARK
Seward serves as the departure point for most trips into this national park that was created in 1980. The park covers 587,000 acres (238,000 hectares) and consists mainly of the Harding Icefield, the rugged coastline where tidewater glaciers calve into the sea, and the offshore islands. The many deep fjords, rich marine life and numerous glaciers make the park a bluewater paddler's dream, though kayakers have to be cautious and experienced in rough water to handle the sections exposed to the Gulf of Alaska.

Information
The Kenai Fjords National Park Visitor Centre (tel 224-3874) is off the Seward Highway near the Harbormaster Office and the Small Boat Harbor. It is open daily from 8 am to 5 pm and has exhibits and slide programmes as well as handouts on the park. There is also a ranger station at Exit Glacier that is staffed and open daily during the summer.

Getting There
Most of the park and all but one of its 36 named glaciers are inaccessible to visitors except through expensive flight-seeing trips or on charter boats. The lone exception is Exit Glacier, which can be reached by a 10-mile (16 km) gravel road. The road leaves the Seward Highway at *Mile 3.7* (six km) at a well-posted junction and winds back almost eight miles (12.8 km) to a bridge and parking area where the Resurrection River trailhead is located.

In 1985, the footbridge over the river was replaced by a vehicle bridge and the road was extended another two miles to the ranger station near the glacier. From the ranger station you can scramble over loose rock and actually touch the dense, blue-tinged glacial ice and view ice towers that loom 150 feet (46 metres) above you. The rangers schedule a variety of activities during the summer, most of them on Saturday and Sunday, that include campfire talks, walks to the glacier and all-day hikes to the Harding Icefield. There is also camping nearby.

For the best view of the 36-mile (57.6 km) wide Harding Icefield and the glaciers it fans out of, contact Harbour Air (tel 224-5720) in Seward about their daily flight-seeing tours. The other approach to the park is to view its rugged coastline and tidewater glaciers on a charter boat. Kenai Fjords Tours (tel 224-3668) runs an eight-hour tour of the park with boats departing at 8 am daily except Thursday. The fare is $65 per person and tickets may be purchased at the Fish House near the Small Boat Harbor.

Hiking
Besides the scramble from the ranger station to the glacier, the only other developed hike in the Exit Glacier area is the trek to Harding Icefield. The hike to the icefield is a difficult ascent which follows a steep, roughly-cut and sometimes slippery route on the north side of the glacier, beginning at its base.

The all-day trek is well worth it for those with the stamina, as it provides spectacular views of not only the icefield but of Exit Glacier and the valley below. The upper section of the route is snow covered for much of the year. A ranger-led hike to the icefield departs the station on Saturdays at 10 am. Bring a lunch and good boots if you plan to join.

Kayaking
Bluewater paddles out of Resurrection Bay along the coastline of the park are challenges for experienced kayakers only,

but reward those who undertake such an adventure with daily wildlife encounters and close-up views of the glaciers from a unique perspective. Alaska Treks & Voyages (tel 224-3960) rents out both rigid and inflatable kayaks from the Seward Small Boat Harbor at a weekend rate of $70 and a weekly rate of $130. The outfitter also runs a 10-day trip along the park's coastline for $987 per person or overnight or weekend tours for $100 per person per day.

One way to get around the outfitter's fee for those experienced at kayaking but unsure about the Gulf of Alaska is to be dropped off and picked up in one of the many protected fjords. Contact the National Park Service for information on such bays, and then make arrangements with the *MV Maxine* (tel 288-3177) to charter you and your kayak out to the area.

HOPE HIGHWAY TO HOPE
The paved road leads almost 18 miles (28.8 km) north to the historical community of Hope and the northern trailhead for the Resurrection Pass Trail. Hope experienced a minor stampede in 1896 when news of a gold strike bought over 3000 prospectors to the cluster of cabins and to nearby Sunrise, a tent city. Within a few years the majority had left to look elsewhere and today Hope is a small village with a summer population of 190. Nothing remains of Sunrise. Even if you are not planning to hike Resurrection Pass Trail, Hope is a great side trip; the tucked-away town in a very scenic area lets you step back in time. Hitching is not hard, but plan on two to three days for this venture rather than a rushed overnight stop.

At *Mile 16* (25.6 km) of the highway is the junction to Palmer Creek and Resurrection Creek Rds. Turn left onto Resurrection Creek Rd and in 0.7 miles (1.1 km) Palmer Creek Rd branches to the left. Near the junction is the unattended Hope airstrip. Four miles (6.4 km) down

Resurrection Creek Rd is the northern trailhead of the Resurrection Pass Trail. Palmer Creek Rd is a scenic drive that leads seven miles (11.2 km) to USFS Coeur d'Alene Campground (six sites, free use). Beyond the campground the road is not maintained but leads another five miles to alpine country above 1500 feet (457 metres) and ends at the ruins of the abandoned Swetmann mining camp. From the old mining buildings it is easy to scramble through the tundra to several small alpine lakes.

To reach downtown, turn right on Hope Rd at *Mile 16.5* (26.6 km) of Hope Highway. Hope Rd leads down to the waterfront and passes many of the town's historical buildings and abandoned log structures that have become favourites among photographers.

Places to Stay & Eat
Hope has a post office, general store, laundromat and a couple of lodges and cafés. Within town there is the *Seaview Café & Motel* (tel 782-3364) on Hope Rd where you can get a meal, a beer or a single room for $18, doubles are $25.

Camping sites abound all around Hope but the USFS maintains *Porcupine Campground* (24 sites, $5 fee), 1.3 miles (two km) beyond Hope at the end of Hope Highway. Near the campground is *Davidson Enterprises*, a general store that sells groceries, gasoline and liquor.

Gold Panning
There are about 125 mining claims throughout the Chugach National Forest but most of today's prospectors are recreational miners out there for the fun, searching their pans or sluice box for a little colour. Some of the more serious ones actually make money from their time spent along the creeks, but most are happy to take home a bottle with a few flakes in it.

The Hope area provides numerous opportunities for the amateur panner, including a 20-acre (8 hectare) claim the

USFS has set aside near the Resurrection Pass trailhead for recreational mining. There are usually some regulars out there who don't mind showing newcomers how to swirl the pan. Other panning areas include Sixmile Creek between *Mile 1.5* (2.4 km) and *Mile 5.5* (8.8 km) of Hope Highway, and many of the creeks along the Resurrection Pass Trail.

Panning Technique The only piece of equipment that is absolutely necessary is a gravity-trap pan, one that measures 10 to 20 inches (25 to 50 cm) across and can usually be bought at any good Alaskan hardware or general store. Those who have panned for a while also show up with rubber boots and gloves to protect hands and feet from icy waters, a garden trowel to dig up loose rock, a pair of tweezers to pick up gold flakes and a small bottle to hold their find.

Panning technique is based on the fact that gold is heavier than the gravel it lies in. Fill your pan with loose material from cracks and crevices in streams or around large boulders where gold might have washed down and become lodged. Add water to the pan and rinse and discard larger rocks, keeping the rinsing in the pan. Continue to shake the contents towards the bottom by swirling the pan in a circular motion and wash off the excess sand and gravel by dipping the front into the stream. You should be left with heavy black mud, sand, and if you are lucky, a few flakes of gold. Use tweezers or your fingernail to transfer the flakes into a bottle filled with water.

Hiking

Gull Rock Trail From Porcupine Campground there are two fine trails to scenic points overlooking Turnagain Arm. The first is an easy 4.5-mile (7.2 km) walk to Gull Rock, a rocky point 140 feet (43 metres) above the Turnagain shoreline. Along the way there are the remains of a cabin and a sawmill to explore. Round trip to Gull Rock is four to six hours.

Hope Point This is not a trail but more of a route that follows an alpine ridge for incredible views of Turnagain Arm. Begin at the entrance sign to Porcupine Campground and follow an unmarked trail along the right-hand side of the small Porcupine Creek. After 0.3 mile (0.5 km) the trail leaves the side of the creek and begins to climb a bluff to the right, reaching an outcropping with good views of Turnagain Arm in 45 minutes or so. From here you can follow the ridge above the treeline to Hope Point, elevation 3708 feet (1131 metres). Other than an early summer snowfield, there is no water after Porcupine Creek.

STERLING HIGHWAY TO KENAI

It is only 58 miles (93 km) from Tern Lake Junction to Soldotna along Sterling Highway, not much more than an hour's drive, yet the stretch contains so many hiking, camping and canoeing opportunities that it would take you a month to enjoy them all. Surrounded by the Chugach National Forest and Kenai National Wildlife Refuge, Sterling Highway and its side roads touch over a dozen trails, 20 campgrounds and an almost endless number of lakes, rivers and streams in which to wet a fishing line or dip a canoe paddle.

Do not rush through this area just to reach Kenai or Soldotna. If you are driving, make good use of your freedom to explore the handful of back roads. If you are hitching, don't hesitate to give up a ride to spend a day camping or hiking somewhere. There will always be another ride passing your way once you are ready to return to the road.

Mileposts along the highway show distance from Seward, making Tern Lake Junction, the start of the Sterling Highway, *Mile 37* (59.5 km). The first campgrounds appear eight miles (12.8 km) from the beginning at *Mile 45* (72.4 km). Just past the Sunrise Motel is the junction to Quartz Creek Rd. Follow the road south 0.3 mile (0.5 km) to USFS Quartz Creek

Campground (41 sites, $6 fee) on the shores of Kenai Lake or three miles (4.8 km) to USFS Crescent Creek Campground (13 sites, $5 fee).

Crescent Creek Trail

About 0.5 mile (0.8 km) beyond the second USFS campground is the marked trailhead to this footpath, which leads 6.5 miles (10.4 km) to the outlet of Crescent Lake and a USFS cabin (reservations needed, $10 per night). The trail is an easy one and is beautiful in September during the autumn colours, and from the cabin there is access to the high country. Make cabin reservations in Anchorage. At the east end of the lake is Carter Lake Trail to Seward Highway, but no path connects the two.

Another 0.5 mile (0.8 km) west on Sterling Highway is a large look-out and observation point for Dall sheep in the Kenai Mountains and mountain goats in the Cecil Rhode Mountains directly across Kenai Lake. Displays explain the life cycle of the animals. The Kenai River Bridge is at *Mile 47.8* (76.9 km) and immediately after it is Snug Harbor Rd, which leads south 12 miles (19.3 km) to Cooper Lake and the eastern trailhead to Russian Lakes Trail (see the Wilderness chapter).

The Kenai River parallels the highway for the next 10 miles (16 km) where several gravel look-outs offer good views. At *Mile 50.7* (81.6 km) is USFS Cooper Creek Campground (27 sites, $5 fee) where there are camping sites on both sides of the highway. Several of those on the north side of the highway are scenically located on the Kenai River.

The final USFS campground is at *Mile 52.8* (85 km), two miles (3.2 km) to the west and 16 miles (25.6 km) from Tern Junction. Russian River Campground (84 sites, $6 fee) is a beautiful spot where the Russian and Kenai rivers merge. Both the Cooper Creek and Russian River campgrounds lie on prime red salmon spawning areas and tend to fill up by noon

in late summer. The Russian River is so popular that they charge you $2 just to park and fish.

One mile (1.6 km) down on Russian River Campground Rd is the trailhead and parking area for Russian Lakes Trail, while 0.25 mile (0.4 km) west of the campground on Sterling Highway is the well-marked entrance to the Resurrection Pass Trail (see the Wilderness chapter).

Once beyond the Resurrection Pass trailhead, you leave Chugach National Forest, administered by the Forest Service, and enter the Kenai National Wildlife Refuge (formerly named Kenai National Moose Range), managed by the US Fish & Wildlife Service. The first campground in the refuge is Kenai-Russian River Recreational Area (10 sites, fee) at *Mile 55* (88.5 km). West of the confluence of these two salmon-rich rivers, this campground is heavily used from mid to late summer by fishermen. A privately owned ferry carries anglers to the opposite bank of the Kenai River here, using cables and the current to propel it across in both directions. It is an interesting sight during the height of the salmon season as a couple of hundred fishermen will be lined up at 5 am to catch the first trip across.

Fuller Lake Trail

This three-mile (4.8-km) trail begins at *Mile 57.2* (92.1 km) of the highway and ends at Fuller Lake just above the treeline. The trailhead, an old road blocked by logs, is marked. Halfway up you reach Lower Fuller Lake, where you cross a stream over a beaver dam and continue over a low pass to Fuller Lake. At the lake the trail follows the east shore and then branches. The fork to the left leads up a ridge and becomes Skyline Trail. This trail is not maintained and is unmarked above the bushline. It follows a ridge for 6.5 miles (10.4 km) and descends to *Mile 61* (97.6 km) of Sterling Highway. Those who want to hike both trails should plan on overnighting at Fuller Lake.

Just past the Fuller Lake trailhead is the junction of Skilak Lake Loop Rd at *Mile 57.8* (93 km) and the Kenai National Wildlife Refuge visitor station. The log cabin is open daily from 10 am to 7 pm and is the source of handouts, maps and brochures on the refuge. The 19-mile (30.4 km) loop road is a scenic side trip to an already scenic highway and is a popular and often crowded recreational avenue. There are seven free, well-marked USFS campgrounds along the road; from east to west they are:

Jim's Landing (five sites) near the junction
Hidden Lake (30 sites) at *Mile 3.6* (5.8 km)
Upper Skilak Lake (10 sites)
Lower Ohmer (four sites) at *Mile 8.6* (13.8 km)
Engineer Lake (eight sites) at *Mile 9.7* (15.6 km)
Lower Skilak Lake (14 sites) at *Mile 14* (22.5 km)
Bottinentnin Lake (three sites) at *Mile 19* (30.6 km).

Kenai River Trail
Located 0.6 mile (0.9 km) past the visitor station, this trail winds 6.3 miles (10 km) to Skilak Lake and then swings into the Hidden Creek Loop. The 1.4-mile (2.2 km) loop trail curves back to its beginning at *Mile 4.6* of Skilak Lake Rd. Both trails are easy walks along level terrain.

Skilak Lookout Trail
This trail begins at *Mile 5.5* (8.8 km) of Skilak Lake Rd and climbs 2.6 miles (4.1 km) to a knob that offers a panoramic view of the surrounding mountains and lakes at 1450 feet (442 metres). Plan on four to five hours for the round trip.

Seven Lakes Trail
At *Mile 9.7* (15.6) is the spur to Engineer Lake and the start of this five-mile (eight km) trail to Sterling Highway. The trail is easy walking over level terrain and passes Hidden Lake and Hikers Lake before ending at Kelly Lake campground, on a side road off Sterling Highway.

If you choose to stay on Sterling Highway past the Skilak Lake Rd junction, you pass the small campground at Jenny Lake at *Mile 60* (96 km) and the side road at *Mile 69* (110.4 km) that leads south to Peterson Lake Campground (three sites, free) and Kelly Lake Campground (three sites, free) near one end of the Seven Lakes Trail. The west junction with Skilak Lake Rd is reached at *Mile 75.3* (121.2 km).

At *Mile 81* (130.3 km) you arrive in the small town of Sterling (population 2400). Sterling meets the usual travellers' needs with restaurants, lodges, gas stations and grocery stores. Just beyond the town is Izaak Walton Campground (17 sites, free) at the confluence of the Kenai and Moose rivers. A display explains the nearby archaeological site where excavations suggest that the area was used by Eskimo 2000 years ago. The recreational area is heavily used all summer, as fishermen swarm here for the salmon runs while paddlers end their Swan Lake trip at Moose River Bridge. Canoe rentals and transportation are available at the bridge to the Swan Lake and Swanson River canoe trails (see the Wilderness chapter).

At *Mile 85* (136 km) Swanson River Rd turns north for 18 miles (29 km), with Swan Lake Rd heading east for three miles (4.8 km) at the end. The roads are accesses to the Swanson River and Swan Lake canoe routes (see the Wilderness chapter) and three campgrounds: Dolly Varden Lake Campground (12 sites, free) 14 miles (22 km) up Swanson River Rd, Rainbow Lake Campground (three sites, free) another two miles (3.2 km) beyond, and Swanson River Campground (eight sites, free) at the very end of the road. Even without a canoe, this is a good area to spend a day or two as there are trails to many of the lakes which offer superb fishing.

Across Sterling Highway from Swanson River Rd is the entrance to Scout Lake Loop Rd, where Scout Lake Campground

(14 sites, free) is located. Also reached from this road is the Alaska State Parks office (tel 262-5581), which offers handouts, natural displays and information on the remote Kachemak Bay State Park to the south.

KENAI

Kenai (population 6000) is the second-oldest permanent settlement in Alaska, as it was established by Russian fur traders in 1791 and offers good views of the active volcanoes across the inlet and a little Russian history and colour that often get lost in the town's massive oil industry. It doesn't, however, have the charm of Seward or Homer.

It is located at the mouth of the Kenai River on Cook Inlet, where to the south-west you can view Mt Redoubt and Mt Iliamna and to the north-west the Alaska Range. You reach the heart of the city by going north on Kenai Spur Rd at *Mile 94.2* (151.6 km) of Sterling Highway.

Things to See

The Kenai Spur Road leads to **Moosemeat John's Cabin** which is the visitor centre at the corner of Main St. Built in the 1920s, the cabin was moved to its present site in 1976 and is the source of information on the Kenai area. It's open Monday to Friday from 9 am to 5 pm and Saturday from 10 am to 4 pm.

From the visitor centre follow Overland Avenue to **Fort Kenay**, two blocks towards Cook Inlet. Inside the fort is the **Kenai Historical Museum** with a collection of artefacts dating back to the town's Russian origins and its gold-mining days. Around the fort (constructed as part of the Alaska Centennial in 1967) are several old homes moved there for restoration. The fort and museum are open Monday to Friday from 10 am to 5 pm, Saturday from 12 noon to 3 pm and Sunday from 12 noon to 4 pm. Donations are accepted.

Across Mission St from the fort is the **Russian Orthodox Church**, built in 1896

and today the oldest Orthodox church in Alaska. West of the church is the blue-domed **St Nicholas Chapel**, built in 1906 on the burial site of Father Igumen Nicolai, Kenai's first resident priest. There are no regularly-scheduled tours of either building but both have become a photographer's delight.

Head south-east on Mission and you will be travelling along **The Bluff**, a good vantage point from which to view the mouth of the Kenai River or the mountainous terrain on the west side of Cook Inlet. At the corner of Main St and Mission Avenue is the **Beluga Whale Lookout**. From here it is possible to see herds of white whales in the late spring and early summer as they ride the incoming tides into the Kenai River to feed on salmon.

Places to Stay

Hotels Hotels in this area are expensive and tend to be filled during the king salmon runs in June and July. Some exceptions include the *Harbour View* (tel 283-4133), which offers singles for $26 and doubles for $37 on Fireweed Avenue in downtown Kenai.

If you are heading north of Kenai towards Captain Cook state park (see section below) there is the *Hunger Hut* (tel 776-9911) with singles for $25 and doubles for $40 in Nikisha at *Mile 23* (36.8 km) of the Kenai Spur Rd.

Camping Within Kenai, *City Campground* (40 sites, fee), is in a pleasant wooded area overlooking Cook Inlet. The campground is within walking distance of town; you follow Kenai Spur Rd through the city centre and then turn left on Forest Drive.

Places to Eat

There's *Kentucky Fried Chicken* in the Kenai Mall on Kenai Spur Rd in the centre of town; or else try a good $2.50 breakfast at *Sourdough Sal's* on Sterling Highway near the Soldotna post office.

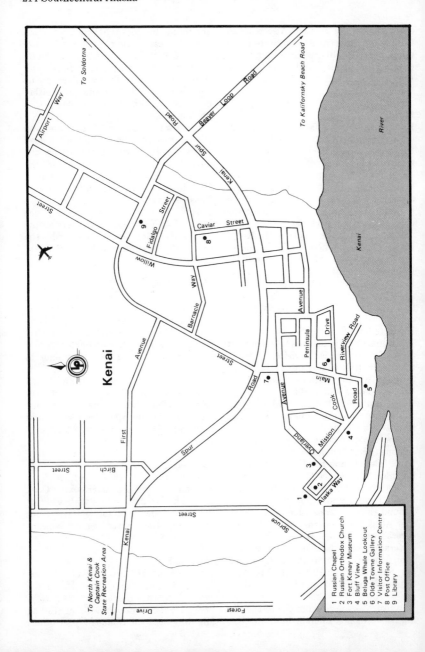

Kenai

To Soldotna

To Kalifornsky Beach Road

Kenai River

To North Kenai &
Captain Cook
State Recreation Area

1 Russian Chapel
2 Russian Orthodox Church
3 Fort Kenay Museum
4 Bluff View
5 Beluga Whale Lookout
6 Olde Towne Gallery
7 Visitor Information Centre
8 Post Office
9 Library

Four Seasons, on the highway just north of the Kenai Spur Rd junction, serves seafood dinners that cost $12 to $15 and a $6 Sunday buffet.

SOLDOTNA

Soldotna (population 3000) is strictly a service centre at the main junction of Sterling Highway. The town was born when the Kenai Spur Rd and Sterling Highway were completed in the 1940s. Today it is little more than a service centre for the fishermen and guides who work the Kenai River in hopes of catching an 80-plus-pound (36-kg) king salmon. Alaska Department of Fish & Game report the Kenai River to be the most heavily-fished stream in the state, as hundreds of thousands of anglers flood the area annually and congest the waterway with powerboats.

Things to See

Information on the town can be obtained at the Soldotna Tourist Centre (tel 262-9814), just past the junction of Kenai Spur Rd and Sterling Highway. The centre, which has a large fishwheel in front of it, is open 9 am to 5 pm daily.

The most interesting thing to do in Soldotna is to drive through it, and turn onto Kalifornsky Beach Rd just after passing the bridge over the Kenai River. The road heads north at first and passes Centennial Park Campground and then the Kenai campus of the **University of Alaska**. The **Damon Memorial Museum**, a log cabin with a small collection of artefacts, is 1.5 miles (2.4 km) past the university.

Eventually the road heads west, then south after passing a junction to Kenai. It continues south for 16 miles (26 km) along the Cook Inlet and offers some splendid views on the waterway and the Alaska Range before rejoining Sterling Highway at the small settlement of Kasilof.

Opposite the Kalifornsky Beach Rd near the Kenai River is the junction to Funny River Rd. Turn here and turn right immediately on Ski Hill Rd, following it for a mile to reach **Kenai National Wildlife Refuge Visitor Centre** (tel 262-7021). Open from 8 am to 4.30 pm weekdays and 10 am to 6 pm weekends, the centre features a good series of wildlife displays, daily slide shows in its theatre, and naturalist-led outdoor programmes on the weekends. There are also three short trails (maps available) that begin at the centre and wind into the nearby woods and lakes.

Places to Stay

Youth Hostel There is a *Youth Hostel* (tel 262-4369) in Soldotna at 444 West Riverside Avenue which has space for about 20 people. The cost is $8 per night for members and $11 for non-members and it is best to call ahead at this one.

Camping There is *Centennial Park Campground* (108 sites, $4 per night) at the corner of Sterling Highway and Kalifornsky Beach Rd, and *Swiftwater Park* campground (20 sites, $4 per night) on East Redoubt Avenue at *Mile 94* (151.2 km) of the highway. Both are on the Kenai River.

Places to Eat

Fast (and cheap) restaurants include *Dairy Queen*, which serves hamburgers on the corner of Kenai Spur Rd and Sterling Highway; and Alaska's latest *McDonald's* half a mile down the highway.

Captain Cook State Recreation Area

By following the Kenai Spur Rd north for 36 miles (57.6 km), you will reach this uncrowded state recreation area that encompasses 4000 acres (1600 hectares) of forests, lakes, rivers and beaches along Cook Inlet. The area offers swimming, camping and the beauty of Cook Inlet in a setting that is unaffected by the salmon stampede to the south.

Kenai Spur Rd ends in the park after first passing Stormy Lake, where there is a bath house and a swimming area along the water's edge. Also within the park is Bishop Creek Campground (12 sites) and Discovery Campground (57 sites), which is located on the inlet.

The best hiking in the park is along the saltwater beach, but don't let the high tides catch you off guard. Those paddling Swanson River Canoe Trail (see the Wilderness chapter) will find the park an appropriate place to end the trip.

STERLING HIGHWAY TO HOMER

From Soldotna, Sterling Highway rambles south, hugging the coastline and opening up to grand views of Cook Inlet every so often. The stretch is 78 miles (126 km) long and passes through a handful of small villages near some great clamming areas, ending at the charming village of Homer. Take your time in this area; the coastline and Homer are worth every day you decide to spend here.

Kasilof

A fishing village of 1200, Kasilof is the first town outside Soldotna. At *Mile 108.8* (175 km) of Sterling Highway, turn west for 3.6 miles (5.8 km) on Kalifornsky Beach Rd to reach Small Boat Harbor on the Kasilof River, the heart of the town. Another mile south, Sterling Highway crosses a bridge over the Kasilof River, where on the other side is Kasilof River State Wayside (11 sites, free) on the riverbank. An intersection is reached at *Mile 111.5* (179.4 km), with Coho Loop Rd heading north-west towards the ocean and Tustumena Lake Access Rd south-east.

Just east on the lake road is the Kasilof Incubation Facility, a state-owned salmon hatchery open to the public from 8 am to 4.30 pm daily. Another 0.3 mile (0.5 km) down the access road is the Johnson Lake recreation area (43 campsites, free) with entry into the rainbow trout lake. At the end of the seven-mile (11.2 km) road is Tustumena Lake Campground (10 sites, free), which really lies on the Kasilof River a mile from the large lake.

Clam Gulch

Before reaching the hamlet of Clam Gulch (population 120) you pass at *Mile 117.4* (188.9 km) the junction of a two-mile (3.2 km) gravel road. Just west on the road is Clam Gulch State Recreation Area, offering covered picnic tables, outhouses and an overnight parking area near which you can pitch a tent. More importantly, the road is access to the beaches along the Cook Inlet and the start of the area's great clam digging. The village of Clam Gulch is less than a mile south on Sterling Highway and has a post office, gas station and lodge.

Clam Digging Almost all of the beaches on the west side of the Kenai Peninsula have a good supply of razor clams, considered by locals to be a true delicacy from the sea. You first have to purchase a sport-fishing licence (one-day visitor's licence is $5, 10-day $15), then obtain a shovel and a large bucket to carry your bag limit of 60 clams.

There is good clamming from April through to August, though the best time is July, right before spawning time. Wait for the tide to drop at least one foot from the high water mark – or better yet, to its lower levels of four to five feet down. Look for the clam's footprint in the sand, a dimple mark left behind when it withdraws its neck. Shovel a scoop or two next to the mark and then reach in the sand for the clam. You have to be quick, since a razor clam can bury itself and be gone in seconds.

The best way to cook clams is right on the beach over an open fire while soaking in the mountain scenery across Cook Inlet. Use a large, covered pot and steam them in salt water or, better yet, in white wine with a clove of garlic.

Ninilchik

This is the next town and has a camping area and good clamming beach. At *Mile 134.4* (216.3 km) is Ninilchik State Recreation Area (35 sites, free) which includes covered picnic tables, out-houses and a trail to the Ninilchik River. Beyond it, 0.5 mile (0.8 km), is a short access road to the town's Russian Orthodox church which was built in 1901. The historic church is on a wide bluff and commands a view of Cook Inlet in front.

Just past the spur to the church, Sterling Highway crosses a bridge over Ninilchik River and then another side road heads west for the ocean, where there is beach camping, toilets and more clam digging. Historic signs on this road point the way to old Ninilchik Village, which includes several log buildings.

Present-day Ninilchik (population 450) is 0.5 mile (0.8 km) further south on the highway at *Mile 135.5* (218 km). It was moved after the Good Friday earthquake sank the original town three feet. Next to the village is Ninilchik View State Campground (12 sites, free) overlooking the ocean. The Kenai Peninsula State Fair, the 'biggest little fair in Alaska' is held annually in town at the end of August.

At *Mile 137.3* (221 km) is Deep Creek State Recreation Area, on the beach near the mouth of the creek. It is used for beach camping, surf fishing and clamming. Higher up is Stariski Creek State Recreation Site (12 campsites, free), on a bluff at *Mile 152* (244.4 km) overlooking Cook Inlet. The town of Anchor Point (population 1500) is another five miles (eight km) south on the highway and is a fishing hot spot during the summer. Within town are gas stations, a post office, grocery stores and the *Anchor River Inn* (tel 235-8531), which has single rooms starting at $25 and doubles at $30.

Anchor River Rd, which begins behind the Anchor River Inn, leads to Silver King State Recreation Area (20 sites, free) and ends 1.5 miles (2.4 km) to the south at a beautiful stretch of beach that has good views across the inlet of Mt Redoubt and Mt Iliamna and interesting tidal pools to explore. The Old Sterling Highway branches off this road and leads south to rejoin the new highway at *Mile 164.8* (265.2 km).

From Anchor Point, Sterling Highway climbs up the bluffs overlooking Homer and Kachemak Bay about five miles from town. If driving, take this section slowly, as there are some great viewing points that will be missed by the hasty. One of the best is 3.2 miles (5.1 km) north of Homer.

HOMER

Arriving in Homer is like opening one of those pop-up greeting cards – it's an unexpected thrill. A couple of miles before town, Sterling Highway provides a few teasers that whet your appetite but never fully prepare you for the charming fishing village that lies at the end. As the road makes a final turn east along the bluffs, Homer unfolds completely. It's an incredible panorama of mountains, white peaks, glaciers and a beautiful body of water known as the Kachemak Bay. The bay is broken by the Homer Spit, a long strip of land that leads back to the town of 3200 residents, the handful of cross streets and the incredible colour that is Homer.

The community is supported by its fishing industries and the influx of tourists that arrive each summer. However, it is known around the state as the arts capital of Southcentral because of the large number of artists and galleries in the area. It is little wonder that they choose Homer; the scenery is inspiring and the climate exceptionally nice.

Homer is protected from the severe northern cold by the Kenai Mountains north and east of it, which gives the town one of the mildest climates in the state. Summer temperatures rarely go above 70°F (21°C) nor fall much below 0°F (-17.8°C) in winter. Annual precipitation is only 28 inches (710 mm), much of it snow.

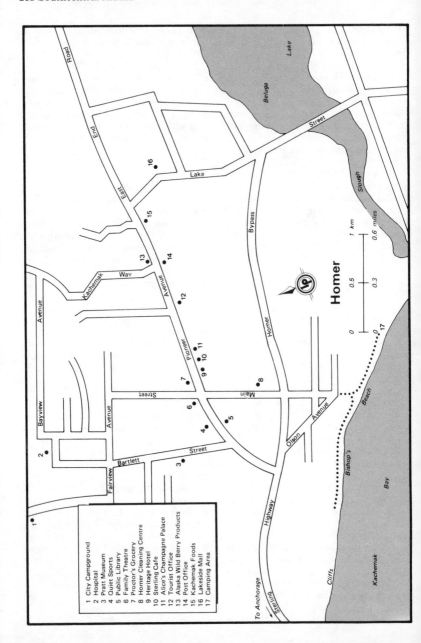

Homer

1 City Campground
2 Hospital
3 Pratt Museum
4 Quiet Sports
5 Public Library
6 Family Theatre
7 Proctor's Grocery
8 Homer Cleaning Centre
9 Heritage Hotel
10 Sterling Cafe
11 Alice's Champagne Palace
12 Tourist Office
13 Alaska Wild Berry Products
14 Post Office
15 Kachemak Foods
16 Lakeside Mall
17 Camping Area

Things to See

Information, handouts and maps on the Homer area can be obtained from the Visitor Information Centre in the small log cabin on Pioneer Avenue west of the post office. The centre is open daily in the summer from 10 am to 6 pm. West on Pioneer Avenue and north on Bartlett St is the **Pratt Museum**, which features Eskimo and Indian artefacts, historical displays and exhibits on marine life in Kachemak Bay. By far the most intriguing aspect of the museum is its marine aquariums that house such living creatures as octopus, sea anemones and other wildlife from the sea. The museum is open daily in the summer from 10 am to 5 pm and charges $1.50 for admission. Check to see when the Homer Society of Natural History will be showing its films and slide shows.

Nearby on West Pioneer is the main office of the Alaska Maritime National Wildlife Refuge, which features information, maps and exhibits on the wildlife in its preserve. The centre is open from 8 am to 5 pm weekdays.

Art Galleries The beautiful scenery that has inspired numerous artists to gather here also gave rise to a handful of galleries in town displaying more than the usual ivory carvings and gold nugget jewellery you see everywhere else. The oldest gallery is the *8 x 10 Studio* in a log cabin at 581 Pioneer Avenue. The gallery houses Toby Tyler's oil, water-colour and pastel works of local scenery and natural subjects. A few doors down Pioneer Avenue is the *Homer Artist Gallery*, founded by Hazel Health, a homesteader and ex-mayor of Homer. The *Pratt Museum* also has an art gallery that exhibits work by artists from around the Kenai Peninsula.

The Spit This long needle of land is a five-mile (eight-km) sandbar into Kachemak Bay and during the summer is the centre of activity in Homer as well as the heart of its fishing industry. It draws thousands of tourists and backpackers every year, making the Spit not only a scenic spot but an interesting mecca of fishermen, cannery workers, visitors and charter boat operators.

The hub of all this activity is the Small Boat Harbor at the end of the Spit, one of the best facilities in Southcentral and home base for over 700 boats. On each side of the harbour's entrance is a cannery. Nearby are Glacier and Cannery Row boardwalks – rows of gray Cape Cod buildings that house charter boat operators, a small visitor centre, gift shops and a couple of fast-food eateries, all connected by wooden sidewalks.

The favourite activity on the Spit, naturally, is beachcombing, especially at dawn or dusk when you can view the sunset or sunrise. You can stroll for miles along the beach, where the marine life is as plentiful as the driftwood, or you can go clamming at Mud Bay, on the east side of the Spit. Blue mussels, an excellent shellfish overlooked by many people, are the most abundant. Locals call the clams and mussels 'Homer grown'.

Another popular activity is a shrimp, clam or crab boil. Grab your campstove and large metal pot, purchase some fresh seafood from either Alaska Sea Ventures or C-Foods next to the ferry dock, and buy a can of beer from Homer Liquor & Wine at the end of the Spit. Then head down to the beach to enjoy your Alaskan feast while watching the tide roll in and the sun set. No beach fires are allowed between Land's End and the Whitney Fidalgo access road.

Skyline Drive North of town are bluffs that rise gently to 1100 feet (335 metres) and are referred to by locals as 'the Hill'. These green slopes, broken up by colourful patches of wildflowers, provide excellent views on a clear day of the glaciers that spill out of the Harding Icefield across the bay. The best views are obtained from Skyline Drive, which runs along the bluff above Homer. Follow Pioneer Avenue east out of town where it turns into East End Rd and then turn onto East Hill Rd up the bluffs to Skyline Drive. Many roads, including East End, are paved and are ideal for cycling (see the Getting There & Around section).

Kachemak Bay This beautiful body of water extends 30 miles (48 km) into the Kenai Peninsula and features a coastline of steep fjords and inlets with a backdrop of the glacier-capped peaks of the Kenai Mountains. Marine life and birdlife are plentiful in the bay, but it is best known for its rich fishing grounds, especially halibut. Over 20 charter fishing boats operate out of the Spit's Small Boat Harbor and charge between $80 to $100 per person for a day of fishing.

For those who have no desire to hook an 80-lb halibut but still want to see the bay, there is the Gull Island trip offered by Rainbow Tours (tel 235-7272). The 1½-hour tour departs daily at 9 am, 12 noon and 4 pm from the Spit and cruises across the bay to view the Gull Island bird rookery, which includes puffins among the nine nesting species. The fare is $15 per person. Kachemak Bay Ferry Tours (tel 235-7847) runs a daily four-hour tour of the bay, highlighted by a visit to the artist community at Halibut Cove.

Places to Stay

Youth Hostel Homer had a year-round Youth Hostel in 1985 but lost the use of the building the following winter. The AYH chapter is still there, so it might pay to check with the visitors centre to see if the hostel has found a new location.

Hotels There are six hotels in the area but most singles begin at $40 to $50 and climb from there in price. All are heavily booked during the summer. At the *Driftwood Inn* (tel 235-8019) on Olson Lane and Bunnel near Bishop Beach, there are some singles for $30. If two of you are checking in, it's $35. Other rooms range in price up to $60.

At the *Heritage Hotel* (tel 235-7787) in the middle of Pioneer Avenue, there are triple rooms without baths for $58.

Camping Beach camping is allowed along the entire west side of the Spit, which makes a beautiful spot to pitch a tent. The nightly fee is $3 if you are pitching your tent in the city-controlled sections near the end, and there are toilets next to the Harbormaster Office, the place to check in.

The *City Campground* is on a hill overlooking the town and can be reached by following the signs up Bartlett Avenue. There is a $3 nightly fee at the City Campground and a 14-day limit applies at both campgrounds. Campers looking to get clean should head over to the Homer Cleaning Centre, just south of Pioneer on Main St, where you can take a shower ($2.50) and wash your clothes at the same time.

Places to Eat

At the end of the Spit you'll find a couple of fast-food places in *Boardwalk Fish & Chips* on Cannery Row and *Glacier Drive-In*, which serves local halibut and shrimp as well as hamburgers. There is also the *Land's End Restaurant* and the *Porpoise Room*, which overlooks the Small Boat Harbor. Both specialise in seafood and charge from $12 to $20 for a complete dinner.

Within the Lakeside Mall on Lake St there is *The Soup Bowl*, known for its seafood chowder. It also serves a good $3.50 breakfast. Other early-morning places include the *Sterling Café* next to the Heritage Hotel on Pioneer Avenue and popular with locals; *Wallace's Bake Shop* just down the street; and the *Fresh Sourdough Coffee Shop* on Ocean Drive 0.5 mile (0.8 km) from the Spit, for those camping on the beach.

The *Willow Wind* is a good health-food restaurant on Ocean Drive on the way to the Spit and features seafood and vegetarian dinners.

Nightlife

Homer's most famous drinking hole is on the Spit. The *Salty Dawg Saloon*, a log cabin bar with a lighthouse tower over it, has the the same claim to fame as Juneau's Red Dog Saloon, right down to the sawdust on the floor and an amazing collection of local artefacts (junk?) on the walls. The place is worthy of at least a look at the collection, if not a few beers while you study them. Nearby is the *Waterfront Bar*, a hangout for fishermen. In town on Pioneer Avenue is *Alice's Champagne Palace*, which has live music almost nightly.

Events

Summer events in Homer begin in May with the almost month-long Spring Arts Festival. This event began as an outlet for local artists to display their work and has since evolved into a festival with dancers, musicians and craftspeople.

Fourth of July is usually a three-day event that includes a parade, a foot race, various local contests such as a grease pole climb, and arts and crafts booths.

Hiking

For all its natural beauty, Homer lacks good public trails. The best hiking is along beaches, while most trails encountered off the road system are private paths that usually lead to somebody's homestead or cabin.

Bishop Beach Hike This hike, which begins at the foot of Main St and Olson Avenue, makes an excellent afternoon stroll or a 10-mile (16 km) trek north of Homer. The views of the bay and Kenai Mountains are superb, while the marine life seen scurrying along the sand at low tide is fascinating. Check a tide book, available from most gas stations or sports stores, to leave before low tide and return before high tide. High tides cover most of the sand, forcing you to scramble onto the base of the nearby cliffs. Within two miles (3.2 km) is a rocky spit that extends far out at low tide; within five miles (eight km) from the foot of Main St you reach Diamond Ridge Rd off Sterling Highway, where you can hitch back to town.

Homer to Anchor River The same beach can also be hiked all the way to Anchor River, an eight-mile (12.8 km) walk. From there you can continue hitching north through the rest of the Kenai Peninsula.

Kachemak Bay State Park

This park, along with the adjoining Kachemak Bay State Wilderness Park to the south of it, makes up 350,000 acres (142,000 hectares) of mountainous and glacial wilderness, accessible only by bush plane or boat. Visitor facilities are a primitive campground near Glacier Spit and a few rough trails inland. The most popular hike is the three-mile, one-way trail from near Rusty Lagoon Campground (five sites, free) to the lake at the base of Grewingk Glacier, the beautiful ice flow seen from Homer.

Also within the park is Halibut Cove, once a thriving fishing community and today home for a small group of artists and craftspeople. A two-mile (3.2 km) trail extends from Halibut Cove to Grewingk Glacier Lake. From the back of the cove a four-mile (6.4 km) path heads south past China Poot Lake and ends at the top of Poot Peak.

Getting There The state park makes an excellent side trip for anybody who has a tent and a spare day and wants to escape the overflow of RVers on the Spit. Rainbow Tours (tel 235-7272) provides drop-off and pick-up service for backpackers who want to overnight at Glacier Spit and spend a day hiking up to the nearby glacier.

You could also spend three or four days paddling the many fjords of the park, departing from Homer and making overnight stops at Glacier Spit or Halibut Cove. A strong paddler, using the tides, can reach Glacier Spit in half a day. Kayaks can be rented from Quiet Sports (tel 235-8620), where doubles cost $50 per day, $105 for three days or $170 for the week.

Getting There & Around

Air ERA (tel 235-5205), the contract carrier for Alaska Airlines, provides two daily flights between Homer and Anchorage from the Homer airport, 1.7 miles (2.7 km) east of town on Kachemak Drive. One-way fare is $62, or you can go standby for $48. Homer Air (tel 235-8591) and Cook Inlet Aviation (tel 235-8163) provide air taxi service to Seldovia with a round-trip ticket priced at $41 per person.

Boat The state ferry *MV Tustumena* provides twice-weekly service between Homer and Seldovia and Homer and Kodiak, where you can continue on to the rest of the Southcentral ports. The ferry terminal (tel 235-8449) is at the end of the Spit. One-way fare for Homer-Seldovia is $9 and Homer-Kodiak $34.

Rainbow Tours departs from the Spit at 10.30 am for a daily sailing to Seldovia. The trip takes 1½ hours and the fare is $30 round trip or $20 one way.

Bicycle The best way to get around Homer or to tackle Skyline Drive is to rent a bicycle from Quiet Sports (tel 235-8620) on Pioneer Avenue within town. The shop has a limited number of bikes that it rents for $8 per day.

SELDOVIA

Across the bay from Homer and in a world of its own is Seldovia, a small fishing village of 600. The town's nickname is 'City of Secluded Charm' and it lives up to it in a slow-moving, sleepy manner. Although in recent years tour boats have made it a regular stop, the village has managed to retain much of its old Alaskan charm and can be an interesting and inexpensive side trip away from Alaska's highway system.

The Good Friday earthquake caused the land beneath Seldovia to settle four feet, allowing high tides to flood much of the original town. In the reconstruction of Seldovia, the village became an urban renewal project, as much of its waterfront and beloved boardwalk were torn out while Cap's Hill was levelled to provide fill material. Today a small remnant of the early boardwalk can be seen if you walk a short distance to the left of the ferry terminal. The town's most popular sight is the St Nicholas Russian Orthodox Church. Built in 1891, the church was recently restored and is open to visitors between 1 and 2 pm on weekdays. It is just off Main St, overlooking the town.

Places to Stay & Eat

The town's hotel, the *Boardwalk* (tel 234-7816), charges $58 for a double. There are also two bed & breakfast places and *Seldovia Lodge* (tel 234-7654), which consists of old trailer units. It's best to camp for free on spectacular Outside Beach, where there are picnic tables and pit toilets. The stretch, known for good surf fishing of silver salmon and great sunsets, is 1.9 miles (three km) from town as you follow Seldovia St towards Jakalof Bay and then take the left-hand fork one mile (1.6 km) from Main St.

On Main St you find the *Kachemak Café*, *The Centurian Restaurant*, three bars and *Stampers Family Market* for groceries and supplies. Public rest-rooms, showers and water are available at the Harbormaster's Office at the Small Boat Harbor.

Hiking

For those who have a spare day in Seldovia, two trails head off from the Jakalof Bay Rd. The first is a privately built trail that climbs steeply above the tree line to Gunsight Mountain. It leaves the road eight miles (12.8 km) east of town but is unmarked, making it wise to inquire locally about its exact location. The second is a two-mile (3.2-km) path to the Tutka Lagoon salmon-rearing facility.

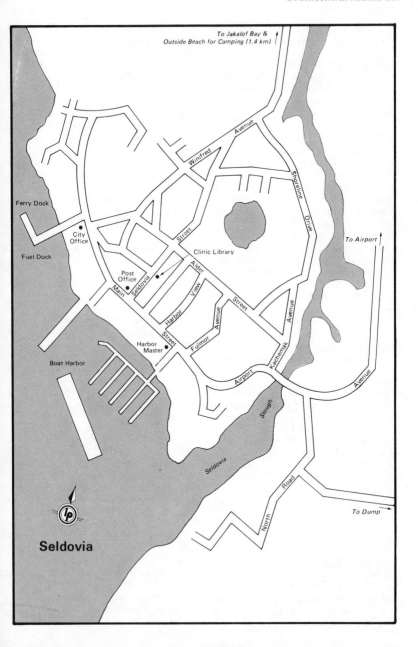

To Jakalof Bay &
Outside Beach for Camping (1.4 km)

Winifred Avenue

Shoreline Drive

Ferry Dock

City
Office

Street

To Airport

Fuel Dock

Clinic Library

Post
Office

Alder

Seldovia

View

Main

Harbor

Street

Fulmor

Avenue

Street

Kachemak Avenue

Harbor
Master

Boat Harbor

Airport

Avenue

Slough

Seldovia

North Road

To Dump

Seldovia

It departs from Jakalof Bay Rd 12 miles (19.2 km) out of town and is posted.

Getting There & Around
Bicycles can be rented from Josh's Bikes & Fishing (tel 234-7603) or from High Tide Originals (tel 234-7850), who run one of the bed & breakfast places in town. For travel on the water, Boardwalk Hotel rents out skiffs.

The state ferry stops at Seldovia twice a week on a round-trip sailing from Homer. One-way fare for Homer-Seldovia is $9. Rainbow Tours (tel 235-7272 in Homer) sails daily between the two towns, departing Homer at 10.30 am and Seldovia at 8 am. The fare is $30 round trip or $20 one way, or you can fly; it's a scenic 12-minute flight that passes over the Kenai Mountains and Kachemak Bay. Both Homer Air (tel 235-8591) and Cook Inlet Aviation (tel 235-8163) offer several flights daily; a round-trip ticket costs $41.

Kodiak Island

KODIAK
South-west of the Kenai Peninsula, 84 miles (140 km) in the Gulf of Alaska, is Kodiak, a city of 6500 that can make a lot of claims in the North Country. The town is on the eastern tip of Kodiak Island, the largest island in Alaska at 3670 square miles (9542 square km) and the second largest in the US. The fishermen of Kodiak can claim the largest fleet in the state, with over 2000 boats. That in turn has made the town the third largest commercial fishing port in the country, while residents proudly call their city the 'King Crab Capital of the World.'

Kodiak Island is home for the famed Kodiak brown bear, the largest terrestrial carnivore in the world. There is an estimated 2400 of them on the island and some males have reached the weight of 1500 lb (675 kg).

Kodiak can claim some of the foggiest weather in Southcentral. Greatly affected by the turbulent Gulf of Alaska, the city is often rainy and foggy with occasional high winds. The area receives 80 inches (2000 mm) of rain per year and has an average temperature of 60°F (16°C) during the summer. On a clear day, however, the scenery is equal to that in any other part of the state. Mountains, craggy coastlines and some of the most deserted beaches accessible by road are Kodiak's most distinctive features.

The island and especially the city can also claim some of the most turbulent history in Alaska. The Russians first landed on the island in 1763 and made the settlement of Kodiak the capital of Russian-America in 1792 before moving it to Sitka 12 years later. In 1912, Kodiak had its first disaster when Mt Katmai on the nearby Alaska Peninsula erupted. The explosion not only created the Valley of 10,000 Smokes in Katmai National Park, but it blanketed the then sleepy fishing village with 18 inches (45 cm) of ash that caused great harm to wildlife, fish and homes. The ash can still be seen today at Fort Abercrombie when you lift up the moss growing on trees.

The second disaster was worse. The Good Friday earthquake in 1964 shook the entire island, and the following tidal wave levelled downtown Kodiak, destroyed the boat harbour and wiped out the local fishing fleet. Processing plants, canneries and 158 homes were lost; damages totalled $24 million. The natural disasters are now part of Kodiak's turbulent history and today the city thrives as the fishing capital of Alaska, with 15 fish-processing plants employing thousands during the summer. The island is also the site of Alaska's largest Coast Guard Station, which occupies the old US naval base. Four large Coast Guard cutters patrol out of Kodiak, seizing foreign vessels that illegally fish in US waters and assisting distressed ships caught in the violent storms of the North Pacific.

Top: Russian church in Ninilchik on the Kenai Peninsula (ADT)
Bottom: View of Homer Spit in Homer (ADT)

Top: Interior Alaska lake with canoe (ADT)
Bottom: The coastline near Kodiak on Kodiak Island (ADT)

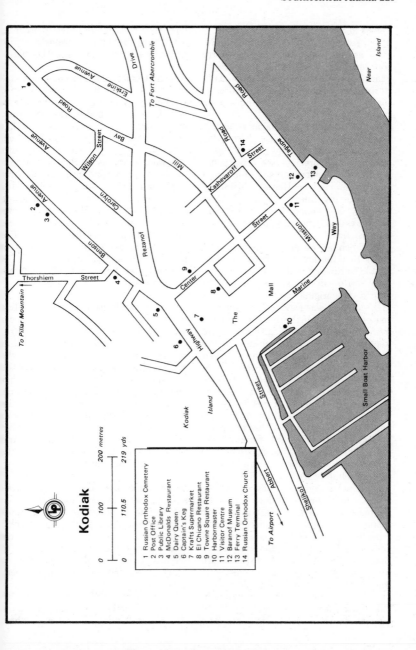

Kodiak

| 0 | 100 | 200 metres |
| 0 | 110.5 | 219 yds |

1 Russian Orthodox Cemetery
2 Post Office
3 Public Library
4 McDonalds Restaurant
5 Dairy Queen
6 Captain's Keg
7 Krafts Supermarket
8 El Chicano Restaurant
9 Towne Square Restaurant
10 Harbormaster
11 Visitor Centre
12 Baranof Museum
13 Ferry Terminal
14 Russian Orthodox Church

Things to See

You'll reach the Visitor Centre (tel 486-4070) as soon as you leave the state ferry terminal. Located at Centre St and Marine Way, the centre is open daily during the summer and is the source of many free handouts, including a good map of the city.

Across the street is the **Baranof Museum** housed in the Erskine House, built by the Russians between 1792 and 1799 as a storehouse for precious sea otter pelts. The museum contains many items from the Russian period of Kodiak's history as well as many fine examples of Aleut basketry. The hours are 10 am to 3 pm weekdays and 12 noon to 4 pm weekends; admission is $1.

Just behind the museum on Mission Rd is **Holy Resurrection Church**, serving the oldest Russian Orthodox parish in the New World – it was established in 1794. One of the original clerics was Father Herman, who was elevated to sainthood in Kodiak in 1970 in the first canonisation ever performed in America. His relics are kept in a carved wooden chest near the altar. Also within the church are polished brassware, several icons and rare paintings. The church is open to visitors from 1 to 3 pm on weekdays. Its blue-and-white onion-domed features make for great photography if you can squeeze out the huge gas storage tank that flanks it.

To the left from the ferry terminal you can follow Marine Way as it curves past **Small Boat Harbor**, the heart and soul of Kodiak. Crab boats, salmon seiners and halibut schooners cram the downtown docks, while more boats dock across the channel at St Herman Harbor on Near Island. An afternoon on the docks leads to friendly encounters with fishermen and the chance to see catches unloaded or nets being repaired. Although no tours are available, **canneries** can be seen clattering and steaming around the clock during the summer on nearby Shelikof St, or you can take the free ferry across the channel to **St Herman Harbor** to view more boats. The

ferry runs continuously, departing from Dock 2 (ask at the Harbormaster Office for its location) of Small Boat Harbor.

Fort Abercrombie State Historical Park This military fort was built in 1941. Its two eight-inch (20 cm) guns, left over from WW I, were installed by the US Army who waited for a Japanese invasion that never came. Today it is a state historical park, sitting majestically on the cliff over wooded Monashka Bay. Restoration has begun with remounting of the guns and repair of the bunkers. A self-guided tour winds through the WW II relics on Miller Point and past the beautiful views of ocean and rocky shorelines where inviting tidal pools are fun to explore. The park, 4.5 miles (7.2 km) north-east of town off Monashka Bay Rd, has 14 camping sites. Nearby is the Frank Brink Amphitheatre.

Pillar Mountain Placement of a DEW-line site and later a communications saucer on top of the 1270-foot (387-metre) mountain has resulted in a road that climbs to a scenic overlook behind the city and provides excellent views of the surrounding mountains, ocean, beaches and islands. One side seems to plunge straight down to the harbour below, while the other overlooks the green interior of Kodiak Island. Pick up the bumpy dirt road by heading up Thorsheim St and turning left on Maple Avenue, which runs into Pillar Mountain Rd.

Kodiak Island Roads Over 100 miles (160 km) of paved and gravel roads head from the city into the wilderness that surrounds Kodiak. Some are rough jeep tracks manageable only by four-wheel-drive vehicles, but many can be driven or hitched along to isolated stretches of beach, great fishing spots and superb coastal scenery.

To the south of Kodiak, Chiniak Rd winds 47.6 miles (76.6 km) to Cape Greville, following the edge of three plendid bays along the way. The road provides access to some of the best coastal cenery in Alaska and opportunities to iew sea lions and puffins offshore, specially at Cape Chiniak near the south nd.

Just past *Mile 30* (48 km) you arrive at he junction with Pasagshak Bay Rd that vinds 16.4 miles (26.4 km) due south to 'asagshak River State Recreation Site. 'his small campground (seven sites, free) s famous for its silver and king salmon ishing as well as for a river that reverses ts flow four times a day with the tides. 'hese scenic areas, and not the city, are he true attractions of Kodiak Island. nybody who has the time (and patience) hitch-hike, or the money to rent a car see the Getting Around section), should xplore these roads.

laces to Stay

outh Hostel There was a short-lived 'outh Hostel in Kodiak that ceased to xist after 1984. Check with the visitor entre to see if it has been reorganised; herwise, plan on either spending a undle on accommodation or hitching iiles out of town to camp.

lotels Of the three hotels in town, *Kodiak tar Motel* (tel 486-5657) on 119 Brooklyn 'errace is the cheapest by a few dollars, 'ith doubles going for $64 a night. All end to be heavily booked during the immer.

amping There are no campgrounds in wn, and camping within the city limits illegal. The closest campground is 'uskin River State Recreation Site (18 tes, free), four miles (6.4 km) south on ezanof Drive, on the way to the airport. 'he spot provides picnic shelters, pit iilets, trails through nearby wooded reas and good fishing on Buskin River or irf fishing in the ocean. Nearby is the odiak National Wildlife Refuge head-uarters and visitor centre.

There is also camping at *Fort Aber-crombie State Historical Park* (14 sites, free), the most scenic campground in which to pitch a tent; and at *Pasagshak River State Recreation Site*. All have a seven-day limit.

Places to Eat

McDonald's has reached Kodiak and now you can head up Thorsheim St near the police station and fire department for a cheap but filling dinner of Big Macs, shakes and fries. *Towne Square Restaurant* has home-baked goods and good deli sandwiches for some of the best prices in town. Located in the Bakery Building on Centre St downtown, it is also a good place for breakfast.

Further up the price range is *Captain's Keg* next door to the Dairy Queen on Rezanof Drive. The restaurant has a huge salad bar and features chicken, ribs and pizza.

For local seafood or an inexpensive breakfast, or to rub elbows with fishermen over early morning coffee, try *Kodiak Café* next to the Small Boat Harbor on Marine Way; or try *Mecca Harborview* across the street, an eatery known for its excellent clam chowder.

Nightlife

Clustered around the downtown waterfront and Small Boat Harbor are a handful of bars that cater to Kodiak's fishing industry. At night they are interesting places, overflowing with fishermen, deck-hands and cannery workers drinking hard and talking lively. One is the *B & B Bar* across from the harbour, which claims to be Alaska's oldest bar, having served its first beer in 1899. Another is *Anchor Bar* on Shelikof Avenue, which also has washers and dryers and sells laundry supplies. At this unique pub, you can order a beer while waiting for your wash to run through.

For music at night there is *Solly's Office* in the mall, which is a restaurant/lounge featuring country music. *Beachcombers*, a little over a mile (1.6 km)

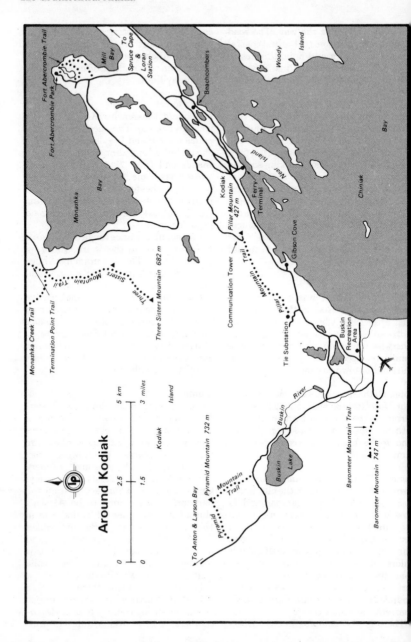

Around Kodiak

north of the ferry terminal on Mission Rd, offers rock & roll.

Events

Kodiak's best event, if you happen to be around in late May, is its week-long Crab Festival, featuring a parade, foot and kayak races, fishermen's skills contests and a lot of cooked king crab.

There is also the State Fair & Rodeo held in mid-August at the Bell Flats rodeo grounds, a Fourth of July celebration, and the Great Buskin Raft Race in June that combines a raft race with five mandatory beer stops.

If you enjoy local pageantry, make an effort to see 'Cry of the Wild Ram', which depicts Kodiak's Russian days in a high-spirited manner complete with cannons roaring and wooden stockade bursting into flames. It is held the first two weeks of August in the Frank Brink Amphitheatre, a magnificent outdoor theatre near Fort Abercrombie. The play takes place rain or shine and tickets are $10 per person. Contact Kodiak-Baranof Productions (tel 486-5291) for ticket information.

Hiking

There are dozens of hiking trails in the Kodiak area but unfortunately very few are maintained and the trailheads are not marked along the roads. Once on the path, windfall could make following it difficult or even totally conceal it. Still, hiking trails are the best avenue to the natural beauty of Kodiak Island. Before starting out, contact the Kodiak area ranger of the Alaska Division of Parks (tel 486-6339) for exact location and condition of trails.

Pillar Mountain Two foot trails depart from Pillar Mountain Rd. The first begins near the KOTV satellite receiver near the lower city reservoir and provides an easy walk north to Monashka Bay Rd. The second begins at the communications tower at the top of the mountain and is a

descent of the south-west side. It ends at the Tie Substation, where a gravel road leads out to Chiniak Rd about one mile (1.6 km) north-east of Buskin River State Recreation Site. Plan on an afternoon for either trail.

Barometer Mountain Trail The trail is a popular one but there's a steep climb of five miles (eight km) to the 2452-foot (748-metre) summit. To reach the beginning, follow Chiniak Rd south of Buskin River Campground and turn right on the first road immediately after passing the end of the airport's runway. Look for a well-worn trail on the left. The trek begins in thick alder before climbing the hogback ridge of the mountain and providing spectacular views of Kodiak and the bays south of the city.

Termination Point Trail This is another popular hike along a five-mile trail that starts at the end of Monashka Bay Rd and branches into several trails near the point. Most of the hiking is done in virgin spruce forest.

Kodiak National Wildlife Refuge

The 1.8 million-acre (754,700 hectare) preserve, which covers the majority of Kodiak Island, is the chief stronghold of the Alaska brown bear. An estimated 2400 bears reside in the refuge and surrounding area, for one of the world's highest densities. The refuge is known worldwide for brown bear hunting and to a lesser degree for salmon and steelhead fishing. There are no maintained trails within the preserve, and cross-country hiking is extremely hard due to thick bush. Access into the park is by charter plane or boat out of Kodiak – both expensive.

Cabins US Fish & Wildlife Service administers nine free-use cabins in the refuge that should be reserved in advance. Cabin reservations are selected by four annual lotteries, each covering usage for certain months. Cabins that are not reserved can be obtained on a first-come first-serve basis. The closest units to Kodiak – Uganik Island Cabin and Veikoda Bay Cabin – are both on the ocean with good beaches nearby. If you are planning your trip, write to Kodiak National Wildlife Refuge (PO Box 825, Kodiak, Alaska 99615) about reserving a unit. If you're already in Kodiak, call the refuge headquarters (tel 487-2600) to check if any cabins are available.

Getting There & Around
Air Mark Air, in conjunction with Alaska Airlines, provides daily flights between Kodiak and Anchorage with a one-way ticket costing $215. The airport is five miles (eight km) south of town on Chiniak Rd.

Boat The state ferry *MV Tustumena* calls on Kodiak three times a week from either Seward or Homer, stopping first at Port Lions, a nearby village on Kodiak Island.

The ferry terminal (tel 486-3800) is downtown. One-way to Homer is $34 and to Seward $38.

Car Rental There are four car-rental companies in Kodiak, including *Rent-A-Heap* (tel 486-5200) that will provide you with wheels to explore the island's outer edges. The used cars go for $20 per day plus 20c per mile.

Bicycle Cyclists will find Kodiak's roads an interesting ride, especially the 12-mile (19.2 km) Anton Larsen Bay Rd that leads from near Buskin River State Campground over the mountainous pass to the west side of the island, where you will find quiet coves and shorelines to explore. Plan on two hours for the ride to Anton Larsen Bay. The ride down Chiniak Rd can be equally impressive. Within town, Elkay Bicycle Shop (tel 486-4219) on Malutin Lane just off Mill Bay Rd handles repairs and parts.

Anchorage

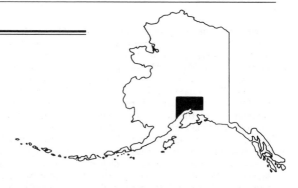

Anchorage, the hub of Alaska's road system, the air crossroads of the world and home for half the state's residents, is a city of prosperity, money and much debate.

Those who live in the Anchorage area claim there is no other city like it in the world. It's Alaska's Big Apple and the state revolves around it. Everything you could possibly want is only a short hop away from the urban area which houses 205,000 people. Glaciers, mountains, hiking trails or whitewater rivers to raft are all 20 minutes away. Within a couple of hours driving is the recreation paradise of the Kenai Peninsula and a handful of state and national preserves which offer unlimited camping, hiking and fishing.

Yet in Anchorage you can enjoy all the comforts and attractions offered by any large US city, including a state-of-the-art performing centre, enclosed shopping malls, and bars and nightclubs that buzz late into the night.

However, many residents around the state look at the city, shake their heads and say, 'Anchorage is great. It's only 20 minutes from Alaska'. To them, everything that Alaska is, Anchorage isn't. The city is a mass of uncontrolled urban sprawl or, in down-to-earth terms, a beer can in the middle of the woods. It has billboards, traffic jams and dozens of fast-food restaurants on a single road. Its trees are ripped out for trailer parks and shopping centres. For the reasons these

people have chosen to live and work in Alaska, Anchorage isn't one of them.

You either hate the city or you love it. If you are a visitor, it is inevitable that you pass through it at least once, if not several times. Anchorage has the advantage of being north of the Kenai Mountains, which shield the city from the excess moisture experienced by Southcentral. The Anchorage Bowl – the city and surrounding area – receives only 14 inches (355 mm) of precipitation annually. Nor does the area have the extreme temperatures of the Interior. The average temperature in January is 13°F (-11°C), while at the height of the summer it's only 58°F (14°C). The area does have more than its share of overcast days, especially in early and late summer.

Although Captain James Cook sailed up the inlet in 1778 looking for the mythical Northwest Passage, Anchorage wasn't born until 1914 when surveyors chose the site as the work camp and headquarters for the Alaska Railroad; by 1915 it was a tent city of 2000. The area's growth occurred in sudden spurts, caused by increased farming in the Matanuska Valley to the north in the 1930s, the construction of military bases during WW II, and the discovery of oil in Cook Inlet in the late 1950s.

Two events literally reshaped the city. The Good Friday earthquake devastated much of downtown Anchorage and resulted in the rebuilding of entire sections of town. Later the city prospered when oil was discovered in Prudhoe Bay, and Anchorage served as the headquarters for much of the Trans-Alaska pipeline construction.

Today Anchorage is truly the heart of Alaska and the centre of the state's commerce and financial communities. Though the wide bowl which Anchorage lies in is boxed in by the Chugach Mountains to the east and Cook Inlet to the west, the city continues to sprawl and seems to be in a constant state of rebuilding. It's the fastest-growing city in Alaska, and little wonder. Almost two-thirds of the state's population lives in the greater Anchorage trading area, making them the recipients of the greatest proportion of the state's recent oil money. Major construction projects have blossomed suddenly like wildflowers on the first warm spring day and now there's talk of bringing the Winter Olympics to Anchorage in the 1990s. As long as oil gushes from Prudhoe Bay, Anchorage will prosper like few cities in America have ever done before.

Information
There are three Visitor Information Centres in Anchorage. The main one is the log cabin (tel 274-3531) on the corner of 4th Avenue and F St, open daily during the summer from 8.30 am to 6 pm. Along with the many services and handouts already described, this centre operates an 'Emergency Language Bank' of 27 languages designed to help any foreign traveller in distress. They also have the 24-hour 'All About Anchorage' recording (tel 276-3200) that lists current events taking place in the city that day. The other two visitor information centres are at the domestic and overseas terminals of the International Airport and are staffed for most incoming flights.

Backpackers and hikers can head over to the National Park Service (tel 271-4243) at 2525 Gambell St for information and handouts on any national park in Alaska. Or you can visit the Alaska Division of Parks (tel 561-2020) at 619 Warehouse Avenue for information or state parks. The Chugach National Forest Office (tel 279-5541) at 2221 East Northern Lights Boulevard has information on any USFS national forest, trail or cabin. The Bureau of Land Management (Pinnell Mountain Trail) also maintains an office (tel 271-5555) at 701 C St, as does the US Fish & Wildlife Service (Kenai National Wildlife Refuge) at 1011 East Tudor Rd (tel 562-2271). If you're just arriving in Alaska at Anchorage, make good use of these agencies to gather the latest information for the rest of your trip.

Anchorage Convention & Visitors Bureau

Things to See
If you fly in, you arrive in the south-west corner of the city. If you drive in – from the south on Seward Highway or the north on Glenn Highway – the roads lead you through the city toward Cook Inlet

Whichever way you arrive, it's best to head downtown. There is bus transportation from the airport and both highways end (or begin if you are leaving) less than one mile (1.6 km) from each other.

Downtown is a somewhat undefined area boxed in by 3rd Avenue to the north, 10th Avenue to the south, Minnesota Drive to the west and Ingra St (Seward Highway) to the east. Begin any visit to the city at the Visitor Information Centre (tel 274-3531) on the corner of 4th Avenue and F St. The centre is housed in a log cabin complete with sod roof and is open daily from 10 am to 6 pm in the summer. Among the handouts and maps they provide is the 'Anchorage Visitors Guide', which describes among other things a three to four-hour walking tour of downtown.

Those not up to walking the tour can catch the free double-decker bus provided by People Mover. The route (No 10) almost parallels the tour, minus a street here and there, and allows you to see most of the following attractions without having to hoof it. It does not stop at the Visitor Centre, however, so you have to walk two blocks west on 5th Avenue and a block south on G St to catch it at the Transit Centre. The bus passes the centre every half hour.

The beautiful thing about Anchorage is the simplicity with which most of the streets are laid out, especially downtown. Numbered avenues run north to south and lettered streets east to west. The tour begins by heading north on E St, where on the corner of 2nd Avenue it passes the **US Geological Survey** office and the **Alaska Railroad Depot** across the street from each other. The USGS office is the place to go for topographic maps for any part of the state. The Railroad depot features historical photos in its lobby, totem poles outside and Engine No 1 on a platform. The small locomotive was built in the 1900s for construction of the Panama Canal and was later shipped to Alaska for use on the railroad.

The tour continues west on 2nd Avenue and then swings onto Christensen Drive, where at the corner of 3rd Avenue it comes to the **Port of Anchorage** observation deck. From here you can view the mouth of Ship Creek and the Port of Anchorage, which handles more than 400 tankers and cargo ships annually.

Turn east on 3rd Avenue and then south on G St until you reach the **Old Federal Building** on the corner of 4th Avenue. Built in the 1930s, the building is on the National Register of Historic Places and was the focal point of celebrations following the passage of the Alaska Statehood Act in 1958. Today it houses the Alaska Public Lands Information Centre, where exhibits, films and handouts covering all of Alaska public parks, preserves and wilderness areas are available. It's an excellent stop-off for anybody who has just arrived in Alaska and plans to spend a summer hiking or backpacking in the woods. On the front lawn stands *The Northern Lights* as depicted by a local sculptor.

West on 4th Avenue and a half block north on K St is the eye-catching large statue entitled *The Last Blue Whale*. Inside the adjoining building is Fred Machetanz's famous painting *The Hunt*.

Nearby at the west end of 3rd Avenue is **Resolution Park** and the **Captain Cook Monument**. From the viewing deck you have an excellent view of the surrounding mountains, including the Talkeetnas to the north-west and the snow-covered Alaska Range to the west. On a clear day you can see Mt McKinley and Mt Foraker to the west, while to the east is Mt Susitna, known as 'The Sleeping Lady'. It marks the south-west end of the Alaska Range. There is also a panorama of Cook Inlet; often the large white caps you see are Beluga whales feeding on salmon fry or smelt.

The tour drops down to 6th Avenue, where near the corner of H St is **Oomingmak Musk Ox Producers Co-op**. The cooperative handles a variety of garments made of arctic musk ox wool and hand-knitted in isolated Eskimo villages. Inside, slide shows and displays demonstrate this cottage industry. East on 6th Avenue at the corner of G St is the **People Mover Transit Centre**, where you can pick up a local bus to any section of the city (see the Getting Around section).

Across from the bus station on the north side of 6th Avenue is the new **Performing Arts Complex**, due to be completed in 1987. Nearby is the **Sydney Laurence Auditorium**, home of the Alaska Repertory Theatre.

You then swing north on F St, where at the corner of 5th Avenue is a replica of a **Japanese formal garden** that was completed in 1978. East of it is the new **Egan Civic & Convention Centre**. Eventually the tour heads to the **Anchorage Historical & Fine Arts Museum** (tel 264-4326) near the corner of 7th Avenue and A St. In 1984, the museum was expanded to triple its size and now is an impressive centre for displays on Alaskan history and native culture as well as an art gallery that features work by regional, national and international artists. It is open Monday through Saturday from 9 am to 6 pm and until 9 pm on Tuesday and Thursday. On Sunday, hours are 1 to 5 pm and admission is free. Among the special events the museum stages during the summer are free showings of Alaskan films daily at 3 pm.

Less impressive is Anchorage's other museum, **Alaska Wildlife & Natural History Museum** (tel 272-3510), at 833 West 4th Avenue. The centre contains 30 stuffed animals and various exhibits of live ones, plus films and photographs of Alaskan wildlife. Hours are 9 am to 6 pm daily and admission is \$5.

Parks The most scenic park in the city is Earthquake Park at the west end of Northern Lights Boulevard on the Knik Arm (bus No 93 from the Youth Hostel). There is little evidence of the 1964 disaster, but interpretive and illustrated signs detail the powerful force that shook Anchorage and killed 115 persons. The best part of the park is the excellent panorama of the city skyline set against the Chugach Mountains; on a clear day you can see Mt McKinley and Mt Foraker to the north.

If the weather is hot enough, several lakes in the area offer swimming. The closest one is Goose Lake, three miles (4.8 km) east of downtown on Northern Lights Boulevard (bus Nos 3 or 93). Before or after your dip, take a stroll through the University of Alaska at Anchorage, the largest campus in the state university system. It is connected to Goose Lake Park by footpaths. There is also swimming at Spenard Lake, three miles (4.8 km) on Spenard Rd and then west on Lakeshore Drive (bus No 7), and at Jewel Lake, 6.5 miles (10.4 km) from downtown on Diamond Boulevard (bus No 7).

Within the downtown area there is Delaney Park, known locally as 'The Park Strip' because it stretches from A to P Sts between 9th and 10th Avenues. The green strip, the site of the 50-ton bonfire that highlighted statehood in 1959, and later where Pope John Paul II gave an outdoor mass in 1981, is a good place to lie down on a hot afternoon.

Military Bases Elmendorf Air Base and Fort Richardson were established during WW II as the major northern military outposts for the US, and continue today to contribute to Anchorage's economy. In the early 1940s Elmendorf housed one of the nation's strongest air stations and now is home base for F-15 Eagles, T-33s and other huge aircraft. The base offers a weekly summer tour that allows you to view the hangars and planes along with the rest of the facility. Call ahead (tel 552-2282) to find out times and reserve a seat on the bus. There is also a wildlife museum with over 200 Alaskan mammals, fish and birds in Building 4-803 (ask the guard for directions) that is open from 7.45 am to 4.45 pm weekdays and 10 am to

3 pm Saturday (bus No 14 from the Transit Centre).

Fort Richardson (tel 863-8113) also has a wildlife museum with 250 specimens, along with a golf course and salmon hatchery. The museum, Building 600, is open 9 am to 5 pm weekdays, 10 am to 4 pm Saturday and noon to 4 pm Sunday (bus No 75). Both museums are free.

National Park Service The National Park Service Information Centre (tel 271-4243) is at 2525 Gambell St between Fireweed Lane and Northern Lights Boulevard and is open 8 am to 5 pm weekdays (bus Nos 2 or 3). It should be the first stop for anybody who is planning a summer of hiking and wilderness trekking, as it is the source of numerous handouts and maps about the state's many national parks. Even if you didn't bring a pair of hiking boots, stop by to see the larger reference area that contains a photo series on Alaskan wildlife and scenery. The centre also shows a nature film daily at 12.15 and 3 pm.

Lake Hood Air Harbor Those enchanted by Alaska's bush planes and small air-taxi operators will be overwhelmed by Lake Hood, the world's busiest floatplane base (and ski plane base in the winter). Almost every type of small plane imaginable can be seen buzzing on and off the lake's surface. The floatplane base can be reached by bus No 93 from the Youth Hostel and makes an interesting afternoon trip when combined with a swim in adjoining Lake Spenard.

Ship Creek From mid to late summer, king, coho and pink salmon spawn up Ship Creek, the historical site of Tanaina Indian fish camps. There is a good viewing platform on the north side of the creek, 0.5 mile (0.8 km) from the Railroad Depot, where you can watch the return of the salmon. Follow C St north as it crosses Ship Creek Bridge and then turn right on Whitney Rd.

Places to Stay

Youth Hostel Anchorage has one of the main *Youth Hostels* (tel 276-3635) in the Alaska Council. It is on the west side of the city in the Sands Apartment Complex at the corner of 32nd Avenue and Minnesota Dr, one block south of Benson Boulevard. The cost is $7.75 for members and $9.75 for non-members, and there is a three-night maximum stay unless special arrangements are made with the house-parents. Check-in is from 5 to 9 pm and check-out from 7 to 9 am. Along with sleeping arrangements, there is a family room, kitchen facilities, showers and a laundry room. You can store extra gear there for 50c a day. While not in the most popular area of Anchorage, the hostel is near numerous restaurants, bars, a shopping centre and the routes of several People Mover buses that provide cheap and quick access to other areas. From the airport take bus Nos 93 or 6, which pass right in front of it. Other buses that come within a block or so are Nos 7, 3, 31, 9 and 60. The Anchorage Youth Hostel Chapter is searching for a new location downtown and hopes to obtain a place by 1988. Call the Alaska Division of Parks (tel 561-2020) to find out if it has already moved.

Hotels Anchorage has over 35 hotels and motels and 3700 rooms for rent, so late arrivals and independent travellers with no reservations have few problems finding an available bed. However, trying to find a single under $40 and a double under $50 is the tricky part. One of the cheaper ones downtown is the *Palace Hotel* (tel 277-6313) on 4th Avenue and Barrow, which offers singles for $25 and doubles for $30 with shared baths.

A much better stay for only a few dollars more is the *Midtown Hotel* (tel 338-7778) at 604 West 26th St, just off Arctic Boulevard between Fireweed Lane and Northern Lights Boulevard (bus No 9 from the Transit Centre). The Midtown has singles for $28 and doubles for $30

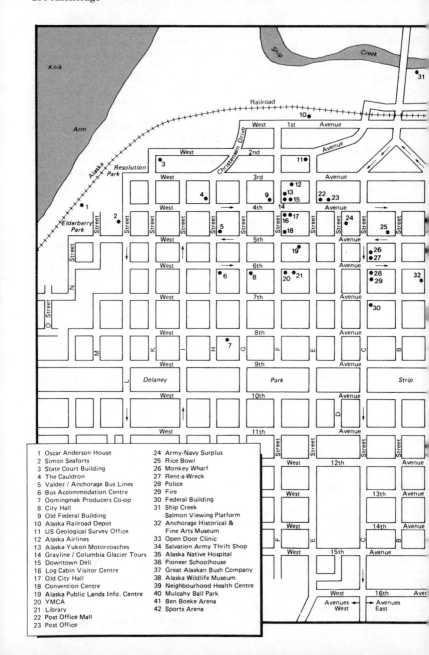

1 Oscar Anderson House
2 Simon Seaforts
3 State Court Building
4 The Cauldron
5 Valdez / Anchorage Bus Lines
6 Bus Accommodation Centre
7 Oomingmak Producers Co-op
8 City Hall
9 Old Federal Building
10 Alaska Railroad Depot
11 US Geological Survey Office
12 Alaska Airlines
13 Alaska-Yukon Motorcoaches
14 Grayline / Columbia Glacier Tours
15 Downtown Deli
16 Log Cabin Visitor Centre
17 Old City Hall
18 Convention Centre
19 Alaska Public Lands Info. Centre
20 YMCA
21 Library
22 Post Office Mall
23 Post Office
24 Army-Navy Surplus
25 Rice Bowl
26 Monkey Wharf
27 Rent-a-Wreck
28 Police
29 Fire
30 Federal Building
31 Ship Creek
   Salmon Viewing Platform
32 Anchorage Historical &
   Fine Arts Museum
33 Open Door Clinic
34 Salvation Army Thrift Shop
35 Alaska Native Hospital
36 Pioneer Schoolhouse
37 Great Alaskan Bush Company
38 Alaska Wildlife Museum
39 Neighbourhood Health Centre
40 Mulcahy Ball Park
41 Ben Boeke Arena
42 Sports Arena

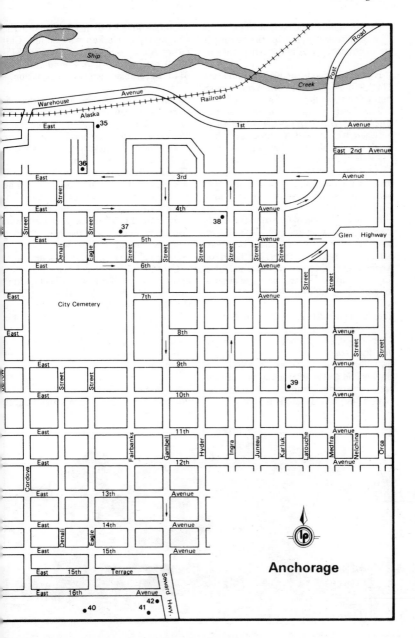

Anchorage

with shared bath, and is eight blocks from Chester Creek Greenstrip, the beautiful series of parks that divides Anchorage in half.

Higher in price is the *Kobuk Hotel* (tel 274-1650) at 1104 East 5th Avenue near Ingra St. It has doubles for $47.

The best place downtown is the *Anchorage Hotel* (tel 272-4553 on E St between 4th and 3rd Avenues, as it has singles or doubles with baths for $40.

For late arrivals at the International Airport there is the *Tradewinds* (tel 243-3965) a mile away at 4332 Spenard Rd, with singles with baths for $28 and doubles for $32.

If you are driving in late from the north there is *John's Motel* (tel 277-4332) at 3543 Mt View Drive off Glenn Highway before you begin to enter the heart of Anchorage. This small motel, which also has hook-ups for RVers, provides singles for $40 and doubles for $50.

Bed & Breakfast A large number of Anchorage residents have organised bed & breakfast accommodation by opening up the spare bedroom for summer travellers. Most begin at $35 to $45 for singles and $50 to $60 for two people and are on the fringes or in the suburbs of the city. They provide a clean bed, a good breakfast and local insight to both the city and the Alaskan way of life. Call either Alaska Private Lodging (tel 345-2222) or Stay With A Friend (tel 274-6445) to arrange such accommodation.

Camping The Anchorage Parks & Recreation Department maintains two parks where there is overnight camping. The closest to downtown is *Lion's Camper Park* in Russian Jack Springs Park south of Glenn Highway on Boniface Parkway. The campground has 10 tent sites, 50 RV spaces, hot showers and rest-rooms. The surrounding park features tennis courts, hiking trails and a picnic area. The campground is 2.5 miles (four km) from downtown and can be reached within a block by bus No 8; it is also within walking distance of bus route Nos 5, 12 and 45.

Centennial Park has 83 sites, showers and rest-rooms but is 4.6 miles (7.4 km) from downtown on Glenn Highway. Take the Muldoon Rd exit south of the highway and turn west onto Boundary Avenue for half a block. Bus Nos 3 and 75 run past the corner of Muldoon and Boundary. The cost is $10 per night and there is a limit of seven days.

Places to Eat
Downtown For those on a strict budget

you have a choice of fast-food places: *McDonald's* on the corner of 4th Avenue and E St, *Wendy's* down the street at 239 4th Avenue, and *Burger King* at 520 West 5th Avenue. All now compete for the breakfast trade as well as for the lunch and dinner crowd looking for a quick burger. Just as easy on the money pouch is the *Federal Building Cafeteria* off C St between 7th and 8th Avenues. It's open from 7 am to 1.30 pm weekdays and serves breakfast and lunches in pleasant surroundings where you don't feel like gulping down your food.

More notable and a little higher in price is the *Downtown Deli* near the McDonald's on 4th Avenue, unquestionably the city's best-known delicatessen and also one of its best. Good Chinese cuisine is available at the *Rice Bowl* near the corner of 5th Avenue and C St, where complete dinners cost from $10 to $17. In the same price range and nearby in the lower level of the Sunshine Mall on 4th Avenue is the *Tea Leaf* for spicy Szechwan dishes.

Good health-food restaurants downtown include *The Cauldron* at 328 I St, known for its homemade soups, large salads and nightly folk music; and *The Bread Factory* at 825 I St. For pizza try *Legal Pizza* at 330 H St, which has a salad bar and serves beer and wine.

Those looking to make an evening out of dinner have a long list of places to choose from. One of the best that won't set you back too much is *Simon & Seafort's Saloon & Grill* at 420 L St between 4th and 5th Avenues. The restaurant has the interesting decor of a turn-of-the-century grand saloon and a nice view of Cook Inlet. The seafood is excellent and dinners average $14 to $17.

Midtown The area roughly from Debarr Rd to Tudor Rd east of Minnesota Drive is occasionally referred to as 'midtown' and the restaurants here are easier to reach for those staying at the Youth Hostel. *McDonald's* is at 800 West

Northern Lights Boulevard and the *Burger King* is even closer to the Youth Hostel along the same road.

Skipper's has all the fish, salad and chowder you can consume for $6 and is within walking distance from the Youth Hostel at the corner of Spenard and Minnesota. There is also a Skipper's at 5668 DeBarr Rd.

Shakey's is a pizza parlour with all the pizza, chicken and salad you can eat for $5 Monday to Friday between 12 noon and 2 pm. There are several in the city, including one at 2950 Minnesota Drive, just north of the Youth Hostel. The best pizza in this area, however, is at *One Guy From Italy*, near the Youth Hostel at the corner of Minnesota Drive and Benson Boulevard. Open daily, the eatery offers over 20 kinds of pizza plus other good Italian dishes.

Harry's at 101 West Benson Boulevard is a good old Irish pub dedicated to Harry Truman, the man who refused to move from his home on the side of Mt St Helens when the volcano began erupting in 1980. The decor is dedicated to him, with a statue of the old-timer and walls of photos of his mountainous home. The place is also a good restaurant, where you can get a meal of sandwiches, hamburgers and salads for under $7.

Nightlife
There is every kind of drinking hole in Anchorage, a city where you can hike all day in the mountains and dance all night in its bars. One of the more colourful places is *Chilkoot Charlie's*, or 'Koots' as the locals call it, at 2435 Spenard Rd in the midtown and Youth Hostel area. The bar hops at night as it features a band and dancing in one room, a long bar in the other, sawdust on the floor and rusty artefacts all over the walls. Liquor prices are reasonable and even better at happy hour, from 4 to 8 pm when drinks are two for one.

On the same road but much classier is *Spenardo DaVinci's* at 3103 Spenard.

The nightclub has dancing and entertainment nightly, along with a laser light and sound show. There's no cover charge from Sunday to Thursday but it can still be an expensive place to drink unless you hit happy hour on Monday to Friday from 4 to 7 pm, when drinks are two for one and hors-d'oeuvres are free.

Other places for music on Spenard are *Midnight Express* at 2612, which features live music – usually country rock; and *Fly By Nite Club* at 4811, which draws an older crowd in their late 20s and 30s for blues and jazz music. Nearby, *Harry's* at 101 West Benson has entertainment and delicious ice-cream drinks that can be enjoyed from its 'step-down bar.'

In downtown Anchorage you have the *Monkey Wharf* at 529 C St, which offers entertainment, dancing and live monkeys behind the bar. There's also *Great Alaskan Bush Co*, the city's notorious strip joint on 4th Avenue. Great views of the area can be obtained for the (steep) price of a drink at the *Crow's Nest* at the top of the Captain Cook Hotel on 5th Avenue and K St; or at *Penthouse Lounge* at the top of the Sheffield House Hotel at 720 West 5th Avenue, where floor-to-ceiling windows let you marvel at Mt McKinley on a clear day.

Noteworthy bars on the fringes of the city include the *Peanut Farm* at 5227 Old Seward Highway. It's a good old bar with bowls of peanuts on the tables for those who prefer drinking to dinner. *Upper 1* is for travellers waiting for their flight or for anyone who enjoys watching jumbo jets land and take off.

Events

Anchorage has a civic opera, a symphony orchestra, several theatre groups and a concert association that brings a number of dance companies and art groups to the city every year. Big-name performers arrive more frequently now that the Performing Arts Centre has been completed. For a daily report on all cultural events around the area, call the All About Anchorage phone line (276-3200) for its recorded message.

Those watching their funds carefully should keep in mind the free concerts given during the summer around town. The 'Meet Me At The Plaza' series offers lunchtime entertainment every Friday at the corner of 5th Avenue and F St. 'Cabaret 550' offers similar programmes at noon on Tuesday at corner of 7th Avenue and E St. Every Thursday at 7 pm you can attend the 'Concerts in the Park' series in Delaney Park Strip. The Anchorage Historical & Fine Arts Museum also sponsors free movies at night; film classics are shown on Tuesday at 7.30 pm and Alaska wilderness programmes are shown on Wednesday at the same time.

The city has numerous movie theatres, including *Capri Cinema* (tel 272-3211), bus No 75; *Denali Theatre* (tel 279-2332), bus Nos 3 and 7; *Fireweed Theatre* (tel 277-3825), bus No 2; *Fourth Avenue Theatre* (tel 272-1024) downtown; and *Totem Theatre* (tel 333-8222), bus Nos 5 and 75.

Summer festivals include a large Fourth of July celebration; a Renaissance Faire with Shakespeare-type costumes and plays in early June at the Tudor Centre; and the Alaska Festival of Music, a two-week event in early September featuring concerts, theatre and opera performances. Smaller events worth attending are Kite Day in early June, when kite-flyers show up in full force for a colourful time in Delaney Park; and the city's summer solstice in mid-June, which is wrapped around the Mayor's Midnight Sun Marathon and the Campbell Creek Classic (during which anything that floats is paddled down the local river).

Getting Around

Airport People arriving at the International Airport have a couple of ways to reach the city. Several limousine services, including International Bus Service (tel 248-2272), run mini-buses from the baggage area to major hotels downtown; plan on $7 one way. Even cheaper is to wait a little and catch People Mover bus No 6, which departs roughly every hour from Monday to Saturday from the lower level near gate 33. The fare is 75c and the bus will pass the Youth Hostel on the way.

Bus Anchorage has a good public bus system in the People Mover. All buses except No 93 begin at the People Mover's terminal in the Transit Centre in the Municipal Building on the corner of 6th Avenue and G St downtown. The fare is 75c or $10 for 20 tokens and drivers do not carry any change. If the trip requires more than one bus, ask the driver for a transfer, which allows you to ride free on the connecting bus. Full service is Monday to Friday, with reduced service on Saturday and 10 buses that run on Sunday, none of which go to the International Airport. For information on any route call the Ride Line at 264-6543.

Car Rental When there are three or more of you, renting a used car is often an affordable and ideal way to see Anchorage, the surrounding area or the Kenai Peninsula. Rates for used cars begin at $15 a day plus 15c a mile for the oldest compacts and go up from there. You have to deposit $200 to $300 or use a major US credit card. For the cheapest rentals contact Rent-A-Wreck, which has an office at the International Airport (tel 561-2218) and downtown at 6th Avenue and C St (tel 276-8459); Rent-A-Dent (tel 243-2277) at 4580 West 5th Avenue; or Rent-A-Rat at 1005 East 5th Avenue.

Bicycle Anchorage has 112 miles (179 km) of paved bicycle paths that parallel major roads or wind through many of its parks and greenbelt areas. One of the more popular routes is the four-mile path through the Chester Creek Greenbelt from UAA and Goose Lake Park to Westchester Lagoon overlooking Knik Arm.

During the summer Earth Cycle loans out fat-tyre, single-speed bicycles at the corner of 4th Avenue and F St near the Visitors Centre Log Cabin. There is no charge for use of the bikes as long as you supply a $5 deposit and a picture I.D. The bikes are available Monday to Saturday from 9 am to 5 pm. You can also rent 10-speeds from Goose Lake Rental (tel 276-2960), a concessionaire in the park.

Hiking

With the Chugach Mountains at its doorstep, Anchorage boasts of many excellent day hikes that begin on the outskirts of the city and quickly lead into the beautiful alpine area to the east. Most of them begin in the Hillside area of the city that butts against Chugach State Park, the second largest state preserve at 495,000 acres (198,000 hectares), and can be reached by the People Mover bus system. For park maps and trail information contact the Chugach State Park office at 2601 Commercial Drive (tel 279-3413). Park rangers also lead hikes throughout the area on Saturday and Sunday during the summer, and the park office maintains a recorded message (tel 274-6713) listing what hikes are planned and where the gathering point is. The Sierra Club (tel 276-4048) at 241 East 5th Avenue assists hikers and paddlers looking for partners to share wilderness outings.

Flattop Mountain Trail Because of its easy access, this trail is the most popular hike near the city. The path to the 4500-foot (1372 metre) peak is not difficult and from the summit there are good views of Mt McKinley to the north and most of Cook Inlet. The trail begins at the Glen Alps entrance to the state park. Catch bus No 92 and start from the corner of Hillside and Upper Hoffman Rd. Walk 0.7 mile (1.1 km) along Upper Hoffman and then turn right on Toilsome Hill Drive for two miles (3.2 km). It will switch-back steeply uphill to the Glen Alps park entrance, a parking lot where trailhead signs point the way to Flattop Mountain, the upper trail of the two that begin here. The round trip is four miles (6.4 km) with some scrambling over loose rock up steep sections near the top. Plan on three to five hours for the entire hike.

Rabbit Lake Trail People Mover Bus No 92 also provides transportation to this trail, which leads to the beautiful alpine lake nestled under 5000-foot (1525 metre) Suicide Peak. Leave the bus at the corner where Hillside Drive curves into DeArmoun Rd. Extending to the east here is Upper DeArmoun Rd. Follow it for one mile (1.6 km) and then turn right onto Lower Canyon Rd for 1.2 miles to reach the trailhead parking lot. The trail begins by paralleling Upper Canyon Rd, a rough jeep track, for 3.5 miles (5.6 km) and then continues another two miles (3.2 km) from its end to the lake. Total mileage for a round trip from the corner of Hillside Drive and DeArmoun Rd is 15.4 miles (24.6 km), or a six to nine-hour hike. You can camp on the lake's shore for a scenic evening in the mountains.

Wolverine Peak Trail The path climbs to the 4455-foot (1358 metre) triangular peak that can be seen to the east of Anchorage. It makes for a strenuous but rewarding full-day trip resulting in good views of the city, Cook Inlet and the Alaska Range.

Take bus Nos 94 or 92 and start at the intersection of Hillside Drive and O'Malley Rd. Head up Upper O'Malley Rd to the east for 0.5 mile (0.8 km) to a 'T' intersection and turn left onto Prospect Drive for 1.1 miles (1.7 km). This ends at the Prospect Heights entrance and parking area of the state park. The marked trail begins as an old homesteader road that crosses South Campbell Creek and passes junctions with two other old roads in the first 2.3 miles (3.7 km). Keep heading east, and the old road will become a footpath that climbs above the

bush line and eventually fades out. Make sure to mark its whereabouts in order to find it on the way back. From here it is three miles (4.8 km) to the peak.

Round trip from the corner of O'Malley Rd and Hillside Drive is 13.8 miles (22 km), a nine-hour hike. Many people just trek to the good views above the bush line, shortening the trip to 7.8 miles (12.5 km).

Rendezvous Peak Route The trek to the 4050-foot (1235 metre) peak is an easy five-hour round trip or less from the trailhead and rewards the hiker with incredible views of Mt McKinley, Cook Inlet, Turnagain and Knik Arms and the city far below. Take bus No 75 for 6.5 miles (10.4 km) out Glenn Highway to Arctic Valley Rd. Turn right on Arctic Valley Rd (this section is also known as Ski Bowl Rd) and head seven miles (11.2 km) to the Arctic Valley Ski Area at the end. From the parking lot a short trail leads along the right-hand side of the stream up the valley to the north-west. It ends at a pass where a short ascent to Rendezvous Peak is easily seen and climbed.

The round trip from the ski area parking lot is only 3.5 miles, but it is a much longer day if you can't thumb a ride up Arctic Valley Rd.

The Ramp This is another of the many alpine summit hikes from the east side of the city that includes hiking through tranquil tundra valleys and good possibilities of seeing Dall sheep during the summer. Begin at the Glen Alps entrance to the state park (see Flattop Trail above). Instead of following the upper trail of the two that depart from the parking lot to Flattop, hike the lower one as it extends 0.5 mile (0.8 km) to the power line. Turn right and follow the power line for two miles (3.2 km), past 13 power poles, to where an old jeep trail crosses over from the left and heads downhill to the south fork of Campbell

Creek. The trail crosses the creek and continues up the hill beyond it to a valley on the other side. Hike up the alpine valley to Ship Lake Pass, which lies between The Ramp at 5240 feet (1598 metres) to the north, and The Wedge at 4660 feet (1421 metres) to the south. Either peak can be climbed.

The round trip from the Glen Alps entrance is 14 miles (22.4 km) or an eight to ten-hour hike.

Williwaw Lakes Trail This hike leads to the handful of alpine lakes found at the base of Mt Williwaw. It makes a pleasant overnight hike and what many consider the most scenic outing in the Hillside area of Chugach State Park. The hike begins on the same lower trail as The Ramp does, from the Glen Alps entrance parking lot (see Flattop Trail above). Hike it 0.5 mile (0.8 km) to the power line and then turn right. This time walk only about 300 yards and then turn left on a trail marked by a 'Middle Fork Loop Trail' sign. This trail leads down and across the south fork of Campbell Creek and then north for 1.5 miles (2.4 km) to the middle fork of the creek. Here you reach a junction; continue on the right-hand trail and follow the middle fork of Campbell Creek until you reach the alpine lakes at its end.

The entire round trip from Glen Alps is 16 miles (25.6 km), or seven to nine hours of easy hiking.

Tours
City Tours The cheapest tour of the city is on board the People Mover's free double-decker bus that departs from the Transit Centre and passes most of the attractions downtown, including the Anchorage Historical & Fine Art Museum, Resolution Park, the Alaska Wildlife Museum and the Alaska Railroad Depot.

Historic Anchorage Inc, the city's non-profit historical society, offers one-hour guided tours of downtown on Monday, Wednesday and Friday at 1.30 and 3 pm when there is interest. The historical

walking tours are $4. Interested persons should purchase tickets at the Historic Anchorage Inc office (tel 562-6100) in Suite 202 on the upper floor of the Old City Hall next to the Visitors Centre Log Cabin on 4th Avenue.

For the deluxe motorcoach tour of Anchorage, contact either Gray Line (tel 277-5581) at 4th Avenue and F St, or Alaska Sightseeing (tel 276-1305) at 327 F St. Both offer a tour for around $17; Alaska Sightseeing takes half an hour longer and includes Elmendorf Air Force Base.

Area Tours Both Gray Line and Alaska Sightseeing offer a daily six-hour Portage Glacier/Turnagain tour for $25 per person. Gray Line also has a Matanuska Valley Tour that includes Palmer and a visit to an Alaskan farm. You have to be hard pressed for something to do to take the farm tour, but it departs daily at 8.30 am and costs $25. A better and much cheaper way to spend an afternoon is to hop on People Mover bus Nos 74, 76 or 78 for the scenic trip north of Anchorage along Eagle River, through Chugiak and to Peter's Creek. The 48-mile (77 km) round trip takes about two hours and costs a mere 75c. Those who take the first bus out in the morning have been known to spot a moose between Fort Richardson and Eagle River.

Package Tours Travellers on a tight schedule will find a variety of package tours available in Anchorage to other areas of the state. They include everything – hotel, transportation and meals – and are a way to cover a lot in a day or two if you are willing to pay the price.

The most popular trip out of the city is the cruise past Columbia Glacier to Valdez and the return to Anchorage along scenic Richardson and Glenn highways. Both Gray Line and Alaska Sightseeing (see above for address) offer the tour as a two-day/one-night package at $225 per person, based on shared accommodation.

The two giant travel companies, along with a few other mega-corporations, have package tours everywhere, shuffling tour groups to such unlikely places as Fort Yukon, Barrow and Kotzebue. The one exception to this Fodor-type travel is Alaska-Denali Transit (tel 276-6443) at 608 West 4th Avenue. This new company offers low-cost bus tours where a tent and sleeping bag are mandatory. Included in their summer itinerary is a two-day excursion of the Kenai Peninsula for $50 per person, a three-day round trip to the Brooks Range above the Arctic Circle for $100 and a three-day drive of the Interior highways for $100. You can even purchase tickets for these trips at the Youth Hostels. Hopefully this is not a fly-by-night outfit and by the time you arrive there should be more trips available.

Outfitters

Anchorage is home base for a large number of guide companies that run hiking, kayaking and rafting trips to every corner of the state. Check the Wilderness chapter for the complete list and descriptions of their expeditions, and don't be shy about calling them at the last minute. Often you not only get a place in the group but can score a hefty discount as well for filling up a leftover spot. Those who don't have the time or the money for a 10-day float or a trek in the Brooks Range should not overlook the day trips out of the city.

Alaska Mountain Adventures (tel 248-3961) runs daily glacier treks that include transportation to and from Anchorage, all gear (boots, crampons, ice axe), training in glacier walking and an unorthodox view of the frozen monument. The cost is $75 per person.

Alaska River & Ski Tours (tel 276-3418) offers one to three-day weekend floats, including a single-day outing on the Kenai River, for $79 per person and an expanded two-day adventure on the same river for $139.

The ultimate in whitewater lies 80 miles (128 km) north-east of Anchorage in the Matanuska River. The Lions Head portion of the river is rated Class IV and V on the International Whitewater Scale and is an exhilarating, drenching experience. Nova Riverrunners (tel 745-5753) in Palmer run the trip and charge $50 per person for the 3½-hour float or $83 if you need round-trip transportation from Anchorage.

Getting There

Air The International Airport, 6.5 miles (10.5 km) west of downtown, is one of the busiest in the country, handling 130 flights daily from the 14 major airlines that serve it. From here you can catch a flight to anywhere in Alaska. Alaska Airlines (tel 243-3300) and its system of contract carriers provide the most intrastate routes to travellers.

Samples of one-way fares from Anchorage are: $111 to Fairbanks, $176 to Juneau, $70 to Cordova and $213 to Nome. Far cheaper flights are available if you book round-trip tickets two weeks in advance. ERA provides flights to Valdez ($79 one way) and you book them through Alaska Airlines. Markair (tel 266-6233) provides service to seven towns including Fairbanks, Kodiak, Barrow and King Salmon. AAI (tel 243-4329) provides scheduled service to Valdez, Kenai, Seward and Homer. A sample of AAI stand-by fares are Anchorage to Kenai $28, to Valdez $62 and to Homer $45.

Rail The Alaska Railroad (tel 265-2494) maintains its office in the depot at 419 West 1st Avenue and provides service both north and south of Anchorage. To the north the Denali Express train departs Anchorage daily, except Wednesday and Saturday, at 8.30 am, reaching Denali Park at 2.30 pm and Fairbanks at 6 pm. On Wednesday and Saturday the local train departs Anchorage at 8.30 am and makes all stops along the way to Anchorage. One-way fare to Denali is $54.50 and to Fairbanks is $78.25.

To the south the Whittier shuttle departs Anchorage at 11 am Monday to Friday for Portage and then continues on to the Prince William port to connect with the *MV Bartlett* for the cruise past the Columbia Glacier to Valdez. On Saturday and Sunday the same train departs at 6 am for Portage. One-way fare to Whittier is $10.75 and to Portage is $5.50.

Beginning in 1987, the railroad will be providing passenger service to Seward for the first time since the 1950s. The train will depart at 8 am and reach Seward at noon. It will then leave at 1 pm to return to Anchorage. Round-trip fare will be $36.

Boat The State Marine Ferry doesn't service Anchorage but does have an office (tel 272-4482) in the city at 213 West 5th Avenue. Here you can obtain information, make reservations or purchase advance tickets. If you know the dates on which you want to make the Columbia Glacier cruise, it is highly recommended that you purchase your ticket as far in advance as possible for this popular sailing.

Bus The concern of the vast majority of travellers who have just arrived in Alaska is how to get to Denali National Park. The cheapest way by bus is Alaska-Denali Transit (tel 276-6443) at 608 West 4th Avenue. They offer a one-way fare to the park for $30. The summer service departs daily at 8.30 am from city hotels, including the Youth Hostel, where you can also purchase your ticket. The company is new but plans to expand its fleet of vans and daily service to such places as the Kenai Peninsula, Tok and Haines.

Alaska-Yukon Motorcoaches (tel 276-1305), which picks up passengers at the Sheffield Hotel on the corner of 5th Avenue and G St, offers a daily run to Valdez by highway for $75, and by way of Prince William Sound for $140. It also offers service to Haines three times a week for $250. The Haines run is a three-day trip with overnight stops (at your own expense) at Glennallen and Destruction Bay. You can also catch a daily bus to Glennallen for $45.

White Pass & Yukon Motorcoaches (tel 227-5581) departs from the Westward Hilton at 500 West 3rd Avenue. It has a weekly run that departs Saturday for either Haines or Skagway, with overnight stops (at your own expense) at Tok and Haines Junction. One-way fare to Haines is $135, to Skagway $145 and to Tok $60.

Seward Bus Lines (tel 562-0712) takes on passengers at Inlet Inns on 6th Avenue and H St and departs daily at noon for Seward. One-way fare is $20.

Valdez-Anchorage Bus Lines (tel 561-5806) departs from the Sheraton Hotel at 6th Avenue and Denali at 8 am on Monday, Thursday and Saturday for Valdez. One-way fare is $55 to Valdez and $34 to Glennallen.

Hitch-hiking Hitching out of Anchorage can be made a lot easier by first spending 75c and hopping on a People Mover bus. Travellers heading north should take bus Nos 75, 78 or 102 to Peter's Creek Trading Post on Glenn Highway. If you're heading to Portage, Seward or the rest of the Kenai Peninsula, take bus Nos 92 or 101 and get off at the corner of DeArmoun Rd and Seward Highway.

Around Anchorage – South

Travellers who arrive in Anchorage and head south to the Kenai Peninsula will immediately be struck by Alaska's splendour; they no sooner leave the city limits than they find themselves following the edge of the spectacular Turnagain Arm. An extension of Cook Inlet, the arm is known for having some of the highest

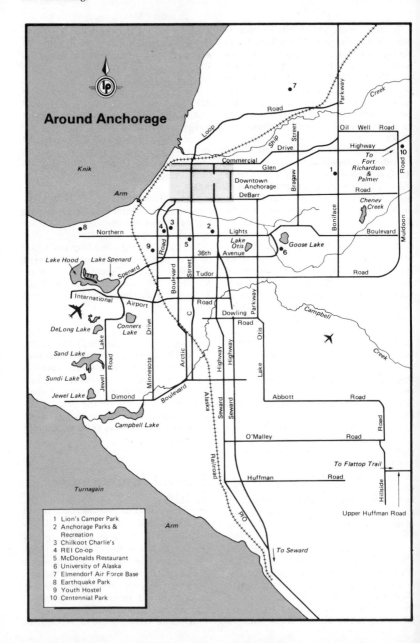

Around Anchorage

1 Lion's Camper Park
2 Anchorage Parks & Recreation
3 Chilkoot Charlie's
4 REI Co-op
5 McDonalds Restaurant
6 University of Alaska
7 Elmendorf Air Force Base
8 Earthquake Park
9 Youth Hostel
10 Centennial Park

tides in the world while giving way to constant views of the Kenai Mountains to the south. Seward Highway along the arm hugs the water and at times has been carved out of the mountainside; it runs side by side with the Alaska Railroad. A bike path shoulders much of the road and when completed will connect the bike trails in Anchorage with those in Girdwood.

Seward Highway begins as New Seward Highway in Anchorage on the corner of 5th Avenue and Gambell St at a junction with Glenn Highway. It heads south and reaches the coast near Rabbit Creek Rd. From here the mileposts on the road measure distance to Seward.

At *Mile 118* (190 km) or nine miles (14.4 km) south of downtown Anchorage, the highway passes the first of many gravel look-outs overlooking Turnagain Arm. In one mile (1.6 km) it reaches two small look-outs overlooking Potter Marsh Waterfowl Nesting Area, a state game refuge. There are display signs at the look-outs where often you can marvel at arctic terns and Canada geese nesting nearby. Some 130 species of birds and waterfowl have been spotted in this refuge at Anchorage's back door.

HIKING
Old Johnson Trail
Just before *Mile 115* (185 km) is the posted northern trailhead of this 11-mile (17.6 km) path. The route was originally used by native Indians and later by Russians, trappers and gold-miners at the turn of the century. Today it provides you with an easy hike and a 'mountain-goat's-eye view' of Turnagain Arm, alpine meadows and Beluga whales feeding in the waters below.

From Potter the trail heads south-east and reaches McHugh Picnic Area in 3.5 miles (5.6 km); Rainbow, access to Seward Highway, in 7.5 miles (12 km): and its southern end at Windy Corner in 9.5 miles (15.2 km). Plan on five to seven hours for the entire walk.

In the next 10 miles (16 km) the highway passes numerous look-outs, many with scenic views of Turnagain Arm. Just beyond *Mile 112* (179.2 km) is McHugh Creek Picnic Area (30 picnic tables) and the second access point to the Old Johnson trailhead. At *Mile 103.6* (166.7 km) is Indian, consisting mainly of a couple of bars and a restaurant.

Indian Valley Trail
Just west of the restaurant and Indian Creek is a gravel road that leads 1.3 miles (two km) past a pump station and ends near Indian Creek, where there is parking space and the posted trailhead for this six-mile (9.6 km) path to Indian Pass. The trail is easy, with only an occasional ford of Indian Creek, and leads to the alpine setting of the pass. Plan on five to seven hours for the round trip of 12 miles (19.2 km).

Bird Ridge Trail
Another 1.5 miles (2.4 km) along Seward Highway is a large marked parking area to the north. From here the trail to the ridge begins with an uphill climb to a power line access road, follows it for 0.3 mile (0.5 km) and then turns left and climbs Bird Ridge, which runs along the valley of Bird Creek. The hike is steep in many places but quickly leaves the bush behind for the alpine beauty above. You can hike over four miles on the ridge itself, reaching views of the head-waters of Ship Creek below. Viewing points of Turnagain Arm are plentiful and make the trail a good mountain hike.

Bird Creek State Campground (25 sites, free) is reached just beyond *Mile 101* (161.6 km). The campground is scenic and is known for its fine sunbathing, but is often full by early afternoon during the summer, especially on weekends. The next 10 miles (16 km) after Bird Creek Campground contains 16 turn-offs, all good spots to watch the tidal bores. Bores, barrelling walls of water that often exceed 10 feet (three metres) in height as they rush 15 miles an hour back across the mud flats, are created twice a day by the powerful tides in the arm. To avoid missing the turbulent incoming waves, get the time of low tide from either of Anchorage's two daily newspapers and add two hours and 15 minutes. At that time the bore will be passing this point along the highway. Arrive early and then continue down the road after the bore passes your look-out to view it again and again and again . . . .

GIRDWOOD

At *Mile 90* (144.8 km) is the junction with the access road to Girdwood, a small hamlet of 300 residents two miles (3.2 km) up the side road. Girdwood has a post office, restaurant, grocery store and Kinder Park, site of the town's annual Forest Fair usually held in the first week of July. The two-day event features a variety of entertainment, arts and crafts booths, contests and food in a delightful small-town atmosphere.

Another mile (1.6 km) down the road is the Alyeska Ski Area. The ski resort hums during the winter and is also a busy place during the summer, when tour groups leave the buses to wander through the gift shops and expensive restaurants or participate in hot-air balloon flights and horse-drawn carriage rides. The best thing about the resort is the scenic chairlift ride to Skyline Restaurant, 2000 feet (612 metres) above the valley floor. The 20-minute ride costs $15 per person but the views of the surrounding area and Turnagain Arm are incredible. Plus it is a lazy person's way to good alpine hiking.

Places to Stay A small but charming Youth Hostel in the area can be reached by turning right onto Timberline Drive before the ski lodge and then turning right again on Alpine Rd for 0.4 mile (0.6 km). The Alyeska *Youth Hostel* is in a cabin with wood heat, gas lighting and a kitchen area and includes the use of a wood-burning sauna. Unfortunately the

hostel only has six beds, so it is crucial to make reservations if you can by sending the first night's fee, name and time and date of arrival to Alyeska Hostel, PO Box 10-4099, Anchorage, Alaska 99510; or call ahead at 277-7388 to try to secure space. The hostel is only open Wednesday to Sunday and nightly fees are $8 for members and $10 for non-members. Again, this might change by 1987 or 1988, as the chapter is searching for a larger space closer to Alyeska Ski Lodge.

Alyeska Glacier View Trail

Begin by taking the chairlift to the Skyline Restaurant and then scramble up the knob behind the sun-deck. From here you follow the ridge into an alpine area where there are views of the tiny Alyeska Glacier. The entire round-trip hike is less than one mile (1.6 km). You can continue up the ridge to climb the so-called summit of Mt Alyeska, a high point of 3939 feet (1201 metres). The true summit lies further to the south but is not a climb for casual hikers.

Crow Creek Trail

Two miles (3.2 km) up the Alyeska Access Rd and just before Girdwood is the junction with Crow Creek Rd, a bumpy gravel road. It extends 5.8 miles (9.3 km) to a parking lot where the marked trailhead to this short but beautiful alpine hike is located. It is four miles (6.4 km) to Raven Glacier, the traditional turn-around point of the trail, and with transportation hikers can easily do the eight-mile (12.8-km) round trip in four to six hours. However, this highly recommended trail, which features gold-mining relics, an alpine lake and usually Dall sheep on the slopes above, offers many possibilities for longer trips. There is a USFS cabin three miles (4.8 km) up the trail ($10 per night) that has to be reserved in advance through the USFS office in Anchorage. You can also camp around Crow Pass, turning the walk into a pleasant overnight trip. Or you can continue and complete the three-day, 25-mile (40 km) route along the Old Iditarod Trail to the Chugach State Park Eagle River Visitor Centre (see the 'Around Anchorage – North' section).

From the Alyeska Access Rd, Seward Highway continues south-east and at *Mile 81* (129.6 km) reaches the Wetland Observation Platform constructed by the Bureau of Land Management. The platform features interpretive plaques on the ducks, arctic terns, bald eagles and other wildlife that can often been seen from it. Portage, the departure point for foot traffic and cars going to Whittier on the Alaska Railroad, is passed at *Mile 80* (128 km).

There is not much left to Portage, which was destroyed by the Good Friday earthquake, other than a few structures sinking into the nearby mud-flats. The shuttle train departs from the loading ramp three times a day from Monday to Friday at 1.20, 4.20 and 6.40 pm; the first trip connects with the *MV Bartlett*, the state ferry that cruises from Whittier to Valdez. On Saturday and Sunday there are two additional trips to Whittier at 8 and 10.30 am. One-way fare between Whittier and Portage is $5.25.

PORTAGE GLACIER

Another mile (1.6 km) beyond the loading ramp is the junction with Portage Glacier Access Rd. The road leads 5.4 miles (8.7 km) past three campgrounds to a visitor centre overlooking Portage Glacier. The magnificent ice floe is five miles (eight km) long and one mile (1.6 km) wide at its face, and is Southcentral's version of the drive-in glacier.

Known as the Portage Glacier Recreation Area, USFS officials say that over 300,000 people visit the spot annually, and with the new visitor centre they estimate the number will escalate to almost one million by 1990. This is becoming obvious already each summer when a constant stream of buses and cars passes though.

However, even if crowds are what you're trying to avoid, Portage Glacier should not be missed. The glacier, with its lake and icebergs, is classic Alaskan imagery, while the Begich, Boggs Visitor Centre, completed in 1986, is well worth viewing.

The centre, which cost $8 million to build, houses among other things a simulated ice cave which you can walk through, an iceberg you can touch, a 200-seat theatre with free films shown regularly, and an enclosed observation deck.

If you're planning to camp in the area, take in some of the activities sponsored by the centre. They include nature walks, gold-panning demonstrations and a hike to Byron Glacier to search for iceworms. The three campgrounds are scattered along the road from Seward Highway and consist of Beaver Pond (nine sites, $5 fee), Black Bear (12 sites, $5 fee) and Williwaw (38 sites, $5 fee).

Williwaw is a particularly pleasant spot as there is a salmon spawning observation deck near it and there's also a one-mile (1.6 km) nature walk through beaver and moose habitat that begins in the campground.

Byron Glacier Trail

Check with rangers about a planned trail to the face of Portage Glacier. Otherwise, hiking in the area consists of this easy one-mile (1.6 km) path to the base of Byron Glacier that begins near the visitor centre. Once you reach the permanent snow in front of the glacier, look for iceworms in it. The worms, immortalised in a Robert Service poem, are black, thread-like and less then an inch (2.5 cm) long. They survive by consuming algae and escape the heat of the sun by sliding between ice crystals of glaciers and snowfields.

From Portage, Seward Highway turns south and heads for the scenic town of Seward on Resurrection Bay, 128 miles (205 km) from Anchorage (see the South-central chapter).

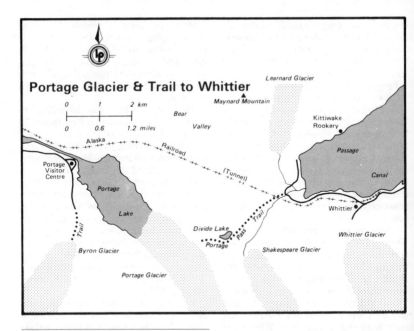

Portage Glacier & Trail to Whittier

Around Anchorage – North

The 189-mile (304 km) Glenn Highway begins at the corner of Medfra St and 5th Avenue (*Mile 0*), just west of Merrill Field Airport in Anchorage, and extends to Glennallen and the Richardson Highway. The first 42 miles (68 km) heads north to Palmer, the trade centre of the Matanuska Valley, where the highway forms a junction with George Parks Highway. From here Glenn Highway curves northeast for Glennallen in a section that is covered in the Interior chapter. Mileposts on the highway show distances from Anchorage.

In the first eight miles (12.8 km) you pass the exits to Elmendorf Air Force Base, Centennial Campground and Arctic Valley Rd to Fort Richardson (see the Things to See section). At *Mile 11.5* (18.5 km) is the turnoff to Eagle River State Campground (36 sites, free), just up Hiland Rd. The scenic campground is in a wooded area on the south banks of the Eagle River. The spot is popular and has a four-day limit. Don't drink the glacier-fed water of the Eagle River. Also, don't plan on getting a tent space if you arrive late.

At *Mile 13.6* (22 km) is the exit for Eagle River, a town of 9000, and Eagle River Rd. This 12.7-mile (20.4 km) road ends at the Eagle River Visitor Centre for Chugach State Forest. The log cabin centre (tel 694-2108) is open daily, except Wednesday, from 10 am to 5 pm and features wildlife displays, handouts for hikers, naturalist programmes and telescopes with which to view Dall sheep in the surrounding mountains.

Old Iditarod Trail
The visitor centre also serves as the northern trailhead for this 25-mile (40

km) historical trail. The route was used by gold-miners and dog-sled teams until 1918, when the Alaska Railroad was completed from Seward to Fairbanks. Today it is a three-day hike through excellent mountain scenery and up to Crow Pass, where you can view nearby Raven Glacier and Crystal Lake. From here you hike down the Crow Pass Trail and emerge on Crow Creek Rd, seven miles (11.2 km) away from Seward Highway (see the 'Around Anchorage – South' section above).

Although the route involves fording several streams, including Eagle River itself, and some climbing to the pass, it is an excellent hike – one of the best in the Southcentral and Anchorage regions. It is also a way to bypass Anchorage, for those who want to avoid big-city hassles and head straight for the Kenai Peninsula. Backpackers in Anchorage can reach the junction of Eagle River Rd on People Mover bus Nos 74, 76 and 78 and from there hitch to the visitor centre. Bring a stove, as campfires are not allowed in the state park.

Thunderbird Falls Trail

North-bound on Glenn Highway, Thunderbird Falls Exit is reached at *Mile 25.2* (40.6 km) and leads 0.3 mile (0.5 km) to a parking area and trailhead. The one-mile (1.6-km) trail is a quick and easy hike to the scenic falls formed by a small, rocky gorge. The Indian village of Eklutna (population 25 or so) is reached by taking the Eklutna Rd exit at *Mile 26.5* (42.6 km) of Glenn Highway. The village is west of the highway and contains the St Nicholas Russian Orthodox Church (built in the 1830s), a hand-hewn log chapel, and brightly coloured spirit houses in a cemetery nearby.

Eklutna Rd bumps and winds east for 10 miles (16 km) to the west end of Eklutna Lake, the largest body of water in Chugach State Park, with a length of seven miles (11.2 km). Here you'll find Eklutna Lake State Recreation Area (17

sites, free). The road continues east past the campground and around the lake, but vehicles are prohibited due to numerous wash outs. Motorcycles and bicycles may be used along this section, however.

Twin Peaks Trail

From the campground parking lot, head across a bridge to the picnic area and look for the marked trailhead. The trail is an abandoned road that heads four miles above the tree line to the passes between Twin Peaks. It is well marked in the beginning and forks after 0.25 mile (0.4 km), rejoining the spur 0.5 mile (0.8 km) later. Above the tree line the road turns into a hard-to-follow trail. At this point, scrambling in the alpine area is easy, and the views of Eklutna Lake below are excellent. Plan on several hours, depending how far you go above the tree line, and keep a sharp eye out for Dall sheep.

Bold Peak Trail

This route is another good hike from the lake shore to the alpine area below Bold Peak, 7522 feet (2294 metres). The drawback is that you have to walk (or bike) 5.5 miles (8.8 km) from the Eklutna Lake picnic area to the trailhead due to wash outs that have closed the remainder of Eklutna Lake Rd to vehicles.

Heading east around the lake, look for a large stream that flows underneath the road through four large culverts. After crossing it, walk another 150 yards (136 metres) and turn sharply left on an old road. The trailhead is posted 50 yards (45 metres) up the road. From here the trail climbs steeply, reaching the bushline in 1.5 miles (2.4 km) and ending in another mile (1.6 km). Great views are obtained here, while those people with the energy can scramble up nearby ridges.

To actually climb Bold Peak requires mountaineering skill and equipment. The round trip, from the campground and picnic area, is a 16-mile (25.6 km) hike and takes eight to 10 hours.

PALMER

From Eklutna Lake Rd, Glenn Highway continues north, crosses bridges over the Knik and Matanuska rivers at the northern end of Cook Inlet, and at *Mile 35.3* (56.8 km) reaches a major junction with George Parks Highway. At this point Glenn Highway curves sharply to the east and leads into Palmer (population 2500) seven miles (11.2 km) away.

Although a railroad station was built here in 1916, the town was really born in 1935, when it was selected for an unusual social experiment during President Franklin Roosevelt's New Deal relief programmes. Some 200 farming families, hit hard by the Great Depression in the Midwest, were moved north to raise crops and livestock in the Matanuska and Susitna valleys. The failure rate was high within this transplanted agricultural colony, but somehow Palmer survived and today is the only community whose economy is based primarily on farming. It is the farms of the Matanuska Valley that grow the 60-lb (27 kg) cabbages and seven-lb (3.1 kg) turnips as a result of the midnight sun that shines up to 20 hours a day during the summer.

Within Palmer itself there isn't a lot to do except stop at the Visitors Centre, a rustic log cabin near the corner of Fireweed Avenue and South Valley Way in the centre of town. Open from 9 am to 5 pm daily, the centre has a small museum in the basement with relics from its 'colony' era. More farming relics and an odd assortment of planes, cars and trucks can be viewed at the Alaska Historic & Transportation Museum on the state fairgrounds one mile (1.6 km) south of town off Glenn Highway. The museum is open from 8 am to 4 pm daily and admission is free.

Things to See

Farms If you have a vehicle, a drive through the back roads of the Palmer area and past the farms makes an interesting afternoon. To view a few of the colony farms that survived along with the original barns they built, head north-east nine miles (14.4 km) on Glenn Highway and exit onto Farm Loop Rd. Old Glenn Highway, which departs from the present highway right before the bridges across Knik and Matanuska rivers and rejoins it in Palmer, can also provide views of area farms, especially on Bodenberg Loop Rd that runs off it. Keep an eye out for vegetable stands if you're passing through during mid to late summer.

Places to Stay

There is no Youth Hostel in Palmer. The cheapest hotel in town is the *Pioneer Hotel* (tel 745-3425) at the corner of North Alaska and Arctic Sts, where a single is $35 per night and a double is $40.

Camping in town is possible at *Deneke Park*, where there is a large grassy area for people to pitch tents. The park also has tables and coin-operated showers. The nightly fee is $3. From the visitors centre, head north along South Valley Way and turn right onto East Cottonwood Avenue just past the Alaska State Troopers office. The park is on the corner of East Cottonwood and South Denali St.

Events

The best reason to stop in Palmer (and some feel the only reason) is the Alaska State Fair, an 11-day event that ends on Labor Day. The fair features produce and livestock from the surrounding area, horse shows, a rodeo, a carnival and the largest cabbages you'll ever see. Within the state fairgrounds is the outdoor Borealis Theatre; during the third week of July it is the site of a bluegrass festival, worth attending if you are passing through. Those in Anchorage should check with the Alaska Railroad, which occasionally runs special trains to Palmer for these events.

Hiking

The best hike near Palmer is the climb to the top of Lazy Mountain, elevation 3720

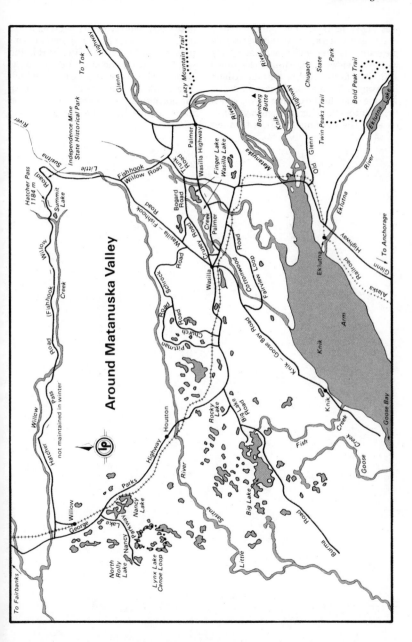

Around Matanuska Valley

feet (1134 metres). The 2.5-mile (four km) trail is steep at times, but makes for a pleasant trek that ends in a alpine setting with good views of the Matanuska Valley and its farms below. From Glenn Highway in Palmer, head east on Arctic Avenue, the third exit into town, which turns into Old Glenn Highway. After crossing the Matanuska River, turn left onto Clark-Wolverine Rd and then left in 0.5 mile (0.8 km) at a 'T' junction. This puts you on unmarked Huntly Rd, and you follow it for one mile (1.6 km) to the Equestrian Centre parking lot at its end. The trailhead is marked 'Foot Trail' on the north side of the parking lot. Plan on three to five hours for the round-trip hike.

The Interior

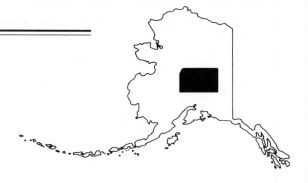

Between Anchorage and Fairbanks is an area commonly referred to as the Interior and affectionately referred to as 'the Golden Heart of Alaska'. It is the 'great, big, broad land way up yonder' that was searched over by miners and immortalised by such poets as Robert Service, and which is immediately visualised when somebody says 'the Last Frontier'.

The Golden Heart is bordered by dramatic mountain chains, with the Alaska Range lying to the south and the Brooks Range to the north. In between is the central plateau of Alaska, a vast area of land that gently slopes to the north and is broken up by such awesome rivers as the Yukon, Kuskokwim, Koyukuk and Tanana. It is the home of Mt McKinley, the highest peak (20,320 feet, 6193 metres) in North America, and of Denali National Park & Preserve, the number one attraction in the state which offers superb hiking, camping and fishing. It is the stamping grounds for brown bear, moose, caribou and Dall sheep, whose numbers are unmatched anywhere else in the US.

It can also be enjoyed by even the most impecunious traveller because it's accessible by road. The greater part of Alaska's highway system forms a triangle between the state's two largest cities and allows cheap travel by bus, train, car or thumb. George Parks Highway leaves Anchorage and winds 358 miles (573 km) to Fairbanks, passing Denali National Park along the way. Glenn Highway spans 189 miles (302 km) between Anchorage and Glennallen and then continues another 125 miles (200 km) to Tok in a section known as the Tok Cut-Off. Richardson Highway passes Glennallen from Valdez and ends at Fairbanks, 368 miles (589 km) away. Dividing the triangle from east to west is Denali Highway, 136 miles (218 km) long and at one time the only road to Denali National Park.

All four roads are called highways, though they are rarely more than two-lane roads. All of them pass through spectacular scenery, offer good possibilities of spotting wildlife and are lined with turnoffs, campgrounds and hiking trails. For the most part the towns along them are small, colourless service centres, although a few have managed to retain their rustic gold-rush and frontier flavour from yesterday. The real attraction of the Interior is not these crossroads of gas stations, motels and cafés, but what lies in the hills and valleys beyond the highway.

In this land of mountains and spacious valleys, the climate varies every possible way. In the winter, the temperatures drop to -60°F (-51°C) for days at a time. In the summer, they can soar above 90°F (32°C). From one day to the next the daily weather changes. Most of that is caused by the mountain ranges, which keep the weather different from one part

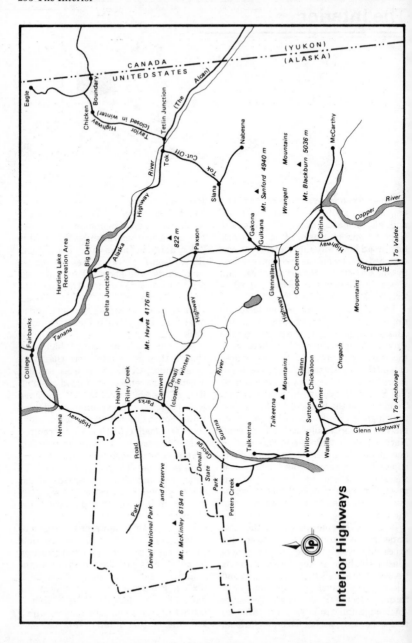

Interior Highways

Top: Anchorage skyline (AVB)
Bottom: Dog sled races during the Fur Rendezvous in Anchorage

Top: Mt. McKinley from Denali National Park and Preserve (AVB)
Bottom: The Nenana River Gorge and the Alaska Railroad en route to Denali National Park and
    Preserve (JD)

of the region to the next. The norm for the summer is long days with warm temperatures between 60°F and 70°F (15°C to 21°C). However, it is common for Denali National Park to experience at least one snowfall in the lowlands between June and August. Here, more than anywhere else in the state, it is important to have warm clothes while still being able to strip down to a T-shirt and hiking shorts. Most of the area's 10 to 15 inches (250 to 380 mm) of annual precipitation comes in the form of summer showers, with cloudy conditions common, especially north of Mt McKinley. In the park, the grand mountain is hidden for two days out of three.

Getting Around

Bus transportation is available on every highway except Denali, and there is a train service between Anchorage and Fairbanks (see the Getting Around chapter or sections below). Bus routes and even the companies themselves change often in Alaska, so it pays to double-check motorcoach departures with a phone call. The hitch-hiking is surprisingly good during the summer, as the highways are cluttered with the stream of recreational vehicles and summer tourists arriving from down south. Avoid back-tracking if you can, even if it means going out of your way on an alternative route. All the highways offer their own roadside scenery that is nothing short of spectacular.

George Parks Highway

A large number of travellers, and most overseas visitors, arrive in Alaska through Anchorage and venture north along George Parks Highway. The road, which was opened in 1971, provides a direct route to Denali National Park while passing through some of the most rugged scenery Alaska has to offer. The road begins at a junction with Glenn Highway 35.3 miles (56.8 km) north of Anchorage. Mileposts read distance from Anchorage and not from the junction.

WASILLA

From its junction with Glenn Highway, George Parks Highway heads north and passes numerous roadside stands selling fresh produce from the Matanuska Valley farms before reaching the town of Wasilla (population 3900) in seven miles (11.2 km). At one time the community was a mining supply centre and in the 1970s was little more than a sleepy little town servicing local farmers. From 1980 to 1983 the population of Wasilla doubled when Alaskans who wanted to work in Anchorage but not live there began moving in to make it a dormitory community of the large city. Today there is even talk of building a bridge across the Knik Arm to shorten the drive to Anchorage, while shopping malls and businesses have mushroomed along the highway.

The town's museum doubles as the visitor centre (tel 376-2005) and is in the Wasilla Community Hall on Main St just off the highway. The centre is open daily from 10 am to 6 pm Tuesday to Saturday and from 1 to 6 pm on Sunday and Monday. Admission to the museum is $1; it contains some tools and other relics from the early farmers and miners in the area as well as a handful of restored buildings in the back.

The historical society that runs the Wasilla museum also maintains the Musher's Hall of Fame in Knik, 14 miles (22.4 km) south of town on Knik Rd (also known as Goose Bay Rd). The museum is open from 11 am to 5 pm Wednesday through Sunday and contains memorabilia on the Iditarod dog-sled race, Alaskan mushers and their teams.

Wasilla serves as the second starting point for the famous 1049-mile (1600-km) race to Nome, while Knik, the home for many Alaskan mushers, is check-point number four on the route. For more on this uniquely Alaskan race, stop in at the Iditarod Race headquarters upstairs in Teeland's Country Store off the highway in Wasilla. The office is open weekdays from 9 am to 5 pm and sells an assortment of race paraphernalia.

Independence Mine State Park

This fascinating state historical park is the only reason anybody should stop in Wasilla. The 272-acre (110 hectare) park is 21 miles (31.5 km) away from town and is entirely above the tree line. Within the beautiful bowl-shaped valley of the park are the remains of 16 buildings that were built in the 1930s by the Alaska-Pacific Mining Company and for 10 years were second only to Juneau's A-J Mine as the leading gold producer in Alaska. Today it looks like a ghost town, with weather-beaten buildings surrounded by the craggy Talkeetna Mountains. The Alaska Division of Parks administers and staffs the site and is busily restoring the old mess halls, bunk houses and mills that still stand. Facilities include a museum and visitors centre which can supply maps and a walking tour of the area. Although you cannot enter the buildings, signs outside explain the history and use of the remaining structures. You can camp in the area but bring a campstove as fires are prohibited. Within a mile of the park there is also *Hatcher Pass Lodge* (tel 745-5897), which offers both lodging and meals.

To reach the park, follow Wasilla's Main St east as it turns into Wasilla-Fishhook Rd and extends 10.5 miles (16.8 km) to a junction with Fishhook-Willow Rd. Turn left on this road and the park will be reached in another 10.5 miles (16.8 km). Hitch-hiking is better than on most backcountry roads in Alaska, as 150,000 visitors annually endure the bumps and dust to view the mining relics. You can also rent a used car from Kohrings Rent-A-Car (tel 376-5784) in Wasilla, which charges $15 per day plus 15c per mile,

making a single-day trip to the park a $25 affair. Wasilla is a regular stop for the Alaska Railroad local trains.

AROUND WASILLA

From Wasilla, George Parks Highway continues in a westerly direction for the next 10 miles (16 km) and then curves north, reaching Willow at *Mile 69* (111 km). Before entering the small village, you pass two side roads to the west that lead to state recreation areas offering lakeside campgrounds and canoe trails.

Big Lake

At *Mile 52.3* (84.2 km), where the highway curves north, is the junction with Big Lake Rd. Head 3.3 miles (5.3 km) down the road and turn right at the gas station for 0.5 mile (0.8 km) to reach Rocky Lake State Campground (10 sites, free). A few hundred yards further along Big Lake Rd is a fork known as 'Fisher's Y' where the hamlet of Big Lake (gas station, grocery store, post office) is located. The right fork leads 1.6 miles (2.6 km) to Big Lake East State Campground (15 sites, free), the left fork 1.7 miles (2.7 km) to Big Lake South State Campground (13 sites, free).

Big Lake is connected to several smaller lakes by dredged waterways making it possible to paddle for miles though you have to share the lake with power-boaters. Another possible trip (if you can figure out how to get back) is to paddle Fish Creek, which begins in Big Lake and flows into the Knik Arm. The start of this canoe trail is where the left fork of Big Lake Rd crosses the creek. The trip is a 13-mile (21 km) paddle and ends at the Knik Rd bridge west of Knik.

Nancy Lake

George Parks Highway continues from Big Lake Rd, passes the village of Houston (population 800) and Little Susitna River City Campground (80 sites, free), and reaches the junction with Nancy Lake Parkway at *Mile 67.2* (108

m). The parkway leads to the northern
ortion of Nancy Lake State Recreation
rea, a lake-studded park that offers
amping, fishing, canoeing and hiking
ossibilities. Although it lacks the
ramatic scenery of the country to the
orth, the state park with its 130 lakes is
till a scenic spot and one worth stopping
t for a couple of days if you do not have a
ime limit. Nancy Lake Parkway extends
6 miles (10 km) to the west and ends at
outh Rolley Lake Campground (106
ites, free).

liking For those without a canoe, you can
till reach the backcountry by one of two
rails. Chicken Lake Trail begins at *Mile*
7 (9.2 km) of the parkway and extends
hree miles (4.8 km) south to the lake and
nother 2.5 miles (four km) to the east
hore of Red Shirt Lake. A round-trip
ike on the trail is a pleasant 11-mile
17.6 km) overnight trek. More popular is
win Shirt Lakes Trail that begins near
he campground at the end of the
arkway. The trail leads 3.5 miles (5.6
m) south to the northern end of Red
hirt Lake after passing Red Shirt
)verlook and its scenic views of the
urrounding lake country.

addling The most popular canoe trail is
he Lynk Lake Loop, a two-day, 16-mile
26 km) trip that passes through 14 lakes
nd over an equal number of portages.
he trail begins and ends at the posted
Milo Lakes Canoe trailhead on *Mile 4.7*
7.6 km) of the parkway. The portages are
ell marked and many of them are
lanked where they cross wet sections.
he route includes nine primitive camp-
ites, accessible only by canoe, but bring a
ampstove because campfires are prohib-
:ed in the backcountry. The largest lake
n the route is Lynx Lake and you can
xtend your trip by paddling south in it
vhere portage leads off to six other lakes
nd two more primitive campsites in
keetna Lake. Nancy Lake Resort (tel
95-6284) on George Parks Highway, 2.7

miles (4.3 km) south of the junction to the
state recreation area, rents canoes.

Getting There The state recreation area
can be reached from the Alaska Railroad
by taking the local train to Willow, and
then hitching or hiking 1.8 miles (2.9 km)
south on George Parks Highway to the
junction with Nancy Lake Parkway.

WILLOW
The next town on the highway is Willow
(population 150), a small village that
became famous in the 1970s as the place
selected for the new capital that was to be
moved from Juneau. The capital-move
issue was put on the back burner in 1982,
however, when funding for the immense
project was defeated in a general state
election.

Today Willow is a small service centre
with the usual visitor facilities of gas
station, restaurant and grocery store.
Two miles (3.2 km) north of it is the
junction to Fishhook-Willow Rd that
leads 31.6 miles (51 km) to Independence
Mine State Park and eventually to Glenn
Highway by way of Hatcher Pass. By
driving just 1.3 miles (2.1 km) up the road
you reach Willow Creek State Campground (17 sites, free).

TALKEETNA
At *Mile 98.7* (158.8 km) of George Parks
Highway a side road heads off to the
north-east and leads 14.5 miles (23.3 km)
to Talkeetna (population 400), the most
interesting and colourful town along the
highway.

The village was once a pioneer mining
and trapping settlement that was established in 1901 and today retains much of
that early Alaskan flavour along its
narrow dirt roads lined with log cabins
and clapboard businesses. Main St, the
only paved road in the village, begins with
a 'Welcome to beautiful downtown
Talkeetna' sign at the town park and ends
at the banks of the Susitna River. From
here it is possible to hike along the gravel

banks of the river to camp, fish or take in the scenic views of the surrounding mountains.

On Main St is the Talkeetna Museum in the old schoolhouse built in 1936. It is open Wednesday to Sunday from 9 am to 5 pm and Monday and Tuesday from 12 noon to 4 pm. The displays centre on the town's early history and two of its more famous characters – Ray Genet and Don Sheldon. Genet was an Alaskan mountain climber who made a record 25 climbs to the summit of Mt McKinley before dying near the summit of Mt Everest in Nepal. Sheldon was a bush pilot who pioneered many of the routes used today to carry climbers to Mt McKinley.

The colourful legends of both men add considerably to the mountaineering atmosphere that is felt, seen and heard in Talkeetna during the summer. The town, though small, is the jumping-off spot for most climbing expeditions to North America's highest peak, and the scores of climbers from around the world give the place an international feel. The vast majority of climbers use the West Buttress route, developed by Bradford Washburn, which means flying in ski-planes from the town's airstrip to the Kahiltna Glacier. From here at 7000 feet (2134 metres) they begin climbing for the South Peak, elevation 20,320 feet (6193 metres). The National Park Service operates an office (tel 733-2512) to handle the numerous expeditions during the summer while the climbers themselves are often encountered in the local bars, hotels and roadhouses and make for an intriguing evening of conversation.

Other attractions of the town include the town's Moose Dropping Festival, held on the second Saturday of July. It features, among other things, a moose-dropping throwing contest. Several air-taxi operators run flight-seeing tours of Mt McKinley that can be expensive but awe-inspiring experiences on a clear day. At times is is possible to see climbing parties en route to the top. Contact K2

Aviation (tel 733-2291) or Talkeetna Air Taxi (tel 733-2218), which charges $85 per person for its flight-seeing tour of the mountain.

Places to Stay & Eat

Plans call for a Youth Hostel to open up in one of the Main St houses by 1987; travellers should check at the museum to see if the facility has been completed. There is also a Youth Hostel back out on George Parks Highway, three miles (4.8 km) north of the junction to Talkeetna Spur Rd. The *Susitna Ranch Youth Hostel* (tel 733-2775) is a year-round hostel that offers 10 dorm beds as well as space in cabins.

There are five hotel/lodges in town, of which the best is the *Fairview Inn* (tel 733-2423). The historical hotel was built in the early 1920s and was visited by President Harding in 1923 during his golden spike ceremony that completed the Alaska Railroad. Singles are $20 per night and doubles $25, but rooms are limited. The inn also has a lively bar that is a good place to meet climbers while someone occasionally strums away on the 'bar guitar'.

There is a *City Campground* at the end of Main St on the banks of the river. More spots to pitch a tent can be found along the river's gravel bars a short hike away.

The best place for a hearty meal, though it will cost you $12, is the *Talkeetna Road House* (tel 733-2341) in the heart of town, where dinners are served family style and you eat with lodge guests and the family that runs the place. You must contact them before 3 pm so they can set a place for you at dinner. Better yet is to go there in the morning for coffee and the best home-baked cinnamon rolls found on George Parks Highway.

Getting There On Wednesday and Saturday during the summer the Alaska Railroad reaches Talkeetna from Anchorage, bound for Fairbanks. A south-bound train stops here on Thursday and Sunday. Drop by the museum, the town's unofficial visitor centre, for more information.

Hitching along the spur road to the highway can be slow going at times, especially in early morning for those in a rush to reach Anchorage or Denali National Park.

DENALI STATE PARK

The reserve of 421,120 acres (170,385 hectares), the second largest state park in Alaska, is entered when you cross the southern boundary at *Mile 132.2* (213 km) of George Parks Highway. The park covers the transition zone from low coastal environment to the spine of the Alaska Range and provides numerous views of its towering peaks, including Mt McKinley and the glaciers on its south slopes. The park is largely undeveloped but does offer a handful of turnoffs, trails and one campground that are reached from the highway which splits the preserve in half.

Less than three miles (4.8 km) from the southern boundary at *Mile 135.2* (217.6 km) is Ruth Glacier Overlook, where the glacier is less than five miles (eight km) to the north-west. Displays at the paved look-out also point out Mt McKinley, Mt Hunter, Moose Tooth and several glaciers. Byers Lake State Campground (61 sites, free) is reached at *Mile 147* (236.6 km) and provides tables, an out-house and access to Byers Lake.

Hiking

There are currently several trails under consideration or construction in the park and interested hikers should contact the Alaska Division of Parks office in Anchorage (see the Anchorage chapter) about the status and location of them.

Long-established routes include a four-mile (6.4 km) trail from Byers Lake Campground to Curry Ridge and a second trail that leads south to the rest area and bridge over Troublesome Creek at *Mile 137.3* (221 km) of the highway. At

Mile 163.8 (263.6 km) there is the trailhead and parking area for Little Coal Creek Trail, which climbs to the tree line of Indian Ridge. Once on top of the ridge you can easily continue hiking through the alpine tundra.

BOARD PASS TO DENALI NATIONAL PARK ENTRANCE

The northern boundary of the state park is at *Mile 168.6* (271.3 km) of George Parks Highway, and nine miles (14 km) beyond that is the bridge over Honolulu Creek where the road begins a gradual climb to Board Pass. Within 18 miles (29 km) you begin viewing the pass and actually reach it at *Mile 203.6* (327.7 km), where there is a paved parking area. Board Pass, elevation 2300 feet (701 metres), is the point of divide where rivers to the south drain into Cook Inlet and those to the north empty into the Yukon River. The area is worth stopping at in order to spend some time hiking. The mountain valley, surrounded by white peaks, is unquestionably one of the most beautiful spots along George Parks Highway or the Alaska Railroad line, as both use the low gap to cross the Alaska Range.

From the pass the highway begins a descent and after 6.3 miles (10 km) comes to the Cantwell post office just before *Mile 210* (336 km) at the junction with Denali Highway (see section below). The rest of Cantwell (population 100) lies two miles (3.2 km) west on Denali Highway. Another scenic spot is reached at *Mile 234* (377 km) on the east side of the highway, where there are fine views of Mt Fellows, elevation 4476 feet (1364 metres). The mountain is well photographed because of the constantly changing shadows on its sides. The peak is especially beautiful at sunset.

The entrance to Denali National Park & Preserve is at *Mile 237.3* (382 km), where just inside the park are two campgrounds. The next public campground is in Fairbanks. The highway around the park entrance has become a tourist strip of private campgrounds, lodges and other businesses, all living off Alaska's biggest draw-card.

Denali National Park

The name has been changed and the boundaries altered, but the park is still unquestionably Alaska's most-visited and probably most-loved attraction. Few people leave Denali National Park disappointed. Most visitors, especially backpackers, depart amazed at what they saw and loaded with canisters of exposed film.

Situated on the northern and southern flanks of the Alaska Range, 237 miles (382 km) from Anchorage and about half that distance from Fairbanks, Denali is a wilderness that can be enjoyed by those who never sleep in a tent. As a result of the 1980 Alaska Lands Act, the old Mt McKinley National Park was enlarged by four million acres (1.6 million hectares) and the area was redesignated and renamed. Today the park comprises six million acres (2.4 million hectares) or an area slightly larger than Massachusetts. Within it roam 37 species of mammals, ranging from moose, caribou, Dall sheep and brown bears to foxes and snowshoe hares, while 130 different species of bird have been spotted.

The main draw of the park is Mt McKinley, an overwhelming sight if you catch it on a clear day. At 20,320 feet (6194 metres), the peak of this massif is almost four miles high, but what makes it stunning is that it rises from an elevation of 2000 feet (610 metres). What you see from the park road is 18,000 feet (5490 metres) – almost three miles – of rock, snow and glaciers reaching for the sky. In contrast, Mt Everest is the highest mountain in the world at 29,028 feet (8848 metres) but rises only 11,000 feet (3353 metres) from the Tibetan Plateau.

Combine the park's easy viewing of wildlife and the grandeur of Mt McKinley with the free shuttle bus system and the fine accommodation at the park entrance and you have the source of its only complaint – crowds. From late June through to early September, Denali is a busy and popular place. Riley Creek campground overflows with recreational vehicles, nearby Morino campground is crowded with backpackers, and the hotel is bustling with large tour groups. The pursuit of shuttle-bus seats, backcountry permits and campground reservations at the visitors centre often involves lines like the ones at Disneyland.

Although crowds disappear once you are hiking in the backcountry, many people prefer to visit the park in early June or late September to avoid them. Mid to late September can be particularly pleasant, for not only are the crowds gone but so are the bugs. This is also when the area changes colours and valleys go from a dull green to a fiery red.

It is wise to arrive at the park early in the day if possible, as all the campgrounds are filled on a first-come first-serve basis. In the middle of the tourist season, campgrounds are often filled by 10 am and there is little you can do but look for accommodation outside the park. Except for Morino Campground near the entrance, which is a walk-in for backpackers, sites at all park campgrounds are obtained by registering first at the Riley Creek Visitor Centre. Popular ones like Wonder Lake are booked solid for days at a time.

The same holds true for backcountry permits, which allow you to camp in the backcountry. The park is divided into 37 zones and only a regulated number of backpackers are allowed into each section at a time. You have to obtain a permit for the zone you want to stay overnight in, and that usually means waiting a day or two at Riley Creek until one opens up. Denali National Park cannot be a quick side trip in the middle of the summer. Plan to spend at least three days or more

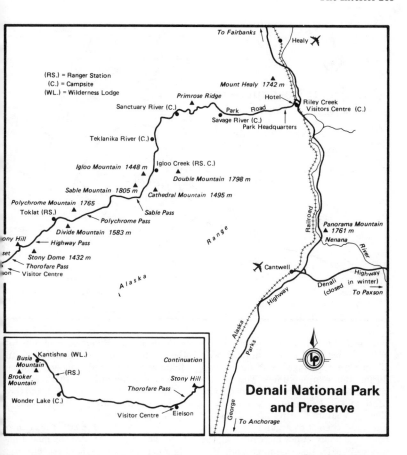

(RS.) = Ranger Station
(C.) = Campsite
(WL.) = Wilderness Lodge

To Fairbanks
Healy
Mount Healy 1742 m
Primrose Ridge
Hotel
Sanctuary River (C.)
Park Road
Riley Creek Visitors Centre (C.)
Savage River (C.)
Park Headquarters
Teklanika River (C.)
Igloo Creek (RS. C.)
Igloo Mountain 1448 m
Double Mountain 1798 m
Sable Mountain 1805 m
Cathedral Mountain 1495 m
Polychrome Mountain 1765
Toklat (RS.)
Sable Pass
Polychrome Pass
Railroad
Divide Mountain 1583 m
Panorama Mountain 1761 m
ony Hill
Highway Pass
Nenana
set
Stony Dome 1432 m
River
Thorofare Pass
Cantwell
Highway
son
Visitor Centre
Denali (closed in winter)
To Paxson
Alaska
Range
Alaska Highway

Busia Mountain
Kantishna (WL.)
Continuation
Brooker Mountain
(RS.)
Stony Hill
Thorofare Pass
Wonder Lake (C.)
Visitor Centre
Eielson
George Parks
To Anchorage

Denali National Park and Preserve

---

if you want to spend a night in one of its campgrounds and a day riding the shuttle bus to Wonder Lake.

Information

Riley Creek Visitor Centre near the entrance of the park can supply information and handouts as well as permits, and also sells topographic maps and publications relating to Denali. Outside there is a 24-hour recorded weather report, worth listening to if you have just obtained your backcountry permit. The centre is open daily during the summer from 5.30 am to 8 pm. Eielson Visitors Centre at *Mile 66* (106.2 km) is also a source of information, handouts, topographic maps and backcountry permits. The ranger staff hold their own hikes and naturalist programmes. Eielson Visitors Centre is open daily during the summer from 9 am to 8 pm.

Along the Park Road

The park road begins at George Parks Highway and winds 91.6 miles (147.4 km) through the heart of the park, ending at Kantishna, an old mining settlement and

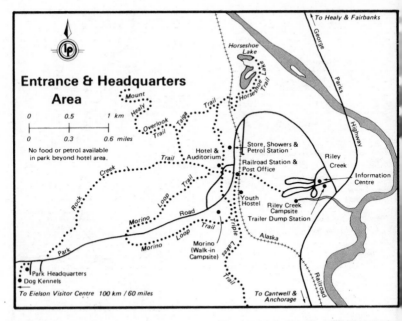

Entrance & Headquarters Area

No food or petrol available in park beyond hotel area.

To Healy & Fairbanks

Horseshoe Lake

Mount Healy Overlook Trail

Taiga Trail

Store, Showers & Petrol Station

Hotel & Auditorium

Railroad Station & Post Office

Riley Creek

Information Centre

Rock Creek

Trail

Loop Trail

Youth Hostel

Riley Creek Campsite

Trailer Dump Station

Morino Loop

Road

Triple Lakes

Morino Loop

Morino (Walk-in Campsite)

Alaska

Park

Park Headquarters

Dog Kennels

To Eielson Visitor Centre 100 km / 60 miles

To Cantwell & Anchorage

Parks Highway

George

Railroad

the site of two wilderness lodges. Those with vehicles can drive only as far as *Mile 12* (19.2 km) to Savage River Campground during the summer unless you have a special permit, rather difficult to obtain. Most of the free shuttle buses run to Eielson Visitors Centre, *Mile 66* (106.2 km), and then turn around for a round trip of 7.5 hours. A few more drive all the way to Wonder Lake Campground, *Mile 84* (135.2 km), for a 10-hour round trip.

Mt McKinley is not visible from the park entrance or the nearby campgrounds and hotel. Your first glimpse of it comes between *Mile 9* (14.4 km) and *Mile 11* (17.6 km) before Savage Creek Campground, if you are blessed with a clear day. The park's weather, despite its Interior location, is cool, with long periods of overcast and drizzle during the summer. The rule of thumb stressed by National Park Service rangers is that the grand mountain is hidden two out of three days.

From Savage River the road dips into the river valleys of Sanctuary and Teklanika, and Mt McKinley disappears behind the foothills. Both these rivers make for excellent hiking areas, and three of the five backcountry campgrounds are situated along them.

After passing through the canyon formed by Igloo and Cathedral mountains, the road climbs to Sable Pass, elevation 3880 feet (1183 metres) at *Mile 38.5* (62 km). The canyon and surrounding mountains are excellent places to spot Dall sheep, while the pass is known as prime habitat for Toklat brown bears. From here the road drops to the bridge over East Fork Toklat River at *Mile 44* (71 km). The area is a wildlife zone, as foot traffic is prohibited within a mile (1.6 km) of the park road from *Mile 37* (59.5 km) to *Mile 42* (67.2 km).

Hikers will enjoy treks that lead from the bridge over the east fork of the Toklat River along the riverbanks both north and south. By hiking north you can complete a six-mile (9.6 km) loop that ends at the Polychrome Pass overlook at *Mile 46.3* (74.5 km). The pass is a rest stop for the shuttle buses and a popular spot for visitors. The scenic area has an elevation of 3500 feet (1067 metres) and gives way to views of the Toklat River to the south. The alpine tundra above the road makes good hiking and an excellent place to photograph Dall sheep.

The road crosses two single-lane, wooden bridges over Toklat River and climbs near Stony Hill, elevation 4508 feet (1374 km) at *Mile 61* (98 km). This is the first spot for an exceptional view of Mt McKinley, while another 0.25 mile (0.4 km) down the road is a look-out for viewing caribou. From the look-out, a short scramble north takes you to the summit of Stony Hill. After climbing through Thorofare Pass, elevation 3900 feet (1189 metres), the road descends to Eielson Visitors Centre at *Mile 66* (106.2 km).

The centre is known for its excellent view of Mt McKinley and the surrounding peaks of the Alaska Range as well as Muldrow Glacier. It offers interpretive displays and conducts a series of its own programmes, including hikes, afternoon naturalist talks and demonstrations. One programme worth sticking around for is the hour-long 'Tundra Walk' that takes place daily at 1 pm and again at 3 pm. Catch the 9 am or 11 am shuttle bus at Riley Creek to make it to the centre for the walk. Several day and overnight hikes are possible from the centre, including one around Mt Eielson (see the Wilderness chapter) and another to Muldrow Glacier.

The park road leaves the visitor centre and drops to the valley below, passing at *Mile 74.4* (119.7 km) a sign for Muldrow Glacier. At this point the glacier lies about one mile (1.6 km) to the south, and the terminus of the 32-mile (51 km) ice floe is clearly visible, though darkened by a blanket of vegetation. Wonder Lake Campground is reached at *Mile 84* (135.2 km). Here the beauty of Mt McKinley is doubled on a clear day, with the mountain's reflection in the lake's surface. Ironically, the heavy demand for the 20 sites at Wonder Lake and the numerous overcast days caused by Mt McKinley itself prevent the majority of visitors from ever seeing this remarkable panorama. If you do experience the reddish sunset on the summit reflecting off the still waters of the lake, cherish it as a priceless moment.

Places to Stay

Those opposed to sleeping in a tent have alternatives at the main entrance of the park. The *Denali National Park Hotel* (tel 683-2155 in the summer) offers a variety of rooms, including single-person roomettes for $19 per night and compartments in original Pullman sleepers of the Alaska Railroad for $28 single and $32 double. Their regular rooms begin at $81 for singles and climb steadily. Needless to say, reservations are highly recommended, though last-minute cancellations occasionally make the Pullman sleepers available.

Cheaper is the *Youth Hostel* south of the train depot, where converted railroad cars supply space for your own bedding at $2 per night. There are no showers, cooking facilities or even heat. Showers are available behind the Chevron Gas Station near the hotel.

The campgrounds at the main entrance are *Riley Creek Campground* and *Morino*. First, stop at the nearby visitor centre to be assigned a site in Riley Creek, the largest and nicest campground in the park. There are 102 sites (of which most are gone before noon), with piped-in water, flush toilets and an $8 nightly fee. Morino is a free walk-in campground for backpackers without vehicles, providing only a metal cache to keep your food away from the bears. Though it is listed as having only 10 sites, there is usually a spot to pitch a tent. The other five campgrounds are spread along the park road, four of them within the first 34 miles (54.4 km). They are:

Savage River (29 sites, $8 fee) is at *Mile 12* (19.3 km)

Sanctuary River (seven sites, free) is at *Mile 22* (35.4 km)

Teklanika River (50 sites, $8 fee) is at *Mile 29* (46.6 km)

Igloo Creek (seven sites, free) is at *Mile 34* (54.4 km)

Wonder Lake (20 sites, $8 fee) is at *Mile 84* (135.2 km)

You may have to spend a day waiting for an open campsite somewhere, and there is a 14-day limit on staying in one campground or a combination of them.

Outside the Park For a park of six million acres, Denali occasionally stuns visitors who arrive in late afternoon or early evening and find that there is no place to stay. They are informed by National Park Service rangers of private accommodation outside the park, and these people make a good living from the overflow.

Included among these are several private campgrounds where you can expect to pay $10 to $15 for a campsite. The closest is *Lynk Creek Campground* (tel 683-2547) one mile (1.6 km) north of the park entrance on George Parks Highway. *Canyon Campground* (tel 683-2379) is three miles (4.8 km) north of the park. Six miles (9.6 km) south of the entrance is *Grizzly Bear Campground* (no phone) which offers campsites, tents for rent and cabins with cooking facilities. Near Healy, a small town 11 miles (17.6 km) north of the park entrance, there is *KOA Kampground* (tel 683-2379), which provides free bus rides to Riley Creek Visitors Centre.

If there are three or four in your party, consider *Denali Cabins* (tel 683-2643 during the summer), where you can get a large cedar cabin with outdoor hot tub for $60 per night. The cabins are six miles (9.6 km) south of the park entrance at *Mile 231* (369.6 km).

Places to Eat
There are two restaurants and one bar in the park, all located off the lobby of the Denali National Park Hotel. The *Denali Dining Room* serves full meals in pleasant surroundings but is overpriced for most budget travellers. Breakfast after 8 am, however, can be a leisurely and reasonable $6 affair when it is pleasant to sit around drinking the fresh coffee for a spell. The *Whistle Stop Snack Shop*, also off the lobby, is open from 11 am until midnight and serves hamburgers and sandwiches.

The *Gold Spike Saloon* – two lounge cars side by side – is the hotel's bar that hops at night with an interesting mixture of climbers, hikers, visitors and park employees. An even more interesting gathering of travellers can be found in the hotel lobby itself, where around the giant stone fireplace you'll find retired couples dragging large suitcases, foreign tour groups being herded here and there, and backpackers munching on dried banana chips from their daypacks.

McKinley Mercantile, a block from the hotel, sells a variety of fresh and dried food, some canned goods and other supplies. The selection is limited and high priced. Your best bet is to stock up in Fairbanks or Anchorage before leaving for the park. The small park grocery store is open daily from 8 am to 8 pm. Once you leave the main entrance area, there are no more visitor services in the park.

Activities
Riley Creek Visitors Centre offers a variety of programmes during the summer, all of them free. One of the most popular is the dog-sled demonstration. The park keeps the dogs for winter maintenance of the park and holds demonstrations daily at 11 am, 3 and 4 pm behind park headquarters, 3.5 miles (5.6 km) west on the park road. The talk explains the current and historical role of the dogs and the teams pull a ranger on a wheeled sled. A free bus leaves the centre half an hour before each demonstration.

The centre also offers daily nature walks at 4 pm from the park hotel and longer hikes throughout the park. Check the centre's bulletin board for the time and place of the day hikes. The auditorium behind the park hotel is the site of a daily slide programme at 12.30 and 7 pm that covers the history, wildlife or mountaineering aspects of the park. There are also daily campfire programmes at Riley Creek campground at 7.30 pm and at Savage River and Teklanika River campgrounds various nights of the week.

Hiking

Even for those who have neither the desire nor the equipment for an overnight trek (see the Wilderness chapter), hiking is still the best way to enjoy the park and to obtain a personal closeness with the land and its wildlife. The best way to undertake a day hike is to ride the shuttle bus and get off at any valley, riverbed or ridge that sparks your fancy. There are few trails in the park as most hiking is done across open terrain. When you've had enough, return to the road and flag down the first bus going your way.

You can hike virtually anywhere in the park that hasn't been closed because of impact on wildlife. Popular areas include Teklanika River south of the road, Toklat River, the ridges near Polychrome Pass and the tundra areas near Eielson Visitors Centre (see Park Road section above for location of routes). On a day hike, always take piped water with you, as water found in the park must be boiled or treated before drinking. The few maintained trails in the park are found around the main entrance area.

Horseshoe Lake Trail This trail is a leisurely 0.5-mile (0.8 km) walk from the hotel to an overlook of the lake. An additional 0.7 mile (1.2 km) takes you down a steep trail to the lake. At Riley Creek Visitors Centre, trail guides are available to describe plants and animals along the way.

Triple Lakes Trail A moderate nine-mile (14.4 km) hike from the railroad depot runs along the tracks and ends at George Parks Highway. After crossing Riley Creek train trestle, the trail skirts off the tracks, follows the creek drainage and passes Triple Lakes. The trail emerges on the highway just north of McKinley Village, seven miles (11.2 km) from the park entrance.

Morino Loop Trail This leisurely walk of 1.5 miles (2.5 km) begins off the road through Riley Creek Campground and offers good views of Hines and Riley creeks. Eventually the trail swings through Morino campground and back to Riley Creek Campground.

Mt Healy Trail Behind the west wing of the park hotel is the trailhead for the steep hike up Mt Healy. The trail is three miles (4.8 km) long and climbs 1700 feet (518 metres), but offers fine views of the Nenana Valley. Plan on five to six hours for the round trip.

Rock Creek Trail A moderate two-mile (3.2 km) walk connects the hotel area with the park headquarters/dog kennels area. The trail passes Rock Creek near the headquarters and then passes through mixed aspen/spruce forest before emerging on the service road behind the hotel. This is a pleasant way to arrive at the dog-sled demonstrations.

Rafting

The Nenana River and the impressive gorge it carves is a popular whitewater area. Several rafting companies offer daily floats here during the summer. The most exciting run is called 'Healy Express' and consists of 22 miles (35 km) of whitewater and canyon, ending near the town of Healy, 10 miles (16 km) north of the park. This float is offered twice daily during the summer with the departure point at McKinley Village, seven miles (11.2 km) south of the park entrance. Two companies that run the float are Nova (tel 745-5753), who depart the village at 8 am and 2 pm; and Denali Raft Adventures (tel 683-2234), who depart at 8.30 am and 2.30 pm. Both charge $42 for the four-hour adventure in getting wet.

Denali Raft Adventures also offers several shorter and less exciting floats that last two hours on the river and cost $27 per person. Check the park hotel for information and times.

Getting There

Air AAI (tel 683-2261), which shares an office with Wilderness Air in the Railroad Depot, offers a daily flight to Anchorage that departs the Denali Park airstrip at 1.30 pm and arrives in Anchorage at 2.45 pm; one-way fare is $81.

Rail The most enjoyable way to arrive at the park is aboard the Alaska Railroad (see the Getting Around chapter) with its double vistaliner coaches that provide sweeping views of Mt McKinley or the Susitna and Nenana river valleys along the way. Check the chapters on Anchorage and Fairbanks for departure times for those cities. All trains arrive at Denali Park between 2 and 2.30 pm at the Railroad Depot between Riley Creek Campground and the park hotel, and only stay long enough for passengers to board.

Within the depot is a post office, some lockers and the offices for local air-taxi operators. There is daily express service south to Anchorage, except Thursday and Sunday when there is only a local train. North-bound express service is offered daily except Wednesday and Saturday. The one-way fare to Anchorage is $54.50; to Fairbanks is $29.50.

Bus Bus service is available both north and south of Denali Park. Alaska Yukon Motorcoaches departs from the park hotel daily at 2 pm and arrives in Anchorage at 7.30 pm; one-way fare is $55. Alaska Hyway Tours provides service

daily to Fairbanks, with a bus departing the park hotel at 3.30 pm. Then there is Alaska-Denali Transit (tel 683-2798 in the park), which departs from the railroad depot daily at 2.30 pm for Anchorage and charges $30 for the one-way trip.

Getting Around

Shuttle Bus What makes the park and its wildlife so accessible is the park road that runs the length of the preserve and the free shuttle buses that use it. The buses leave the Riley Creek Visitors Centre every half hour from 6 am to 2 pm and then every hour until 6 pm. Between 6 and 7 pm an overnight bus departs for Wonder Lake, returning the next morning. The buses either head out to Eielson Visitors Centre or to Wonder Lake before turning around. Use of the buses is free but there is a heavy demand for the 40 seats on each one. To get a seat on the 6 am bus, arrive at the visitors centre at 5.30 am and pick up a plastic bus token from one of the rangers. For the 6.30 am bus, arrive at 6 am to pick up a token, and so on. The token guarantees you a seat on the next available bus. Lose a little sleep to make it to the first runs of the day, as the wildlife is superb in the early morning and competition for the buses between 8 and 10 am is fierce.

The free bus system was put into effect in 1972 to prevent the park road from becoming a busy highway of cars and trailers. Today the wildlife is accustomed to the rambling yellow school buses and rarely stop their activities when one passes by. The naturalist on board can't guarantee it, but it's a pretty sure bet that passengers will be able to spot some wildlife on any trip. The most common are brown bears, moose, Dall sheep, red foxes and ptarmigans.

You can also use the bus system to go from one campground to the next deeper in the park. Or stay at the main entrance and take the bus to selected areas for day hikes, for which backcountry permits are not needed. Once in the backcountry, you an stop a bus in either direction on the park road by flagging it down for a ride back. Passengers armed with binoculars and cameras scour the terrain for wildlife. When something is spotted, the name of he animal is called out, prompting the driver to slow down and sometimes stop or viewing and picture taking. The driver also doubles as a park guide and naturalist or a more interesting trip. Some visitors never put on hiking boots, but just ride he shuttle bus.

Tour Bus The park concessionaire operates a bus tour along the park road. The bus departs from the Denali National Park Hotel at 5.30 am, 6 am and 3 pm daily. The six-hour tour, designed primarily for package-tour groups, costs $33.50 per person. Reserve a seat the night before at the hotel reservation desk.

NORTH OF DENALI NATIONAL PARK

From the Denali National Park entrance, George Parks Highway heads north and for the next 50 miles (80 km) parallels the Nenana River, providing many viewing points of the scenic river. One of them is June Creek Rest Area at *Mile 269* (433 km), where a gravel road leads down to the small creek and a wooden staircase takes you up to fine views of the river. Also provided are out-houses, picnic tables and shelters.

Nenana

The only major town before Fairbanks is Nenana (population 540) which you reach at *Mile 305* (488 km) before crossing the Tanana River. Originally a construction camp for the Alaska Railroad, the town made history on 5 July 1923 when President Warren G Harding arrived and drove the golden spike that completed the railroad on the north side of the Tanana River.

Today the community is more famous for the Nenana Ice Classic, a lottery event in which Alaskans try to guess the exact time of break-up on the Tanana River for a pay-off of $150,000. Break-up, the first movement of river ice in April or May, is determined by a tripod which the surging ice dislodges. The movement stops a clock and the official winner is announced. Excitement swells in the small town, and through most of the state for that matter, as break-up time nears in Nenana. Stop at the visitors information centre, a log cabin with a sod roof at the junction of the highway and A St to see a replica of the tripod and the 1974 book of guesses – a volume that measures 12 by 18 inches and almost four inches thick. Outside is the *Taku Chief* river tug, which once pushed barges along the Tanana River.

Travel down Front St, parallel to the river in town, or cross to the north side of the bridge to view fish wheels at work, best seen in late summer during the salmon runs. The wheels, a traditional fish trap, scoop salmon out of the water as they move upstream to spawn.

Ester

From Nenana the highway shifts to a more easterly direction, passes a few more scenic turn-offs and arrives at the old mining town of Ester (population 200) at *Mile 351.7* (566 km). The town was established in 1906 when a sizeable strike was made at Ester Creek, and at one time was a thriving community of 15,000. Today Ester is the home of the *Cripple Creek Resort* (tel 479-2500) and its Malemute Saloon, the restored mess hall and bunk house of the mining camp and a regular stop for every tour bus out of Fairbanks. The hotel is no bargain at $45 a night for singles and $50 for doubles, but the saloon, with its rustic mining days atmosphere and daily recitals of Robert Service poetry, can be a fun place at night.

From Ester it is seven miles (11.2 km) to Fairbanks, the second largest city in Alaska, situated at the end of George Parks Highway at *Mile 358* (576 km) (see the Fairbanks chapter).

The Alcan

Travellers heading north along the Alaska Highway (Alcan) reach the US/Canada border at *Mile 1189.5* (1914.3 km) from Dawson Creek in British Columbia. The spot is marked by a look-out and plaque, while 0.5 mile (0.8 km) further along the highway is the US Customs border station. On the American side of the highway you will notice mileposts at almost every mile. These posts were erected in the 1940s to help travellers know where they were on the new wilderness road. Today they are a tradition throughout the state and are still used for mailing addresses and locations of businesses. They measure the mileage from Dawson Creek, *Mile 0* on the Alcan.

Once in Alaska, two state campgrounds are passed along the Alcan before you reach Tok. At *Mile 1249.4* (2010.7 km) is Deadman Lake State Campground (15 sites, free). At *Mile 1456.7* (2022.5 km) is Lakeview State Campground (15 sites, free) on beautiful Yager Lake.

TOK

Although you enter Alaska just north of Beaver Creek, Tok serves as the gateway to the 49th State. The town of 1200 is 125 miles (200 km) beyond the US/Canada border and is at the major junction between the Alcan that heads north-west to Fairbanks 206 miles (329.6 km) away and the Tok Cut-Off, an extension of Glenn Highway that ends in Anchorage 328 miles (528 km) to the south-west.

Tok was born in 1942 as a construction camp for the Alaska Highway. Originally it was called Tokyo Camp near Tokyo River, but WW II sentiment caused locals to shorten it to Tok. Today the town is a trade and service centre for the almost 4000 residents in the surrounding area.

Near the corner of the Tok Cut-Off and the Alcan is the Tok Visitor Information Centre (tel 883-5667), open daily in the summer from 7 am to 10 pm. The centre offers a mountain of travel information and handouts along with free coffee, a large floor map and rest-rooms. There is also a small museum in the timberline room and wildlife displays consisting of mounted heads or skins. The most important item in the centre for many backpackers is the message board. Check out the board or display your own sign if you are trying to hitch a ride through Canada along the Alcan. It is best to arrange one in Tok and not wait until you reach the international border.

Places to Stay

Youth Hostel Probably the best accommodation is at the *Tok International Youth Hostel* on a side road at *Mile 1322.8* (2116 km) of the Alcan and a mile south of

the highway. That puts it nine miles (14.4 km) west of the town, but it provides 10 beds in a big army tent along with tent sites in a pleasant wooded area. Those biking it to Alaska should note that Tok's bike trails pass near the hostel before ending at Tanacross Junction at *Mile 1325.8* (2133.7 km). The rate per night is $5 per member and $8 for non-members. There is no phone at the Youth Hostel, but the visitor information centre can supply details and rates on it.

Hotels Those travellers bussing up from Haines or Skagway will find themselves stopping overnight in Tok. There are eight hotel/motels in the area; many of them are around the junction of the two highways. The cheapest is *Gateway Motel* (tel 883-4511) across the Alcan from the visitor information centre. The motel has rooms with shared baths that begin at $25 for singles. Just about everything else in town begins at $45 for a single.

Camping The closest private campground is *Golden Bear Motel* (tel 883-2561) just 0.3 mile (0.5 km) south on Tok Cut-Off. The motel has tent spaces for $8 a night and coin-operated showers, but is the first of many tourist traps in the state set up to catch the steady stream of RVers passing through. Among the things it uses as bait is a sad-looking moose called 'Bucky' that is saddled so tourists can have their picture taken on it.

Getting There

Alaska-Yukon Motorcoaches stop at Tok in both directions and utilises Burnt Paw Gift Shop near the junction as its pick-up point. A bus leaves every Tuesday at 10 am for Fairbanks and every Thursday at 1.30 pm for Anchorage. Heading south, a bus departs every Thursday at 8 am and Saturday at 1 pm for Haines, a two-day trip. One-way fare between Tok and Anchorage is $115 and Tok to Haines $150.

On Wednesday a Whitepass & Yukon bus departs the Tok Lodge for Anchorage at 8 am and another one leaves on Saturday for Haines Junction, where there are connections to Haines, Skagway and Whitehorse. One-way fare between Tok and Anchorage is $60, Haines $85, Skagway $100 and Whitehorse $70. You might also check into Norline Coaches and its companion carrier Yukon Stage Lines, which combine services to offer a bus from Tok to Fairbanks on Tuesday and a south-bound bus to Whitehorse on Saturday. They also have a bus that departs Tok on Saturday at 1.30 pm for Dawson Creek. Check with the visitor information centre to see if the service is still available because the company was recently considering dropping several routes and in the past has cancelled runs if there are not enough passengers booked. One-way fare between Tok and Fairbanks is $37; to Dawson it's $55.

TOK TO DELTA JUNCTION

The Alaska Highway leaves Tok to the west and within 10 miles (16 km) you are greeted with views of the Alaska Range which parallels the road to the south. Moon Lake State Campground (15 sites, free) is reached at *Mile 1332* (2144 km), 18 miles (29 km) west of Tok. The state wayside offers tables, out-houses and a swimming area in the lake where it is possible to do the backstroke while watching a floatplane land nearby. Although there are no more official campgrounds until Delta Junction is reached, travellers often stop overnight at Gerstle River State Wayside, a large look-out at *Mile 1393* (2242 km). The scenic spot provides tables and outhouses but no piped-in drinking water.

DELTA JUNCTION

This town of 1000 residents is known as the 'End Of The Alcan' because the famous highway joined the existing Richardson Highway here to complete the route to Fairbanks. The community began as a construction camp and picked up its name from the junction between the two highways. Delta Junction is a service centre not only for travellers but also for the growing agricultural community in the surrounding valleys and the 1200 military personnel and their families stationed at nearby Fort Greely.

The log cabin which houses the town's Visitors Centre is in the 'Triangle', the spot where the Alcan merges into Richardson Highway. Just outside is the large white milepost for *Mile 1422* (2288.4 km), marking the end of the famous highway. This causes much confusion for travellers, as Fairbanks has an even larger milepost at *Mile 1523* (2437 km), proclaiming it to be the end of the road. The debate will never end, but in Delta Junction they argue that the larger city to the north is nothing more than the terminus for Richardson Highway. The community itself is spread out considerably on both highways, with the Triangle as the town's unofficial centre.

The visitors centre is open daily from 9 am to 6 pm in the summer and is the usual source of local information, handouts and free coffee. Those who have just completed the Alcan from Dawson Creek can also purchase an 'End of The Highway' certificate for $1, or can wait until you get to Fairbanks.

There isn't a lot to do in Delta Junction unless you wander in during the Deltana Fair (giant vegetables, livestock shows, parades) on the first weekend in August. If you have the time, head three miles (4.8 km) down Richardson Highway to the scenic look-out across from the FAA facility. The mountainous panorama with the Delta River in the foreground is spectacular from this spot. On a clear day you can easily spot Mt Hayes, 13,832 feet (4218 metres) in the centre, and Mt Moffit, 13020 feet (3971 metres) to the left, as well as several other peaks.

Check out the public library behind the city hall in the centre of town if you have run out of reading material after the long haul on the Alcan. The library is open afternoons until 4 pm Monday to Saturday in the summer and runs a paperback swap for travellers.

Places to Stay

Youth Hostel The *Delta Youth Hostel* is a unique log cabin in a wooded retreat nine miles (14.4) north of Delta Junction on the way to Fairbanks. Although it is hassle to get out there without your own vehicle, the hostel is worth finding and is a pleasant place to spend a day or two. Follow Richardson Highway six miles (9.6 km) to *Mile 272* (435 km) as measured from Valdez, and turn right on Tanana Loop Rd. Head one mile (1.6 km) down the road, turn right onto Tanana Loop Extension and then look for the unmarked dirt road that leads left to the hostel; the building is three miles (4.8 km) from the highway. The hostel offers 10 beds and kitchen facilities but has no phone. Rates are $4.25 for members and $7.25 for non-members. Call 895-4627 Monday to Friday between 9 am and 5 pm for more information.

Hotels There are a number of hotel/motels within Delta Junction. *Evergreen Inn* (tel 895-4666) is across from the visitor information centre. *Kelley's Motel* (tel 895-4667) is nearby, on the west side of the highway, and offers singles for $35 and doubles for $40. Also consider *Silver Fox Roadhouse* (tel 895-4157), on the Alcan 18 miles (29 km) before reaching Delta Junction, where there are cabins for $25.

Camping There are two public campgrounds in the area. The closest is *Delta State Campground* (24 sites, free), one mile (1.6 km) north of the visitor information centre. The other is *Clearwater State Campground* (18 sites, free), 13 miles (21 km) away from town. Follow Richardson Highway and turn right on Jack Warren Rd, 2.4 miles (3.8 km) north of the visitor information centre. Head

10.5 miles (16.8 km) east along the the road and look for signs to the campground, which is along Clearwater Creek.

Richardson Highway

The Richardson, Alaska's first highway, begins in Valdez and extends north 266 miles (428 km) to Delta Junction, where the Alaska Highway joins it for the final 98 miles (158 km) to Fairbanks. The road was originally scouted in 1919 by Captain W R Abercrombie of the US Army, who was looking for a way to link the gold town of Eagle with the warm-water port of Valdez. At first it was a telegraph line and footpath, but it quickly turned into a wagon trail following the gold strikes at Fairbanks at the turn of the century.

Today the road is a scenic wonder; it passes through the Chugach Mountains and the Alaska Range while providing access to Wrangell-St Elias National Park. Along the way it is highlighted by waterfalls, glaciers, five major rivers and the Alaska Pipeline, which parallels the road most of the way.

VALDEZ TO DELTA JUNCTION
The first section from Valdez, *Mile 0*, to the junction of Glenn Highway, *Mile 115* (185 km), is covered in the Southcentral chapter. The next 14 miles (22.4 km) to the junction of Tok Cut-Off, which includes the campgrounds at Dry Creek State Recreation Site and Gulkana, is covered in the section below on the Tok Cut-Off. Mileposts along the highway show distance to old Valdez, four miles (6.4 km) from the present city, the new beginning of the Richardson.

Once past Gulkana, the highway parallels the Gulkana River for the next 35 miles (56 km) through land that is owned by Ahtna Native Corporation. Fishing is excellent in this river for king and red salmon from mid-June to mid-July and for rainbow trout and grayling

most of the summer. In order to fish off the shore you must have a permit ($10), issued by the native corporation and available at the Ahtna Lodge at the junction of Richardson and Glenn highways. During the popular salmon runs the permits are also sold along the highway.

At *Mile 147.4* (237.2 km) the road reaches Sourdough Creek BLM Campground (15 sites, free), which provides access into the Gulkana River for canoeists and rafters. Also in the campground is the trailhead for the 1.4-mile (2.2 km) path to Sourdough Creek. On the other side of the highway and to the north is the Sourdough Roadhouse, established in 1903 when the old Valdez Trail to Eagle ran behind it. Today it is a national historical site and, its owners claim, the oldest existing roadhouse in Alaska. Its dining room is open from 6 am to 10 pm and the sourdough pancakes are good.

Gulkana Canoe Route
The Gulkana River from Paxson Lake, *Mile 175* (281.6 km) of the highway, to where Richardson Highway crosses it at Gulkana is a popular canoe, kayak and raft route of 80 miles (128 km). The first 45 miles (72 km) is only for experienced whitewater paddlers or rafters, as it involves several challenging rapids, including Canyon Rapids, Class IV whitewater. Although there is a short portage around Canyon Rapids, rough Class III waters follow. The final 35 miles (56 km) from Sourdough Creek BLM Campground to Gulkana is a pleasant one or two-day paddle of mild water that can be enjoyed by less hardcore canoeists.

All land from the BLM campground south is owned by the Ahtna Native Corporation, which charges boaters to camp on it. The exception is three single-acre sites that are signposted along the riverbanks and have short trails leading back to the highway.

Canoes can be rented in Fairbanks or

rafts can be rented from Taiga Outdoor Rentals (tel 883-5384) in Tok for $25 per day for the adventurous souls who want to run the entire 80 miles (130 km).

Alaska Range Foothills to Fielding Lake

Ten miles (16 km) beyond Sourdough Creek, the highway enters the foothills of the Alaska Range. Gradually there are sweeping views of not only the Alaska Range straight ahead, but the Wrangell Mountains to the south and the Chugach Mountains to the south-west. More splendid views follow; you can see the large plateau to the west where the headwaters of the Susitna River form, and the Glennallen area to the south. At *Mile 175* (281.6 km) is the gravel spur that leads 1.5 miles (2.4 km) west to Paxson Lake BLM Campground (20 sites, free).

The junction with Denali Highway (see next section) is at *Mile 185.5* (298.5 km), where the small service centre of Paxson is located. In another five miles (eight km) north, look for the parking area by the Gulkana River on the left side of the highway, where there are litter barrels and picnic tables. The scenic spot provides views of Summit Lake and the Alaska Pipeline. From mid to late summer this is also a good spot to watch the salmon spawn. After passing the lake, the bridge over Gunn Creek is reached at *Mile 196.7* (316.5 km) and provides views of Gulkana Glacier to the north-east. From here the highway begins climbing to its highest point at Isabel Pass, elevation 3000 feet (914 metres). The pass is at *Mile 197.6* (318 km) and is marked by a historical sign dedicated to General Wilds Richardson, after whom the highway is named. From this point you can view Gulkana Glacier to the north-east and Isabel Pass Pipeline Camp below it.

Three miles north of the pass at *Mile 200.5* (322.7 km), a gravel spur leads 1.5 miles (2.4 km) to Fielding Lake Wayside, where you can camp (seven sites, free) in a scenic area above the treeline. The highway and the pipeline parallel each other from Fielding Lake, and there are several look-outs to view mans' monumental efforts to move oil. One of the best is at *Mile 205.7* (331 km), where the pipeline can be photographed on an incline up a steep hill.

Black Rapids Lake Trail

At *Mile 225.4* (362.7 km) there is a viewpoint with picnic tables and a historical marker pointing out what little ice remains of Black Rapids Glacier to the west. The glacier is known as the 'Galloping Glacier' for its famous three-mile (4.8 km) advancement in the winter of 1936 when it almost engulfed the highway. Across from the marker an easy trail of 0.3 mile (0.4 km) winds through wildflowers to Black Rapids Lake.

Donnelly Creek to Delta Junction

The last public campground before Delta Junction is just before *Mile 238* (383 km), where a short loop road leads west of the highway to Donnelly Creek State Campground (12 sites, free). Two interesting turnoffs are passed in the final 25 miles (40 km) before reaching the Alcan and are worth stopping at.

The first is at *Mile 241.3* (388.3 km) and overlooks the calving ground of the Delta buffalo herd to the west. In 1928, 23 bison were transplanted here from Montana for the pleasure of sportsmen, and today they number almost 400. The animals have established a migratory pattern in the area which includes summering and calving along the Delta River. There is an interpretive display at the turnoff where often you can spot up to 100 animals. Since the herd is two to three miles (3.2 to 4.8 km) away, binoculars are needed.

The other turnoff is just before *Mile 244* (390.4) and has spectacular views of the pipeline and three of the highest peaks in the Alaska Range to the south-west. From south to west you can view Mt Deborah, 12339 feet (3761 metres); Hess Mountain, 11,940 feet (3639 metres) and Mt Hayes, 13,832 feet (4216 metres).

The highway passes Fort Greely just beyond *Mile 261* (417.6 km) and then arrives at the Delta Junction visitor centre on the 'Triangle', where the Alaska Highway merges into the Richardson at *Mile 266* (428 km).

DELTA JUNCTION TO FAIRBANKS
From Delta Junction the Richardson Highway merges with the Alcan for the remaining 98 miles (157 km) to Fairbanks. After passing the junction of the Alcan at *Mile 266* (428 km) of the Richardson, you pass through the farming village of Big Delta (population 300) at *Mile 275.3* (443 km). From the town's bridge across the Tanana River you can look east for an impressive view of the Alaska Pipeline suspended over the water, or look west for equally impressive views of the Alaska Range.

The junction to Quartz Lake State Campground (16 sites, free) is reached at *Mile 278* (445 km). Turn right at the posted road and head straight 2.8 miles (4.5 km) for the campground along the shores of the scenic lake, which provides good fishing for rainbow trout. A trail from the campground leads over to nearby Lost Lake, where there are two more campsites.

For the next 20 miles (32 km) the highway passes a handful of look-outs where there are spectacular views of both the Tanana River in the foreground and the Alaska Range behind it. The three most noticeable peaks are Mt Hayes, elevation 13832 feet (4216 metres) to the south-east; Mt Deborah, 12,339 (3639 metres) to the south-west; and Hess Mountain, 11,940 feet (3761 metres), between them.

The spur that leads to Harding Lake State Campground (89 sites, free) is at *Mile 321.5* (517.4 km). The campground has a ranger office near the entrance and provides picnic shelters and drinking water as well as swimming and canoeing opportunities in the lake. From the campground it is 43 miles (69 km) to

Fairbanks. There are two public campgrounds along the way; at *Mile 346.7* (558 km) is Chena Lakes Recreation Area (78 campsites, fee), and another three miles (4.8 km) north is North Pole Public Park with a few tent sites (both are covered in the Fairbanks chapter). Richardson Highway reaches the south-east corner of Fairbanks at *Mile 363* (580 km).

Tok Cut-Off

The Tok Cut-Off is often considered the northern half of Glenn Highway, but mileposts along the road show distance from Tok and not from Anchorage, as they do once you pass Glennallen.

TOK TO GLENNALLEN
From Tok it is 328 miles (528 km) to Anchorage, which is reached by first travelling the Tok Cut-Off 139 miles (224 km) south-west to Glennallen. The small town lies on the junction of Richardson and Glenn highways, and from there it is another 189 miles (304 km) to Alaska's largest city on Glenn Highway.

Eagle Trail
The first of only two public campgrounds on the Tok Cut-Off is reached at *Mile 15.7* (25.3 km). Eagle Trail State Campground (40 sites, free) is near Clearwater Creek and provides drinking water, toilets, rain shelter and firepits. The historical trail, which at one time extended to Eagle on the Yukon River, can still be hiked on a one-mile (1.6-km) section from the campground. Look for the posted trailhead near the covered picnic shelters.

Porcupine Creek
The second campground is another 45 miles (72 km) south-west along the highway just before *Mile 61* (97.6 km). Porcupine Creek State Campground (12 sites, free) is a scenic spot along the creek and provides tables, toilets and drinking

water. A historical marker and splendid views of Mt Sanford, a dormant volcano with an elevation of 16,237 feet (4949 metres), is situated one mile (1.6 km) along the highway.

Nabesna

At *Mile 65.2* (105 km) is the junction with Nabesna Rd. The 45-mile (72.4 km) side road extends into the Wrangell-St Elias National Park (see the Southcentral chapter) and ends at Nabesna, a mining community of less than 25 residents.

The side trip is a unique experience off the beaten path of Alaska highways; the road is only one of two that lead into the heart of the new national park. The first 30 miles is manageable gravel road, but after that the road is extremely rough, with several streams flowing over it.

There are no tourist facilities in Nabesna and no campgrounds along the way. Good camping spots, however, along with scenic lakes and inviting ridges for backpackers, lie from one end of this road to the other.

Gakona Junction

Officially Tok Cut-Off ends at Gakona Junction, 125 miles (201 km) south-west of Tok, where it merges into Richardson Highway. The village of Gulkana (population 100) is two miles (3.2 km) to the south and you can camp (voluntary fee) along the Gulkana River by the bridge that crosses it in town. The eastern end of Glenn Highway is reached 14 miles (22.4 km) from Gakona Junction.

Glenn Highway

Glenn Highway heads west from Glennallen at *Mile 187* (301 km), with the mileposts along the road showing the distance from Anchorage (*Mile 0*).

GLENNALLEN

Glennallen, referred to by some as 'The Hub' of Alaska's road system, is a service centre of 800 residents two miles (3.2 km) west on Glenn Highway from its junction with Richardson Highway. Because of its strategic location, the town provides a wide range of facilities and services, and serves as the major departure point into Wrangell-St Elias National Park. It is also the home-base for many fishing and hunting guides; otherwise there is little reason to linger here.

Places to Stay

Motels Of the handful of motels, *Park's Place* (tel 822-3334) on Glenn Highway in the heart of town is the cheapest. Singles with shared bath cost $25 a night and doubles are $39. At the nearby *Caribou Lodge* (tel 822-3302), singles are $30 and doubles $35.

Camping The closest public campground is *Dry Creek State Campground* (58 sites, free) five miles (eight km) east of town on Richardson Highway between the Glenn Highway junction and the one with Tok Cut-Off to the north. Hitch-hikers who get caught in Glennallen at nightfall never have to walk far, however, to find a place to pitch a tent.

Getting There

Air Gulkana Air Service (tel 822-5532) provides daily flights to Anchorage on Monday and Friday. One-way fare to Anchorage is $125.

Bus Glennallen is notorious among hitch-hikers as a place for getting stuck in, especially for backpackers at the Glenn Highway junction trying to thumb a ride north to the Alcan. The Ahtna Lodge (tel 822-3289) at the junction is the boarding point for several bus companies and the salvation for somebody who has just spent a long day on the side of the road.

Alaska-Yukon Motorcoaches has a bus departing daily at 11 am for Fairbanks and another at 2 pm for Valdez. On Friday evening a bus stops overnights at

Glennallen and then departs Saturday at 8 am for Tok and eventually Haines. On Fridays a bus departs at 8 am for Anchorage. The fare between Glennallen and Fairbanks is $50, Valdez $30, Haines $180 and Anchorage $45.

The Whitehorse & Yukon bus departs Glennallen on Saturday at 1.30 pm and stops overnight at Tok before continuing on to Haines Junction. One-way fare to Tok is $25 and to Haines Junction $75. Valdez-Anchorage Bus Lines passes through at 12.30 pm on Monday, Thursday and Saturday on its way to Valdez, and on Tuesday, Friday and Sunday to Anchorage. One-way fare to Anchorage is $34 and to Valdez $21. Always call the lodge about current times of buses because the meager system of motor-coaches in Alaska is in a constant state of flux.

GLENNALLEN TO ANCHORAGE
The road runs west from Glennallen through a vast plateau bordered by the Alaska Range to the north and the Chugach Mountains to the south. This is an incredibly scenic section that extends for almost 150 miles (241.4 km) west, and is a good one for spotting wildlife. The lowlands are roamed by moose and caribou, and the timbered ridges are prime habitat for black bears and grizzlies. On the slope of both mountain ranges and often visible from the highway are bands of Dall sheep.

The first public campground is Tolsona Creek State Campground (10 sites, free) at *Mile 172.7* (278 km) on the south side of the highway. The next one is Lake Louise State Recreation Area (20 sites, free) which provides shelters, tables, water and swimming in the lake. The campground is 17 miles (27 km) up Lake Louise Rd from *Mile 160* (256 km) of the highway.

A third state campground is Little Nelchina River (six sites, free) just off the highway at *Mile 137.5* (221.3 km). The 35 miles (56 km) between these three

campgrounds is a hiker's delight, as several trails go from the highway to the nearby mountains and lakes.

Mae West Lake Trail
A look-out with litter barrels marks the trailhead of this short hike at *Mile 169.3* (272.3). The one-mile (1.6-km) trail leads to a long, narrow lake fed by Little Woods Creek.

Lost Cabin Lake Trail
The trailhead is on the south side of the highway at *Mile 165.8* (266.8 km), where a pair of litter barrels have been placed. The trail winds two miles (3.2 km) to the lake and is a berry picker's delight from late summer to early autumn.

Old Man Creek Trail
The trailhead is at *Mile 138.3* (222.6 km), or 0.8 mile (1.3 km) east of Little Nelchina River Campground for those camping there. The trail leads two miles (3.2 km) to Old Man Creek and nine miles (14.4 km) to Cooked Creek, where you can fish for grayling. It ends at the old mining area of Nelchina, 14.5 miles (23 km) from the highway. Here it merges into the old Chickaloon-Knik-Nelchina Trail, a gold miner's route used before Glenn Highway was built.

Today the Chickaloon-Knik-Nelchina route is an extensive system of trails that extend beyond Palmer, with many posted access points along the north side of the highway. The system is not maintained regularly and hikers attempting any part of it should have good outdoor experience and the right topographic maps.

Eureka Summit
From Little Nelchina River the highway begins to climb, and views of Gunsight Mountain (you have to look hard to see the origin of its name) comes into sight. At Eureka Summit you can see not only Gunsight but the Chugach Mountains to the south as well, with Nelchina Glacier spilling down in the middle and the

Talkeetnas to the north. The impressive unobstructed view is completed to the west, where the highway can be seen dropping into the river valleys separating the two chains. Eureka Summit is reached at *Mile 129.3* (208 km) and is the highest point of the highway near the tree line at 3322 feet (1013 metres).

Belanger Pass Trail

The trailhead is at *Mile 123.3* (198.4 km) on Martin Rd across from Tahneta Lodge, and is marked by a 'Chickaloon-Knik-Nelchina Trail' sign. For the most part it is used by miners and hunters in off-road vehicles for access into the Talkeetna Mountains, and at times the mining scars are disturbing. The views from Belanger Pass, a three-mile (4.8-km) hike, are excellent and well worth the climb. From the 4350-foot (1326 metre) pass, off-road-vehicle trails continue north to Alfred Creek, another 3.5 miles (5.6 km) away, and eventually around the north side of Syncline Mountain past active mining operations.

Two miles (3.2 km) beyond the trailhead, Tahneta Pass is reached at *Mile 121* (194.7 km); 0.5 mile (0.8 km) beyond it there is a scenic turnoff. Here you can view the 3000-foot (914 metre) pass. To the east lies Lake Liela, and Lake Tahneta beyond it.

Squaw Creek Trail

This is another miners and hunters trail that begins at *Mile 117.6* (189.3 km) and merges into Chickaloon-Knik-Nelchina Trail. It begins as an off-road-vehicle trail marked by a 'Squaw Creek Trail' sign. It extends 3.5 miles (5.6 km) to Squaw Creek and 9.5 miles (15 km) to Caribou Creek after climbing a low pass between the two. Although the trail can be confusing at times, the hike is a scenic one with a backdrop of Gunsight, Sheep and Syncline mountains.

From here the road begins to descend and the scenic highway becomes stunning as it heads towards the Talkeetna

Mountains, passing an oddly-shaped rock formation at *Mile 114* (183.5 km) known as Lion's Head. About 0.5 miles (0.8 km) beyond it, the highway reaches the first view of Matanuska Glacier; to the north is Sheep Mountain, properly named as you can often spot Dall sheep on its slopes. Numerous turnoffs with good views of the glacier and the Chugach Mountains follow.

At *Mile 101* (162.5 km) you reach Matanuska Glacier State Campground (13 sites, free). The area has sheltered tables, water and trails along a nearby bluff that provide good viewing points of the glacier. Matanuska Glacier is a stable ice floe that is four miles wide (6.4 km) at its terminus and extends 27 miles (43.5 km) back into the Chugach Mountains.

Puritan Creek Trail

Just before the bridge over the creek (also known as Purinton) at *Mile 89* (143 km), there is a short dirt road that heads north of the highway and then east, passing an off-road-vehicle trail that ascends a steep hill to the north. The trail is a 12-mile (19.2-km) walk to the foot of Boulder Creek, though the final seven miles (11.2 km) consist mostly of trekking along the gravel bars of the river. The scenery of the Chugach Mountains is excellent and there are good camping spots along Boulder Creek.

From Boulder Creek it is possible to climb to Chitna Pass and down to Caribou Creek to reach more sections of the Chickaloon-Knik-Nelchina Trail, a system that parallels the Glenn Highway. The adventurous backpacker and one who is knowledgeable with map and compass, could hike for days, exiting at a number of trailheads, including Belanger Pass and Squaw Creek (see above hikes).

In the next 13 miles (20.8 km) the highway passes three public campgrounds. The first is Long Lake State Campground (eight sites, free) at *Mile 85.3* (137.3 km). Along with toilets and firepits, the campground offers access to a fishing hole that is a favourite among Anchorage's residents for grayling. Two miles (3.2 km) west is a gravel spur road that leads to Lower Bonnie Lake State Campground (eight sites, free), a two-mile (3.2 km) side trip from the highway. The third campground is King Mountain State Wayside (22 sites, free) at *Mile 76* (121.6 km). The scenic campground is on the banks of the Matanuska River, with a view of King Mountain to the south-east.

After passing through Sutton at *Mile 61* (98.2 km), a town of 850 residents and site of a former Youth Hostel (ask to see if it has been reorganised), you come to the last public campground before Palmer. Moose Creek State Campground (eight sites, free) is a small site on the creek at *Mile 54.5* (87.2 km) and provides sheltered tables, out-houses and drinking water. Five miles (eight km) beyond Moose Creek is the junction to Fishhook-Willow Rd that takes you to Independence Mine State Park (see Willow section above). The highway then descends into the agricultural centre of Palmer.

From Palmer, Glenn Highway merges into George Parks Highway and continues south to Anchorage, 43 miles (67 km) away (see the Anchorage chapter).

Denali Highway

With the exception of 21 miles (33.6 km) that is paved at the east end, Denali Highway is a gravel road, extending from Paxson on Richardson Highway to Cantwell on George Parks Highway, just south of the main entrance to Denali National Park.

When the 135-mile (216 km) route was opened in 1957 it was the only road to the national park, but became a secondary route after George Parks Highway was finished in 1972. Today Denali Highway is open only from mid-May to October.

Most of it runs along the foothills of the Alaska Range to the north, through glacial valleys where you can see stretches of alpine tundra. There are numerous trails into the surrounding backcountry but none of them are marked. Also in the area are two popular canoe routes. Ask locals at the roadhouses and take along topographic maps that cover the areas where you intend to trek or paddle.

There are no established communities along the way, but a few roadhouses provide food, lodging and gas. If driving, it is best to fill up at Paxson or Cantwell.

From Paxson, *Mile 0*, the highway heads west and passes a one-mile (1.6 km) gravel road to Sevenmile Lake at *Mile 7* (11.2 km). From here the terrain opens up and provides superb views of the nearby lakes and peaks of the Alaska Range. Most of the lakes – as many as 40 in the spring – can be seen from a look-out at *Mile 13* (21 km).

Swede Lake Trail
The trail is passed near *Mile 17* (27.3 km) and leads south three miles (4.8 km) to the lake after passing Little Swede Lake in two miles (3.2 km). Anglers fish the lakes for trout and grayling. Inquire at the Tangle River Inn at *Mile 20* (32.2 km) for directions to the trail and an update on its conditions.

The paved portion ends just beyond *Mile 21* (33.6 km), and in another 0.5 mile (0.8 km) the highway reaches Tangle Lakes BLM Campground (13 sites, free) to the north, on the shores of Round Tangle Lake. A second BLM campground, Upper Tangle Lakes (seven sites, free), is 0.2 mile (0.3 km) down the road on the south side. Both campgrounds serve as the departure point for two scenic canoe routes. Caribou are occasionally spotted on the surrounding hills.

Delta River Canoe Route
The 35-mile (56 km) paddle begins at the Tangle Lakes BLM Campground north of

the highway and ends a few hundred yards from *Mile 212.5* (340 km) of Richardson Highway. You begin by crossing Round Tangle Lake and continue to Lower Tangle Lake, where a waterfall must be portaged around. Following the waterfall is a set of Class III rapids that must either be lined for two miles (3.2 km) or paddled with an experienced hand. Every year the BLM reports numerous canoeists who damage their boats beyond repair on these rapids and are forced to hike 15 miles (24 km) back out to Denali Highway. The remainder of the trip is a much milder paddle.

Upper Tangle Lakes Canoe Route

This route is easier and shorter than Delta River but requires several portages, none of which are marked. All paddlers attempting this route must have topographic maps. The route begins at Tangle River and passes through Upper Tangle Lake before ending at Dickey Lake, nine miles (14.4 km) to the south.

Landmark Gap Trail

At *Mile 25* (40 km) the highway crosses Rock Creek Bridge, where a trail leads north three miles (4.8 km) to Landmark Gap Lake, elevation 3217 feet (981 metres). You can't see the lake from the highway but you can spot the noticeable gap between the Amphitheatre Mountains. A trail from the lake loops around for a pleasant overnight trek.

Glacier Lake Trail

At *Mile 32* (51.2 km), on the north side of the highway, is a parking lot for the three-mile (4.8 km) trail to Glacier Lake, sometimes visible from the road. From Glacier Lake it is possible to continue six miles (9.6 km) to another Sevenmile Lake.

MacLaren Summit

From here the highway climbs MacLaren Summit, elevation 4086 feet (1245 metres), the highest highway climb in the state

other than North Slope Haul Rd. The summit is reached at *Mile 35.2* (56.6 km) and has excellent views of Mt Hayes, Hess Mountain and Mt Deborah to the west and MacLaren Glacier to the north.

The MacLaren River is crossed at *Mile 42* (67.6 km) on a 364-foot (111-metre) multiple-span bridge. Another bridge crosses Clearwater Creek at *Mile 56* (89.6 km), where nearby there are campsites and out-houses. Beginning at *Mile 69* (110.4 km) is the first of many hiking trails in the area, all unmarked and many are nothing more than old gravel roads. Inquire at the Gracious Lodge, a road-house at *Mile 82* (132 km), for the exact location of the trails.

Hatchet Lake Trail

Just before *Mile 69* (110.4 km) is the five-mile (eight km) trail that begins near Raft Creek. Hatchet Lake lies two miles (3.2 km) south of the highway.

Denali Trail

A trail begins on the north side of the road at *Mile 79* (126.4 km), 0.5 mile (0.8 km) before the highway crosses the Susitna River on a multiple-span bridge. It winds for six miles (10 km) to the old mining camp of Denali, first established in 1907. A few of the old buildings still remain. Today gold mining has resumed in the area. Several old mining trails branch off the trail, including an 18-mile (29 km) route to Roosevelt Lake from Denali Camp. The area can provide enough hiking for a two or three-day trip, but tackle these trails only with map and compass in hand.

Snodgrass Lake Trail

Between *Mile 80* and *Mile 81* (128 and 129.6 km) is a parking area for the trail that leads two miles (3.2 km) south to Snodgrass Lake, known among anglers for its grayling.

Butte Lake Trail

The off-road-vehicle trail leads five miles (eight km) south to Butte Lake, known for its large lake trout, often weighing over 30 lb (13.5 kg). The trailhead is at *Mile 94* (150.4 km). Motorised transportation can be arranged through Adventures Unlimited, a roadhouse with lodging and food at *Mile 100* (160 km).

Brushkana River to Cantwell

Brushkana River BLM Campground (17 sites, free) is at *Mile 104.3* (167.8 km) and provides a shelter and drinking water as well as a meat rack for hunters who invade the area in late summer and autumn. The river which the campground overlooks can be fished for grayling and Dolly Varden. From here it is another 20 miles (32 km) to where Denali Highway merges into George Parks Highway. Denali continues for a little more than a mile from here to the small town of Cantwell (population 100). Denali National Park & Preserve is 17 miles (27 km) north on George Parks Highway.

Taylor Highway

Scenic Taylor Highway extends 161 miles (259 km) north from Tetlin Junction, 13 miles (21 km) east of Tok on the Alaska Highway, to the historic town of Eagle on the Yukon River. It is a beautiful but rough drive, as the road is narrow, winding and climbs Mt Fairplay, Polly Summit and American Summit, all over 3500 feet (1067 metres) in elevation.

The highway is the first section to Dawson City, Yukon and offers access to the popular Fortymile River canoe route and much off-road hiking. As with Denali Highway, the problem of unmarked trailheads exists, making it necessary to have the proper topographic maps in hand. Many trails are off-road-vehicle tracks used heavily in late summer and autumn by hunters.

By Alaskan standards there is light to moderate traffic on Taylor Highway during the summer, until you reach Jack Wade Junction, where the majority of it continues east for Dawson City. Hitchhikers thumbing their way to Eagle have to be patient in the final 65 miles (105 km) north, but the ride will come. If you're driving, leave Tetlin Junction with a full tank of gas because roadside services are limited along the route.

From Tetlin Junction, *Mile 0*, the highway heads north, and within nine miles (14.4 km) begins to climb towards Mt Fairplay, elevation 5541 feet (1689 metres). A look-out near the summit is reached at *Mile 35* (56 km) and is marked by litter barrels and an interpretive sign describing the history of Taylor Highway. From here you are rewarded with superb views of Mt Fairplay and the valleys and forks of the Fortymile River to the north. The surrounding alpine area offers good hiking for those who need to stretch their legs.

The first BLM campground is reached at *Mile 49* (78 km) on the west side of the highway. West Fork BLM Campground (six sites, free) offers out-houses but no drinking water; all water taken from nearby streams should be boiled or treated first. Travellers packing along their gold pans can try their luck in West Fork River.

After crossing a bridge over Mosquito Fork of the Fortymile River at *Mile 64.4* (103.6 km), the highway passes the old Chicken post office on a hill beside the road, at *Mile 66.2* (106.5 km). The post office, still operating today, was originally established when Chicken was a thriving mining centre.

The community of Chicken itself (population between 30 and 50) is 0.5 mile (0.8 km) to the north on a spur road that leads east to an airstrip, grocery, restaurant and gas station. The town's name, according to one tale, originated at a meeting of the resident miners in the late 1800s. When trying to come up with a name for the new tent city, somebody suggested Ptarmigan, since the chicken-like bird existed in great numbers throughout the area. All the miners liked it but none of them could spell it. It's been Chicken ever since.

Just north of the spur to the village is Chicken Creek Bridge, built on tailing piles from the mining era. If you look back to the left, you can see the Chicken dredge which was used to extract gold from the creek between 1959 and 1965. Most of the forks of the Fortymile River are virtually covered from one end to the other by active mining claims and often you can see suction dredging for gold from the highway.

Views of the old town site of Chicken, now in the hands of a mining company, can be obtained at *Mile 67.3* (108.3 km) by looking to the west. At *Mile 75.3* (121.2 km) is the bridge over South Fork and the most popular access point for the Fortymile River canoe route.

Fortymile River Canoe Route

This historical river, designated as the Fortymile National Wild River, offers an excellent escape into scenic wilderness for paddlers experienced in lining their canoes around rapids. It also lets them step back into the gold-rush era of Alaska; they will view such abandoned mining communities as Franklin, Steele Creek and Fortymile while undoubtedly seeing some present-day mining. The best place to put in is the bridge over South Fork, because access points south of here on Taylor Highway often are too shallow for an enjoyable trip.

A common trip is to paddle the 40 miles (64 km) to the bridge over O'Brien Creek at *Mile 113* (181 km) of Taylor Highway. This two to three-day trip involves three sets of Class III rapids. A greater adventure would be to continue past O'Brien Creek and paddle the Fortymile River into the Yukon River and from here head north to Eagle at the end of Taylor Highway. Such a trip would be 140 miles (224 km) long

and would require seven to 10 days to cover, along with lining several sets of rapids in the Fortymile River. The planning and organising for such an expedition has to be done carefully and well before you leave for Alaska (see Eagle section about paddling the Yukon).

Walker Fork to American Creek

Walker Fork BLM Campground (34 sites, free) lies on both sides of the highway at *Mile 82* (132 km) and has tables, firewood and a short trail to the limestone bluff overlook. A look-out is reached at *Mile 86* (144.7 km), where you can view the Jack Wade dredge, which operated from 1900 until 1942. For most of its working days the dredge was powered by a wood-burning steam engine and required 10 to 12 cords of wood per day. The old mining camp of Jack Wade is passed four miles (6.4 km) north of the dredge; after being abandoned for 30 years the mine is now being reworked as the result of gold's higher prices.

The Jack Wade junction is at *Mile 95.7* (154 km), and here the Top Of The World Highway (also known as Dawson Highway) winds 3.5 miles (5.6 km) to the Canada/US border and another 75 miles (120 km) to Dawson City. Taylor Highway continues north and begins climbing Polly Summit, elevation 3550 feet (1083 metres). The summit is reached at *Mile 105* (168 km). Five miles beyond it is a scenic overlook where you can view the Fortymile River.

From the summit, Taylor Highway begins a steep descent and drivers must take this section slowly. Along the way there are numerous look-outs with good views as well as a variety of abandoned cabins, old gold dredges and mine tailings. Liberty Creek BLM Campground (seven sites, free) is reached at *Mile 132* (211 km) and is on King Solomon Creek. The campground provides tables, out-houses and firewood. Holiday prospectors should try their luck in the nearby creek.

The last campground before Eagle is

American Creek BLM Wayside (four sites, free) at *Mile 154* (248 km). The wayside is interesting, as there are usually some miners and prospectors staying there. Eagle is another six miles (9.4 km) to the north.

EAGLE

The historic town of Eagle (population 190) had its beginnings in the late 1800s and today is one of the best-preserved boom towns of the mining era in Alaska.

The original community, today called Eagle Village, was established by the Athapaskan Indians long before Francois Mercier arrived in the early 1880s and built a trading post in the area. A permanent community of miners was set up in 1898. A year later the US Army decided to move in and build a fort in its effort to maintain law and order in the Alaskan Interior. A federal court was established in Eagle in 1900 by Judge Wickersham, and the next year President Theodore Roosevelt issued a charter that made Eagle the first incorporated city of the Interior.

Eagle reached its peak at the turn of the century, when it boasted a population of over 1500 residents and the overland telegraph wire was completed from Valdez in 1903. Some residents even went as far as to call their town 'the Paris of the North', though that was hardly the case.

Other gold strikes in the early 1900s, most notably at Fairbanks, began drawing residents away from Eagle and caused the removal of Judge Wickersham's court to the new city in the west. The Army fort was abandoned in 1911, and by the 1940s Eagle's population had dwindled to 10. When Taylor Highway was completed in the 1950s, however, the town's population bounced back up to its present levels.

Things to See

If you're spending a day in Eagle, the best way to see the town and learn its history is to be in front of Judge Wickersham's courthouse at the corner of B St and First Avenue at 10 am. The courthouse is now a museum managed by the Eagle Historical Society, which offers a free walking tour of the town daily during the summer, beginning at the front porch. The tour covers such historical and renovated buildings as the Eagle **City Hall**, where the city council continues to hold regular meetings; the **Customs Building Museum**; and the **post office** on the corner of A St and First Avenue, where a plaque commemorates explorer Roald Amundsen's visit to Eagle. The Norwegian explorer hiked overland to Eagle in 1905 after his ship froze in the Arctic Sea off Canada. From the town's telegraph office he sent word to the waiting world that he had just navigated the Northwest Passage. **Amundsen's cabin**, where he stayed for a spell, is another museum in Eagle.

To the north of town is **Fort Egbert**, which can be reached from Taylor Highway on 4th Avenue. The BLM has been involved in restoring the old army fort, which once contained 37 buildings; several are now open to visitors during the summer. Clustered together in one section of the fort are the restored mule barn, carriage house, dog house and officer's quarters.

Places to Stay

A few cabins are available for rent from *Eagle Frontier Services* (tel 547-2232), a gas station in town, but most people camp at the Eagle BLM Campground (13 sites, free). To reach it follow 4th Avenue, 0.7 mile (1.1 km) south of Eagle on Taylor Highway, north as it runs 1.5 miles (2.4 km) through Fort Egbert to the campground.

Paddling

Yukon River Float During its heyday Eagle was an important riverboat landing for traffic moving up and down the Yukon River. Today it is still a important departure point for the many paddlers who come to float the river through the

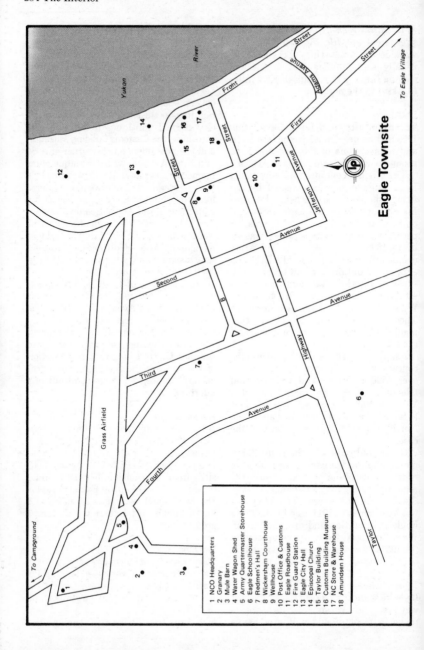

Eagle Townsite

1 NCO Headquarters
2 Granary
3 Mule Barn
4 Water Wagon Shed
5 Army Quartermaster Storehouse
6 Eagle Schoolhouse
7 Redmen's Hall
8 Wickersham Courthouse
9 Wellhouse
10 Post Office & Customs
11 Eagle Roadhouse
12 Fire Guard Station
13 Eagle City Hall
14 Episcopal Church
15 Taylor Building
16 Customs Building Museum
17 NC Store & Warehouse
18 Amundsen House

Yukon-Charley Rivers National Preserve. The 150-mile (240 km) trip extends from Eagle to Circle at the end of Steese Highway out of Fairbanks, and most paddlers plan on six to 10 days for the float. It is not a difficult paddle, but it must be planned carefully with air-taxi operators in order to shuttle boats, equipment and people from Circle.

Tatondak Outfitters (tel 547-2221) in Eagle rents rafts for $60 per day; the rafts will easily hold four people and their gear. The outfitters also run a flying service and will pick up rafters in Circle and return them to Eagle. Budget around $250 for the air service if you and your party can return in a Cessna 185.

For more on rentals and air service before you depart for Alaska, write to Tatondak at PO Box 55, Eagle, Alaska 99738. The National Park Service maintains an Eagle office (tel 547-2233) in a cabin across from the well-house to assist paddlers attempting this route. Write to the National Park Service (PO Box 64, Eagle, Alaska 99738) in advance for more information on travelling the Yukon River.

Fairbanks

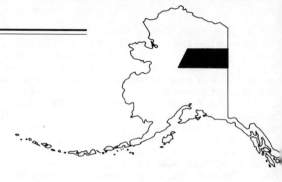

Everyone agrees that Fairbanks is 'extremely Alaska'. The Fairbanks Visitors Bureau made that expression the city's official slogan in a recent ad campaign, but Alaskans had already been saying it years.

Extremes are a way of life in the state's second largest city, with an area population of almost 60,000. On a quick pass through in the summer Fairbanks appears a spread-out, low-rise city with the usual hotels, shopping malls, McDonald's and a university tucked away on the outskirts of town. A second look reveals that this community is different, that the people and the place are one of a kind.

Fairbanks is log cabins, lots of them, from the heart of town to those hidden among the trees on the back roads. It is a semi-professional baseball team that plays games at midnight without the aid of artificial lights. It is a golf course that claims to be the 'world's most northernest', and a college campus where students and staff ski from classroom to classroom much of the year.

Extremely Alaska is the only way to describe Fairbanks weather. During the

summer it is pleasantly warm, with an average temperature of 70°F (21°C) and an occasional hot spell in August that breaks 90°F (32°C). It is long days when each day receives more than 20 hours of light from June to August; this peaks at almost 23 hours on 21 June.

In the winter, Fairbanks is at the other end of the meteorological chart. The temperature stays below 0°F (-18°C) for months and at least once drops to -60°F (-51°C) or even lower for days at a time. The days are short – sometimes as short as three or four hours – and the nights are cold. It's so cold in the winter that parking meters come equipped with electric plugs because cars have heaters around their engines. Beards and moustaches freeze into icicles in only minute at -60°F, and a glass of water thrown out of a second storey window shatters as ice when it hits the ground.

Consider the city's boom-or-bust economy for extremes. Fairbanks was founded in 1901, when E T Barnette was heading up the Tanana River with a boat load of supplies and was swept up by the fast waters of the Chena River. When he stepped ashore at the present site of 1st Avenue and Cushman St, he decided to stay. Fairbanks really came into its own when gold, the metal that gave birth to so many other Alaskan towns, was discovered by Italian prospector Felix Pedro 12 miles (19 km) north of Barnette's trading post. That happened in 1902, and in the next

286

two years a boom town sprang to life amid the hordes of miners stampeding into the area.

After the gold was panned and the mines were shut down, Fairbanks' growth slowed to a crawl. The Alaska Railroad and then WW II and the construction of the Alaska Highway were the next booms in the city's economy, but neither affected Fairbanks like the pipeline. After oil was discovered in Prudhoe Bay in 1968, Fairbanks was never the same. For four years, from 1973 to 1977, the town exploded at its seams as the principal gateway to the North Slope, where construction of the Alaska Pipeline was at its height. From all over the US and the world, workers came looking for four-digit weekly paycheques and filled every hotel room and tent site for miles around. Prices soared, lines at the supermarket became unbearable, and suddenly there were traffic jams in a town that had none before. During this boom everybody tried to profit. Prostitutes flocked to the city despite its winter temperatures. This was truly a twentieth century goldrush.

The aftermath of the pipeline days were just as extreme. The city shrank and unemployment crept towards 25% of the population. But like the weather, Fairbanks residents endured all this, and will endure in the future if a proposed gasline is put through. Fairbanks residents are a hardy and independent breed because they have to be. That, more than the log cabins or the midnight sun, is the city's trademark. The residents tend to be more colourful than most Alaskans, maybe a bit louder, a degree more boastful. They exemplify to the fullest the Alaskan theme of 'work hard, play hard, drink hard'. If you wander into a downtown bar and they seem like a friendly bunch willing to share a story and a drink, remember that the summers are short between those cold, dark winters.

Information
The main source of information is the Visitors Bureau Log Cabin (tel 456-5774) on the corner of 1st Avenue and Cushman St downtown. Among the many services not already mentioned is a recorded telephone message (tel 456-4636) that lists the daily events and attractions in town; a language bank for foreign travellers who need assistance from an interpreter; and an 80-page brochure with accommodation and restaurants written in German, French and Japanese as well as English. The log cabin is open daily during the summer from 8.30 am to 5 pm. Other visitors centres are located in Alaskaland, open daily from 11 am to 9 pm; and near the baggage claim of the Fairbanks International Airport, open daily from 1.30 to 10.30 pm.

Things to See
Fairbanks, the transportation hub for much of the Interior and Arctic Alaska, is a spread-out town that covers 31 square miles (80 square km). Downtown is hard to describe and even harder to recognise. Generally it is considered to be the area bounded by Airport Way to the south, Steese Highway to the east, Cowles St to the west and the banks of the Chena River to the north. Slicing this area in half from north to south is Cushman St, the closest thing Fairbanks has to a main street.

The best way to get oriented in Fairbanks is to begin at the **Visitors Bureau** log cabin (tel 456-5774) overlooking the Chena River on the corner of 1st Avenue and Cushman St. The centre is open daily from 8.30 am to 5 pm and has the usual handouts and maps of the city as well as the booklet *Ghosts Of The Gold Rush* which points out historical highlights of downtown. The staff also sponsors a guided historical walking tour that starts from the log cabin at 10 am and 3 pm daily if the weather is cooperating. The one-hour tour is free; the booklet is $1.50.

Two of the older buildings in the downtown area are churches. The **Immaculate Conception Church**, just across the Chena River Bridge from the

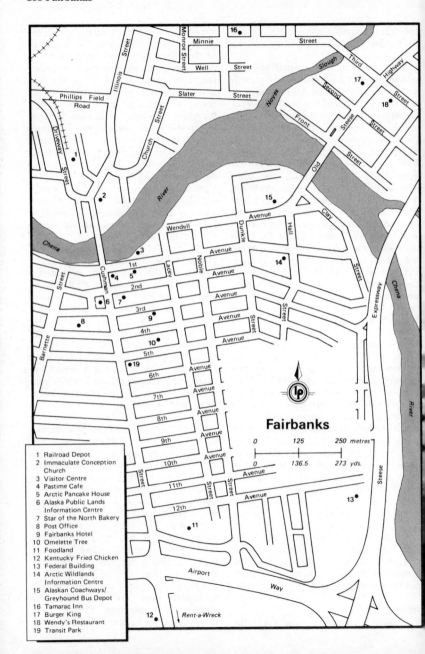

Fairbanks

0	125	250 metres
0	136.5	273 yds.

1 Railroad Depot
2 Immaculate Conception Church
3 Visitor Centre
4 Pastime Cafe
5 Arctic Pancake House
6 Alaska Public Lands Information Centre
7 Star of the North Bakery
8 Post Office
9 Fairbanks Hotel
10 Omelette Tree
11 Foodland
12 Kentucky Fried Chicken
13 Federal Building
14 Arctic Wildlands Information Centre
15 Alaskan Coachways/ Greyhound Bus Depot
16 Tamarac Inn
17 Burger King
18 Wendy's Restaurant
19 Transit Park

Top: Old miner's home at Circle Hot Springs (JD)
Bottom: Old cabin on the Pribilof Islands (ED)

Top: Sod hut in Barrow, Alaska (ADT)
Bottom: Riverboats on the Chena River in Fairbanks (ADT)

Visitors Bureau, was built in 1904 and was moved to its present location in 1911. The church is a National Historic Monument and features beautiful stained glass windows. **St Matthew's Episcopal Church**, at 1035 1st Avenue, is a unique log church built in 1905 which was rebuilt in 1947 immediately after it burned down.

Just south of the Visitors Bureau on the corner of Cushman St and 3rd Avenue is historic **Courthouse Square**. In the basement is the Alaska Public Lands Information Centre (tel 451-7352). The centre is a wealth of information on public lands and on federal and state parks and preserves. You can obtain maps and handouts on a variety of wilderness areas, parks and trails throughout Alaska as well as take in photo displays, historical exhibits, a variety of short videotapes and slide presentations in its auditorium.

Fairbanks has an excellent facility in the **Noel Wien Library** (tel 452-5177) on the corner of Airport Way and Cowles St (MACS bus No 20), a long walk from the Visitors Bureau. Along with a large Alaskana section, the library features an art exhibit and a stone fireplace, so it can be a warm place to be on a rainy day in Fairbanks. Hours are Monday to Wednesday from 10 am to 9 pm, Thursday and Friday 10 am to 6 pm, Saturday 10 am to 5 pm and Sunday 1 to 5 pm.

Don't overlook Fairbanks' outdoor art as you walk around downtown. In 1979, local artists painted murals on 20 buildings, ranging from abstract art to wildlife scenes, as part of a beautification programme. Most of them can be seen in a four-block section beginning at the Visitors Bureau, which has a free handout pointing out the murals.

Alaskaland The city's largest attraction is his 44-acre (18 hectare) pioneer theme park created in 1967 to commemorate the 100th year of American possession of Alaska. Inside are such historical displays as the *Nenana*, a former sternwheeler of

the Yukon River fleet; a street of log cabins relocated from downtown and now called Gold Rush Town; and the Pioneers of Alaska Museum. At the back of the park you'll find the Native Village Museum & Mining Valley, with displays of gold-mining equipment.

The entrance to the park is off Airport Way near Peger Rd. A free shuttle bus, made to look like a train, makes hourly runs each day between the Visitors Bureau and the park. You can also reach the park on MACS bus No 20. Alaskaland (tel 452-4529) is open daily from 11 am to 9 pm. Some visitors find it hokey, while others think it is an enjoyable step back into Alaska's history. Whatever you may think, you can't beat the price – there is no admission fee into the theme park.

University The University of Alaska-Fairbanks is the original and main campus of the statewide college and an interesting place to wander around for an afternoon. The school is four miles (6.4 km) from downtown Fairbanks in a beautiful and unusual setting for a college; it is on a hill that overlooks the surrounding area, and on a clear day it is possible to view Mt McKinley from marked vantage points. Stop at the distinct Wood Centre in the centre of campus first to pick up a map of the college. The building is the student centre and general meeting place on campus, as it provides a cafeteria, pub, game rooms, outdoor patio and showers and laundry service in the basement. There is also a ride board here for those trying to thumb to other parts of the state.

The main attraction of UA-F is the excellent University Museum, which houses native and pioneer artefacts as well as 'Blue Babe', a 36,000-year-old preserved bison. The museum is open daily in the summer from 9 am to 5 pm. On the outskirts of the campus is the Agricultural Experiment Farm, where the university dabbles in growing vegetables of mythical proportions.

Because of its lofty perch, the campus is the best place in Fairbanks to view Mt McKinley on a clear day. A pulloff and marker defining the mountainous horizon is at the south end of Yukon Drive. UA-F is also a good spot to view another polar phenomenon – the Northern Lights. The amazing colours that snake across the sky are best seen away from the centre of town in early or late summer. If you have never seen the Northern Lights before arriving in Fairbanks, be prepared. This far north they are so vivid and active they are bound to keep you up half the night watching them.

You can reach the campus by taking MACS bus Nos 10, 20 or 40 to the commuter terminal. From there, catch the university shuttle bus to the museum and upper portion of the college. Free tours of the experimental farm are offered once a week; days and times can be obtained by calling UA-F at 474-7581. Daily tours of the campus include the museum, library and Geophysical Institute. The campus tour begins at 10 am from the museum.

Pipeline The closest spot to view the Trans-Alaska Pipeline, where some 1.5 million barrels of oil flow daily on their way to Valdez, is eight miles (12.8 km) north of the city on Steese Highway. The turnoff is at Goldstream Rd.

Places to Stay

Youth Hostel The Fairbanks *Youth Hostel* has been on the move ever since the local chapter was organised in the early 1980s. In 1985, it was at the Tanana Valley Fairgrounds (MACS bus No 10) north of town off College Rd, where it consisted of an old military hut with an addition. Nightly rates were $3 for members and $5 for non-members. Plans call for another move, however, and in early 1987 the Youth Hostel hopes to occupy a permanent location at the Chena River State Campground (MACS bus Nos 20 or 70), on the corner of Airport and University.

When arriving in town, call the Alaska Division of Parks at 479-4114 to make sure of the hostel's location.

Hotels Hotel/motel rooms in Fairbanks are expensive even by Alaskan standards. The few with reasonable rates are less than desirable or are a considerable distance from downtown. Check out the room before handing over your money.

Close to the railroad depot and cheap is the *Fairbanks Hotel* (tel 456-6440) at 517 3rd Avenue. Singles without bath are $25 per night and doubles $31. The *Tamara Inn* (tel 456-6406), close to downtown, is north of the Chena River at 252 Minnie St. Singles run $35 and doubles $45, and some units come with cooking facilities.

Other places with good rates and clean rooms are some distance from downtown. *Monson Motel* (tel 479-6770) is near the International Airport on 1321 Karen St (MACS bus No 70) and offers single rooms at a weekly rate of $110 or doubles for $135. South of the university near the corner of Geist Rd and Fairbanks St (MACS bus No 20) is *Borealis Motel* (tel 479-6442), where singles without bath are $30 and doubles are $35. The *Aurora Motel* (tel 456-7361) at 2016 College Rd west of the Tanana State Fairground (MACS bus No 10) has rooms ($35 to $45) and cabins for rent.

Bed & Breakfast The *Fairbanks Bed & Breakfast* (tel 452-4967) is a reservation service for a number of private homes around the city that rent spare rooms to travellers. Plan on $40 to $60 per night for singles or doubles, and call ahead for reservations. The host will often meet you at the railroad depot or airport.

Camping The only public campground in the Fairbanks area is the *Chena River State Campground* (51 sites, free) of University Avenue just north of Airport Way. The campground offers tables, toilets, fireplaces and water, and can be reached by MACS bus Nos 20 or 70.

The other campgrounds in the city are private, and both charge around $9 per night to camp. They are *Tanana Valley Campground* (tel 456-7956) near the airgrounds on College Rd, and *Norlite Campground* (tel 452-4206) on Peger Rd just south of Airport Way and the entrance to Alaskaland. Both have showers and laundry facilities, but Tanana Valley provides more natural wooded surroundings for campers. Norlite is little more than an open field.

Places to Eat

Downtown The best sourdough pancakes in the city are at *Arctic Pancake House* across from the Visitors Bureau log cabin on 1st Avenue.

Other good places with inexpensive Alaskan prices for breakfast (from $4 to $6) are *Star of the North Bakery & Luncheonette* at 543 2nd Avenue, known for their great home-made donuts; and the *Omelette Tree* at 526 5th Avenue, where you can choose from 26 different kinds of egg dishes.

The *Sonshine Inn* at 419 2nd Avenue offers good meals and entertainment at night. The best Chinese food downtown is at *Tiki Cove*, 546 3rd Avenue, where complete dinners cost $10 to $15. For cheap Mexican dishes try the *Tio Taco* at 454 Cushman, south of Airport Way.

Around Town Hungry souls should take in the *Alaskaland Salmon Bake* (free shuttle bus from the Visitors Bureau), where for $12 you not only get grilled salmon but halibut, spare-ribs and trips to the salad bar.

There is a variety of eateries, including *McDonald's* in the Bentley Mall at College Rd and Old Steese Highway, and *Wendy's* nearby at 3rd St and 44th St.

Colleges always give rise to unique and reasonably priced restaurants, and UA-F is no exception. The best eatery near the campus is *Blue Marlin* at 3412 College Rd. The restaurant has an interesting interior with a fireplace and split-level seating. It serves beer and wine and offers excellent pizza, along with salads and sandwiches. At 3374 College Rd is *Food Factory* for cheap subs and sandwiches that can be enjoyed with your favourite beer. Near the corner of College and University Avenue is *Whole Earth Exchange* for bulk natural foods.

More chain restaurants such as *Dairy Queen*, *Big Boys*, *Taco Time* and another *McDonald's* can be found along University Avenue and Airport Way on your way into downtown Fairbanks.

The best place in the area to turn dinner into an evening is *The Pumphouse* two miles (3.2 km) from downtown on Chena Pump Rd. The Pumphouse, once used in the gold-mining era, is now a national historical site that houses a restaurant and saloon. The atmosphere is unique; inside and out there are artefacts and relics from the golden past. Dinners cost from $12 to $20, or you can go there simply to enjoy a drink while taking in the boat traffic on the Chena River.

Nightlife

The bar-rooms are the best place to meet locals in Fairbanks, and it seems you never have to travel far to find one. Rowdy saloons that are throwbacks to the mining days are the area's specialty. *Palace Saloon* at Alaskaland is alive at night with honky-tonk piano, turn-of-the-century can-can dancers and other acts on its newly enlarged stage. The *Malemute Saloon*, seven miles (11.2 km) west of Fairbanks in Ester, also offers ragtime piano and vaudeville acts, but has made a ritual out of reading Robert Service poetry. There are two shows nightly, 9 and 10.30 pm, at this tour-bus haven.

Other lively establishments on the outskirts of Fairbanks are *Senator's Saloon* at the Pumphouse on Chena Pump Rd, *Ivory Jack's* on Goldstream Rd, and the *Howling Dog Saloon* in Fox at the intersection of Steese and Elliott highways 12 miles (19.2 km) north of downtown. All have live music or entertainment. The Howling Dog is the stage for rock & roll bands and an occasional volleyball game played out the back under the midnight sun.

Live music and a college atmosphere are found at the *University Pub* in the Woods Centre at UA-F. In the downtown area, try *Kennedy's Pub* for country music; or try *The Big I Bar*, the local hang-out for city workers and reporters from the *Daily News-Miner*. Both bars are north of the Chena River near the railroad depot on North Turner Rd.

Events

The Goldpanners is Fairbanks' entry in Alaska League Baseball, in which a six-team league of top college and amateur players from around the country compete each summer. More then 80 professionals have played in the Alaska League, including Tom Seaver of the Chicago White Sox and Dave Winfield of the New York Yankees. Games are played at Growden Memorial Park West on 2nd Avenue and tickets are $3 per person.

A variety of free summer concerts takes place in Bicentennial Park on Cushman Avenue, all beginning at 7 pm. Call the Visitors Bureau's 24-hour message on current events (456-4636) for dates of concerts or home baseball games. A quieter and more relaxing evening can be had at Three-D Steam Bath (tel 456-6740) at 308 Wendell, where you'll find old-fashioned steam rooms for two. The place is open to 10 pm daily and until 11 pm Friday and Saturday; the cost is $6 per person or $10 per couple.

Golden Days has grown to be Fairbanks' largest celebration of the summer. Staged during the third week in July, the festival commemorates Felix Pedro's discovery of gold with parades, games, booths, a boat parade on the Chena River and numerous special events. The summer solstice is also well celebrated on 21 June, when the sun shines gloriously for almost 23 hours.

Events include arts and crafts booths, foot races, speedboat races and the traditional Midnight Sun baseball game pitting the Goldpanners against anothe Alaska rival.

Around the second week in August, the Tanana Valley Fair is held at the fair grounds on College Rd. It features a midway, a rodeo, entertainment, and the usual livestock shows and large produce.

Hiking

Two of the best trails in the state are north of Fairbanks and are administered by the BLM. At *Mile 27* (43 km) of Elliot Highway is the four to five-day White Mountain Trail. The trailheads for the even more impressive Pinnell Trail are a *Mile 85.5* (137 km) and *Mile 107.3* (17? km) of Steese Highway (see the Wilderness chapter for both trails). Contact the BLM office in Fairbanks at 356-2025 for more information, trail conditions and availability of the three public-use cabins they rent out.

Creamer's Field Trail A self-guided, two mile (3.2 km) trail winds through Creamer's Field Migratory Wildlife Refuge an old dairy farm that has since become an Audubon bird-lover's paradise, a more than 100 species of bird pass through each year. The refuge is at 1300 College Rd (MACS bus No 10) and the trailhead is in the parking lot adjacent to the Alaska Department of Fish & Game office, where trail guides are available.

Chena Lakes Recreation Area The new facility opened in 1984 as the last phase of an Army Corps of Engineers flood contro project prompted by the Chena Rive flooding of Fairbanks in 1967. Two separate parks, Chena River and Chena Lakes, make up the recreational area and are 18 miles (28.8 km) from Fairbank past North Pole, off the Laurance Rd exi of Richardson Highway. The river park contains a 2.5-mile (four km) self-guided nature trail. The lake park offers swim ning and canoe, sailboat and paddleboat rentals. Between the two parks there are three campground loops providing 78 sites. The day-use fee is $3 and the overnight camping fee is $5. MACS bus No 50 runs past the recreation area on its way to Eielson Air Force Base.

Granite Tors Trail Tors are isolated pinnacles of granite popping out of the tundra. A fine set can be seen from this eight-mile (12.8 km) trail. The trailhead is at the Mile 39 Campground in the Chena River State Recreation Area on Chena Hot Springs Rd, and can be reached by following the levee for a short distance on the west side of the stream. The first set of tors is reached in six miles (9.6 km); the best grouping lies another two miles (3.2 km) away. MACS bus No 30 makes two runs out Chena Hot Springs Rd but turns around at *Mile 24* (38.4 km).

Angel Creek Ridge Trail The trailhead is at *Mile 51* (81.6 km) of Chena Hot Springs Rd. A trail/route follows the ridge for almost 30 miles (48 km) around the Angel Creek Drainage. The trail makes an excellent backpacking trip that provides good alpine hiking with scenic views.

Cabins
Fred Blixt Cabin The public-use cabin is off *Mile 62* (99 km) of Elliott Highway, 10 miles (16 km) before the junction with North Slope Haul Rd. A short spur leads from the road to the cabin, which should be reserved in advance through the BLM office in Fairbanks. The rental fee is $5. *Cripple Creek Cabin* The old trapper's cabin, renovated by the BLM in 1972, is at *Mile 60.5* (96.8 km) of Steese Highway. It is between the highway and the Chatanika River and is reached by a short trail. The cabin, available only from mid-August to mid-May, does not offer a truly isolated setting because Cripple Creek Campground and a YCC Camp are nearby. Still, the surrounding area is

scenic. The rental fee is $5 and the unit should be reserved in advance through the Fairbanks BLM office.

Paddling
Fairbanks offers a wide variety of canoeing opportunities – both leisurely afternoon paddles and overnight trips into the surrounding area. There is an almost equal number of rental places where single-day charges run between $15 and $25 for the boat. For travellers without transportation, three of the rental places are conveniently located near water, avoiding problems of how to get the boat from the store to the dock. They include Beaver Sports (tel 479-2494) at 2400 College Rd; Alaska Raft (tel 456-1851) at 520 Front St, which rents rafts and inflatable canoes; and Chena River Floats (tel 455-6502), which rents inflatable canoes by the hour near the Alaskaland boat dock.

Around Town An afternoon can be spent paddling the Chena River, whose mild currents let you paddle upstream as well as down. You can launch a canoe from almost any bridge crossing the river, including the Graehl St Landing near the north side of Steese Highway, where locals like to paddle upstream and then float back down.

At Alaskaland you can rent a canoe from Chena River Floats and paddle down to The Pumphouse for lunch or dinner. From Beaver Sports, you can put your rented canoe in quiet Noyes Slough and paddle east to Graehl Landing, then west along the Chena River through downtown before paddling back up the Slough. The round trip is a 13-mile (21 km) paddle.

Tanana River Those looking for an overnight or even longer paddle should check into a float down the Chena River from the east (see the Wilderness chapter) or a pleasant two-day trip down the Tanana River. This popular trip usually begins

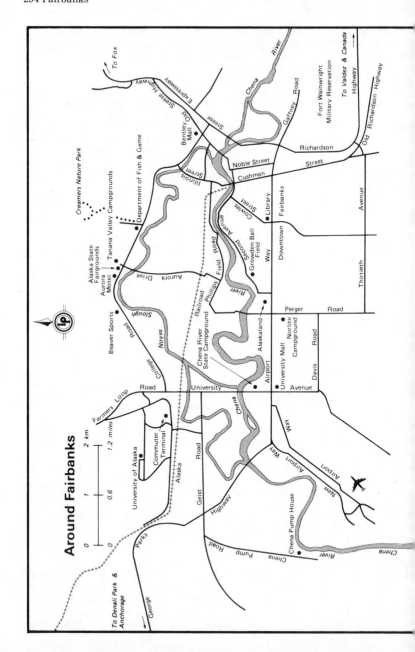

Around Fairbanks

from the end of Chena Pump Rd and terminates in the town of Nenana, where it is possible to return with your canoe to Fairbanks on the Alaska Railroad. The 60-mile (100 km) trip could be done in a single day but would require 10 to 12 hours of paddling.

Chatanika River If you depart from Cripple Creek BLM Campground at *Mile 60* (96.6km) of Steese Highway, this river can be paddled 28 miles (45 km); it parallels the road to Chatanika River State Campground at *Mile 39* (62.8 km). From here the trip could be extended another 17 miles (27 km) to a bridge at *Mile 11* (17.7 km) of Elliott Highway. The river is not a difficult paddle but requires considerable driving because you have to shuttle boats and people between Fairbanks and the two highways. Many locals get around this by paddling only the upper portion that parallels Steese Highway and chaining a bicycle at the end so they can get back to their car.

Outfitters

Check the Wilderness chapter for the list of the many outfitters based in the Fairbanks area. A few offer single-day canoe trips down either the Chena or Chatanika rivers for $75 per person. They usually include your board, lunch, dinner and transportation. A two-day trip cost $150. Contact Gen Bull Moose Canoe Tours (tel 479-4061) or Rafting Alaska (tel 452-7715) about such trips.

Tours

Both Gray Line (Fairbanks Inn, tel 456-7741) and Alaska Sightseeing (Captain Bartlett Hotel, tel 452-8518) offer a three-hour city tour for $17 that includes UA-F, Gold Dredge No 8 on Steese Highway and the Trans-Alaska Pipeline. The tour is scheduled twice daily at 9.30 am and 2.30 pm in small mini-buses. Gray Line offers the cheaper of the two Malemute Saloon tours. It departs at 8 am from Tuesday to Sunday for $18.

You can travel the Chena River on the historic sternwheeler *Discovery* if you're up to parting with $22.50 for the four-hour trip. The boat departs twice daily at 8.45 am and 2 pm in the summer from Discovery Landing, located off the Dale Rd exit at *Mile 4.5* (7.2 km) of Airport Way.

Getting Around

Airport For those arriving at the airport, you can catch MACS bus No 70 outside the terminal for a ride downtown. The public bus runs eight times daily, six days a week and costs $1. There is also limousine service which costs $6 per person for a trip downtown.

Bus Metropolitan Area Commuter Service (MACS) provides local bus transportation throughout the Fairbanks area from Monday to Saturday; there is no service on Sunday. The fare is $1 or a token which can be purchased in advance for 75c from a variety of businesses near or at the Transit Park on the corner of Cushman St and 5th Avenue downtown. The park is the central terminal for the system because all bus routes pass through here. Two of the longer routes take you to *Mile 24* (38.4 km) of Chena Hot Springs Rd for a scenic ride (bus No 30), or south-east past North Pole and Chena lakes to Eielson Air Force Base (bus No 50). For more information contact the MACS office (tel 452-6623) at 3175 Peger Rd or call their Transit Hotline (452-3279) that gives daily bus information.

Car Rental For small travelling parties, splitting the cost of a used car rental is the best and often the cheapest way to see the outlying areas of Fairbanks or to venture to such places as Arctic Circle Hot Springs and Circle on Steese Highway or Manly Hot Springs at the end of Elliott Highway. Rent-A-Wreck (tel 456-8459) at 2105 Cushman, south of Airport Way, has used cars for $14 per day and 14c a mile. Rent-A-Dent (tel 452-3368) at 1408

Turner St offers something in the same range plus a weekly rate of $95 plus 14c a mile. At those prices, a three-day drive to Arctic Circle Hot Springs would run a total of around $90 (including insurance and mileage) that could be divided by up to four people.

Bicycle Three-speed bicycles can be rented at either Alaskaland or from Chena River Floats (tel 455-6502) behind the Visitors Bureau log cabin downtown. Rentals go for $3 per hour and you can get a bike trail map from the Visitors Bureau.

One of the better day trips on a bike is to peddle Farmer's Loop Rd from University Avenue north of UA-F to Steese Highway for scenic views of the city and the surrounding valley.

Getting There

Air The recently enlarged Fairbanks International Airport serves as the gateway for supplies and travellers heading into the Brooks Range and Arctic Alaska. It is almost four miles (6.4 km) south-west of the city and is reached off Airport Way. It is impressive inside, with wall hangings, wildlife displays and Ben Eielson's bi-plane hanging from the ceiling.

Alaska Airlines (tel 452-1661) provides five daily flights to Anchorage, where there are connections to the rest of the state as well as a direct flight between Fairbanks and Seattle. One-way standard fare (the most expensive) to Anchorage is $111.

The other intra-state airline is Mark Air (tel 452-7577), which has three direct flights to Anchorage for the same fare as well as flights to Barrow. Northwest Orient (tel 456-2223) and Japan Airlines (tel 452-6504), among others, also fly out of Fairbanks. A number of air-taxi operators have regularly-scheduled flights and also make mail flights to small communities in the Bush. Frontier Flying Service (tel 452-1014) has flights almost daily to Eagle, Bettles and Anaktuvu Pass.

Rail The Alaska Railroad (tel 456-4155) has an express train departing Fairbanks daily at 10.30 am during the summer except on Thursday and Sunday. The train reaches Denali National Park around 2 pm and Anchorage at 8 pm. On Saturday and Sunday a local train making all stops, departs Fairbanks at 10.30 am. The railroad depot is at 280 North Cushman St, a short walk from the Chena River. One-way fare to Denali National Park is $29.50 and to Anchorage is $78.25.

Bus From Fairbanks, Alaska-Yukon Motorcoaches (tel 452-8518) depart from the Golden Nugget Motel at 900 Noble St daily for Denali and Anchorage at 9.30 am. The company also has a bus departing on Wednesday at 10 am for Tok and then on to Haines. One-way fare to Denali is $25, Anchorage $55 and Haines $250, which does not include accommodation for the overnight stops.

Yukon Stage Lines (tel 456-2299) in conjunction with Norline Coaches depart Fairbanks on Tuesday and Saturday at am for Tok and then for Whitehorse where connections can be made to Skagway or Haines. One-way fare to Tok is $37 and to Whitehorse $93, but double check this company first before depending on its service. Kak Tours (tel 488-2649) provides van service to Arctic Circle Hot Springs and access to the Pinnell Trail during the summer. A round-trip ticket to the springs costs $60.

Hitch-hiking Thumbing is made much easier by jumping on a MACS bus first. Those heading towards Denali National Park and Anchorage on George Parks Highway should take bus No 20 and get off at the corner of Geist and the highway. To head down Richardson Highway towards Delta Junction and the Alcan take bus No 50 to Eielson Air Force Base f you are heading north on Chena Hot Springs Rd, Steese Highway or Elliott Highway, take bus No 30.

HOT SPRINGS
Back around the turn of the century, when gold prospectors were stooping in near-freezing creeks panning for gold, there was one saving grace in the area – the hot springs. There are three of them north of Fairbanks and all were quickly discovered and used by the miners as a brief escape from Alaska's ice and cold. Today the same mineral water – ranging from 120° to 150°F (50° to 65°C) – soothes the aches and pains of frigid travellers passing by. The hot springs include Chena Hot Springs, 56 miles (90 km) east of Fairbanks, Arctic Circle Hot Springs, 135 miles (216 km) north-east on Steese Highway, and Manly Hot Springs, 152 miles (245 km) west on Elliott Highway. There is now mini-bus transportation to Arctic Circle and Chena Hot Springs out of Fairbanks, but the cheapest way to get there, even if there are only two of you, is to rent a used car and drive yourself (see the Getting Around section).

The springs are described in the following sections on Chena Hot Springs Rd and Steese and Elliott highways.

Chena Hot Springs Road

Chena Hot Springs Rd extends 56 miles (90 km) to the hot springs of the same name. The road is paved and in good condition. The resort, the closest of the three to Fairbanks, is also the most developed, as it has been turned into a year-round facility offering downhill skiing in the winter. From *Mile 26* (41.6 km) to *Mile 51* (81.6 km), the road passes through the middle of the Chena River State Recreation Area, a 254,080-acre (102,823 hectare) preserve containing the river valley and the surrounding alpine areas. This is a scenic park that offers good hiking (see above Hiking section), fishing and two public campgrounds. The first is Mile 27 Campground (40 sites, free) at *Mile 27* (43.5 km) of the road, while further to the east is Mile 39 Campground (20 sites, free) near the trailhead for the Granite Tors Trail.

CHENA HOT SPRINGS
At the end of the road is *Chena Hot Springs Resort*, which offers a variety of accommodation and activities during the summer. The most popular activity is hot-tub soaking, done indoors where there are several tubs and pools of various temperatures. The resort has a restaurant and bar. Hotel rooms with half baths begin at $48 for singles; rustic cabins begin at $43. The resort also maintains a campground and charges $5 per couple to pitch a tent. The use of the hot tubs would be an additional $5 per day for each camper.

Getting There Hitch-hiking is not the grand effort it is on Steese or Elliott highways because of the heavy summer usage of Chena River State Recreation Area. Van service to the hot springs is offered by Tours Unlimited (tel 456-1948) in Fairbanks, which charges $25 per person round trip. A used rental car for a two-day trip to the springs would cost between $45 and $50.

Steese Highway

Arctic Circle Hot Springs lies off the 162-mile (261 km) Steese Highway, a miner's trail at one time where today you can still see the signs of old mining camps as well as new ones. The road is paved for the first 44 miles (71 km) and then consists of a good gravel base until the final 30 miles (48 km), where it narrows and becomes considerably rougher. The excellent scenery along the highway and the good accommodation at Arctic Circle Hot Springs make this side trip well worth the time and money travellers put out for it.

The highway starts in Fairbanks, *Mile 0*, at the junction with Airport Way and Richardson Highway. From there it passes the beginning of Chena Hot Springs Rd at *Mile 4.6* (7.4 km) and then Elliott Highway at *Mile 11* (17.7 km), near the service centre of Fox. The golden past of Steese Highway can first be seen at *Mile 9.5* (15.3 km), where it passes the Goldstream Rd exit to Gold Dredge No 8, a five-deck, 250-foot (76 metre) dredge built in 1928 that was named a National Historical Site in 1984. The dredge is privately owned; the cost is $5 to tour it and pan for gold.

At *Mile 16.6* (26.7 km), on the right-hand side of the highway, is a monument to Felix Pedro, whose discovery of gold nearby resulted in the boom town that was to become Fairbanks. Amateur gold panners are often in the nearby stream 'looking for colour'.

The first public campground is Upper Chatanika River State Campground (25 sites, free) along the river at *Mile 39* (63 km). Water and firewood are usually available, but have your bug dope handy – this is mosquito country. The next campground is Cripple Creek BLM Campground (21 sites, free) at *Mile 60* (96.6 km), the site of the uppermost access point to the Chatanika River canoe trail (see Paddling section above). The campground features tables, water and a nature trail nearby.

Access points for the Pinnell Mountain Trail (see the Wilderness chapter) lie at *Mile 85.6* (138 km) and *Mile 107* (172 km). Eagle Summit, elevation 3624 feet (1105 metres), is at *Mile 108* (173.8 km), where a 0.8-mile (1.3 km) trail leads to the top. Eagle Summit is the highest point along Steese Highway, and near 21 June (summer solstice) the midnight sun can be observed skimming the horizon. The

summit is also near a caribou migration route. The last campground before Central is Bedrock Creek BLM Campground (eight sites, free) just beyond *Mile 119* (190.4 km).

Birch Creek Canoe Route

The route begins at *Mile 94* (150.4 km) of Steese Highway, where a short road leads down to a canoe launch on the creek. The wilderness trip is a 140-mile (224 km) paddle to the exit point at *Mile 147* (236.6 km) of the highway. The overall rating of the river is Class II, but there are some Class III and Class IV parts that require lining your canoe. More details on the trip can be obtained from the Fairbanks BLM office (tel 356-2025). Ask for their brochure entitled *Alaska's River Trails – Northern Region*.

ARCTIC CIRCLE HOT SPRINGS

At *Mile 127.5* (205 km), the highway reaches Central (population 800 in the summer) where there is petrol, groceries, a post office, cabins for rent and a BLM information office.

Just beyond the town, Circle Hot Springs Rd heads south and in six miles (9.6 km) passes Ketchem Creek BLM Campground (seven sites, free), where the campsites are on both sides of the river with a footbridge connecting them. Two miles (3.2 km) beyond is *Arctic Circle Hot Springs Resort* (tel 520-5113), first used by miners in 1905 and today a popular spot with Fairbanks residents. The year-round resort maintains an Olympic-sized pool in which 139°F (59°C) mineral water is pumped through at a rate of 386 gallons a minute. There is also a restaurant, hotel and the *Miner's Saloon*. Singles cost $35, doubles $50 and dormitory bunks only $15 per night.

Getting There Hitch-hiking, needless to say, is considerably more difficult on Steese Highway, but not impossible. Beyond renting a used car, there is the van service offered by Kak Tours (tel 488-

2649); a round-trip ticket costs $60 per person.

CIRCLE

Beyond Central, Steese Highway passes the exit point of the Birch Creek canoe route at *Mile 147* (237 km) and ends at Circle (population 70) at *Mile 162* (260.7 km).

Circle is an interesting little wilderness town that lies on the banks of the Yukon River and was the northernmost point you could drive to before North Slope Haul Rd was opened up. A large sign in the centre of town still proclaims this fact. The town is 50 miles (80 km) south of the Arctic Circle, but miners who established it in 1896 thought they were near the imaginary line and gave Circle its present name.

After gold was discovered on Birch Creek, Circle was a bustling log cabin city of 1200 and boasted two theatres, a music hall, eight dance halls and 28 saloons. The Klondike reduced the town to the wilderness hamlet it remains today.

A city-operated campground at the end of Steese Highway consists of tables, out-houses and a grassy area along the banks of the Yukon where you can pitch your tent. Nearby is the Yukon Trading Post, which includes a general store with Arctic Alaska prices, café, bar and motel. The bar is an especially important spot because this is the only place you can go at night (other than your car) to escape the wave of mosquitoes that will attack.

Elliott Highway

From the crossroads of Fox, Elliott Highway extends 152 miles (244.6 km) north and then west to Manly Hot Springs, a small settlement near the Tanana River. The first 28 miles (45 km) are paved and the rest is gravel; sections past the junction with North Slope Haul Rd are often narrow and steep. At *Mile 28* (24 km) are the trailhead, parking lot and information box for the White Mountain Trail to the Borealis LeFevre Cabin (see the Wilderness chapter), a one-way hike of 19 miles (30.6 km).

Tolovana River BLM Campground (seven sites, free) at *Mile 57* (91.7 km) is the only public campground on the highway. The facility, situated along the river where there is good fishing for grayling and northern pike, provides tables and out-houses but no drinking water. The mosquitoes here are of legendary proportions.

At *Mile 71* (114 km) is the service centre of Livengood, where you will find a café and cabins for rent. At this point Elliott Highway swings to a more westerly direction and in two miles (3.2 km) passes the junction with North Slope Haul Rd (see the Bush chapter). From here it is another 78 miles (125 km) to Manly Hot Springs.

MANLY HOT SPRINGS

The town, which has a summer population of 150 or so, is on the west side of Hot Springs Slough, and provides a public campground ($2 per night fee) near the bridge that crosses the slough. Within town, the Manly Trading Post serves as post office, gas station and grocery store.

The *Manly Roadhouse* (tel 672-3161) offers rooms, a restaurant and a bar. The hot springs are in private hands and are presently being developed, presumably to follow the same commercial course as those at Chena Hot Springs and Circle. Until they are officially opened up, soaks can still be arranged at the bath house. The hot springs are a short walk from the campground and can be reached by taking the third left after crossing the bridge over the slough.

The Bush

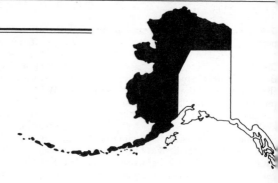

The Bush, the wide rim of wilderness that encircles Anchorage, Fairbanks and all the roads between the two, constitutes a vast majority of the state's area, yet only a trickle of tourists ventures into the region for a first-hand look at rural Alaska.

More than the great mountains or the mighty rivers, cost is the barrier that isolates the Bush. For budget-minded travellers who reach the Great White North with their thumbs and their backpacks, what lies out in the Bush is usually beyond the reach of their pocket-books. Except in a few cases, flying is the only way to an area, often in small chartered planes. Once out there, facilities can be sparse and what is available is very expensive.

Those who do endure the high expenses and extra travel to the outer reaches are blessed with a land and people that have changed little from one era to the next. The most pristine wilderness lies in the many newly created national parks and preserves found away from the road system – parks where there are no visitors centres, campgrounds or shuttle buses running trips into the backcountry. Only nature herself, in all her grandeur, is there to encounter. Traditional villages, where subsistence is still the means of survival, and hearty homesteaders, as independent and ingenious as they come, lie hidden throughout rural Alaska.

There are three general areas in Bush Alaska. Southwest Alaska consists of the Alaska Peninsula, the Aleutian Islands and the rich salmon grounds of Bristol Bay. The Alaska Peninsula extends 550 miles (880 km) from the west shore of Cook Inlet to its tip at False Pass. From there the Aleutian Islands, a chain of over 200, curve another 1100 miles (1800 km) into the Pacific Ocean, lying closer to Hawaii than California does. These areas are trademarked by active and dormant volcanoes, treeless terrain and the worst weather in the state. Alaska's outlying arm is where the arctic waters of the Bering Sea meet the warm Japanese Current, causing considerable cloudiness, rain and fog. Violent storms sweeping across the Pacific add high winds to the area. The major attractions of the region are Katmai National Park & Preserve at the beginning of the Alaska Peninsula, Lake Clark National Park & Preserve across Cook Inlet from Homer, and McNeil River State Game Sanctuary.

Due north is Western Alaska, the flat, treeless plain that borders the Bering Sea north of the Alaska Peninsula to beyond Kotzebue and the Arctic Circle. The flatland is broken up by millions of lakes and slow-moving rivers such as the Yukon, while the weather in the summer is that of cool temperatures, cloudiness and considerable fog and drizzle. The most-visited parts of this region are the towns of Nome and Kotzebue and the Pribilof Islands, north of the Aleutians in the Bering Sea and the location of seal-breeding grounds and bird rookeries.

The third area in the Bush is Arctic Alaska, also known as the North Slope; it lies north of the Arctic Circle. Here the Brooks Range slopes gradually to the north, eventually replaced by tundra plains that end at the Arctic Ocean. The harsh climate and short summers produce 400 species of plants in the treeless tundra that are often dwarfed versions of those further south. Wildlife in the form of polar bears, reindeer, caribou, wolves and brown bears have adapted amazingly well to the rough conditions. The region is characterised by nightless summers and dayless winters.

In Barrow, the northernmost village, the midnight sun never sets from May through to August. Surprisingly, the winters are often milder than those in the Interior. Not surprisingly though, the summers are cool at best and temperatures are rarely warmer than 45°F (8°C).

Within the North Slope region the native town of Barrow attracts a small number of tourists each summer, and backpackers have discovered that Gates of the Arctic National Park & Preserve makes an expensive but intriguing place for a wilderness adventure.

The following places are somewhat geared to tourists, with formal accommodation available most of the time. Still, it is best to be completely self-sufficient whether you are venturing into a new wilderness preserve or into a traditional village set in its ways.

Don't just pick out a village and fly directly to it. It is wise to either have a contact there (someone you know, a guide company or a wilderness lodge) or to travel with someone who does know someone. Although the natives, especially the Eskimos, are generally very hospitable people, there can be much tension and suspicion of strangers in small, isolated rural communities.

Southwest Alaska

There are two ways to see a small part of the Bush without flying. One of them is to drive North Slope Haul Rd. The other is to hop onto the State Marine Ferry when it makes its special run four times each summer along the Alaska Peninsula to the eastern end of the Aleutian Islands. Around 12 May, 9 June, 7 July and 15 September (dates vary slightly from year to year) the *MV Tustumena* continues west to Sand Point, King Cove, Cold Bay and Dutch Harbor on Unalaska Island before back-tracking to Kodiak. The ferry trip is a six-day cruise; the *MV Tustumena*, one of the oldest vessels in the state-operated fleet, leaves Kodiak on Tuesday, returns early Sunday morning and continues on to Seward that day. The boat docks at the villages only long enough to load and unload (one to two hours), but it is sufficient time to get off for a quick look around. On board are dormitory rooms, a cafeteria and a bar.

Round-trip fare for walk-ons to Dutch Harbor from Kodiak is $274; from Seward it is $346. The cruise is interesting and by far the cheapest way to see this section of Alaska, but those with weak stomachs should be warned that the boat ride often gets rough, especially during the September run when it is frequently hit by the stormy autumn weather. For those who want to spend more time at a village, Reeve Aleutian Airways (tel 243-4700 in Anchorage) runs prop-jet service to all the islands as well as the Pribilof Islands and the Alaska Peninsula.

KING COVE
The native town of 460 residents is a commercial fishing base at the western end of the Alaska Peninsula near the entrance of Cold Bay. Surrounded by mountains, King Cove supports a store and a busy harbour during the summer but no restaurants, lodges or campgrounds. Reeve Aleutian Airways charges $225 for

a one-way ticket between King Cove and Anchorage.

COLD BAY

On the west shore of Cold Bay is the town of the same name. The 230 residents are made up mostly of government workers, as the town is a major refueling stop for many flights crossing the Pacific to or from the Orient.

The town also serves as the gateway to the Izembek National Wildlife Refuge, which was established in 1960 to protect some 142 species of birds, primarily the black brant. Almost the entire North American population of brant, some 200,000 of them, arrive in spring and autumn to feed on large eelgrass beds during their annual migration. A 10-mile (16 km) road runs from the town to the Izembek Lagoon; otherwise, travel in the refuge is by foot or plane. Contact the Wildlife Refuge office in Cold Bay (Pouch 2, Cold Bay, Alaska 88571) for more information. Within town there is lodging, meals and groceries. Reeve Aleutian Airways services the community and charges $217 for a one-way ticket from Anchorage.

UNALASKA & DUTCH HARBOR

Unalaska on Unalaska Island and its sister town Dutch Harbor on Amaknak Island – both in the Aleutian chain – lie deep in Unalaska Bay and are connected to each other by a 500-foot (152 metre) bridge. During the summer the population of the two towns can easily exceed 2000, due to the influx of cannery workers who work the plants that process seafood, most notably crab. In 1978, the towns earned more from fishing than any other US port.

The area began as a military development in 1942 when the US Navy established a base at Dutch Harbor; at one time 60,000 servicemen were stationed there. In June 1942 the Japanese opened their Aleutian Islands campaign by bombing Dutch Harbor, and then took

Attu and Kiska islands in the only foreign invasion of American soil during WW II.

Facilities in the two towns include two lodges, restaurants, bars and grocery stores. Reeve Aleutian Airways services the two towns and charges $224 for a one-way ticket to Anchorage.

KATMAI NATIONAL PARK

In June 1912, violent volcanic eruptions and tremors rocked the area now known as Katmai National Park & Preserve, turning wilderness into a dynamic landscape of smoking valleys, ash-covered mountains and small holes and cracks (fumaroles) fuming with steam and gas. After a 1915 scientific exploration trip that revealed the spectacular results of the eruptions to the rest of the world, the area was turned into a national monument in 1918. In 1980, it was enlarged to 3.9 million acres (1.6 million hectares) and redesignated a national park and preserve.

Although the fumaroles no longer smoke and hiss, the park is still a diverse and scenic wilderness, unlike any in Alaska. It changes from glaciated volcanoes and ash-covered valleys to island-studded lakes and a coastline of bays, fjords and beaches. Wildlife is abundant, with more than 30 species of mammals, including large populations of brown bears that sometimes tip the scales past 1000 lb (450 kg). Katmai is also a prime habitat for moose, sea lions, arctic fox and wolves. The many streams and lakes are known around the state as some of the best for rainbow and salmon fishing.

The weather in the park is best from mid-June through to the end of July. Unfortunately this is also when mosquitoes, always heavy in this part of the state, are at their peak. For hiking and backpacking trips the best time is mid-August to early September, when the autumn colours are brilliant, the berries ripe and juicy and the insects scarce.

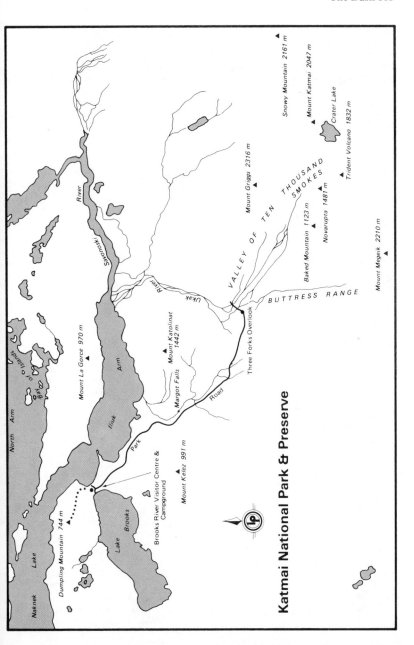

Katmai National Park & Preserve

However, be prepared for frequent storms. You should be ready for rain and foul weather any time in Katmai. Bring warm clothing, as the summer temperatures are in the low 60s F (around 15°C).

Permits

Visits to the game sanctuary are on a permit basis only. Write to the Alaska Department of Fish & Game, 333 Raspberry Rd, Anchorage, Alaska 99502, for an application. Return it with $5 by 1 May for a 15 May lottery drawing. Permits are drawn for only 10 persons a day between 1 July and 25 August.

Information

Katmai is usually not a last-minute place to see. Because of the cost involved in reaching the park, most visitors plan to spend at least four days or more to justify the expenses.

To contact the park beforehand write to: Katmai National Park, PO Box 7, King Salmon, Alaska 99613; (tel 246-3305). In the US, use the toll-free numbers to Mark Air, 1 (800) 426-6784, and Katmailand, 1 (800) 544-0551, for advance reservations. Katmailand is the concessionaire that handles the lodge and canoe rentals.

Brooks Camp

The summer headquarters for Katmai National Park is on the shores of Naknek Lake, six miles (9.6 km) from King Salmon. Facilities here include *Brooks Lodge* where a cabin for two costs $99 per night, a free campground and a restaurant.

A store sells limited supplies of freeze-dried food and campstove fuel; it also rents tents, stoves and canoes. The canoes go for $30 per day or $5 per hour and there is some excellent paddling in the area (see the Wilderness chapter). Scheduled throughout the summer at the park headquarters are naturalist-led walks and evening campfire programmes.

Dumpling Mountain Trail

The only developed trail from Brooks Camp is a half-day trek to the top of Dumpling Mountain, elevation 2520 feet (769 metres). The trail leaves the ranger station and heads north past the campground, climbing 1.5 miles (2.4 km) to a scenic overlook. It then continues another two miles (3.2 km) to the mountain's summit, where there are superb views of the surrounding lakes.

Backcountry

Hiking and canoeing are the best ways to see the unusual backcountry (see the Wilderness chapter). Like Denali National Park, Katmai has few formal trails; backpackers follow river bars, lake shores, gravel ridges and other natural routes. Many hiking trips begin with a ride on the park bus along the dirt road to the Valley of 10,000 Smokes.

The only road in Katmai is 23 miles (37 km) long and ends at Overlook Cabin, where there is a sweeping view of the area. On its daily run, each bus carries a ranger who leads a short hike from the cabin to the valley below. The bus will also drop off and pick up hikers along the road but is not a free shuttle system like at Denali. Round-trip fare is $50.

Getting There

Although the park is closer to Kodiak or Homer, to get from Anchorage to Katmai you first have to fly to King Salmon. A round-trip ticket, if purchased two weeks in advance from Mark Air (tel 243-6275 in Anchorage), costs $241; if you decide to go at the last minute it will be $320. Once at the King Salmon airport terminal you shuffle right over to Peninsula Airways (tel 246-3372) for the second leg of the journey to Brooks Camp in the park. The round-trip fare on the floatplane is $120 and there is no need for reservations.

MCNEIL RIVER

The McNeil River State Game Sanctuary, across from Homer on Cook Inlet, is famous for its high concentration of brown bears from July through August. The bears gather around the mouth of the river where falls slow down the salmon and make for an easy meal. The Alaska Department of Fish & Game has set up a viewing area and allows 10 visitors per day to watch the bears feed. For most visitors, viewing and photographing giant brown bears this close is a once-in-a-lifetime experience.

Getting There

Kachemak Air Service (tel 235-8924), based in Homer, offers a per-seat fare to McNeil River for $230 round trip. They make the trip whether the plane is filled to its capacity of 12 or carries only one passenger. It lands in a tidal area during high tides. For visitors just passing through who do not have a permit to the viewing area, the air-taxi operator offers another alternative – if there are empty seats, you can fly to McNeil River and then immediately return with the plane for a good, if somewhat quick, overview of the bears; the cost is $115 per person.

LAKE CLARK

Apart from backpacking enthusiasts and river runners in Southcentral Alaska, few people know about Lake Clark National Park & Preserve 100 miles (160 km) south-west of Anchorage, yet it offers some of the most spectacular scenery of any of the newly created parks in the state. It is within this 3.6 million-acre (1.5 million hectare) preserve that the Alaska and Aleutian ranges meet. Among the many towering peaks are Mt Iliamna and Mt Redoubt, two active volcanoes clearly seen from Anchorage and the west shore of the Kenai Peninsula.

The park also features numerous glaciers, spectacular turquoise lakes including its centrepiece Lake Clark, and three designated wild rivers that long have been havens for river runners.

Wildlife includes brown and black bears, moose, red foxes, wolves and Dall

sheep on the alpine slopes. Caribou roam the western foothills while the park's watershed is one of the most important producers of red salmon in the world, contributing to 33% of the US catch. Weather in the western section of the preserve, where most of the rafting and backpacking takes place, is generally cool and cloudy with light winds through much of the summer. Temperatures range from 50°F to 65°F (10°C to 18°C) June to August, with an occasional heat wave of 80°F (27°C).

Hiking

Lake Clark is another trail-less park for the experienced backpacker only. Most extended treks take place in the western foothills north of Lake Clark, where open and relatively dry tundra makes ideal hiking. Less experienced backpackers are content to be landed on the shores of the many lakes in the area to camp and undertake day hikes.

There is a summer ranger station at Port Alsworth, but it is best to contact the park headquarters (tel 271-3751) in Anchorage at 701 C St regarding desirable places to hike and camp. You can also write to them before departing for Alaska at: Lake Clark National Park, PO Box 61, Anchorage, Alaska 99513.

Rafting

Float trips down any of the three designated wild rivers – Chilikadrotna, Mulchatna and Tlikakila – are spectacular and exciting since the waterways are rated Class III-IV. Outfitters that run trips along the parks rivers include Tundra Treks (tel 479-2754 in Fairbanks), which has an 11-day float on the Mulchatna River for $1400; and Alaska Treks & Voyages (tel 288-3610 in Moose Pass), which offers a nine-day trip on the Tlikakila River for $1000.

Getting There

Access into the Lake Clark region is by small chartered plane, making the area tough to visit on a limited budget. The cheapest way to reach the park is to book two weeks in advance through Alaska Airlines (tel 243-3300 in Anchorage) a round-trip ticket between Anchorage and Iliamna, a small village 30 miles (48 km) south of the park. The fare is $119 round trip, and Ryan Air, a contract carrier of Alaska Airlines, makes the flight. From Iliamna you have to charter to your destination within the park through air-taxi operators such as Talerik Creek Air Taxi (tel 571-1214) or Iliamna Air Taxi (tel 571-1248).

Western Alaska

PRIBILOF ISLANDS
Out in the Bering Sea, 300 miles (480 km) west of Alaska's mainland and 900 miles (1400 km) from Anchorage, are the Pribilof Islands; desolate, wind-swept places where the abundance of wildlife has made them tourist attractions despite the inhospitable weather. The four islands have two communities: St Paul (population 600) and St George (population 160) consisting of mostly Aleut Indians and government workers.

Although the Pribilof Islands are the home of the largest Aleut villages in the world, seals are the reason for the tourist trade. Every summer the tiny archipelago of rocky shores and steep cliffs becomes a mad scene when 1.5 million fur seals swim ashore to breed and raise their young. The seals spend most of the year at sea between California and Japan, but each summer they migrate to the Pribilofs and become the largest group of mammals anywhere in the world.

Many visitors also venture to the islands to view the extensive bird rookeries. About 190 species of birds totalling about 2.5 million nest at the Pribilofs, making it one of the best seabird colonies in North America. The cliffs are easy to reach and photograph.

Blinds have been erected on the beach for observation of the seals.

Getting There
Because of strict regulations and limited facilities, travellers have little choice but to travel on package tours in order to visit the Pribilofs. Gray Line (tel 277-5581 in Anchorage) offer a three-day tour of the islands that departs Anchorage Tuesdays and Thursdays. The tour, which includes accommodation, meals, air fare and transportation to the beaches and rookeries, costs $697 per person. Exploration Holidays & Cruises offers longer stays of four days for $790 and six days for $925. In Anchorage, you also book these tours through Gray Line or by calling Exploration Holidays' toll-free number 1 (800) 426-0600.

NOME
In 1898 gold was found in Anvil Creek, giving rise to a few tents the miners called Anvil City. The following summer gold was found on the beaches nearby, and when the news finally made its way to Seattle in the summer of 1900, it set off yet another stampede of hopeful miners to Alaska. By the end of that year there were 20,000 people in the town that was now called Nome and would forever be associated around the world with gold and quick fortunes.

Nome suffered from natural disasters like much of Alaska, as fires all but destroyed the town in 1905 and 1934 and a Bering Sea storm overpowered the seawalls in 1974. However, the city survived and today it boasts a population of 3700 and has retained some of its frontier facade along historical Front St.

Nome serves as the transportation hub for much of Western Alaska and during the summer ocean-going barges unloading offshore are a common sight. A surge in gold prices in recent years has also given new life to the mining industry, while the lure of gold still draws people to Nome. These days it's summer tourists rather

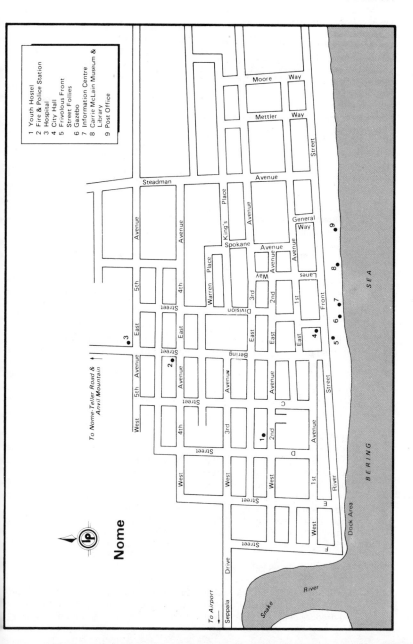

Nome

To Airport

Seppala Drive

To Nome-Teller Road & Anvil Mountain

1 Youth Hostel
2 Fire & Police Station
3 Hospital
4 City Hall
5 Frivolous Front Street Follies
6 Gazebo
7 Information Centre
8 Carrie McLain Museum & Library
9 Post Office

Snake River

Dock Area

BERING SEA

"There's no place like Nome"

NOME

CONVENTION & VISITORS BUREAU

than miners which contribute to Nome's economy.

Things to See

Nome's sights are located along Front St and most travellers have little desire to venture any farther into town. Begin at the **Visitor Bureau** (tel 443-5535), which is part of the Perkins Plaza, Nome's small convention centre, on Front St in the centre of the business district. Their resources include walking tours which describe the city's historical features and buildings.

Behind the bureau is a wooden platform on the rock seawall that provides views of the Bering Sea and Sledge Island. To the east of the bureau on Front St is the **Carrie McLain Museum** on the first floor of the Kegoayah Kozga Public Library. The museum features exhibits on the Bering Land Bridge, Eskimo culture and gold rush history and is open Tuesday to Friday from 9 am to 5 pm and Saturday 1 to 5 pm.

Nome's **public beach** nearby is where in the height of the summer a few local children may be seen playing in the 45°F (7°C) water. On Memorial Day, 20 to 30 residents participate in the annual Polar Bear Swim by plunging into the ice-choked March waters. A warmer swim can be obtained at the **public pool** (tel 443-5717) at the Nome Public School. Admission is $2 per session.

Gold Dredges There are 28 gold dredges, some still being used today, while many others lie deteriorating, in the area surrounding the city. The closest are the reactivated dredges near the north end of the Nome Airport, two miles (3.2 km) north of town. You can't walk through them but you can view them and photograph the mining machinery from 0.5 mile (0.8 km).

Those fascinated by the relics of the gold rush era might consider renting a car and driving the roads that extend into the Seward Peninsula from Nome. It is believed that there are close to 100 dredges scattered throughout the peninsula, many visible from the road. The cheapest place to rent a car is from Q-Trucking Rentals (tel 443-2388), which charges $55 per day plus mileage. Ask the Visitors Bureau about the location of dredges and old steam engines that were used to obtain gold ore.

Places to Stay & Eat

There used to be a Youth Hostel in Nome that made this side trip affordable for backpackers. The hostel, in the United Methodist Church on the corner of 2nd Avenue and C St, ceased operation when a new pastor arrived in 1985. The facilities are still there so it might pay to check with the church to see if it has reopened or if they will provide accommodation. Stop in at the Visitors Bureau about camping on the public beach. The *Polaris Hotel* (tel 443-2000) has singles with shared bath at $40 per night and doubles with private bath at $80.

For dinner go to *Ding How Restaurant* on Front St along the beach for good Chinese food and the best prices in town. Also along Front St are *Snack Shack* for hamburgers and the *Polar Club* for breakfast or home-baked items from its Billikin Bakery.

At night stop in at the *Board of Trade*, the oldest bar on the Bering Sea, and the *Bering Sea Saloon*. Both are on Front St and are good places to meet the locals.

Getting There

Nome is serviced by Alaska Airlines, which offers three daily flights to the town from Anchorage. A round-trip ticket booked two weeks in advance costs $317. Gray Lines (tel 277-5581 in Anchorage) offers a package tour that spends a day in Kotzebue and another in Nome for $393. The price is based on shared accommodation and includes air fare, lodging and meals.

KOTZEBUE

Situated 26 miles (42 km) above the Arctic Circle, Kotzebue is one of the largest native communities in the Bush; over 80% of its 2500 residents are Eskimos. Kotzebue is on the north-west shore of the Baldwin Peninsula in Kotzebue Sound, near the mouths of the Kobuk and Noatak rivers. Traditionally it serves as the transportation and commerce centre for Northwest Arctic Alaska.

More recently it has experienced an increase in tourism mostly through the efforts of NANA, a native corporation, and as the departure point into the new national preserves and parks nearby. NANA also manages a reindeer herd, numbering over 6000 head, on the Baldwin Peninsula. Many residents still depend on subsistence hunting and fishing to survive.

The majority of travellers to Kotzebue are either part of a tour-group package or are just passing through on their way to a wilderness expedition in the surrounding parks. The community is extremely difficult to visit for an independent traveller on a budget.

Things to See

The town is named after Polish explorer Otto von Kotzebue, who stumbled onto the native village in 1816 while searching for the Northwest Passage for the Russians. Much of the town's history and culture can be be viewed at one of two museums. **Ootukahkuktuvik City Museum** features artefacts of natives and early settlers, including a rain parka made of walrus intestine. The museum is open daily in the summer from 8 am to 4.40 pm and is on Kotzebue Way near Tundra Way.

Most tour groups visit the **Museum of Arctic**, where 2nd and 3rd Avenues come together at the south end of town. The centre is owned and operated by NANA and offers a two-hour programme of native culture, demonstrations in Eskimo handicrafts and a visit to the adjoining jade factory as well as a traditional blanket toss. Independent travellers can join the museum tour if they want to part with $25 by contacting the NANA office (tel 442-3301).

Perhaps the most interesting thing to do in Kotzebue is just stroll down **Front St** (also known as Shore Avenue), a narrow gravel road only a few yards from the water. Here you can see salmon drying out on racks, fishing boats crowding the beach to be repaired and locals preparing for the long winter ahead. This is also the best place to watch the midnight sun which rolls along the horizon, painting the sea reddish gold in a beautiful scene of colour and light reflecting off the water. Beginning in early June the sun does not set for almost six weeks. In the centre of town there is a large **cemetery** where spirit houses have been erected over many of the graves.

Places to Stay & Eat

There is no Youth Hostel or public campgrounds in Kotzebue. The only hotel, *Nul-luk-vik* (tel 442-3331), has rates that begin at $100 for singles and climb from there. It is a common practice among backpackers, however, to hike south of town from Front St, 0.25 mile (0.4 km) past the airport, and pitch their tent on the beach. Keep in mind that much of the beach around Kotzebue is difficult to camp on because it is narrow and slanted or is privately owned.

As out of place as it may seem, there is a *Dairy Queen* – undoubtedly the northernmost of the chain – on the corner of 2nd Avenue and Lagoon St. Along with hamburgers and ice-cream, it serves steaks and seafood but is not the cheapest place in town for a meal. Better in price is

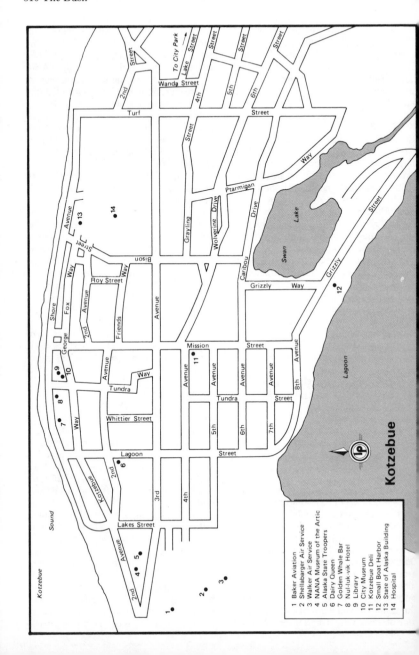

Kotzebue

1 Baker Aviation
2 Shellabarger Air Service
3 Walker Air Service
4 NANA Museum of the Artic
5 Alaska State Troopers
6 Dairy Queen
7 Golden Whale Bar
8 Nul-luk-vik Hotel
9 Library
10 City Museum
11 Kotzebue Deli
12 Small Boat Harbor
13 State of Alaska Building
14 Hospital

Hamburger Hut on Front St, where you can get a hamburger for around $6; or *Kotzebue Deli* on the corner of 4th Avenue and Mission St, where sandwiches cost from $8 to $12.

River Running

Kotzebue provides access to some of the finest river running in Arctic Alaska. The popular ones include the Noatak, the Kobuk, the Salmon (which flows into the Kobuk), and the Selawik (which originates in the Kobuk lowlands and flows west into Selawik Lake). Trips along the Kobuk National Wild River consist of floats from Walker Lake 140 miles (224 km) downstream to the villages of Kobuk or Ambler, where there are scheduled flights to both Kotzebue and Bettles, another departure point for this river. Bering Air (tel 443-5464) charges $70 one way for a Kobuk-Kotzebue ticket and $65 from Ambler. Most of the river is rated Class I, but some lining of boats may be required just below Walker Lake and for one mile (1.6 km) through Lower Kobuk Canyon. Paddlers usually plan on six to eight days for the float.

The Noatak National Wild River is a 16-day float of 350 miles (560 km) from Lake Matcharak to the village of Noatak, where Bering Air has scheduled service to Kotzebue for $40 per person one way. However, the numerous access lakes on the river allow it to be broken down into shorter paddles. The entire river is rated Class I-II. For more information contact the National Park office (tel 442-3890) in the Museum of Arctic, which is open Monday to Friday from 7 am to 5 pm in the summer, or write to the National Park Service before you depart for Alaska at PO Box 287, Kotzebue, Alaska 99752.

Canoes can be rented in town (check with the NPS for names of people renting them) or in Ambler from Ambler Air Service (tel 445-2121), which can also supply drop-offs up the Kobuk River. Keep in mind the arrangement Bering Air has with Alaska Airlines for connecting flights to villages. It is possible to book a round-trip, supersaver flight from Anchorage to Ambler for $432, and from there rent boats and drop-off service from Ambler Air Service. See the list of outfitters in the Wilderness chapter.

Getting There

Alaska Airlines offers a round-trip ticket to Kotzebue, if booked two weeks in advance, for $317 from Anchorage. You can also purchase a round-trip ticket from Anchorage with stopovers in both Nome and Kotzebue for $395. Gray Line offers a daily single-day tour of Kotzebue out of Anchorage for $298 per person.

North Slope

NORTH SLOPE HAUL ROAD

The official name is Dalton Highway, but it is best known in Alaska simply as 'Haul Road'. The stretch of gravel winds 416 miles (666 km) from Elliott Highway to Deadhorse at Prudhoe Bay, the community that houses the workers of what is believed to be the largest oil reserve in the US. Here is the start of the Trans-Alaska Pipeline that carries oil 800 miles (1300 km) to the ice-free port of Valdez on Prince William Sound.

After the road was completed in 1978, it was kept closed to the public except the first 56 miles (90 km) to the Yukon River. In 1981, after a bitter battle in the state legislature, the public was allowed to drive 210 miles (337 km) of the road to Disaster Creek. This section takes you into Brooks Range and near the borders of Kanuti and Yukon Flats national wildlife refuges and Gates of the Arctic National Park & Preserve north of them, to a turnaround spot 205 miles (329 km) south of Prudhoe Bay. At this point a Department of Transportation check station allows only those with permits to continue.

Mileposts

Mile 0 of North Slope Haul Rd is at the junction with Elliott Highway, 73 miles (116.8 km) north of Fairbanks. The beginning is marked by an information centre that covers the route north. At *Mile 25* (40 km) is the second look-out of the road, where there is a good view of the pipeline crossing Hess Creek. There are camping possibilities around the creek, the colour of which draws an occasional amateur gold panner.

The highway begins to descend to the Yukon River at *Mile 47* (75 km), and shortly you will be able to view miles of pipeline. At *Mile 51* (82 km) a rough road leads right 5.4 miles (8.7 km) to the Yukon River. There is a boat launch maintained by the BLM on the north side of the river.

The Yukon River Bridge is reached at *Mile 56* (90 km). The wooden-decked bridge was completed in 1975 and is 2290 feet (698 metres) long. On the other side of the bridge is one of two spots to purchase supplies and gas. Across the road from the bridge is a rough camping area with litter barrels.

Just beyond *Mile 91* (145.6 km) is a look-out with a scenic view of the road and the pipeline to the north. At *Mile 96* (153.6 km) the highway climbs above the tree line into an alpine area where there is good hiking and berry picking. The Haul Rd stays in this alpine section for the next five miles (eight km) before the terrain turns rugged and you pass many impressive rock out-crops and granite tors.

Eventually the road descends into a valley that provides good views of the surrounding mountains. The Arctic Circle is reached near *Mile 117* (187 km) and is marked by a turnoff with parking and litter barrels. From here, for the next 64 miles (102 km), the road passes six streams and small Grayling Lake, all of which offer the angler superb action for grayling.

Coldfoot, a lodge and restaurant that also sells gas and groceries, is reached at *Mile 175* (280 km), while another five miles (eight km) north is the spur to the Marion Creek campsite. The road is now near the boundaries of Gates of the Arctic National Park and the scenery is at its best. Wildlife is plentiful, especially Dall sheep high on the mountain slopes. After you pass *Mile 186* (297.6 km) there is a look-out where you can view the historical mining community of Wiseman west of the road across the Koyukuk River. Buildings from the town's heyday in 1910 still stand, but all are private property – a handful of people remain in Wiseman.

More spectacular mountain scenery begins around *Mile 193* (309 km), with the first views of Sukakpak Mountain to the north and Wiehl Mountain to the east, both 4000 feet (1200 metres) in elevation. Poss Mountain, elevation 6189 feet (1885 metres), comes into view to the east in another 2.5 miles (four km); and the Koyukuk River, a heavily braided stream, is seen near *Mile 201* (321.6 km).

Just before *Mile 204* (326.4 km) is a look-out with a 0.5-mile (0.8 km) trail leading to Sukakpak Mountain. The mounds between the road and the mountain were formed by ice pushing the soil and vegetative mat above it.

Another look-out is passed after *Mile 206* (329.6 km), where there are good views of Snowden Mountain, elevation 5775 feet (1761 metres) 10 miles (16 km) to the north-west. Six miles (9.6 km) north of that is Disaster Creek and the turnaround point for all those without a special permit to continue on to Prudhoe Bay.

Getting There

Cheap used-car rentals are available in Fairbanks (see the Fairbanks chapter), though you'd better ask first if they allow their vehicles on the road. If you're driving, remember that the road is used heavily by tractor-trailer rigs driving at high speeds. Never stop in the middle of the road to observe wildlife or scenery, as the trucks have limited braking ability.

Gas, tyre-repair services and limited food supplies are available where the road crosses the Yukon River, 141 miles (225.6 km) north of Fairbanks, and at Coldfoot Lodge, 37 miles (59 km) south of the turnaround point. At both places gas costs close to $2.50 per gallon ($0.66 per litre).

For more information on the road, or to obtain permits if you think you qualify, contact the Department of Transportation, 2301 Peger Rd, Fairbanks, Alaska 99701; tel 452-1911.

Another way to see the road is to join Haul Road Tours (tel 452-7648) for a two-day tour of the road with an overnight stop in Coldfoot. The cost is $125 round trip from Fairbanks when the van is full with five passengers. You can either camp at Coldfoot or pay another $50 for a bed. Call Haul Road Tours when you're in Fairbanks to see when trips are departing.

GATES OF THE ARCTIC
One of the finest wildernesses left in the world is Gates of the Arctic National Park & Preserve, which straddles the Arctic Divide in the Brooks Range 200 miles (320 km) north-west of Fairbanks.

The entire park area contains 8.1 million acres (5.7 million hectares), which extend 200 miles (320 km) east to west and lies totally above the Arctic Circle. It ranges from the southern foothills of the Brooks Range, across the range's ragged peaks and down onto the North Slope. Most of the park, lying north of the limit of trees, is vegetated with shrubs and tundra and is a habitat for grizzly bears, wolves, Dall sheep, moose, caribou and wolverines. Fishing is considered superb for grayling and arctic char in clear streams and for lake trout in the larger, deeper lakes.

Within this preserve you have dozens of rivers to run, miles of valleys and tundra slopes to hike and, of course, the gates

themselves. Mt Boreal and Frigid Crags are the gates that flank the North Fork of the Koyukuk River; it was through these landmark mountains that Robert Marshall found an unobstructed path northward to the Arctic Coast of Alaska. That was in 1929 and Marshall's naming of the two mountains has remained ever since.

Hiking
The park is a vast wilderness containing no NPS facilities, campgrounds or trails. Backpackers follow the long, open valleys for extended treks or work their way to higher elevations where open tundra and sparse shrubs provide excellent hiking terrain.

Most backpackers enter the park by way of charter air-taxi out of Bettles, which can land on lakes, rivers or river bars. Extended treks across the park require outdoor experience and good map and compass skills. One of the more popular treks is the four to five-day hike from Summit Lake, through the Gates to Redstar Lake. Less experienced backpackers often choose to be dropped off and picked up at one lake and from there explore the surrounding region on day hikes. Lakes ideal for this include Summit Lake, the Karupa Lakes region, Redstar Lake, Hunt Fork Lake or Chimney Lake.

The lone exception to chartering is the trek beginning from North Slope Haul Rd either at Coldfoot or Wiseman, where you enter the park from its eastern border.

River Running
Floatable rivers in the park include the John, the North Fork of the Koyukuk, the Tinayguk, the Alatna and the Middle Fork of the Koyukuk from Wiseman to Bettles. The headwaters for the Noatak and Kobuk rivers are in the park and are described in the above section about river running from Kotzebue. Difficulties of the waterways range from Class I-III. Of the various rivers, the North Fork is one of

the most popular because the float begins in the shadow of the 'Gates' and continues downstream 100 miles (160 km) to Bettles through Class I-II waters. Canoes and rafts can be rented in Bettles and then floated downstream back to the village.

BETTLES

This small village of 100 residents serves as the major departure point to the Gates of the Arctic. Within town there is *Bettles Lodge* (tel 692-5111), Bettles Trading Post, where you can pick up such supplies as freeze-dried food and topographic maps, and a National Park Service office (tel 692-5494).

Canoes and rafts can be rented from Sourdough Outfitters (tel 692-5252), who offer unguided expeditions with arrangements for boats and for drop-off and pick-up air service for independent backpackers. With such arrangements the two-week adventure that combines hiking from Summit Lake to Redstar Lake and then floating down the North Fork to Bettles costs $450 per person.

Outfitters

A number of guide companies run trips through the Gates of the Arctic, including Sourdough Outfitters, who charge $1500 for the two-week hiking and canoeing expedition from Summit Lake. Also look into Tundra Treks (tel 479-2754 in Fairbanks), who run a 10-day float down the John River for $1200; Caribou Wilderness Outfitters (tel 488-4594 in Salcha) for their 10-day float down the North Fork for $1250; and Brooks Range Expeditions (tel 692-5333 in Bettles) for their six-day hike and float on the North Fork for $1000.

Getting There

Access to the park's backcountry is usually accomplished in two steps, with the first being a scheduled flight from Fairbanks to Bettles. Check out Frontier Flying Service (tel 452-1014) or Arctic Circle Air (tel 456-1112) in Fairbanks,

who make regular flights to the small village for a fare of $75 one-way.

The second step is to charter an air-taxi in Bettles to your destination within the park. A Cessna 185 on floats holds three passengers and cost around $225 per hour, and most areas in the park can be reached in under two hours of flying time from Bettles. If your destination is an hour away and there are two persons in your party, the price for drop-off and pick-up is $450 per person. Look into Brooks Range Aviation (tel 692-5444) for air charter out of Bettles.

The alternative to expensive air chartering is to begin your trip from North Slope Haul Rd (Dalton Highway). Haul Road Tours (tel 452-7648) will provide round-trip transportation for as low as $125 if the five-passenger van is full.

Even cheaper for those with time but little money is to thumb the North Slope Haul Rd. A trickle of cars and a couple of hundred trucks use the road daily. While trucks will not stop to pick you up on the roadside, often it is possible to pick up a ride with one at the Hilltop Café, a truck-stop and gas station at *Mile 5.3* (8.5 km) of Elliott Highway.

BARROW

Barrow (population 2900) is the largest Inupiat Eskimo community in Alaska and one of the largest in North America. Although the residents enjoy such modern-day conveniences as a local bus system and gas heating in their homes from the nearby oil fields, they remain very traditional in their outlook on life and seasonal events, symbolised the most by the spring whale hunts.

The town is the northernmost community in the US and as the place where American humourist Will Rogers died. He perished in 1935, 15 miles (24 km) south of Barrow, when the plane carrying him and Wiley Post stalled and crashed into a river during their Fairbanks-to-Siberia trip. Barrow is 330 miles (530 km) north of the Arctic Circle and less than 1200 miles (1920 km) from the North Pole.

Most people visit the native town to say they've been 'at the top of the world' or to view the midnight sun, which never sets from 10 May to 2 August. Otherwise there is little reason to make the expensive side trip to Barrow. Round-trip air fare from Fairbanks is $500 on Mark Air, rooms in the town's two hotels begin at over $100 per night, and occasionally there can be a feeling of tension between natives and independent travellers.

For those set on seeing Barrow, by far the best and most economical way is to book a package tour through Exploration Holidays & Cruises, who offer a two-day trip including air fare, accommodation (shared room) and a city tour for $395 per person. Their toll-free number is 1 (800) 426-0600. Gray Line (tel 456-7741) offers a 12-hour tour of the community out of Fairbanks for $270.

Index

Map references in **bold** type.

Lonely Planet

Lonely Planet published its first book in 1973. Tony and Maureen Wheeler had made a lengthy overland trip from England to Australia and, in response to numerous 'how do you do it?' questions, Tony wrote and they published *Across Asia on the Cheap*. It became an instant local best-seller and inspired thoughts of a second travel guide. A year and a half in South-East Asia resulted in their second book, *South-East Asia on a Shoestring*, which they put together in a backstreet Chinese hotel in Singapore in 1975. The 'yellow book', as it quickly became known, soon became *the* guide to the region and has gone through five editions, always with its familiar yellow cover.

Soon other writers started to come to them with ideas for similar books – books that went off the beaten track and took an adventurous approach to travel, books that 'assumed you knew how to get your luggage off the carousel,' as one reviewer described them. Lonely Planet grew from a kitchen table operation to a spare room and then to its own office. It also started to develop an international reputation as the Lonely Planet logo began to appear in more and more countries. In 1982 *India – a travel survival kit* won the Thomas Cook award for the best guidebook of the year.

These days there are over 60 Lonely Planet titles. Nearly 30 people work at our office in Melbourne, Australia and another half dozen at our US office in Oakland, California.

At first Lonely Planet specialised exclusively in the Asia region but these days we are also developing major ranges of guidebooks to the Pacific region, to South America and to Africa. The list of walking guides is growing and Lonely Planet is producing a unique series of phrasebooks to 'unusual' languages. The emphasis continues to be on travel for travellers and Tony and Maureen still manage to fit in a number of trips each year and play a very active part in the writing and updating of Lonely Planet's guides.

Keeping guidebooks up to date is a constant battle which requires an ear to the ground and lots of walking, but technology also plays its part. All Lonely Planet guidebooks are now stored and updated on computer, and some authors even take lap-top computers into the field. Lonely Planet is also using computers to draw maps and eventually many of the maps will be stored on disk.

The people at Lonely Planet strongly feel that travellers can make a positive contribution to the countries they visit both by better appreciation of cultures and by the money they spend. In addition the company tries to make a direct contribution to the countries and regions it covers. Since 1986 a percentage of the income from each book has gone to aid groups and associations. This has included donations to famine relief in Africa, to aid projects in India, to agricultural projects in Nicaragua and other Central American countries and to Greenpeace's efforts to halt French nuclear testing in the Pacific. In 1988 over $40,000 was donated by Lonely Planet to these projects.

Lonely Planet Distributors

Australia & Papua New Guinea Lonely Planet Publications, PO Box 88, South Yarra, Victoria 3141.
Canada Raincoast Books, 112 East 3rd Avenue, Vancouver, British Columbia V5T 1C8.
Denmark, Finland & Norway Scanvik Books aps, Store Kongensgade 59 A, DK-1264 Copenhagen K.
Hong Kong The Book Society, GPO Box 7804.
India & Nepal UBS Distributors, 5 Ansari Rd, New Delhi – 110002
Israel Geographical Tours Ltd, 8 Tverya St, Tel Aviv 63144.
Japan Intercontinental Marketing Corp, IPO Box 5056, Tokyo 100-31.
Netherlands Nilsson & Lamm bv, Postbus 195, Pampuslaan 212, 1380 AD Weesp.
New Zealand Transworld Publishers, PO Box 83-094, Edmonton PO, Auckland.
Singapore & Malaysia MPH Distributors, 601 Sims Drive, #03-21, Singapore 1438.
Spain Altair, Balmes 69, 08007 Barcelona.
Sweden Esselte Kartcentrum AB, Vasagatan 16, S-111 20 Stockholm.
Thailand Chalermnit, 108 Sukhumvit 53, Bangkok 10110.
UK Roger Lascelles, 47 York Rd, Brentford, Middlesex, TW8 0QP
USA Lonely Planet Publications, PO Box 2001A, Berkeley, CA 94702.
West Germany Buchvertrieb Gerda Schettler, Postfach 64, D3415 Hattorf a H.
All Other Countries refer to Australia address.